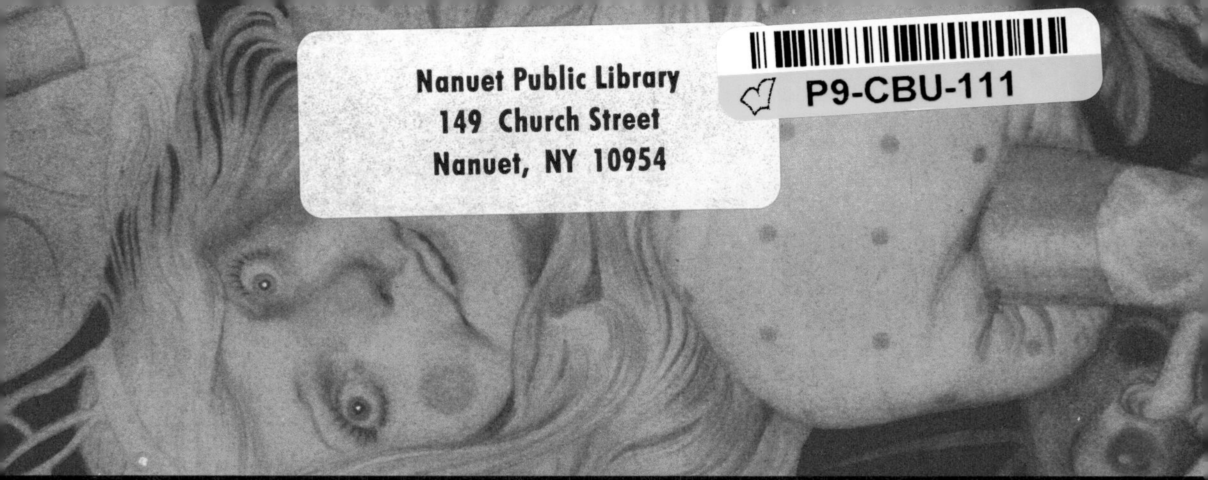

FABLES: CUBS IN TOYLAND

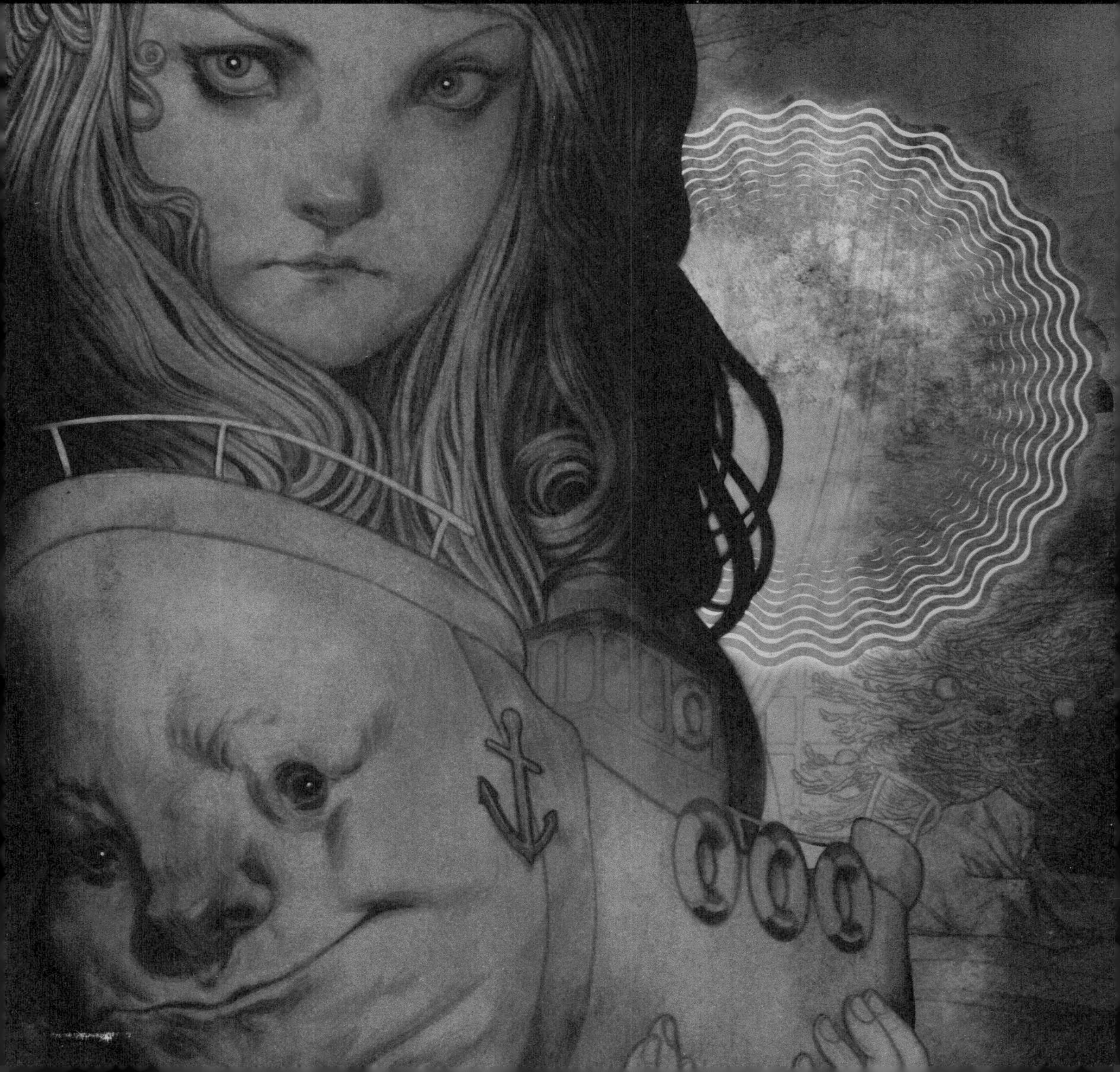

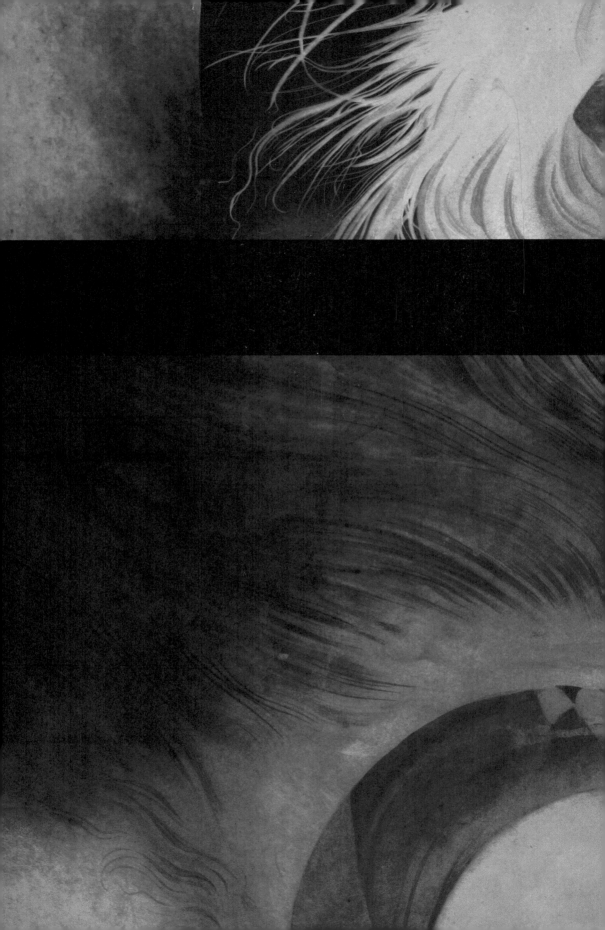

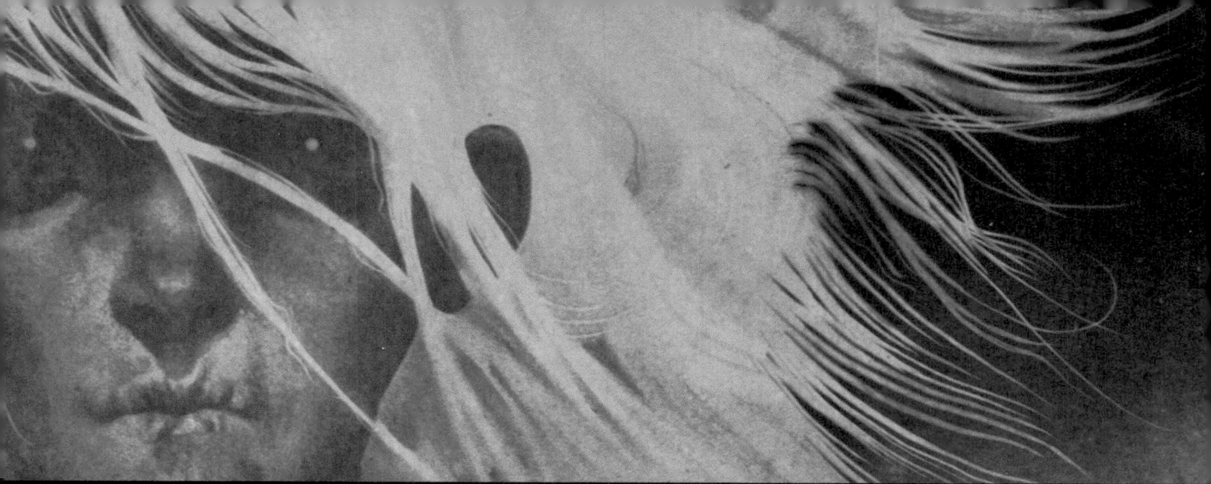

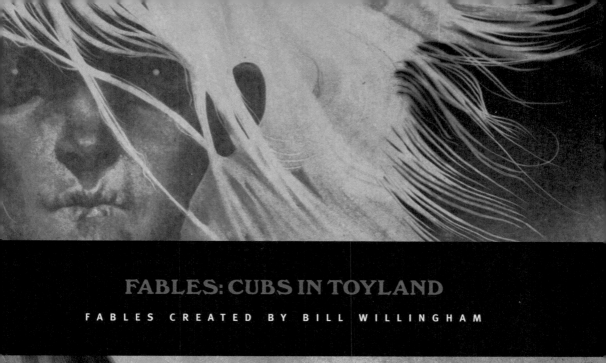

FABLES: CUBS IN TOYLAND

FABLES CREATED BY BILL WILLINGHAM

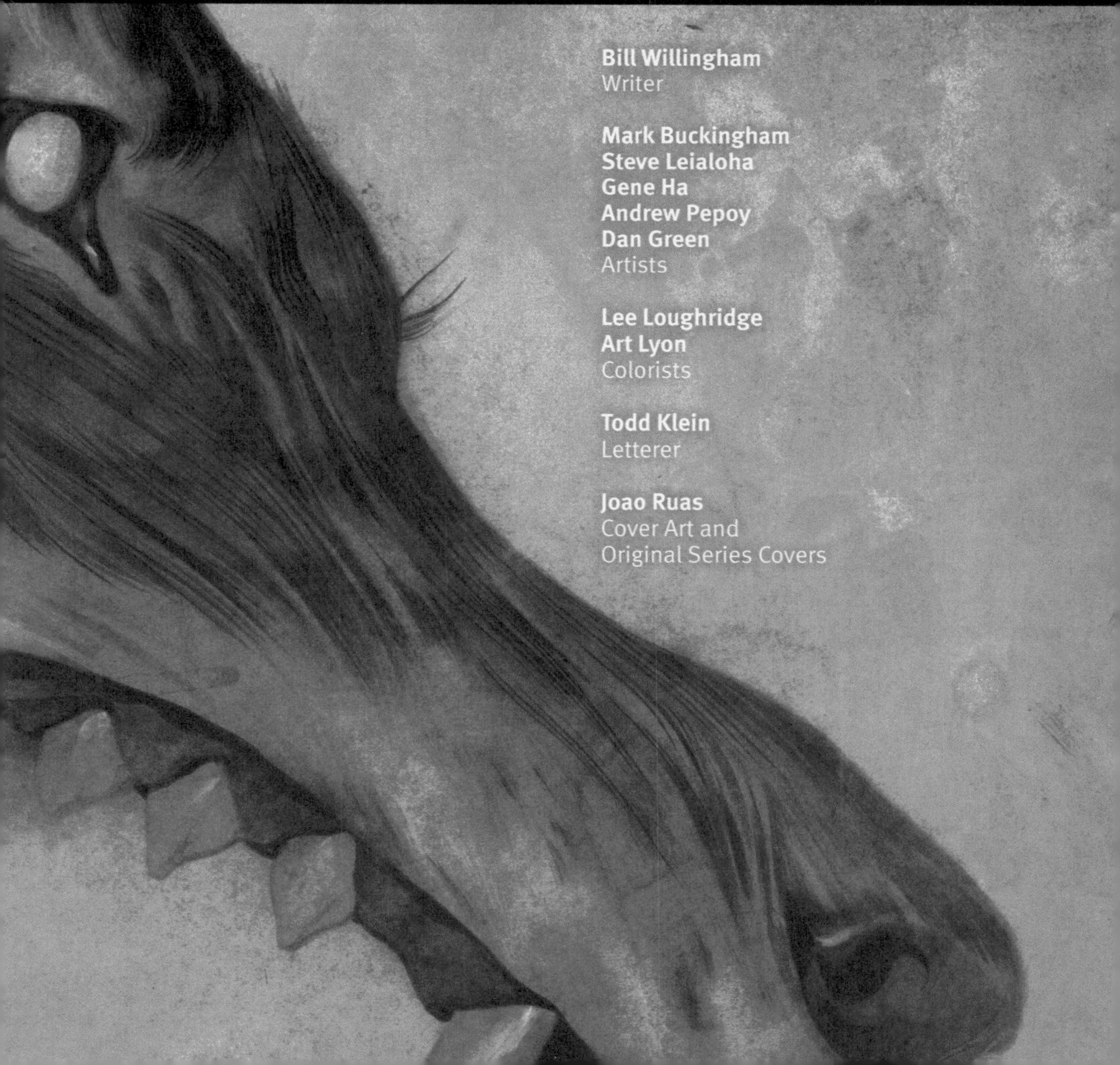

Bill Willingham
Writer

Mark Buckingham
Steve Leialoha
Gene Ha
Andrew Pepoy
Dan Green
Artists

Lee Loughridge
Art Lyon
Colorists

Todd Klein
Letterer

Joao Ruas
Cover Art and
Original Series Covers

SHELLY BOND
Editor – Original Series

GREGORY LOCKARD
Assistant Editor – Original Series

SCOTT NYBAKKEN
Editor

ROBBIN BROSTERMAN
Design Director – Books

KAREN BERGER
Senior VP – Executive Editor, Vertigo

BOB HARRAS
VP – Editor-in-Chief

DIANE NELSON
President

DAN DIDIO and **JIM LEE**
Co-Publishers

GEOFF JOHNS
Chief Creative Officer

JOHN ROOD
Executive VP – Sales, Marketing and Business Development

AMY GENKINS
Senior VP – Business and Legal Affairs

NAIRI GARDINER
Senior VP – Finance

JEFF BOISON
VP – Publishing Operations

MARK CHIARELLO
VP – Art Direction and Design

JOHN CUNNINGHAM
VP – Marketing

TERRI CUNNINGHAM
VP – Talent Relations and Services

ALISON GILL
Senior VP – Manufacturing and Operations

HANK KANALZ
Senior VP – Digital

JAY KOGAN
VP – Business and Legal Affairs, Publishing

JACK MAHAN
VP – Business Affairs, Talent

NICK NAPOLITANO
VP – Manufacturing Administration

SUE POHJA
VP – Book Sales

COURTNEY SIMMONS
Senior VP – Publicity

BOB WAYNE
Senior VP – Sales

This collection of silly politics and serious horror is dedicated with true affection to reluctant FABLES fan Rachel Maddow, who maintains her love/hate relationships with endurance and élan.
— Bill Willingham

For Tilly and Rudy.
— Mark Buckingham

Logo design by Brainchild Studios/NYC

FABLES: CUBS IN TOYLAND

Published by DC Comics. Cover and compilation Copyright © 2013 Bill Willingham and DC Comics. All Rights Reserved.

Originally published in single magazine form as FABLES 114-123. Copyright © 2012, 2013 Bill Willingham and DC Comics. All Rights Reserved. All characters, their distinctive likenesses and related elements featured in this publication are trademarks of Bill Willingham. VERTIGO is a trademark of DC Comics. The stories, characters and incidents featured in this publication are entirely fictional. DC Comics does not read or accept unsolicited submissions of ideas, stories or artwork.

DC Comics, 1700 Broadway, New York, NY 10019
A Warner Bros. Entertainment Company.
Printed in the USA. First Printing.
ISBN: 978-1-4012-3769-1

Library of Congress Cataloging-in-Publication Data

Willingham, Bill.
  Fables. Volume 18, Cubs in toyland / Bill Willingham, Mark Buckingham, Steve Leialoha.
    p. cm.
  "Originally published in single magazine form in Fables 114-123."
  ISBN 978-1-4012-3769-1
  1. Fairy tales—Adaptations—Comic books, strips, etc. 2. Legends—Adaptations—Comic books, strips, etc. 3. Graphic novels. I. Buckingham, Mark. II. Leialoha, Steve. III. Title. IV. Title: Cubs in toyland.
  PN6727.W52F43 2012
  741.5'973—dc23
                                    2012032147

Table of Contents

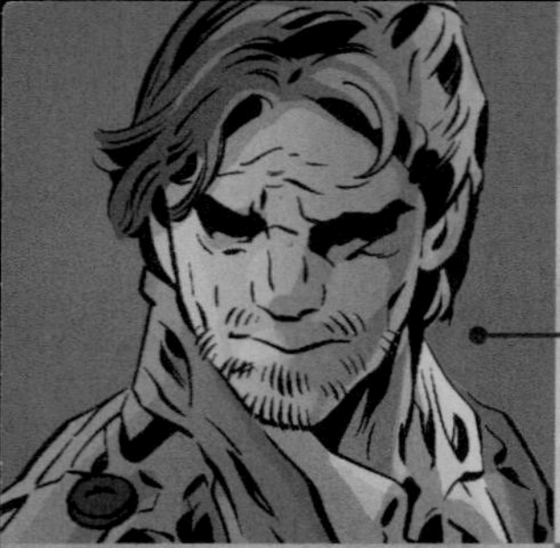

WHO'S WHO IN FABLETOWN

BIGBY

The celebrated Big Bad Wolf and former sheriff of Fabletown.

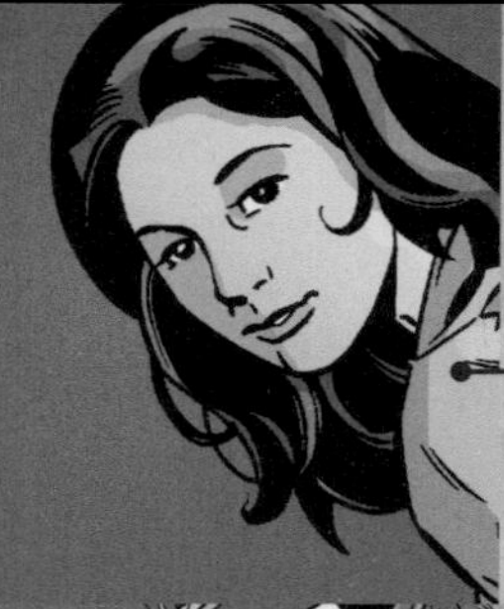

SNOW WHITE

Fabletown's former deputy mayor, wife of Bigby, and moth
to their seven cubs.

THE CUBS

Winter, Darien, Therese, Blossom, Connor, Ambrose and Ghost — seven siblings now on the verge of adulthood's responsibilities.

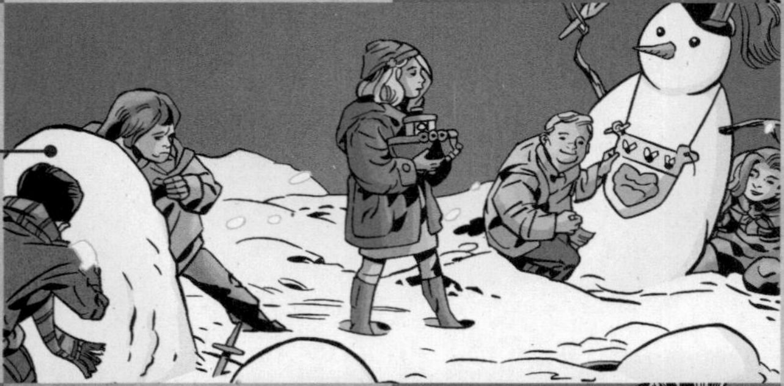

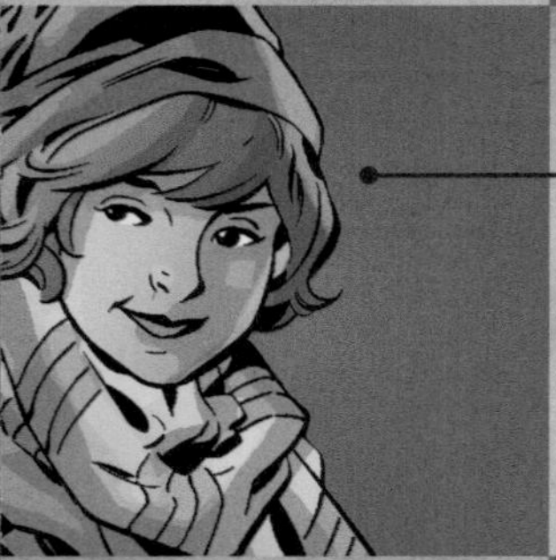

ROSE RED

Leader-in-exile of the Farm — home of the non-human Fables — and sister to Snow White.

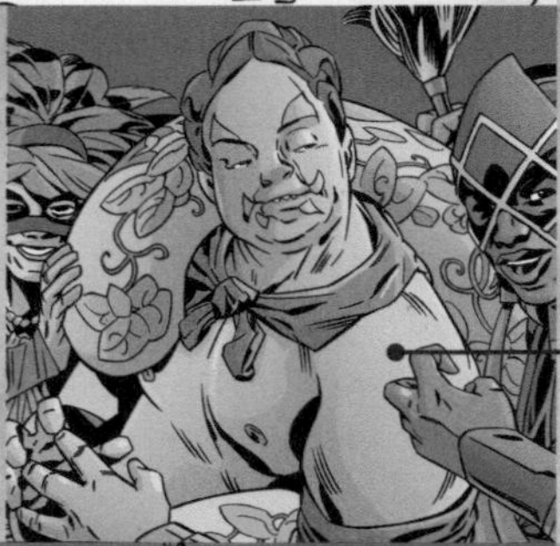

THE CARDINAL WINDS

The North Wind's scheming subordinates from the East, West and South.

THE ZEPHYRS

Loyal retainers of the North Wind.

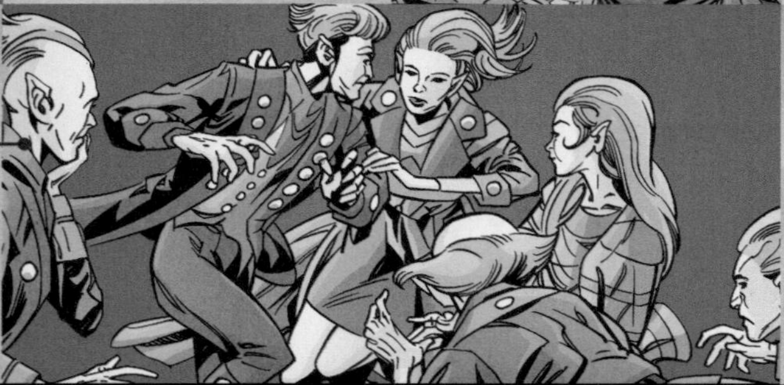

MISS SPRATT

Jack Spratt's revenge-minded widow, now using her maiden name of Leigh Duglas.

KING COLE

The once and future mayor of Fabletown.

PINOCCHIO

Geppetto's first-carved son.

OZMA

The misleadingly youthful-looking leader of Fabletown's wizards and witches.

MADDY

The stealthiest of the Farm-dwelling Fables.

BEAUTY AND THE BEAST

Fabletown's deputy mayor and sheriff, and proud new parents.

MR. TICKY TOCKY TIGER

Also known as Lord Mountbatten, last Viceroy of the Raj, he's been rusted solid for nearly a year.

GRIMBLE

Fabletown's foremost security guard and an infamous bridge troll.

THE STORY SO FAR

Having survived the onslaught of the fearsome Mister Dark, the Free Fables have cautiously begun to reclaim their territories in the Mundane World — including the seemingly never-ending halls of Castle Dark, whose walls still harbor their share of dark secrets. Meanwhile, Winter Wolf — the freshly crowned North Wind — is learning the tools of her exceptionally powerful new trade, leaving her brothers and sisters to ponder what their own fates will be in the grimly fast-approaching realm of adult life.

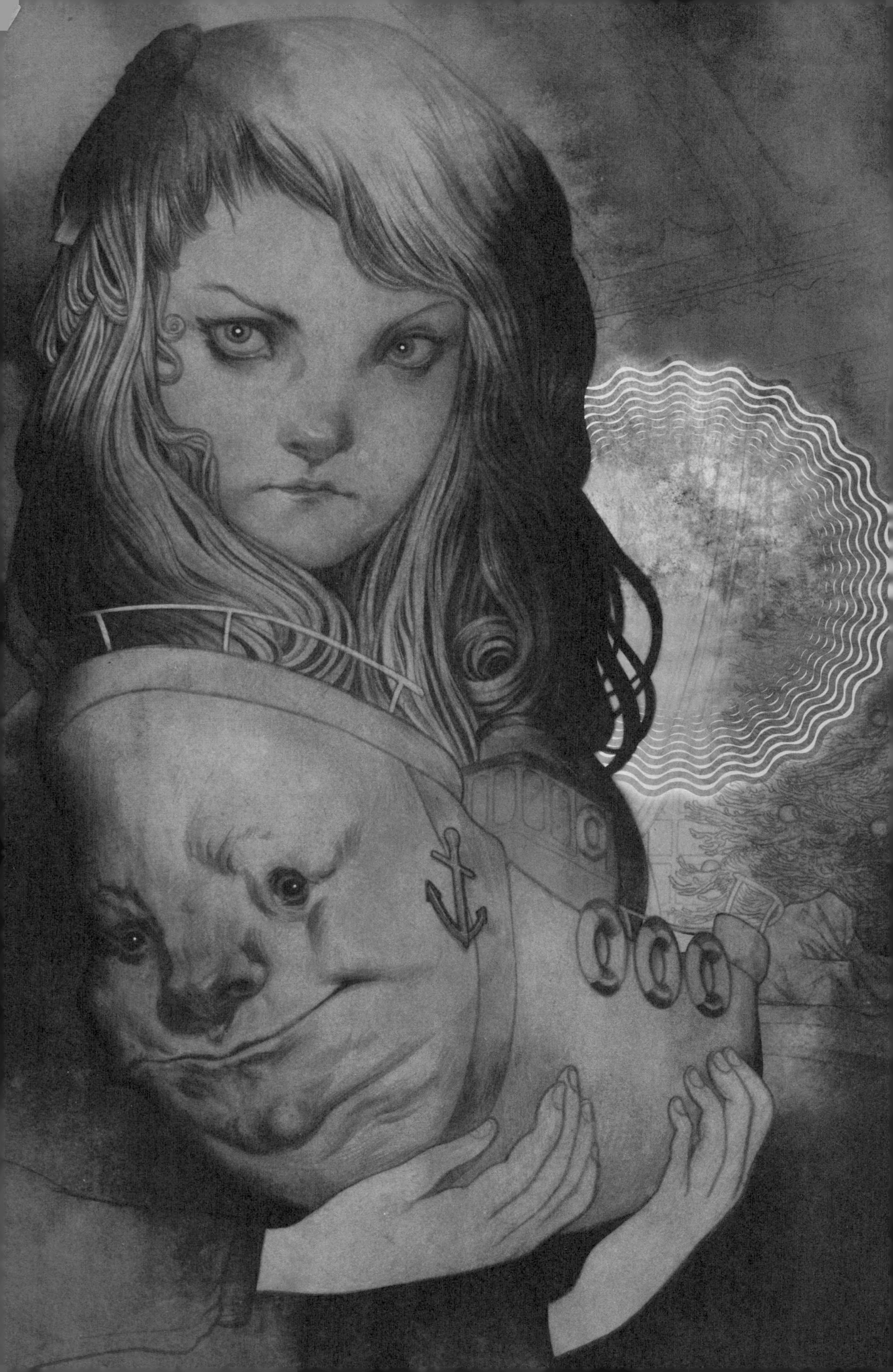

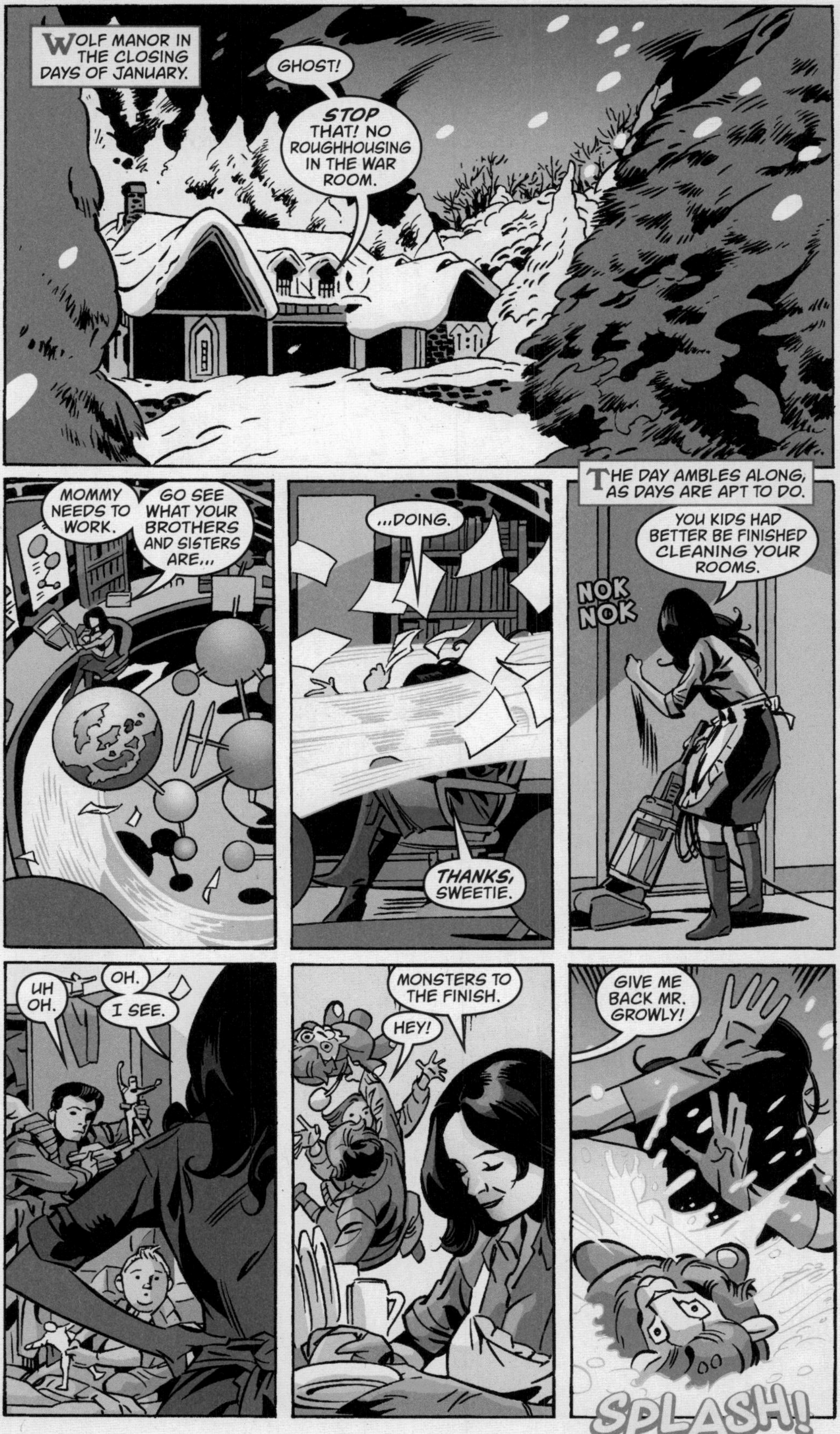
WOLF MANOR IN THE CLOSING DAYS OF JANUARY.
GHOST!
STOP THAT! NO ROUGHHOUSING IN THE WAR ROOM.
MOMMY NEEDS TO WORK.
GO SEE WHAT YOUR BROTHERS AND SISTERS ARE...
...DOING.
THANKS, SWEETIE.
THE DAY AMBLES ALONG, AS DAYS ARE APT TO DO.
YOU KIDS HAD BETTER BE FINISHED CLEANING YOUR ROOMS.
NOK NOK
UH OH.
OH.
I SEE.
MONSTERS TO THE FINISH.
HEY!
GIVE ME BACK MR. GROWLY!
SPLASH!

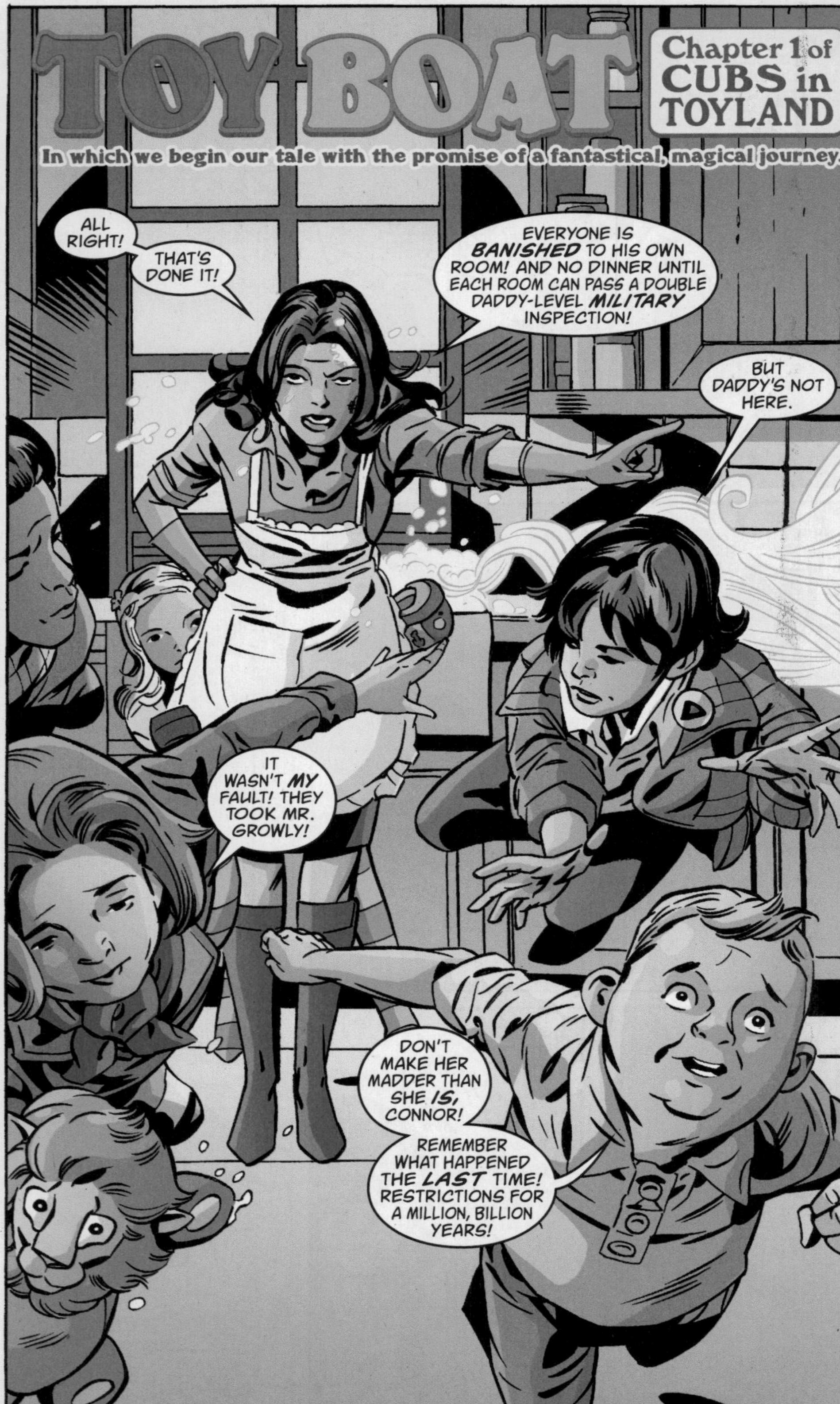
TOY BOAT
Chapter 1 of CUBS in TOYLAND
In which we begin our tale with the promise of a fantastical, magical journey.
ALL RIGHT!
THAT'S DONE IT!
EVERYONE IS BANISHED TO HIS OWN ROOM! AND NO DINNER UNTIL EACH ROOM CAN PASS A DOUBLE DADDY-LEVEL MILITARY INSPECTION!
BUT DADDY'S NOT HERE.
IT WASN'T MY FAULT! THEY TOOK MR. GROWLY!
DON'T MAKE HER MADDER THAN SHE IS, CONNOR!
REMEMBER WHAT HAPPENED THE LAST TIME! RESTRICTIONS FOR A MILLION, BILLION YEARS!

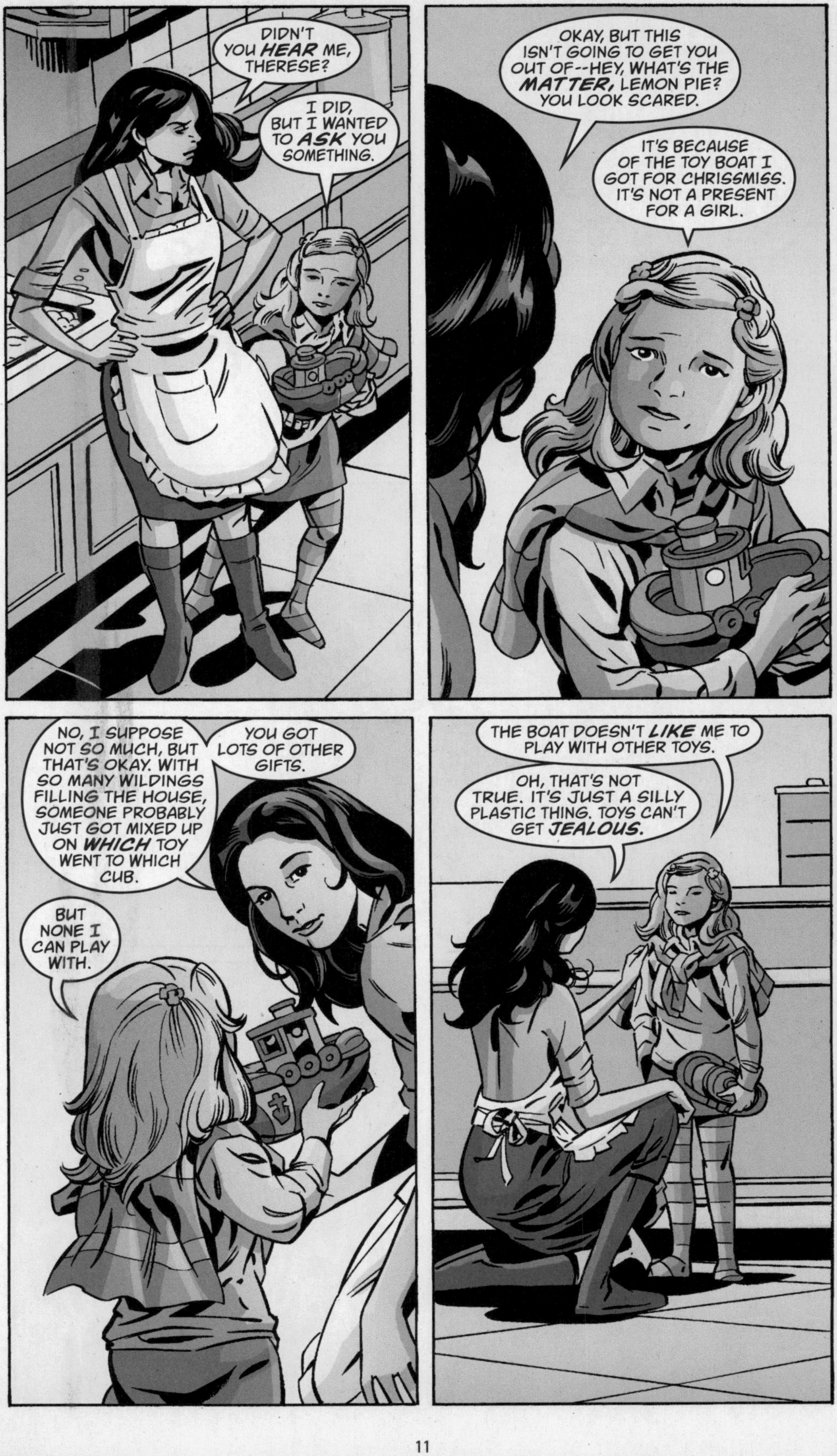
DIDN'T YOU HEAR ME, THERESE?
I DID, BUT I WANTED TO ASK YOU SOMETHING.
OKAY, BUT THIS ISN'T GOING TO GET YOU OUT OF--HEY, WHAT'S THE MATTER, LEMON PIE? YOU LOOK SCARED.
IT'S BECAUSE OF THE TOY BOAT I GOT FOR CHRISSMISS. IT'S NOT A PRESENT FOR A GIRL.
NO, I SUPPOSE NOT SO MUCH, BUT THAT'S OKAY. WITH SO MANY WILDINGS FILLING THE HOUSE, SOMEONE PROBABLY JUST GOT MIXED UP ON WHICH TOY WENT TO WHICH CUB.
YOU GOT LOTS OF OTHER GIFTS.
BUT NONE I CAN PLAY WITH.
THE BOAT DOESN'T LIKE ME TO PLAY WITH OTHER TOYS.
OH, THAT'S NOT TRUE. IT'S JUST A SILLY PLASTIC THING. TOYS CAN'T GET JEALOUS.

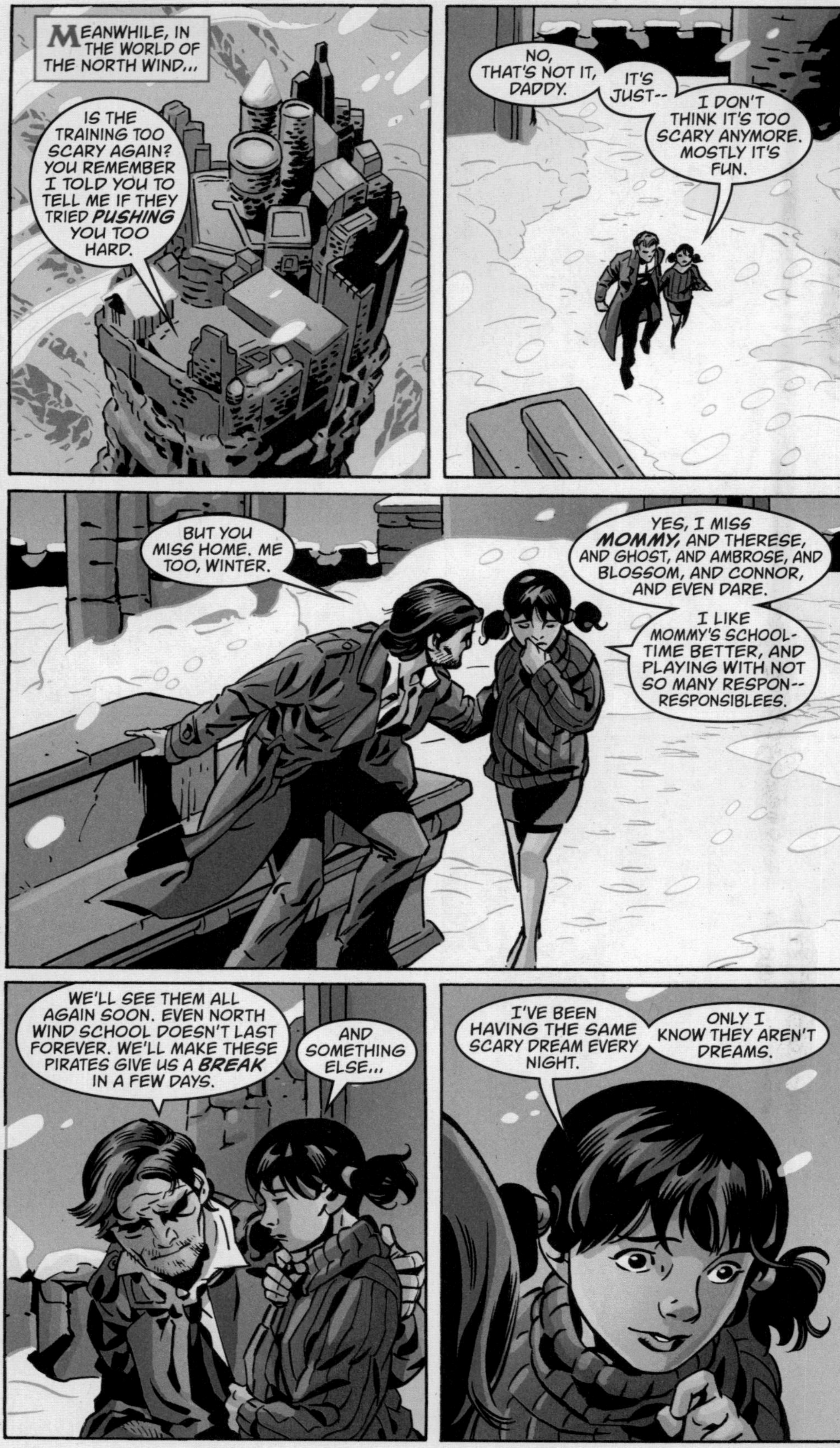
MEANWHILE, IN THE WORLD OF THE NORTH WIND...
IS THE TRAINING TOO SCARY AGAIN? YOU REMEMBER I TOLD YOU TO TELL ME IF THEY TRIED PUSHING YOU TOO HARD.
NO, THAT'S NOT IT, DADDY.
IT'S JUST--
I DON'T THINK IT'S TOO SCARY ANYMORE. MOSTLY IT'S FUN.
BUT YOU MISS HOME. ME TOO, WINTER.
YES, I MISS MOMMY, AND THERESE, AND GHOST, AND AMBROSE, AND BLOSSOM, AND CONNOR, AND EVEN DARE.
I LIKE MOMMY'S SCHOOL-TIME BETTER, AND PLAYING WITH NOT SO MANY RESPON-- RESPONSIBLEES.
WE'LL SEE THEM ALL AGAIN SOON. EVEN NORTH WIND SCHOOL DOESN'T LAST FOREVER. WE'LL MAKE THESE PIRATES GIVE US A BREAK IN A FEW DAYS.
AND SOMETHING ELSE...
I'VE BEEN HAVING THE SAME SCARY DREAM EVERY NIGHT.
ONLY I KNOW THEY AREN'T DREAMS.

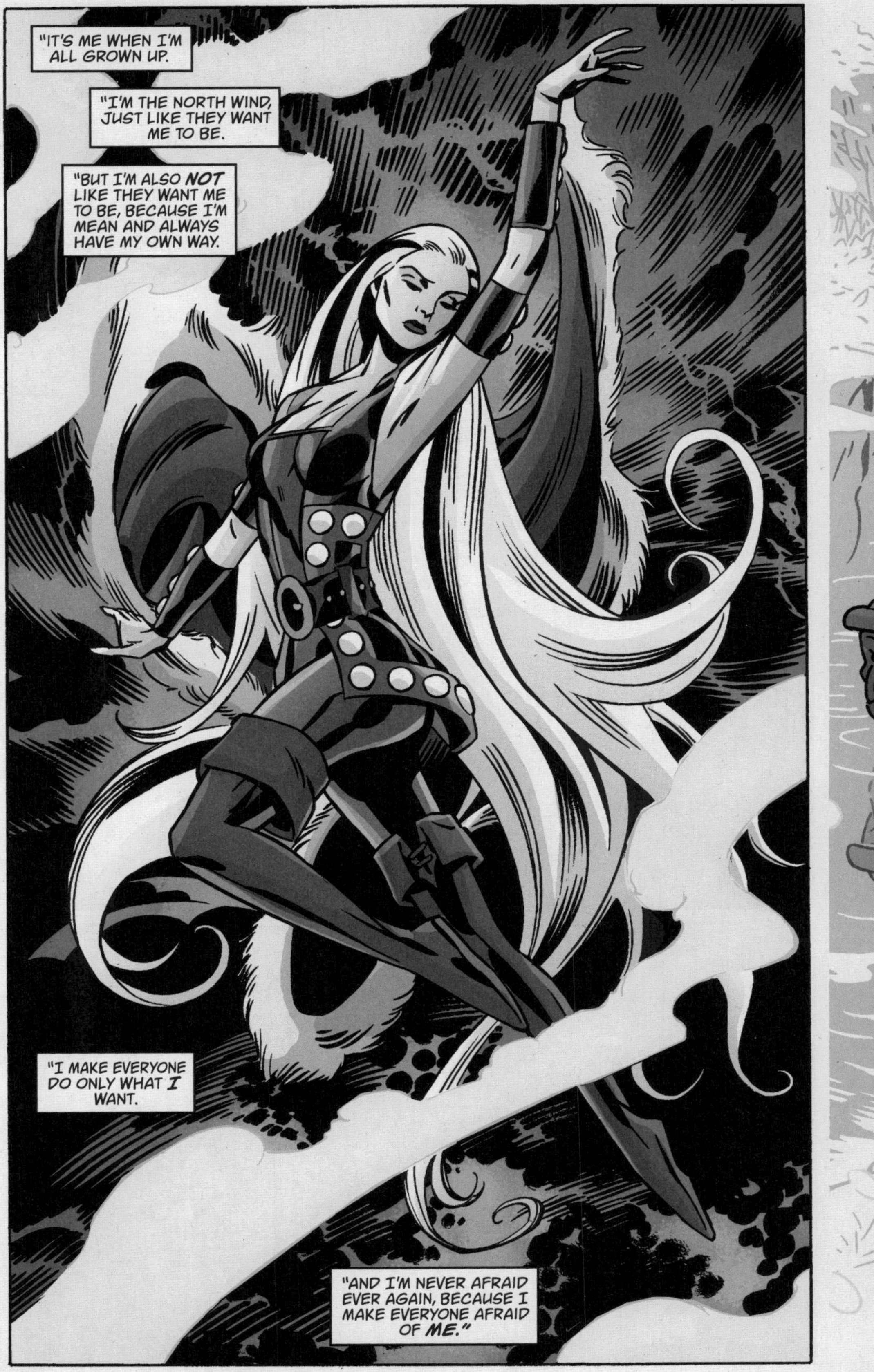
"IT'S ME WHEN I'M ALL GROWN UP.
"I'M THE NORTH WIND, JUST LIKE THEY WANT ME TO BE.
"BUT I'M ALSO **NOT** LIKE THEY WANT ME TO BE, BECAUSE I'M MEAN AND ALWAYS HAVE MY OWN WAY.
"I MAKE EVERYONE DO ONLY WHAT ***I*** WANT.
"AND I'M NEVER AFRAID EVER AGAIN, BECAUSE I MAKE EVERYONE AFRAID OF ***ME.***"

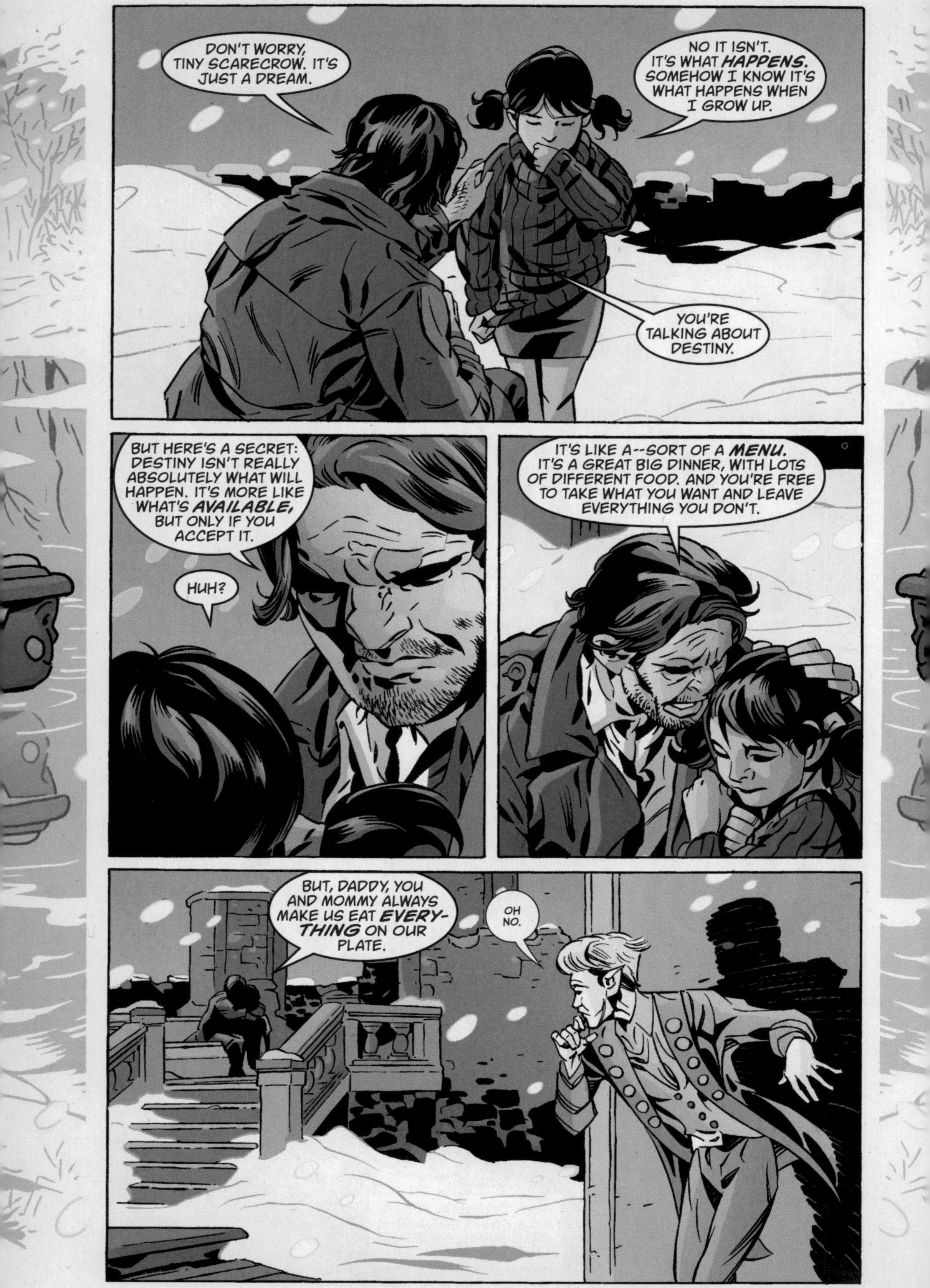
DON'T WORRY, TINY SCARECROW. IT'S JUST A DREAM.
NO IT ISN'T. IT'S WHAT HAPPENS. SOMEHOW I KNOW IT'S WHAT HAPPENS WHEN I GROW UP.
YOU'RE TALKING ABOUT DESTINY.
BUT HERE'S A SECRET: DESTINY ISN'T REALLY ABSOLUTELY WHAT WILL HAPPEN. IT'S MORE LIKE WHAT'S AVAILABLE, BUT ONLY IF YOU ACCEPT IT.
HUH?
IT'S LIKE A--SORT OF A MENU. IT'S A GREAT BIG DINNER, WITH LOTS OF DIFFERENT FOOD. AND YOU'RE FREE TO TAKE WHAT YOU WANT AND LEAVE EVERYTHING YOU DON'T.
BUT, DADDY, YOU AND MOMMY ALWAYS MAKE US EAT EVERY-THING ON OUR PLATE.
OH NO.

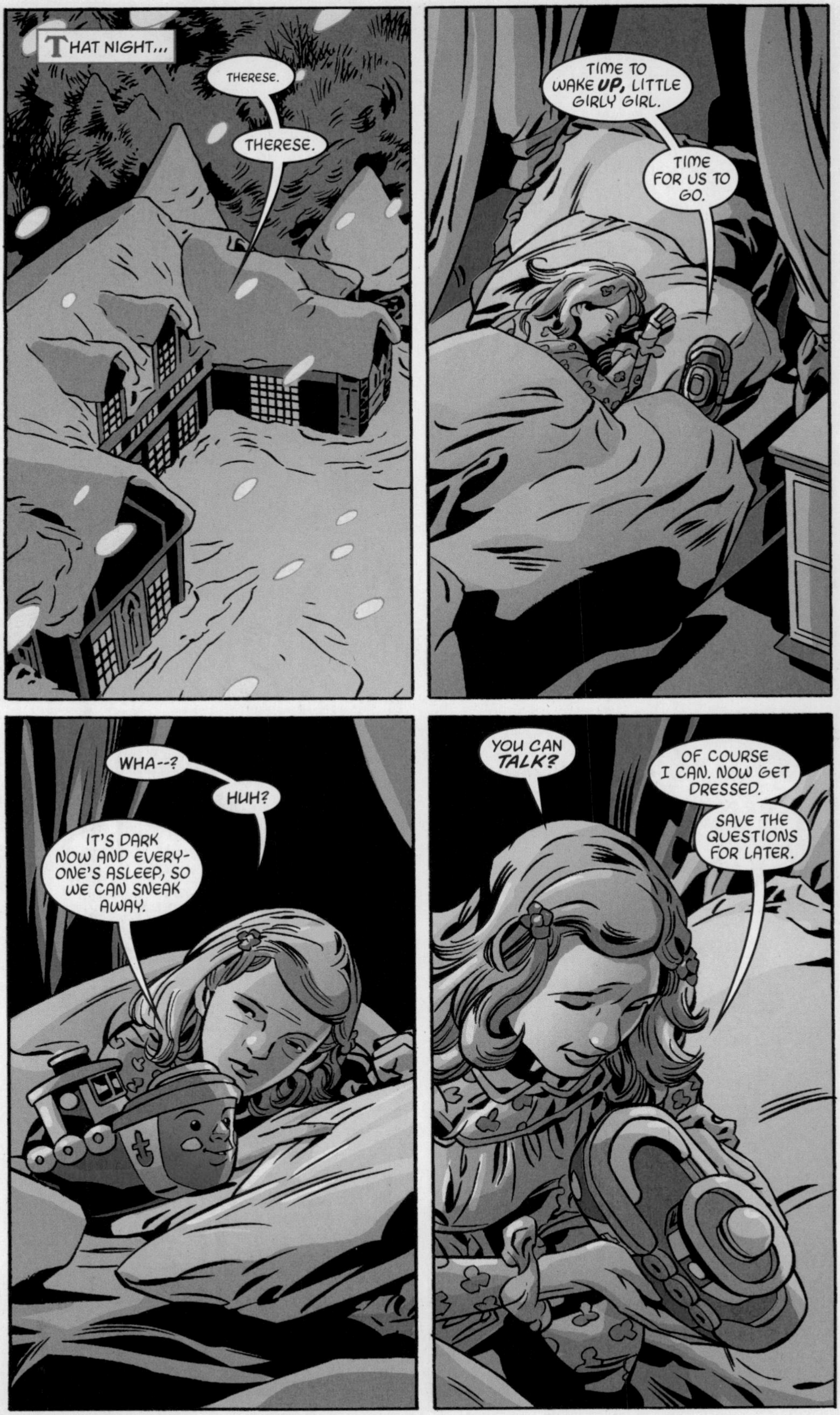
THAT NIGHT...
THERESE.
THERESE.
TIME TO WAKE UP, LITTLE GIRLY GIRL.
TIME FOR US TO GO.
WHA--?
HUH?
IT'S DARK NOW AND EVERY-ONE'S ASLEEP, SO WE CAN SNEAK AWAY.
YOU CAN TALK?
OF COURSE I CAN. NOW GET DRESSED.
SAVE THE QUESTIONS FOR LATER.

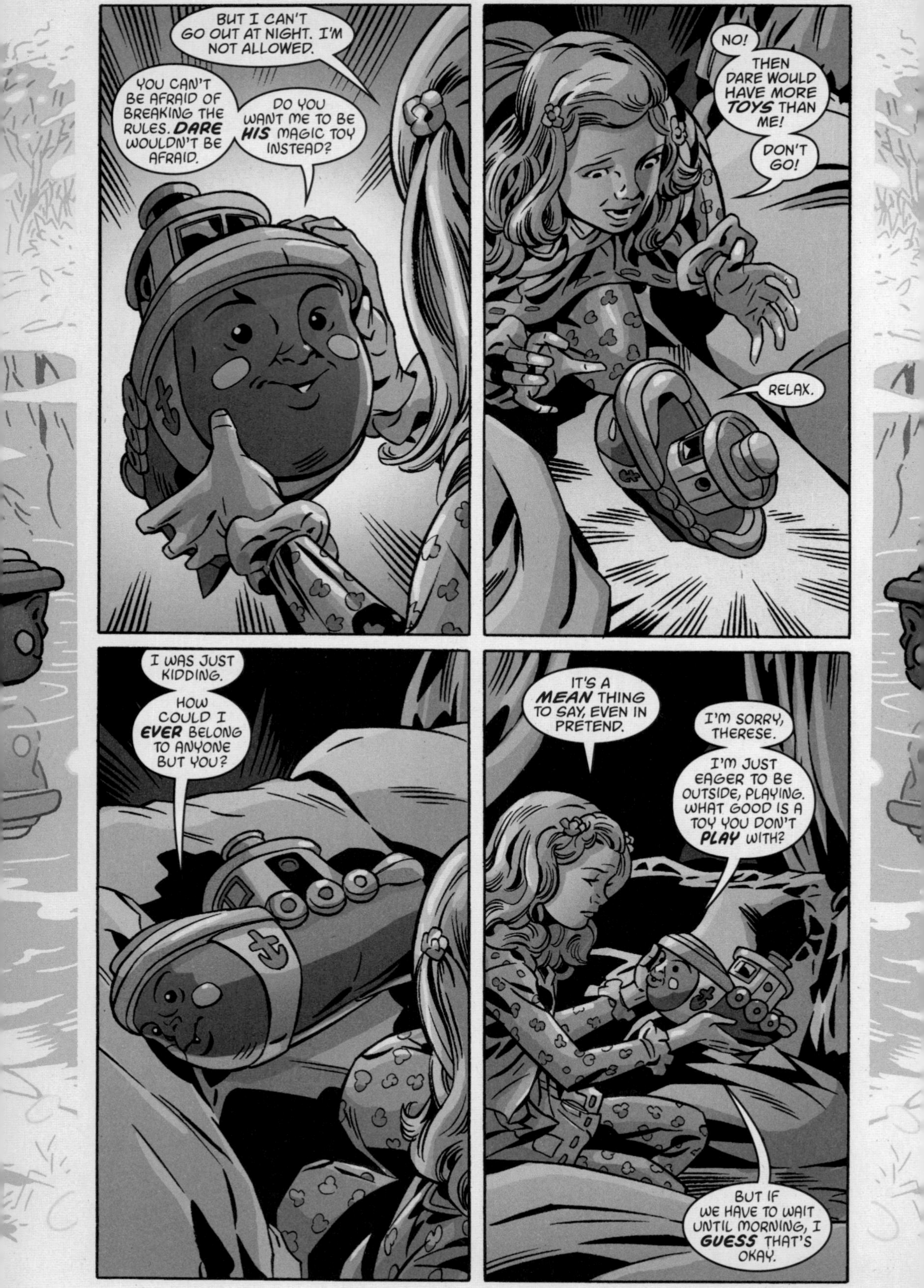
BUT I CAN'T GO OUT AT NIGHT. I'M NOT ALLOWED.
YOU CAN'T BE AFRAID OF BREAKING THE RULES. DARE WOULDN'T BE AFRAID.
DO YOU WANT ME TO BE HIS MAGIC TOY INSTEAD?
NO!
THEN DARE WOULD HAVE MORE TOYS THAN ME!
DON'T GO!
RELAX.
I WAS JUST KIDDING.
HOW COULD I EVER BELONG TO ANYONE BUT YOU?
IT'S A MEAN THING TO SAY, EVEN IN PRETEND.
I'M SORRY, THERESE.
I'M JUST EAGER TO BE OUTSIDE, PLAYING. WHAT GOOD IS A TOY YOU DON'T PLAY WITH?
BUT IF WE HAVE TO WAIT UNTIL MORNING, I GUESS THAT'S OKAY.

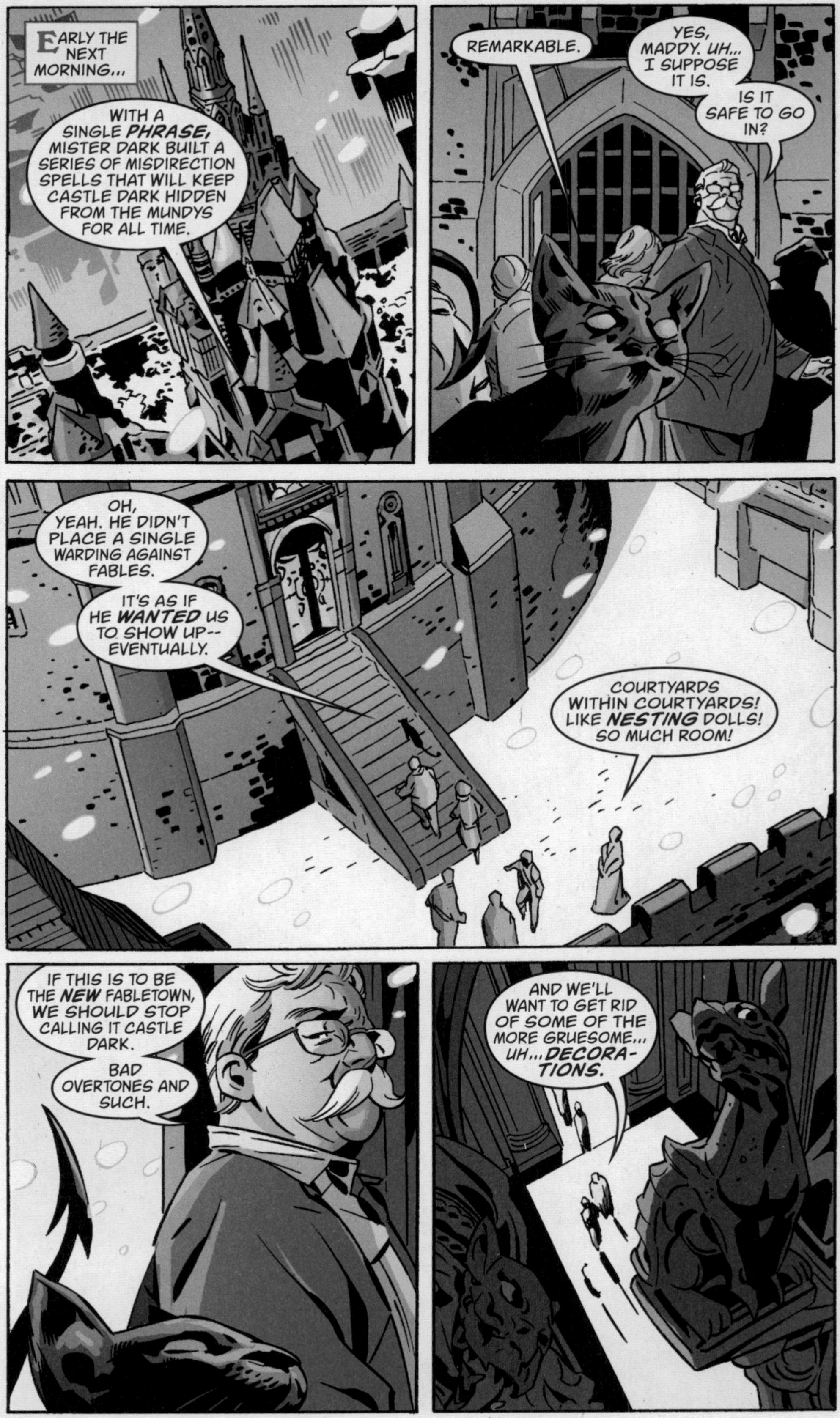
EARLY THE NEXT MORNING...
WITH A SINGLE PHRASE, MISTER DARK BUILT A SERIES OF MISDIRECTION SPELLS THAT WILL KEEP CASTLE DARK HIDDEN FROM THE MUNDYS FOR ALL TIME.
REMARKABLE.
YES, MADDY. UH... I SUPPOSE IT IS.
IS IT SAFE TO GO IN?
OH, YEAH. HE DIDN'T PLACE A SINGLE WARDING AGAINST FABLES.
IT'S AS IF HE WANTED US TO SHOW UP-- EVENTUALLY.
COURTYARDS WITHIN COURTYARDS! LIKE NESTING DOLLS! SO MUCH ROOM!
IF THIS IS TO BE THE NEW FABLETOWN, WE SHOULD STOP CALLING IT CASTLE DARK.
BAD OVERTONES AND SUCH.
AND WE'LL WANT TO GET RID OF SOME OF THE MORE GRUESOME... UH... DECORATIONS.

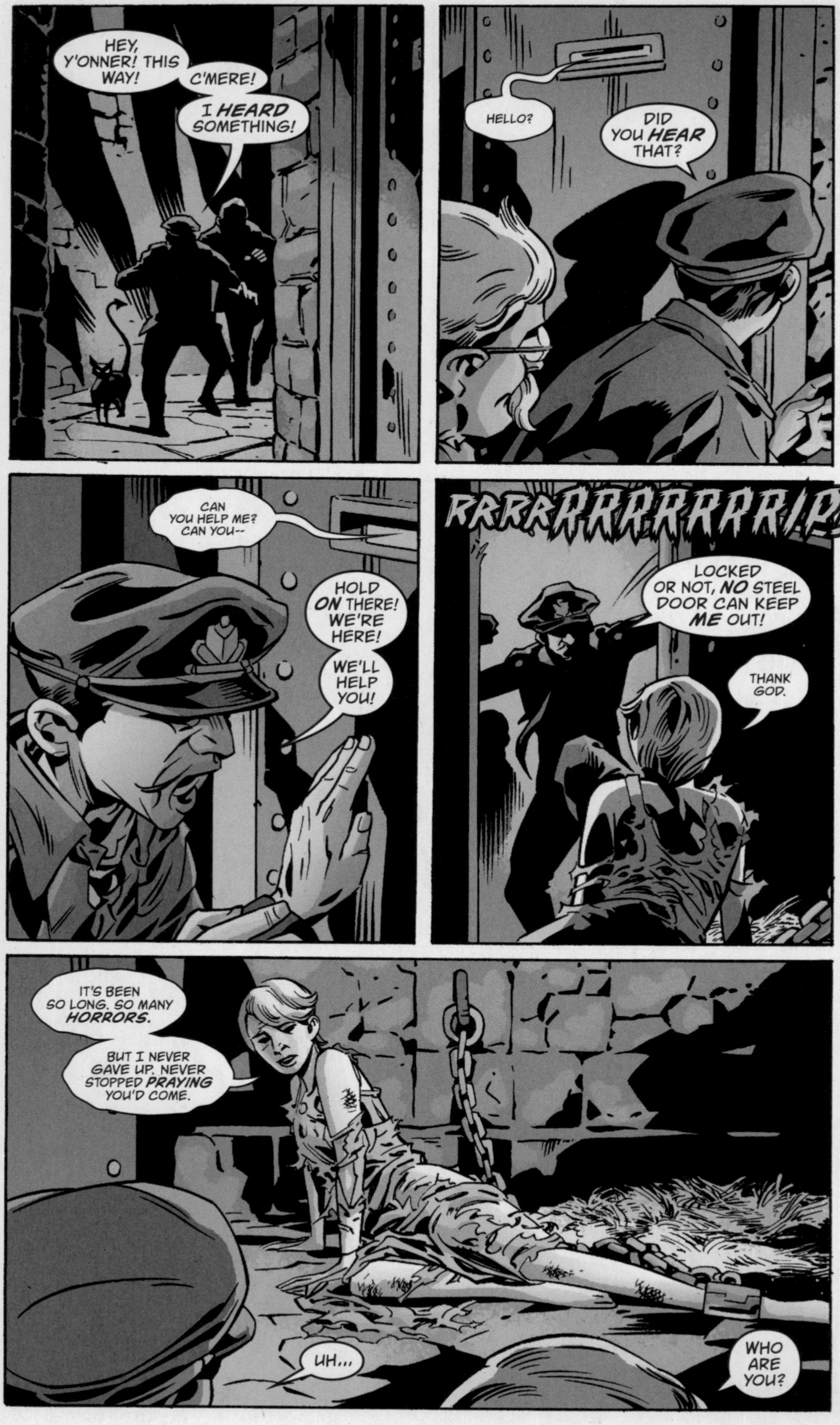

HEY, Y'ONNER! THIS WAY!
C'MERE!
I HEARD SOMETHING!
HELLO?
DID YOU HEAR THAT?
CAN YOU HELP ME? CAN YOU--
HOLD ON THERE! WE'RE HERE!
WE'LL HELP YOU!
RRRRRRRRRRRRRIP!
LOCKED OR NOT, NO STEEL DOOR CAN KEEP ME OUT!
THANK GOD.
IT'S BEEN SO LONG. SO MANY HORRORS.
BUT I NEVER GAVE UP. NEVER STOPPED PRAYING YOU'D COME.
UH...
WHO ARE YOU?

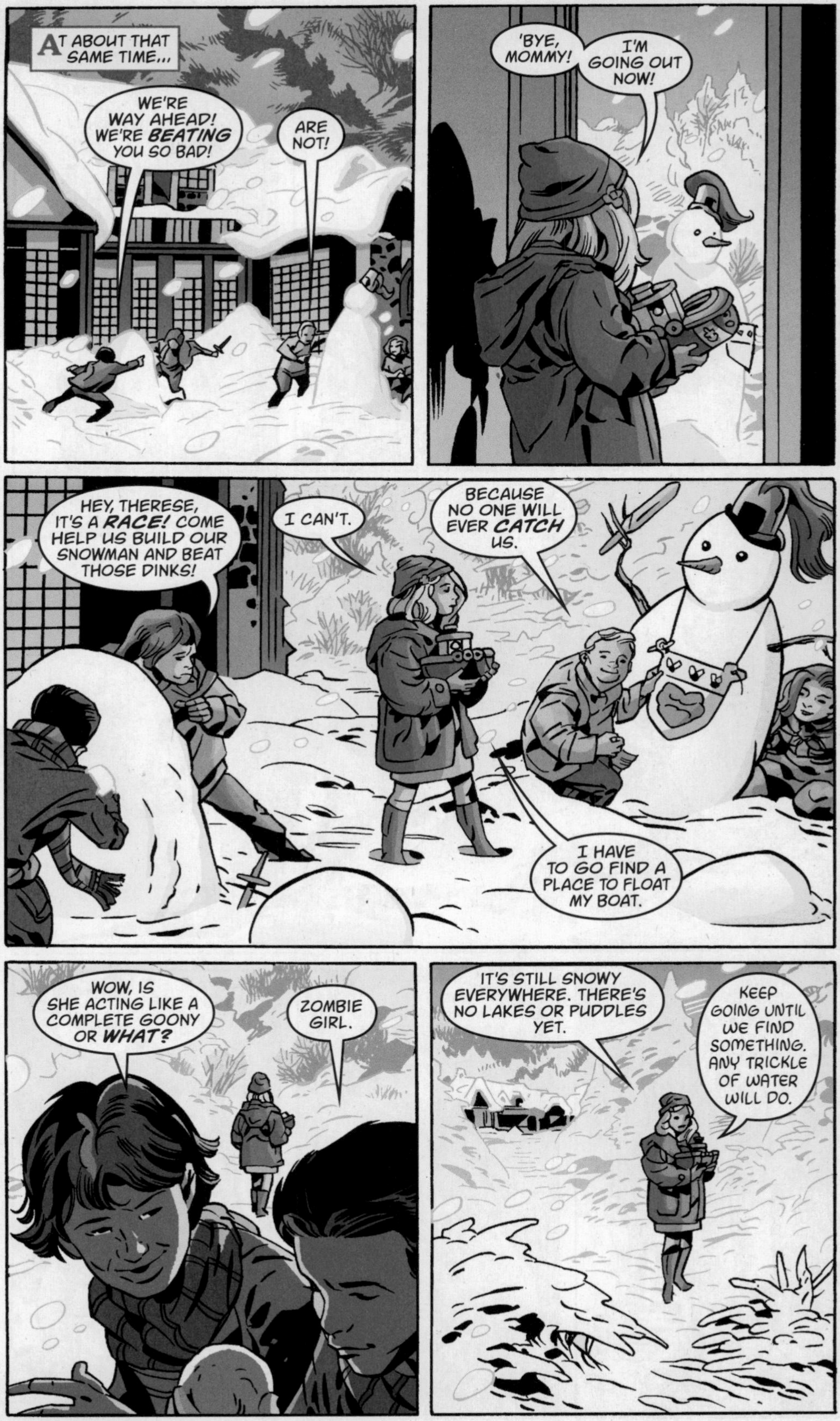
AT ABOUT THAT SAME TIME...
WE'RE WAY AHEAD! WE'RE BEATING YOU SO BAD!
ARE NOT!
'BYE, MOMMY!
I'M GOING OUT NOW!
HEY, THERESE, IT'S A RACE! COME HELP US BUILD OUR SNOWMAN AND BEAT THOSE DINKS!
I CAN'T.
BECAUSE NO ONE WILL EVER CATCH US.
I HAVE TO GO FIND A PLACE TO FLOAT MY BOAT.
WOW, IS SHE ACTING LIKE A COMPLETE GOONY OR WHAT?
ZOMBIE GIRL.
IT'S STILL SNOWY EVERYWHERE. THERE'S NO LAKES OR PUDDLES YET.
KEEP GOING UNTIL WE FIND SOMETHING. ANY TRICKLE OF WATER WILL DO.

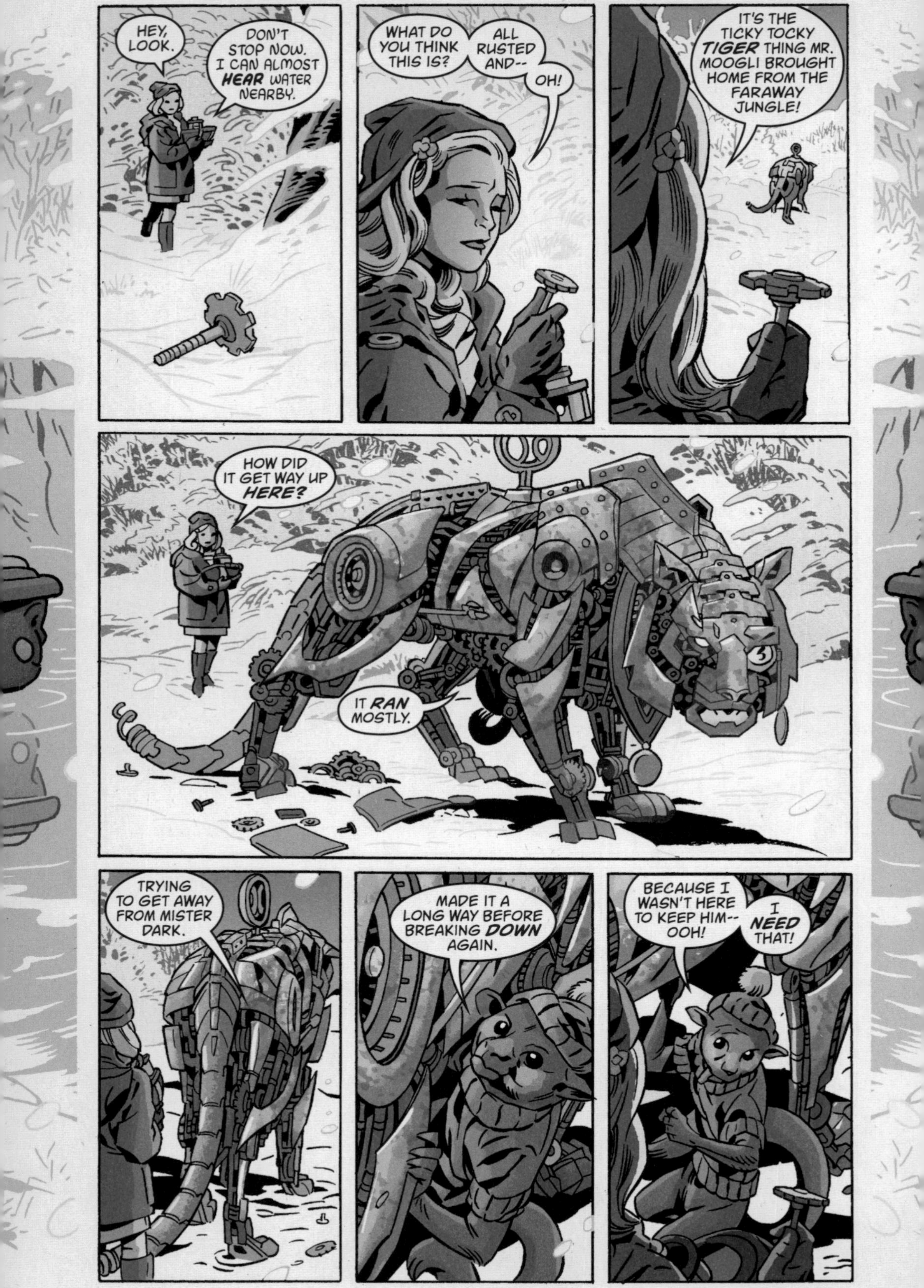
HEY, LOOK.
DON'T STOP NOW. I CAN ALMOST HEAR WATER NEARBY.
WHAT DO YOU THINK THIS IS?
ALL RUSTED AND--
OH!
IT'S THE TICKY TOCKY TIGER THING MR. MOOGLI BROUGHT HOME FROM THE FARAWAY JUNGLE!
HOW DID IT GET WAY UP HERE?
IT RAN MOSTLY.
TRYING TO GET AWAY FROM MISTER DARK.
MADE IT A LONG WAY BEFORE BREAKING DOWN AGAIN.
BECAUSE I WASN'T HERE TO KEEP HIM--OOH!
I NEED THAT!

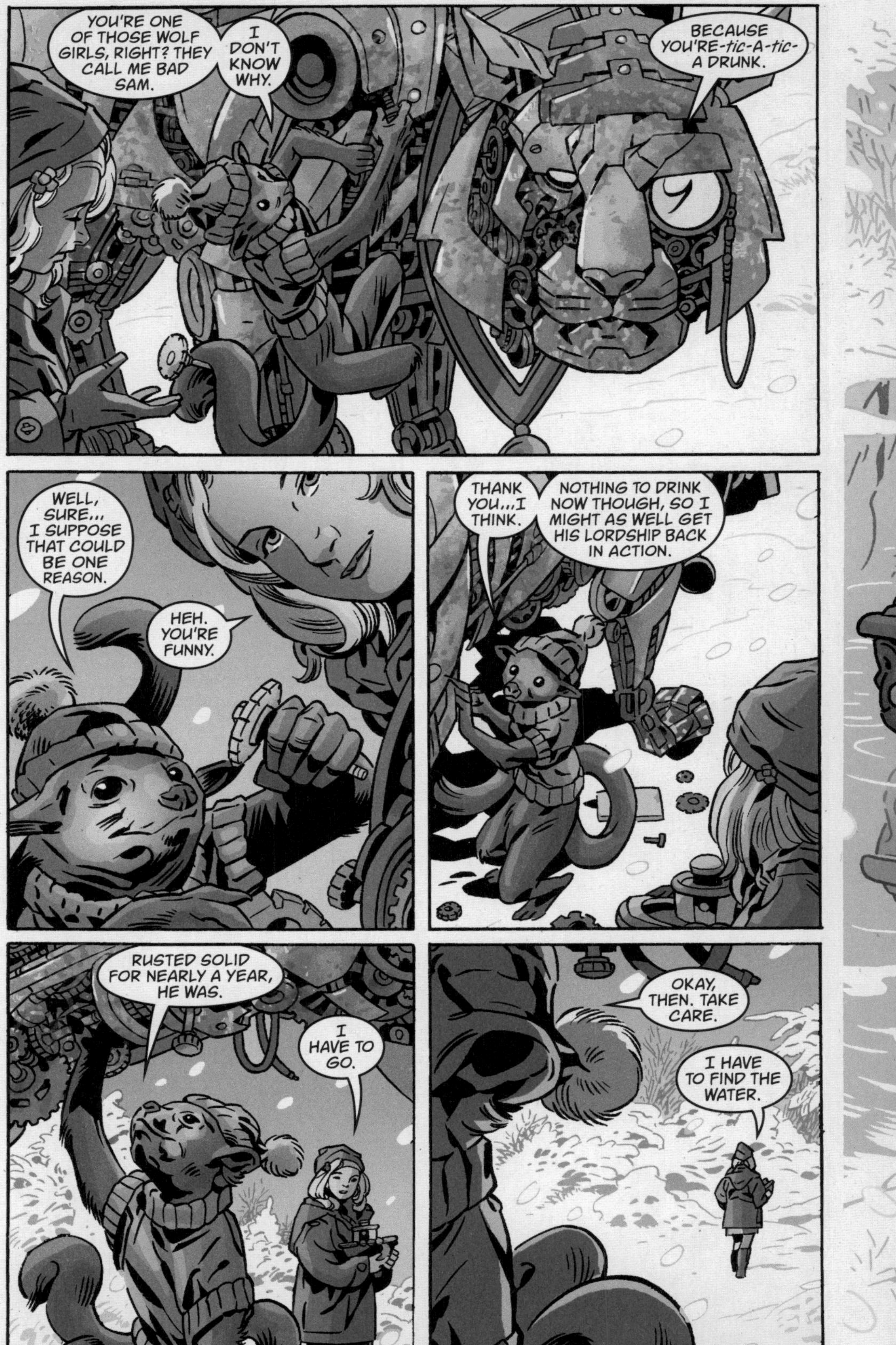
YOU'RE ONE OF THOSE WOLF GIRLS, RIGHT? THEY CALL ME BAD SAM.
I DON'T KNOW WHY.
BECAUSE YOU'RE-tic-A-tic-A DRUNK.
WELL, SURE... I SUPPOSE THAT COULD BE ONE REASON.
HEH. YOU'RE FUNNY.
THANK YOU...I THINK.
NOTHING TO DRINK NOW THOUGH, SO I MIGHT AS WELL GET HIS LORDSHIP BACK IN ACTION.
RUSTED SOLID FOR NEARLY A YEAR, HE WAS.
I HAVE TO GO.
OKAY, THEN. TAKE CARE.
I HAVE TO FIND THE WATER.

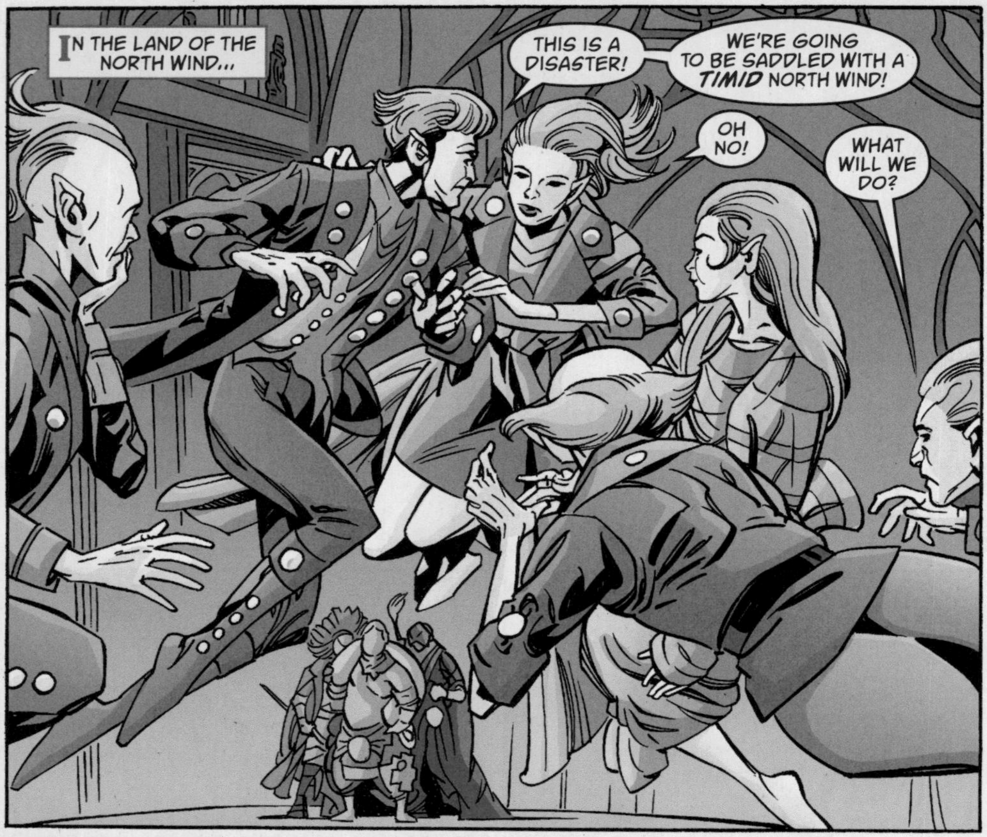
IN THE LAND OF THE NORTH WIND...
THIS IS A DISASTER!
WE'RE GOING TO BE SADDLED WITH A TIMID NORTH WIND!
OH NO!
WHAT WILL WE DO?

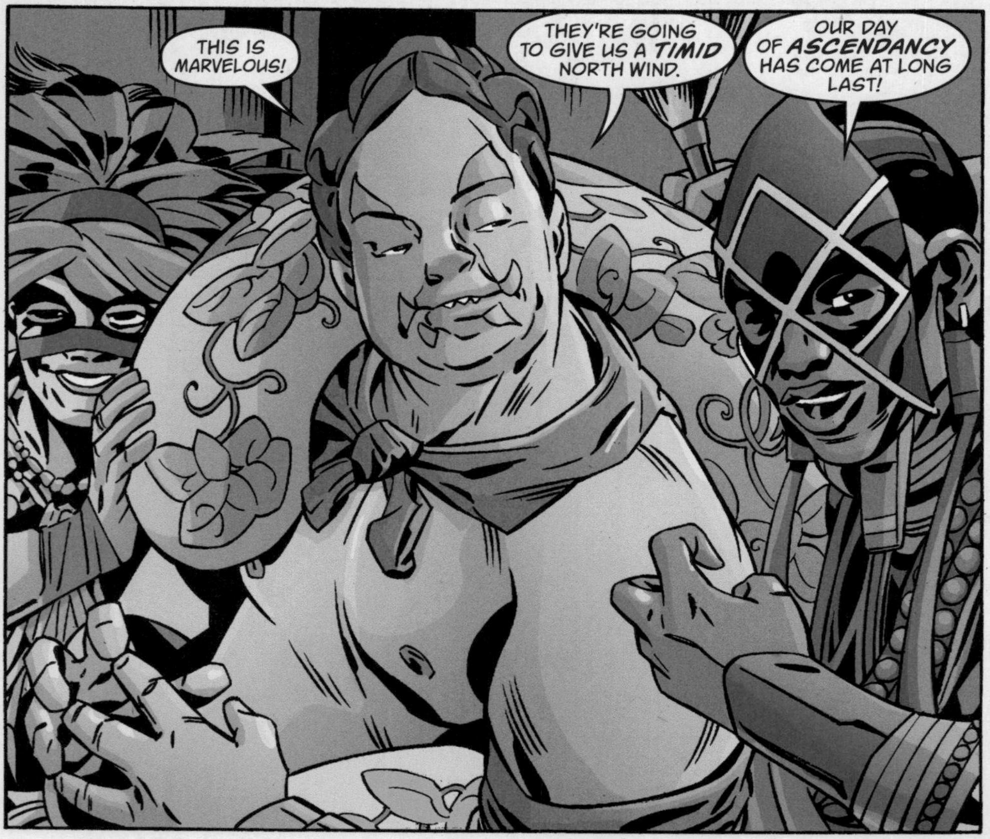
THIS IS MARVELOUS!
THEY'RE GOING TO GIVE US A TIMID NORTH WIND.
OUR DAY OF ASCENDANCY HAS COME AT LONG LAST!

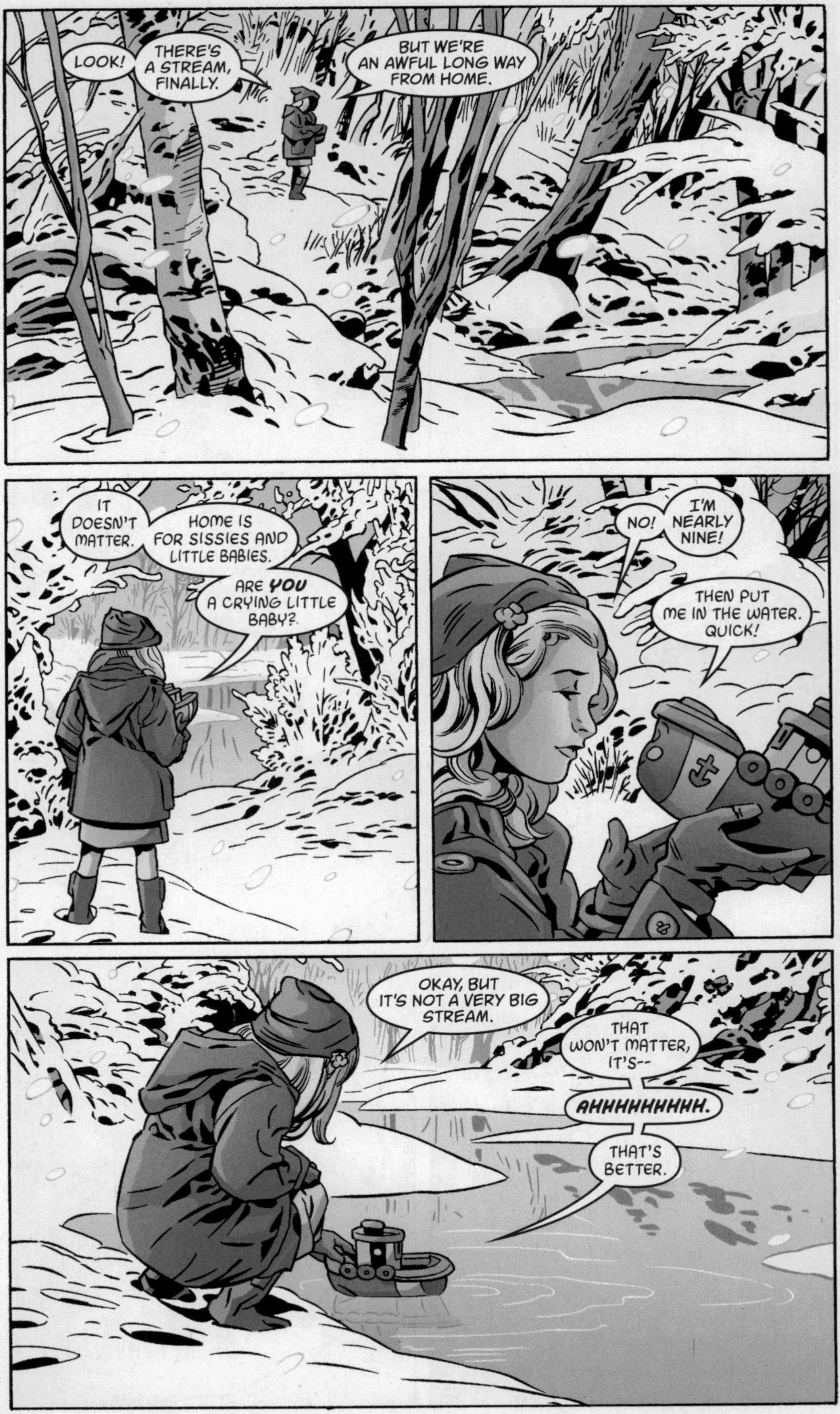
LOOK!
THERE'S A STREAM, FINALLY.
BUT WE'RE AN AWFUL LONG WAY FROM HOME.
IT DOESN'T MATTER.
HOME IS FOR SISSIES AND LITTLE BABIES.
ARE *YOU* A CRYING LITTLE BABY?
NO!
I'M NEARLY NINE!
THEN PUT ME IN THE WATER. QUICK!
OKAY, BUT IT'S NOT A VERY BIG STREAM.
THAT WON'T MATTER, IT'S--
AHHHHHHHHH.
THAT'S BETTER.

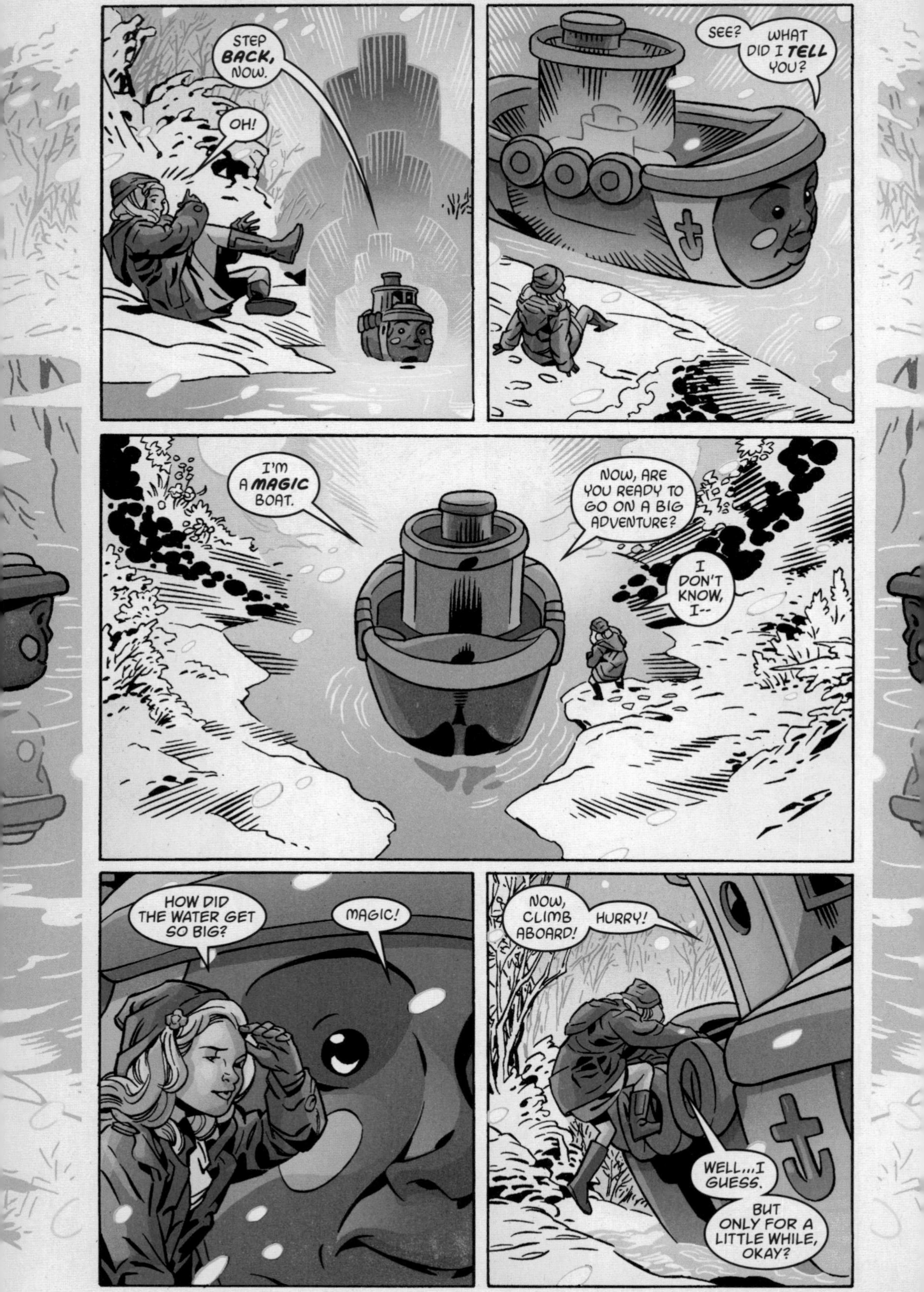
STEP BACK, NOW.
OH!
SEE?
WHAT DID I TELL YOU?
I'M A MAGIC BOAT.
NOW, ARE YOU READY TO GO ON A BIG ADVENTURE?
I DON'T KNOW, I--
HOW DID THE WATER GET SO BIG?
MAGIC!
NOW, CLIMB ABOARD!
HURRY!
WELL...I GUESS.
BUT ONLY FOR A LITTLE WHILE, OKAY?

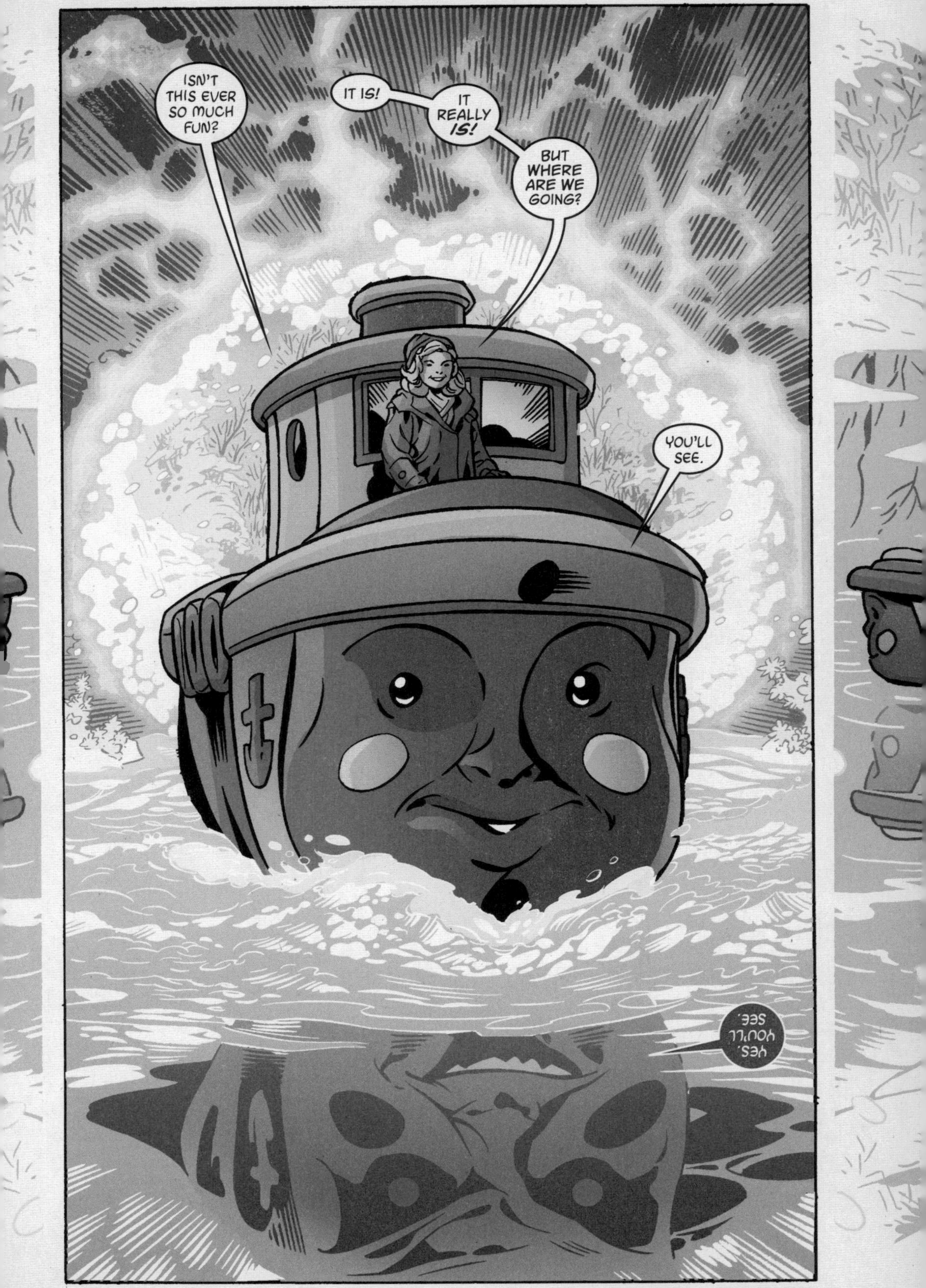
ISN'T THIS EVER SO MUCH FUN?
IT IS!
IT REALLY IS!
BUT WHERE ARE WE GOING?
YOU'LL SEE.
YES, YOU'LL SEE.

NEXT: THE HAPPY WONDERLAND

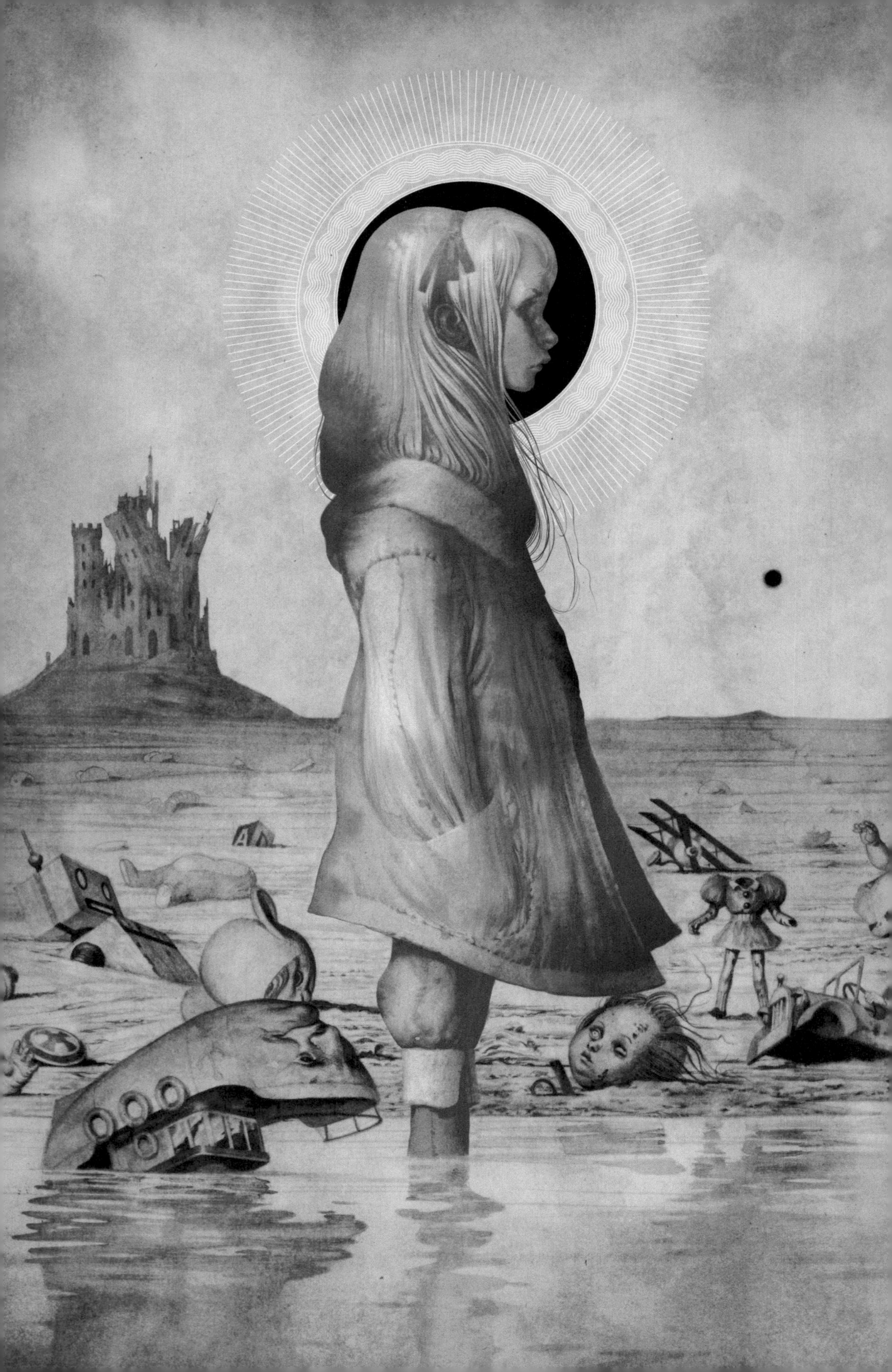

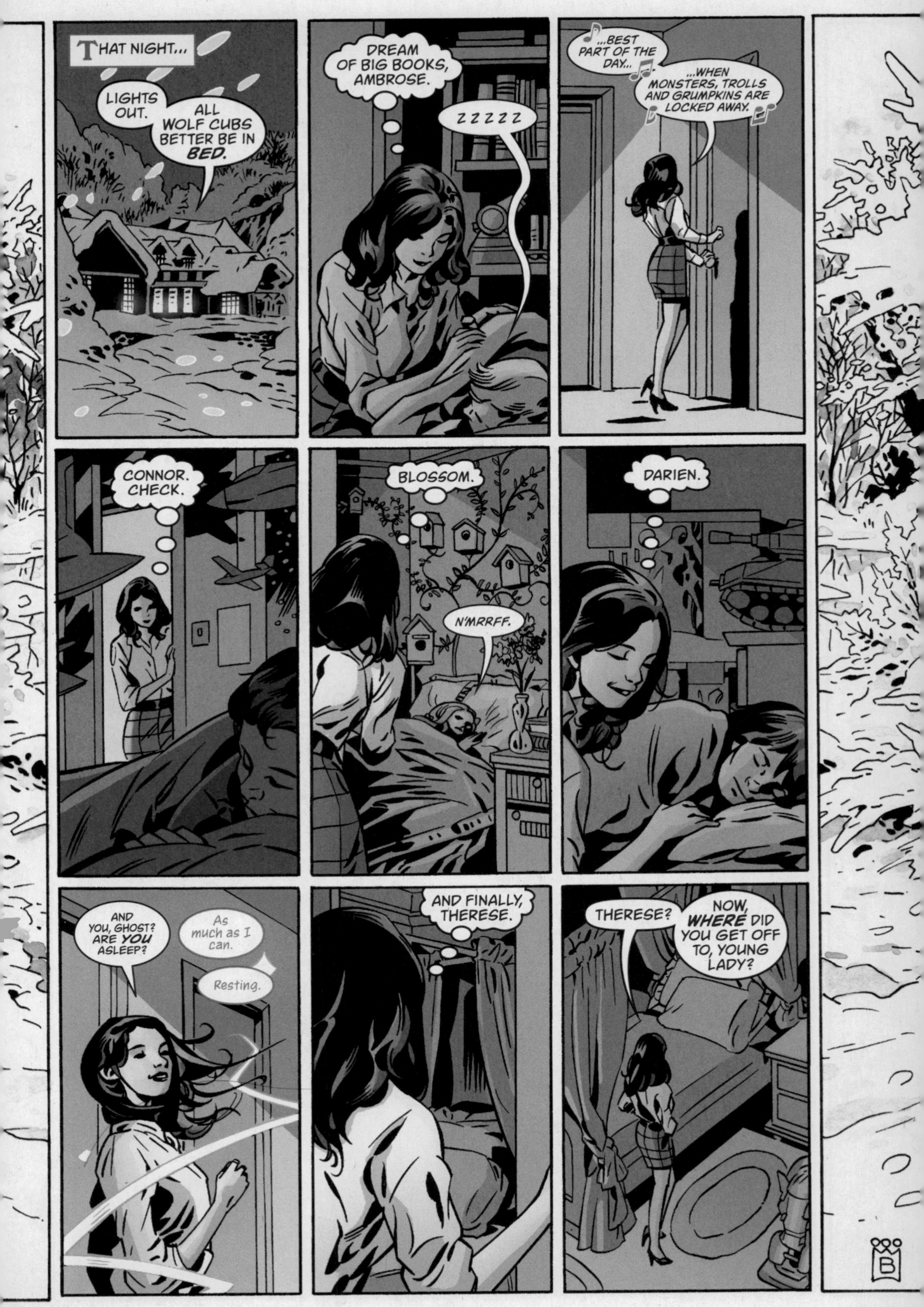

THAT NIGHT...
LIGHTS OUT.
ALL WOLF CUBS BETTER BE IN BED.
DREAM OF BIG BOOKS, AMBROSE.
ZZZZZ
...BEST PART OF THE DAY...
...WHEN MONSTERS, TROLLS AND GRUMPKINS ARE LOCKED AWAY.
CONNOR. CHECK.
BLOSSOM.
N'MRRFF.
DARIEN.
AND YOU, GHOST? ARE YOU ASLEEP?
As much as I can.
Resting.
AND FINALLY, THERESE.
THERESE?
NOW, WHERE DID YOU GET OFF TO, YOUNG LADY?

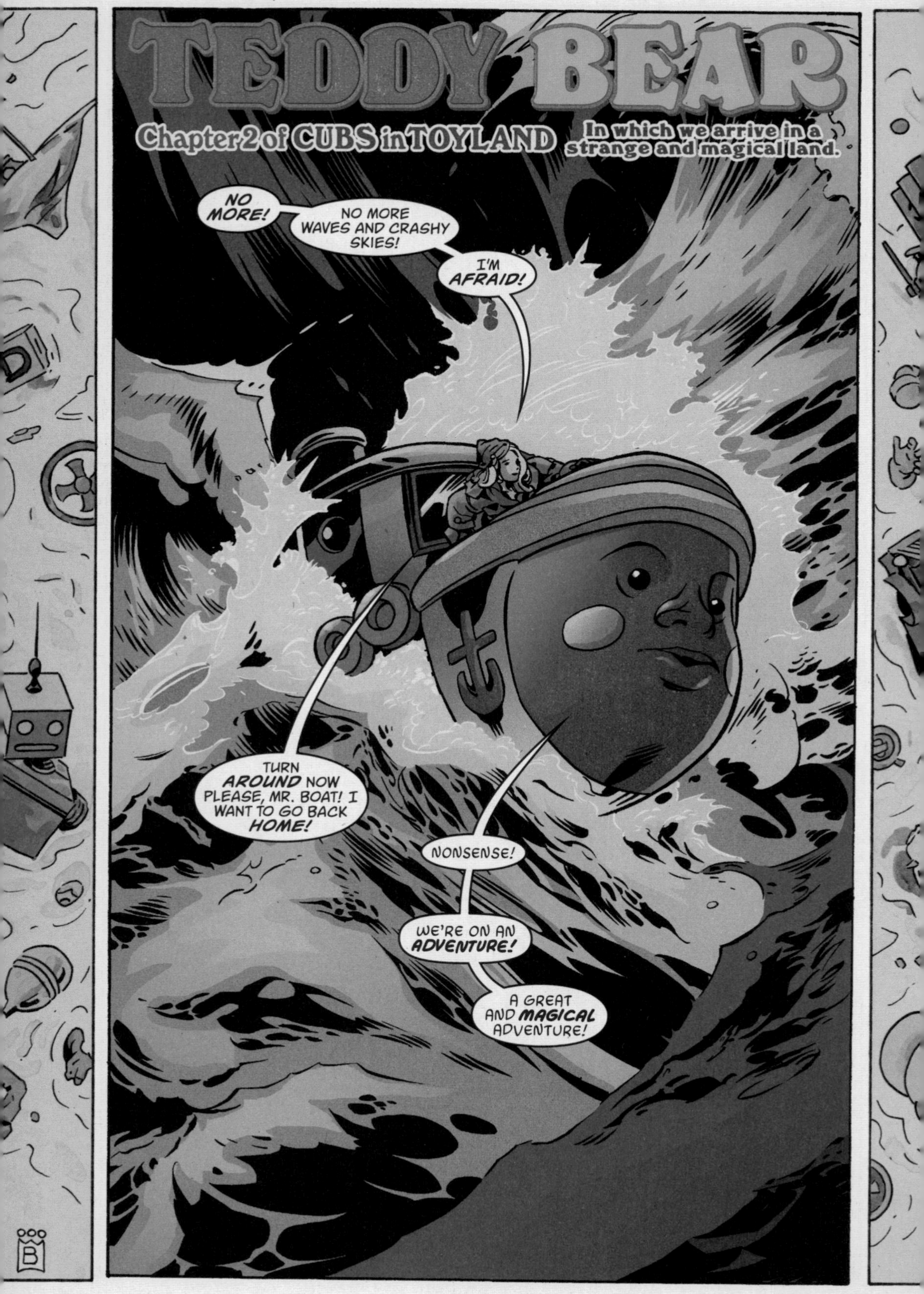
TEDDY BEAR
Chapter 2 of CUBS in TOYLAND
In which we arrive in a strange and magical land.
NO MORE!
NO MORE WAVES AND CRASHY SKIES!
I'M AFRAID!
TURN AROUND NOW PLEASE, MR. BOAT! I WANT TO GO BACK HOME!
NONSENSE!
WE'RE ON AN ADVENTURE!
A GREAT AND MAGICAL ADVENTURE!

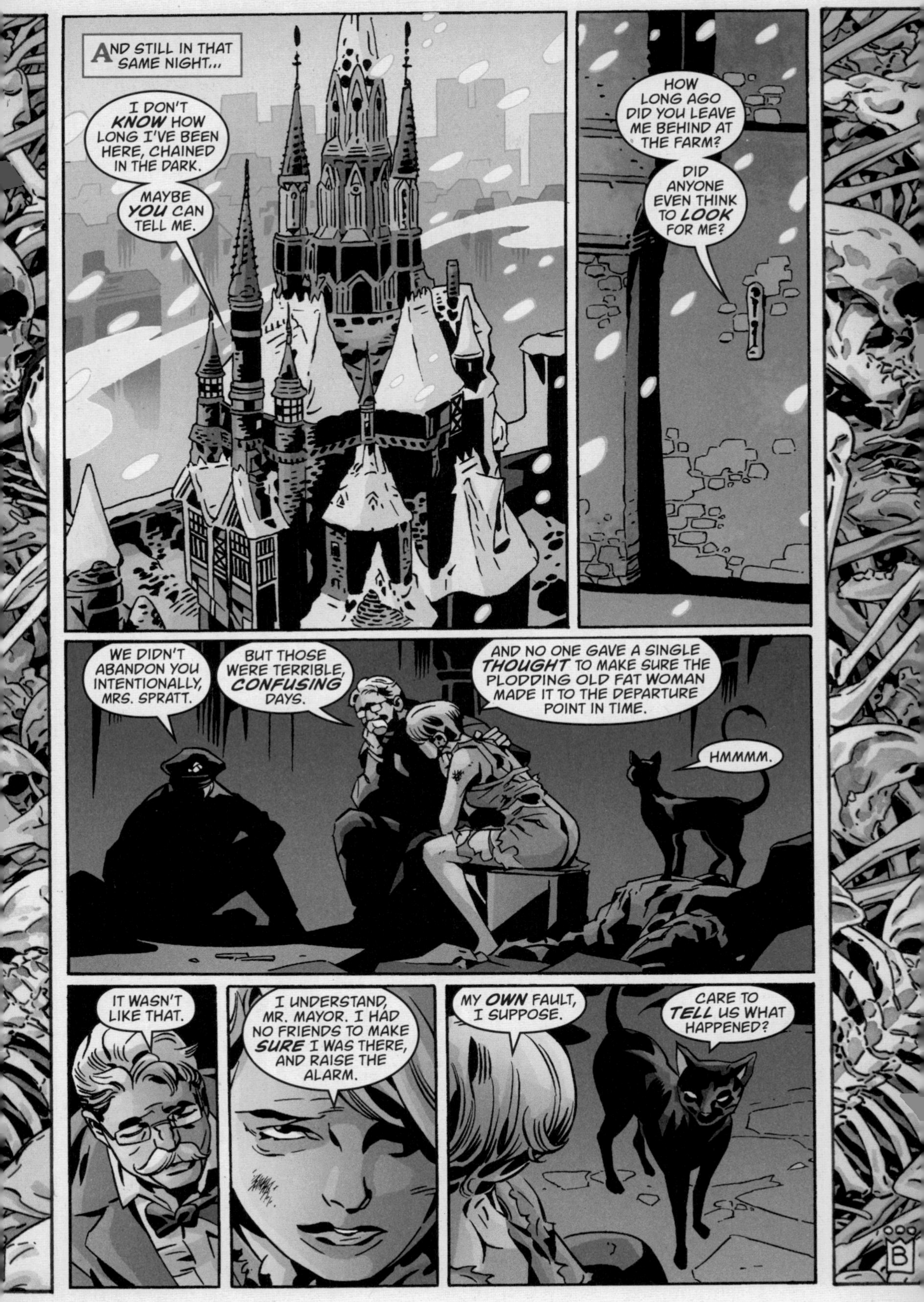
AND STILL IN THAT SAME NIGHT...
I DON'T KNOW HOW LONG I'VE BEEN HERE, CHAINED IN THE DARK.
MAYBE YOU CAN TELL ME.
HOW LONG AGO DID YOU LEAVE ME BEHIND AT THE FARM?
DID ANYONE EVEN THINK TO LOOK FOR ME?
WE DIDN'T ABANDON YOU INTENTIONALLY, MRS. SPRATT.
BUT THOSE WERE TERRIBLE, CONFUSING DAYS.
AND NO ONE GAVE A SINGLE THOUGHT TO MAKE SURE THE PLODDING OLD FAT WOMAN MADE IT TO THE DEPARTURE POINT IN TIME.
HMMMM.
IT WASN'T LIKE THAT.
I UNDERSTAND, MR. MAYOR. I HAD NO FRIENDS TO MAKE SURE I WAS THERE, AND RAISE THE ALARM.
MY OWN FAULT, I SUPPOSE.
CARE TO TELL US WHAT HAPPENED?

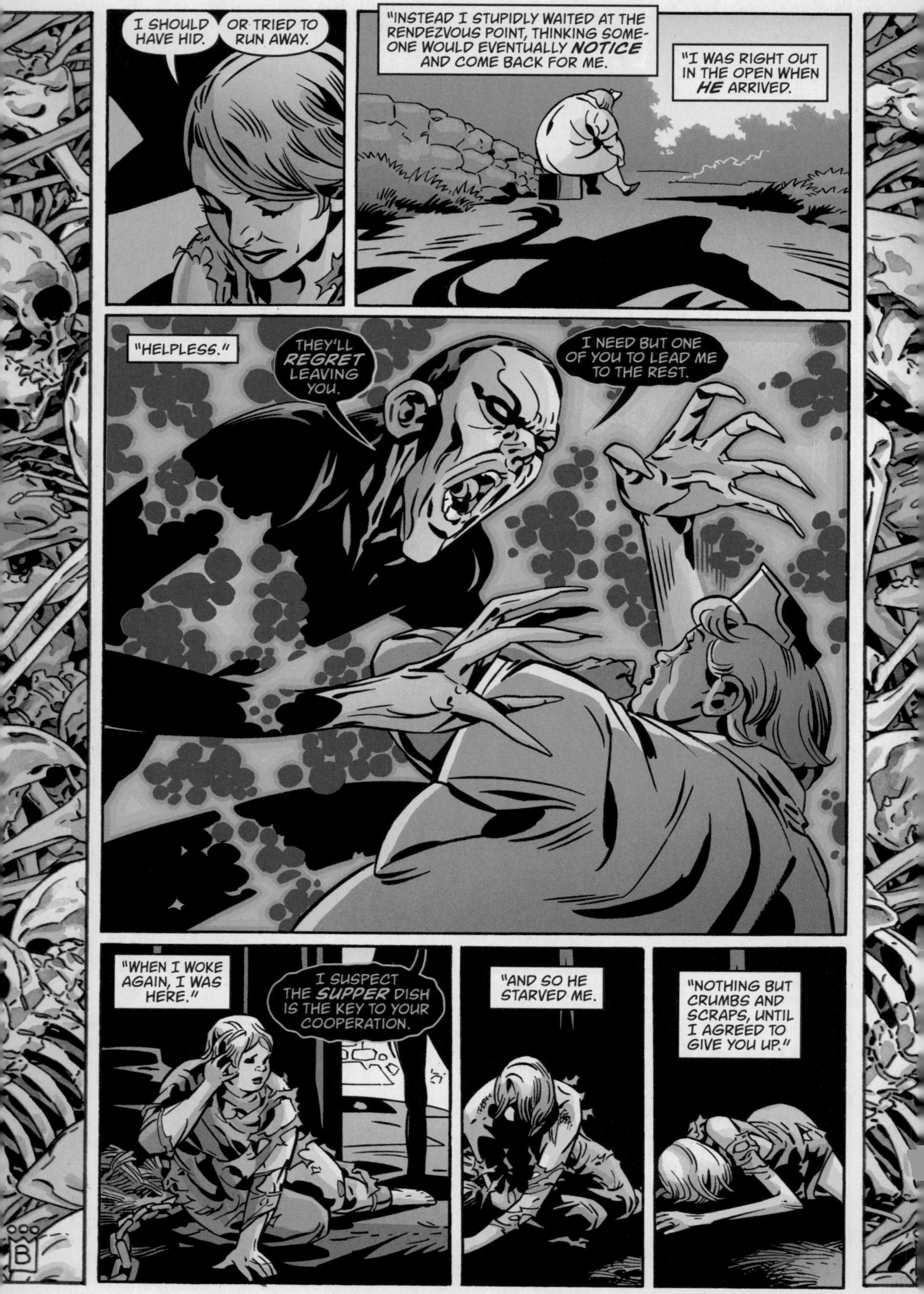
I SHOULD HAVE HID.
OR TRIED TO RUN AWAY.
"INSTEAD I STUPIDLY WAITED AT THE RENDEZVOUS POINT, THINKING SOME-ONE WOULD EVENTUALLY NOTICE AND COME BACK FOR ME.
"I WAS RIGHT OUT IN THE OPEN WHEN HE ARRIVED.
"HELPLESS."
THEY'LL REGRET LEAVING YOU.
I NEED BUT ONE OF YOU TO LEAD ME TO THE REST.
"WHEN I WOKE AGAIN, I WAS HERE."
I SUSPECT THE SUPPER DISH IS THE KEY TO YOUR COOPERATION.
"AND SO HE STARVED ME.
"NOTHING BUT CRUMBS AND SCRAPS, UNTIL I AGREED TO GIVE YOU UP."

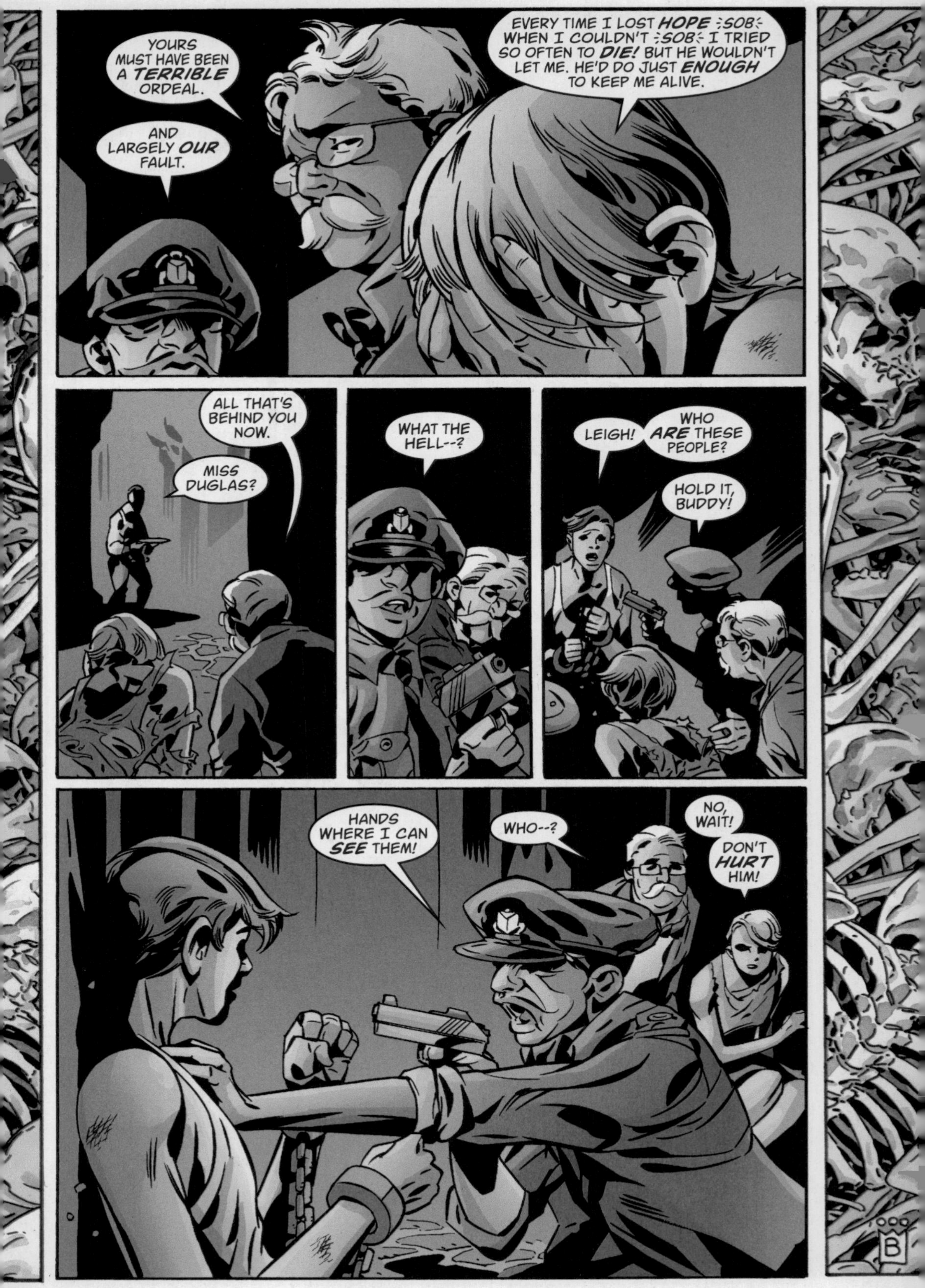
YOURS MUST HAVE BEEN A TERRIBLE ORDEAL.
AND LARGELY OUR FAULT.
EVERY TIME I LOST HOPE :SOB: WHEN I COULDN'T :SOB: I TRIED SO OFTEN TO DIE! BUT HE WOULDN'T LET ME. HE'D DO JUST ENOUGH TO KEEP ME ALIVE.
ALL THAT'S BEHIND YOU NOW.
MISS DUGLAS?
WHAT THE HELL--?
LEIGH!
WHO ARE THESE PEOPLE?
HOLD IT, BUDDY!
HANDS WHERE I CAN SEE THEM!
WHO--?
NO, WAIT!
DON'T HURT HIM!

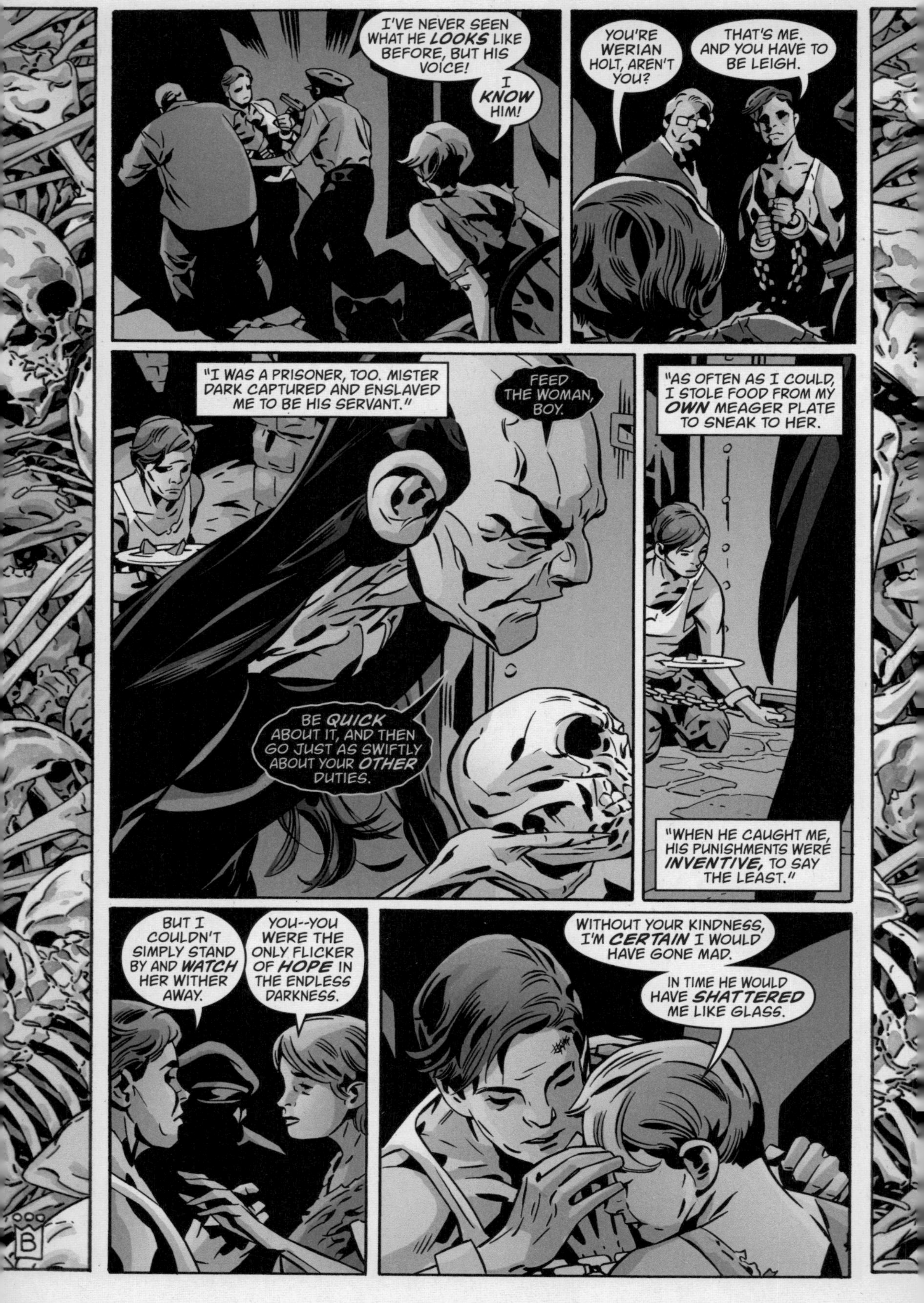

I'VE NEVER SEEN WHAT HE LOOKS LIKE BEFORE, BUT HIS VOICE!
I KNOW HIM!
YOU'RE WERIAN HOLT, AREN'T YOU?
THAT'S ME. AND YOU HAVE TO BE LEIGH.
"I WAS A PRISONER, TOO. MISTER DARK CAPTURED AND ENSLAVED ME TO BE HIS SERVANT."
FEED THE WOMAN, BOY.
BE QUICK ABOUT IT, AND THEN GO JUST AS SWIFTLY ABOUT YOUR OTHER DUTIES.
"AS OFTEN AS I COULD, I STOLE FOOD FROM MY OWN MEAGER PLATE TO SNEAK TO HER.
"WHEN HE CAUGHT ME, HIS PUNISHMENTS WERE INVENTIVE, TO SAY THE LEAST."
BUT I COULDN'T SIMPLY STAND BY AND WATCH HER WITHER AWAY.
YOU--YOU WERE THE ONLY FLICKER OF HOPE IN THE ENDLESS DARKNESS.
WITHOUT YOUR KINDNESS, I'M CERTAIN I WOULD HAVE GONE MAD.
IN TIME HE WOULD HAVE SHATTERED ME LIKE GLASS.

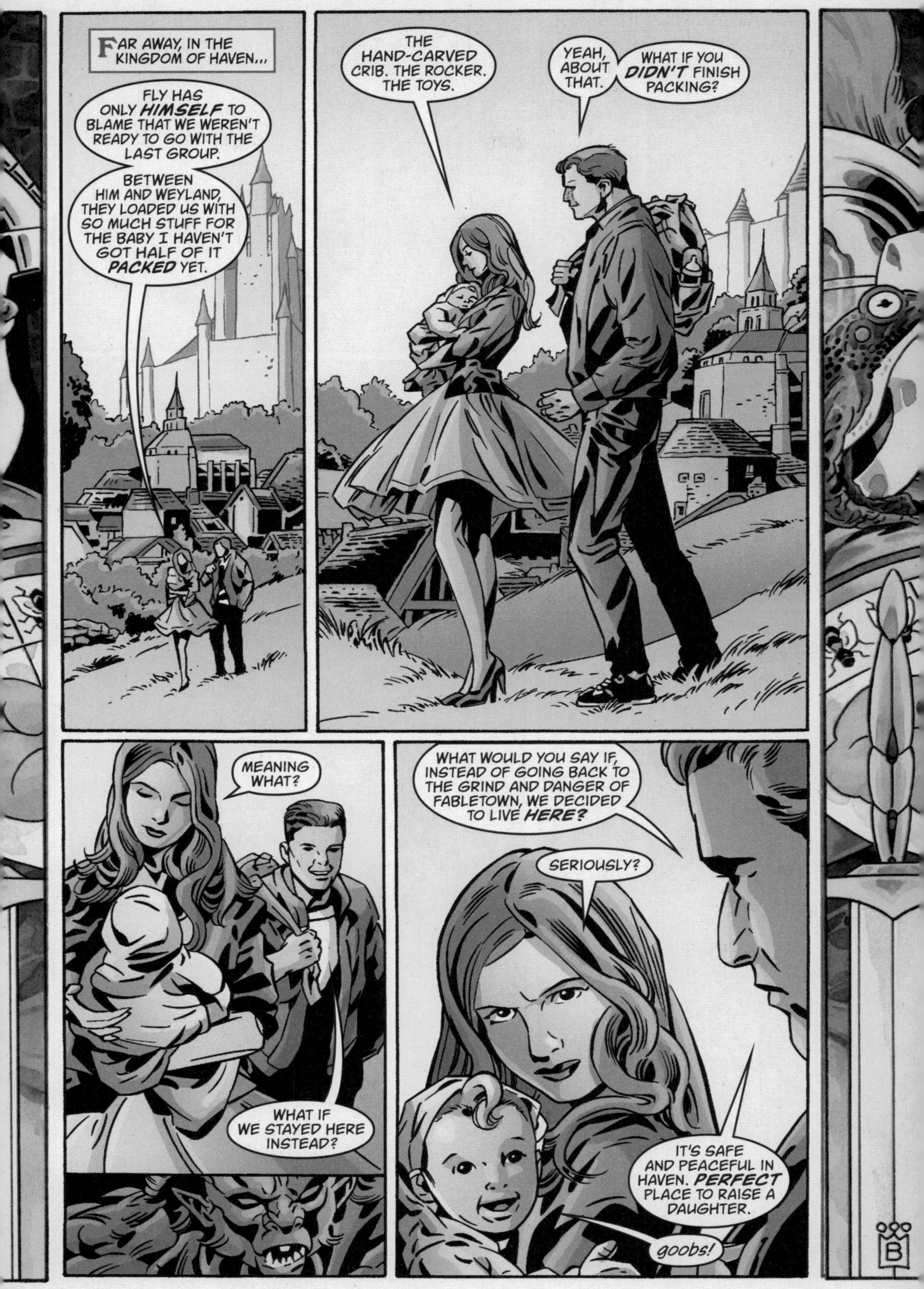
FAR AWAY, IN THE KINGDOM OF HAVEN...
FLY HAS ONLY HIMSELF TO BLAME THAT WE WEREN'T READY TO GO WITH THE LAST GROUP.
BETWEEN HIM AND WEYLAND, THEY LOADED US WITH SO MUCH STUFF FOR THE BABY I HAVEN'T GOT HALF OF IT PACKED YET.
THE HAND-CARVED CRIB. THE ROCKER. THE TOYS.
YEAH, ABOUT THAT.
WHAT IF YOU DIDN'T FINISH PACKING?
MEANING WHAT?
WHAT IF WE STAYED HERE INSTEAD?
WHAT WOULD YOU SAY IF, INSTEAD OF GOING BACK TO THE GRIND AND DANGER OF FABLETOWN, WE DECIDED TO LIVE HERE?
SERIOUSLY?
IT'S SAFE AND PEACEFUL IN HAVEN. PERFECT PLACE TO RAISE A DAUGHTER.
goobs!

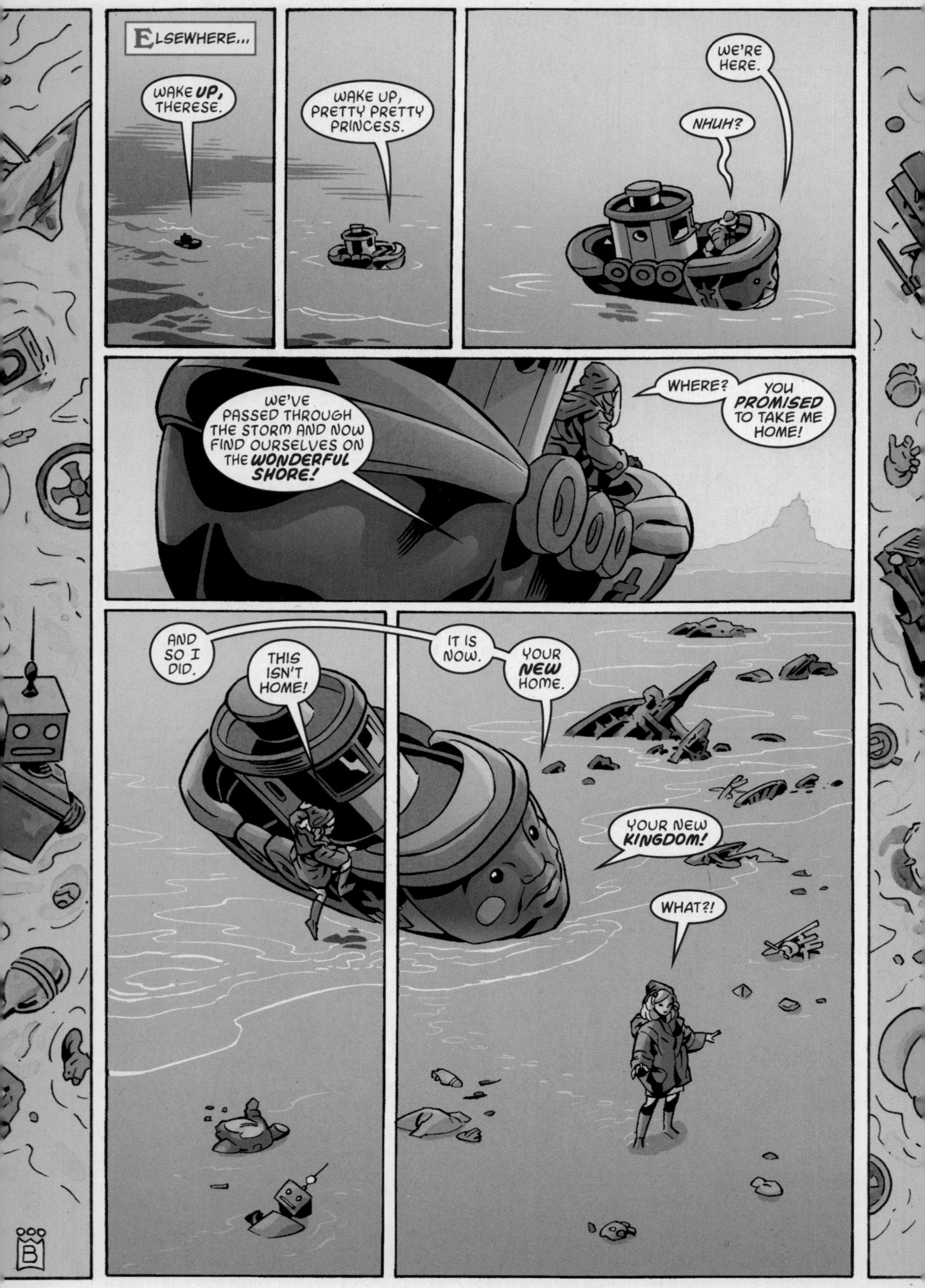
ELSEWHERE...
WAKE UP, THERESE.
WAKE UP, PRETTY PRETTY PRINCESS.
WE'RE HERE.
NHUH?
WE'VE PASSED THROUGH THE STORM AND NOW FIND OURSELVES ON THE WONDERFUL SHORE!
WHERE?
YOU PROMISED TO TAKE ME HOME!
AND SO I DID.
THIS ISN'T HOME!
IT IS NOW.
YOUR NEW HOME.
YOUR NEW KINGDOM!
WHAT?!

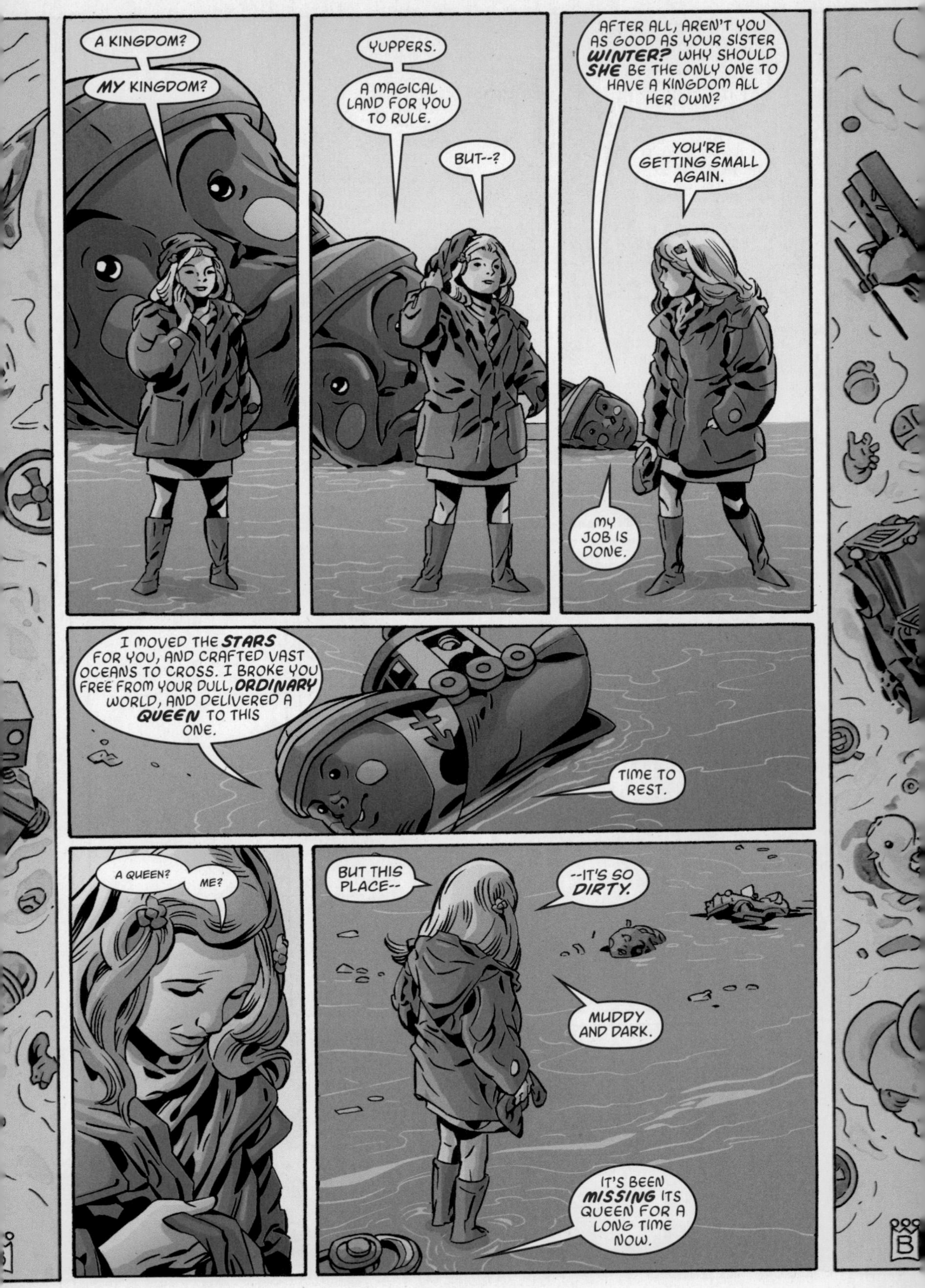
A KINGDOM?
MY KINGDOM?
YUPPERS.
A MAGICAL LAND FOR YOU TO RULE.
BUT--?
AFTER ALL, AREN'T YOU AS GOOD AS YOUR SISTER WINTER? WHY SHOULD SHE BE THE ONLY ONE TO HAVE A KINGDOM ALL HER OWN?
YOU'RE GETTING SMALL AGAIN.
MY JOB IS DONE.
I MOVED THE STARS FOR YOU, AND CRAFTED VAST OCEANS TO CROSS. I BROKE YOU FREE FROM YOUR DULL, ORDINARY WORLD, AND DELIVERED A QUEEN TO THIS ONE.
TIME TO REST.
A QUEEN?
ME?
BUT THIS PLACE--
--IT'S SO DIRTY.
MUDDY AND DARK.
IT'S BEEN MISSING ITS QUEEN FOR A LONG TIME NOW.

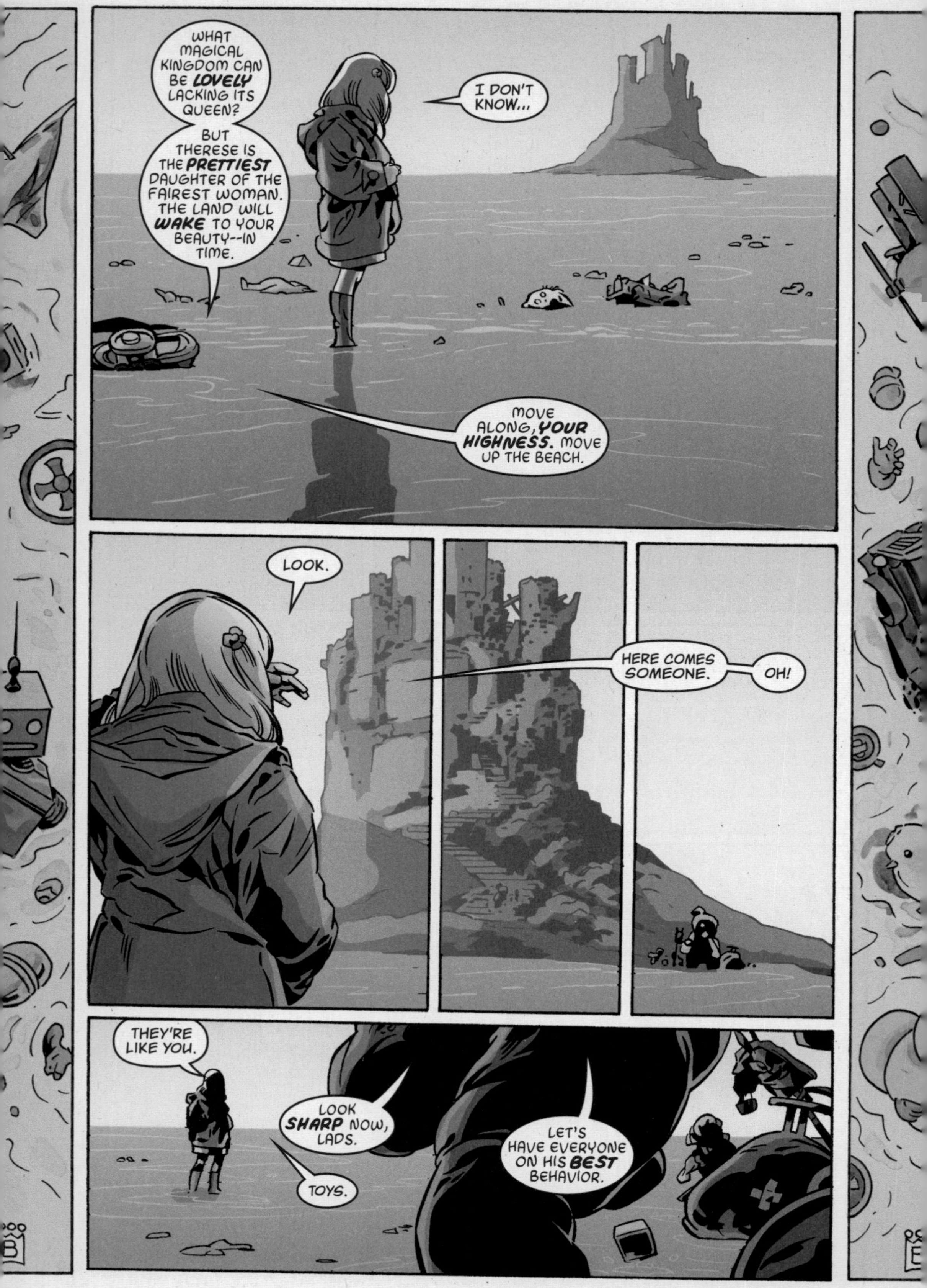
WHAT MAGICAL KINGDOM CAN BE LOVELY LACKING ITS QUEEN?
BUT THERESE IS THE PRETTIEST DAUGHTER OF THE FAIREST WOMAN. THE LAND WILL WAKE TO YOUR BEAUTY--IN TIME.
I DON'T KNOW...
MOVE ALONG, YOUR HIGHNESS. MOVE UP THE BEACH.
LOOK.
HERE COMES SOMEONE.
OH!
THEY'RE LIKE YOU.
LOOK SHARP NOW, LADS.
TOYS.
LET'S HAVE EVERYONE ON HIS BEST BEHAVIOR.

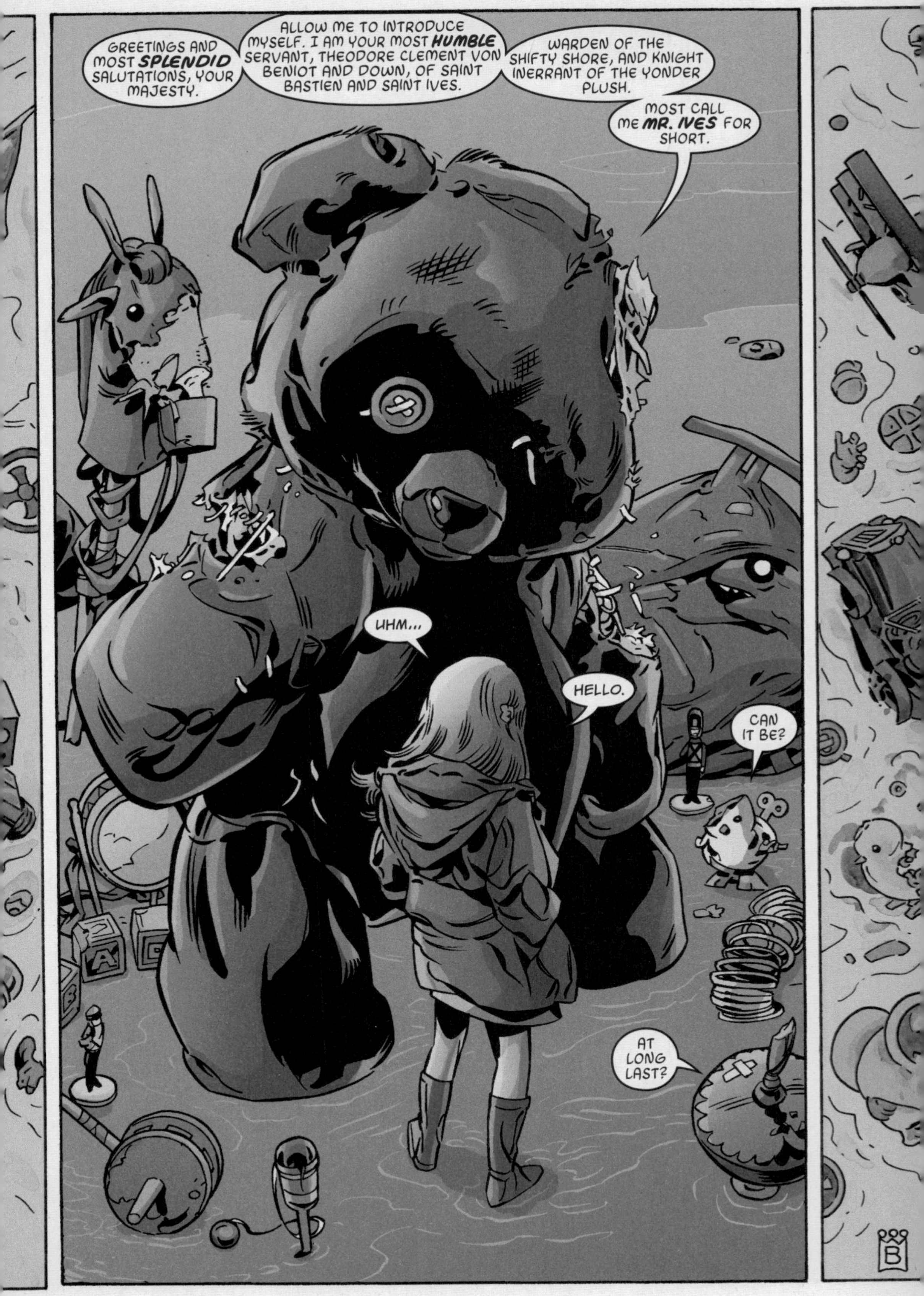
GREETINGS AND MOST SPLENDID SALUTATIONS, YOUR MAJESTY.
ALLOW ME TO INTRODUCE MYSELF. I AM YOUR MOST HUMBLE SERVANT, THEODORE CLEMENT VON BENIOT AND DOWN, OF SAINT BASTIEN AND SAINT IVES.
WARDEN OF THE SHIFTY SHORE, AND KNIGHT INERRANT OF THE YONDER PLUSH.
MOST CALL ME MR. IVES FOR SHORT.
UHM...
HELLO.
CAN IT BE?
AT LONG LAST?

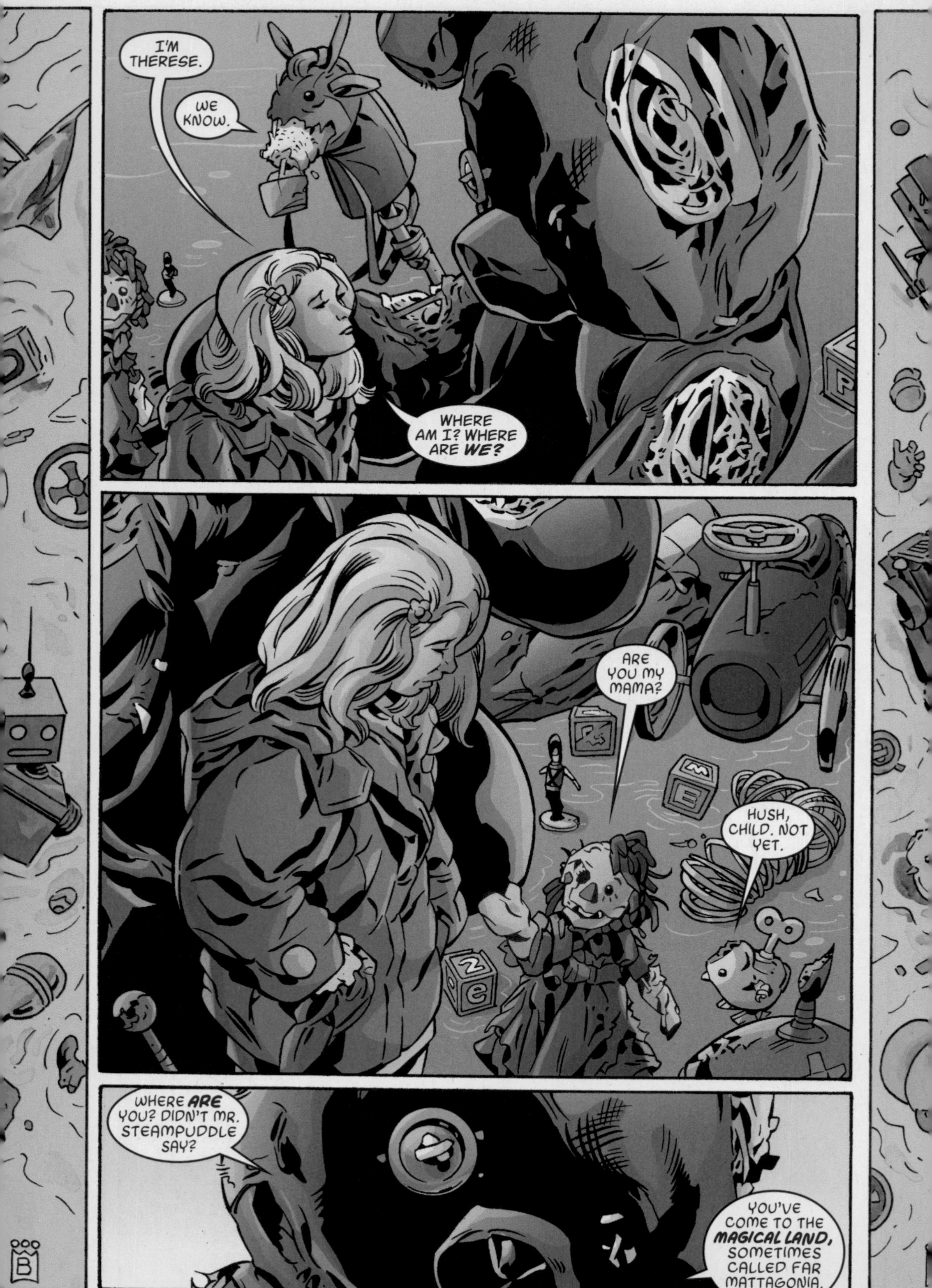
I'M THERESE.
WE KNOW.
WHERE AM I? WHERE ARE **WE?**
ARE YOU MY MAMA?
HUSH, CHILD. NOT YET.
WHERE **ARE** YOU? DIDN'T MR. STEAMPUDDLE SAY?
YOU'VE COME TO THE **MAGICAL LAND,** SOMETIMES CALLED FAR MATTAGONIA.

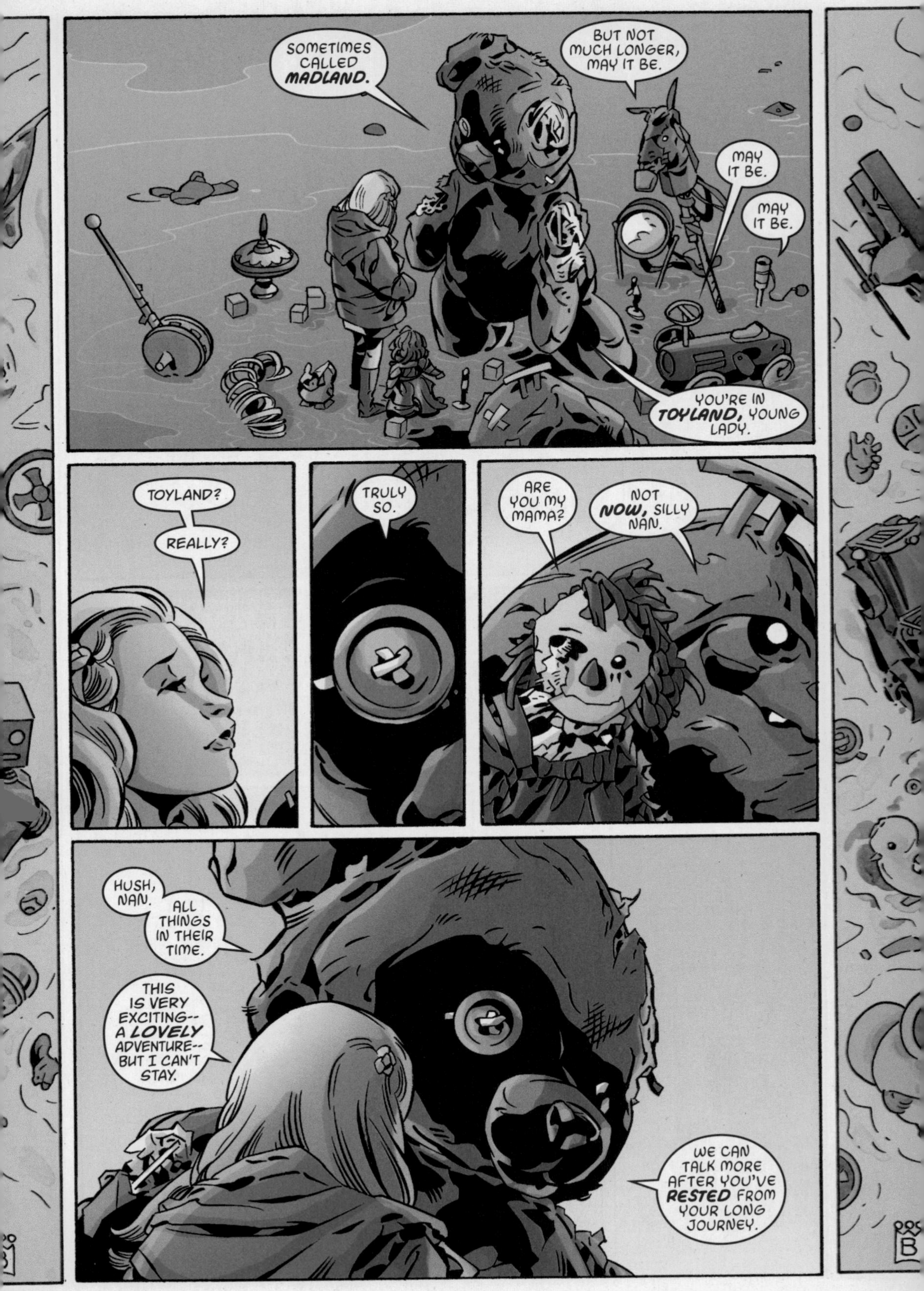

SOMETIMES CALLED MADLAND.
BUT NOT MUCH LONGER, MAY IT BE.
MAY IT BE.
MAY IT BE.
YOU'RE IN TOYLAND, YOUNG LADY.
TOYLAND?
REALLY?
TRULY SO.
ARE YOU MY MAMA?
NOT NOW, SILLY NAN.
HUSH, NAN.
ALL THINGS IN THEIR TIME.
THIS IS VERY EXCITING-- A LOVELY ADVENTURE-- BUT I CAN'T STAY.
WE CAN TALK MORE AFTER YOU'VE RESTED FROM YOUR LONG JOURNEY.

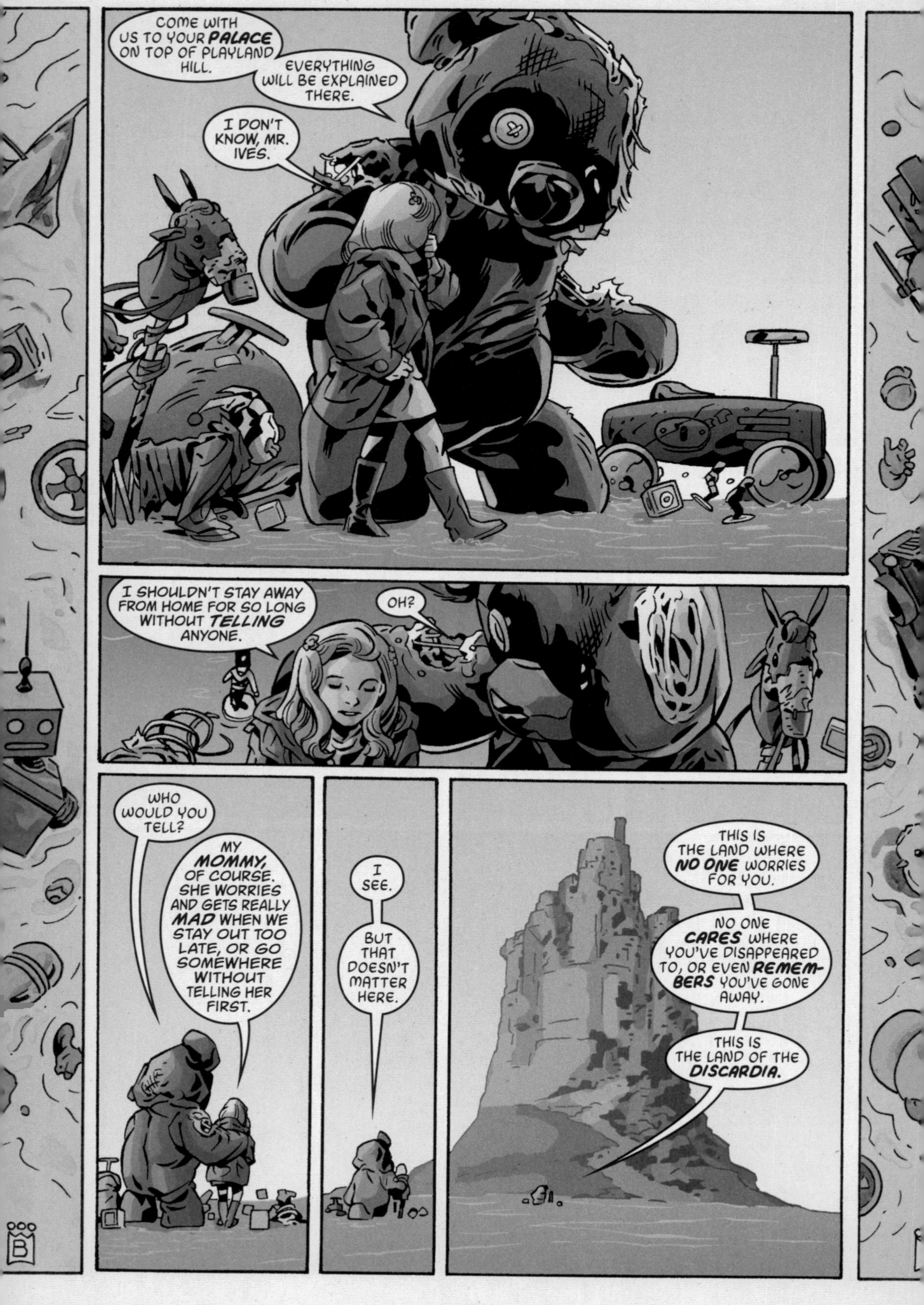
COME WITH US TO YOUR PALACE ON TOP OF PLAYLAND HILL.
EVERYTHING WILL BE EXPLAINED THERE.
I DON'T KNOW, MR. IVES.
I SHOULDN'T STAY AWAY FROM HOME FOR SO LONG WITHOUT TELLING ANYONE.
OH?
WHO WOULD YOU TELL?
MY MOMMY, OF COURSE. SHE WORRIES AND GETS REALLY MAD WHEN WE STAY OUT TOO LATE, OR GO SOMEWHERE WITHOUT TELLING HER FIRST.
I SEE.
BUT THAT DOESN'T MATTER HERE.
THIS IS THE LAND WHERE NO ONE WORRIES FOR YOU.
NO ONE CARES WHERE YOU'VE DISAPPEARED TO, OR EVEN REMEMBERS YOU'VE GONE AWAY.
THIS IS THE LAND OF THE DISCARDIA.

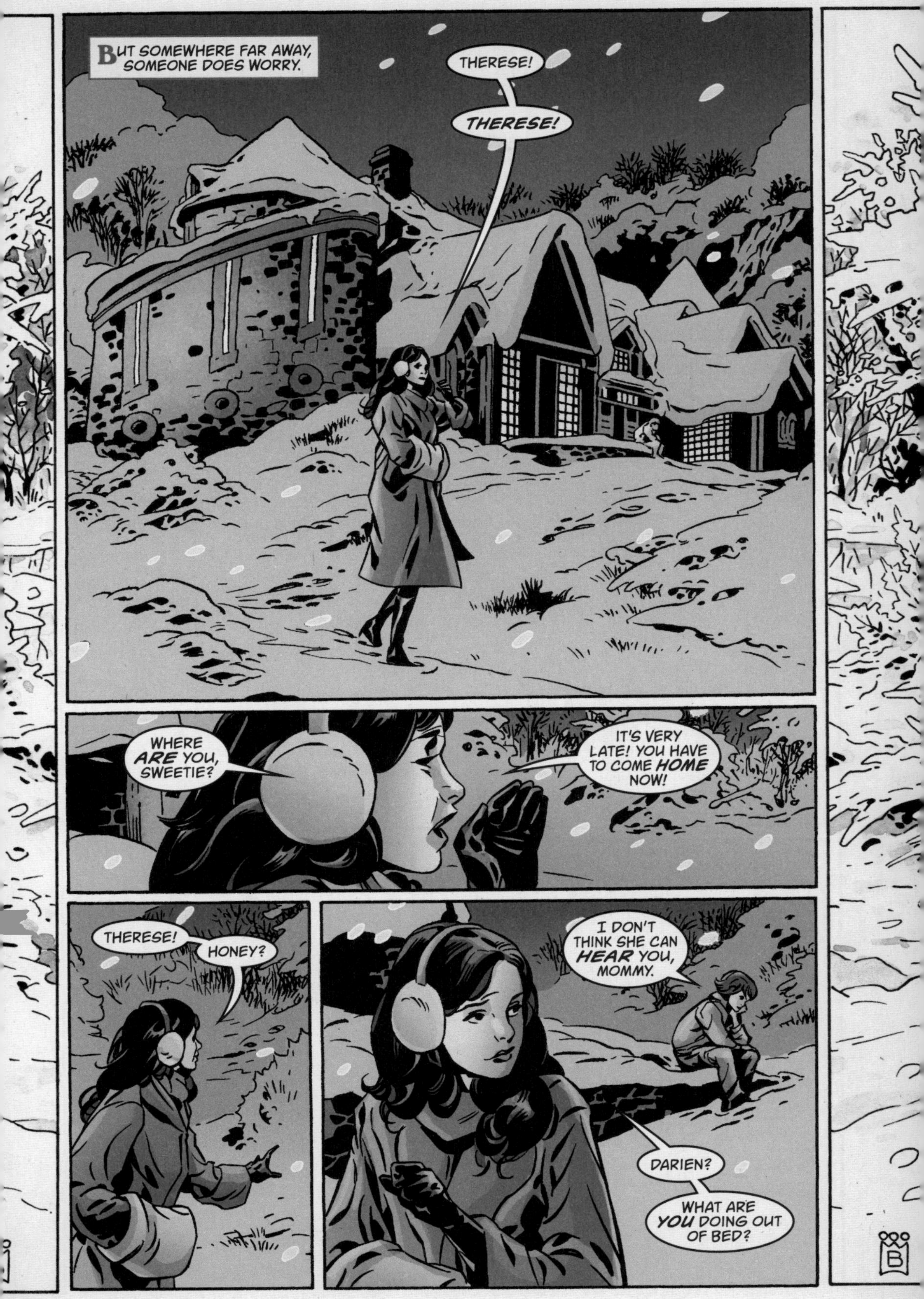
BUT SOMEWHERE FAR AWAY, SOMEONE DOES WORRY.
THERESE!
THERESE!
WHERE ARE YOU, SWEETIE?
IT'S VERY LATE! YOU HAVE TO COME HOME NOW!
THERESE!
HONEY?
I DON'T THINK SHE CAN HEAR YOU, MOMMY.
DARIEN?
WHAT ARE YOU DOING OUT OF BED?

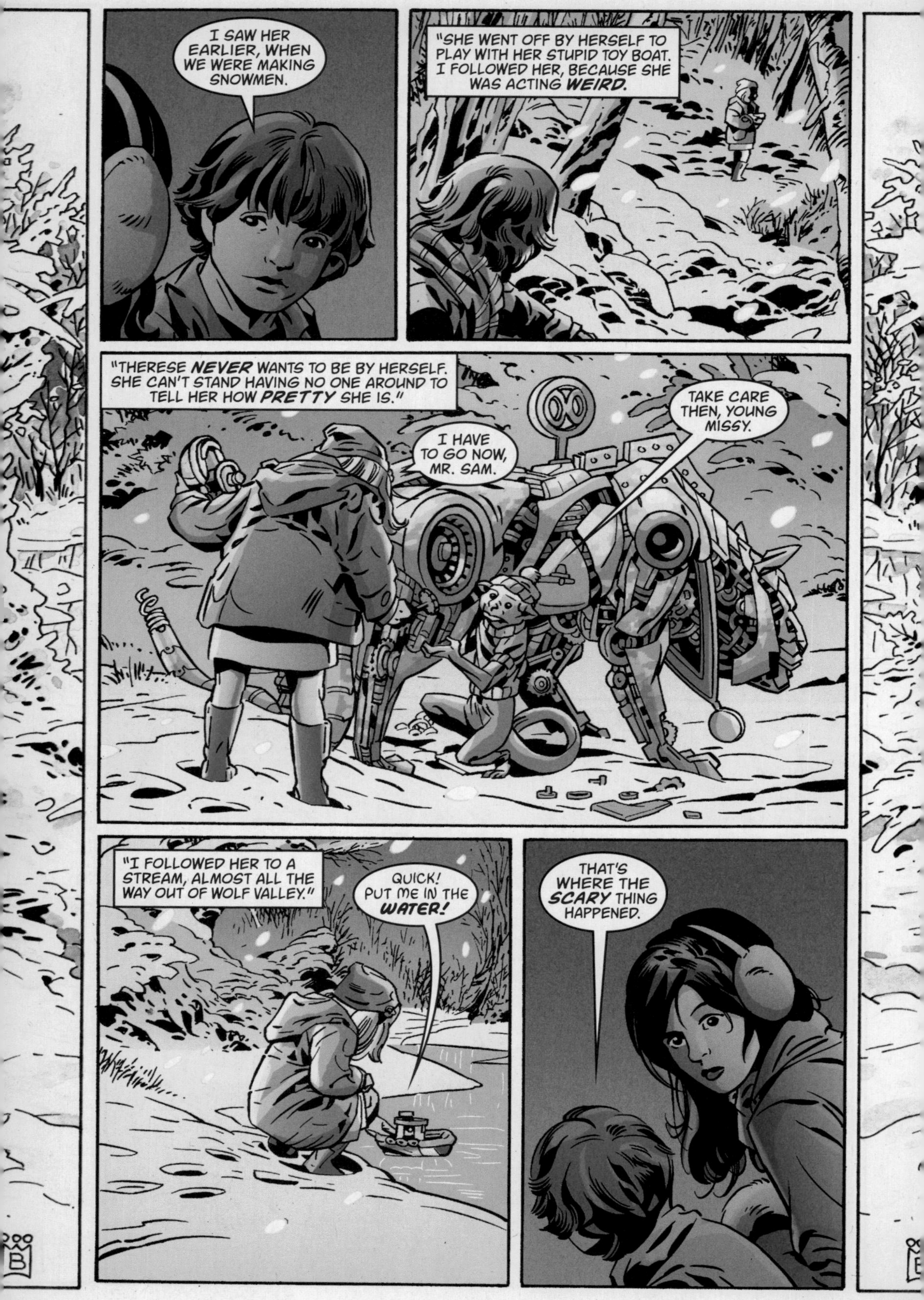
I SAW HER EARLIER, WHEN WE WERE MAKING SNOWMEN.
"SHE WENT OFF BY HERSELF TO PLAY WITH HER STUPID TOY BOAT. I FOLLOWED HER, BECAUSE SHE WAS ACTING WEIRD.
"THERESE NEVER WANTS TO BE BY HERSELF. SHE CAN'T STAND HAVING NO ONE AROUND TO TELL HER HOW PRETTY SHE IS."
I HAVE TO GO NOW, MR. SAM.
TAKE CARE THEN, YOUNG MISSY.
"I FOLLOWED HER TO A STREAM, ALMOST ALL THE WAY OUT OF WOLF VALLEY."
QUICK! PUT ME IN THE WATER!
THAT'S WHERE THE SCARY THING HAPPENED.

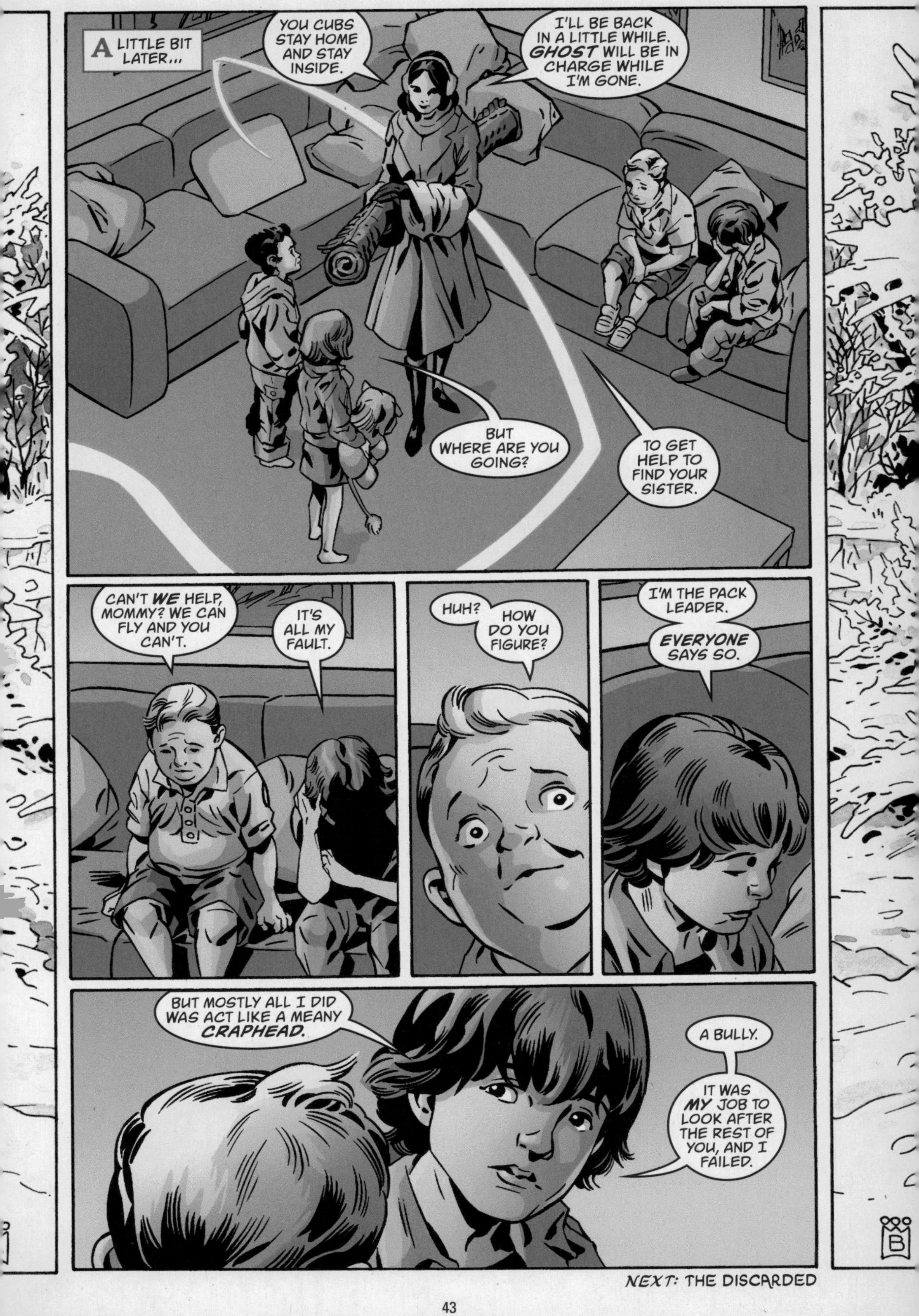
A LITTLE BIT LATER...
YOU CUBS STAY HOME AND STAY INSIDE.
I'LL BE BACK IN A LITTLE WHILE. GHOST WILL BE IN CHARGE WHILE I'M GONE.
BUT WHERE ARE YOU GOING?
TO GET HELP TO FIND YOUR SISTER.
CAN'T WE HELP, MOMMY? WE CAN FLY AND YOU CAN'T.
IT'S ALL MY FAULT.
HUH?
HOW DO YOU FIGURE?
I'M THE PACK LEADER.
EVERYONE SAYS SO.
BUT MOSTLY ALL I DID WAS ACT LIKE A MEANY CRAPHEAD.
A BULLY.
IT WAS MY JOB TO LOOK AFTER THE REST OF YOU, AND I FAILED.

NEXT: THE DISCARDED

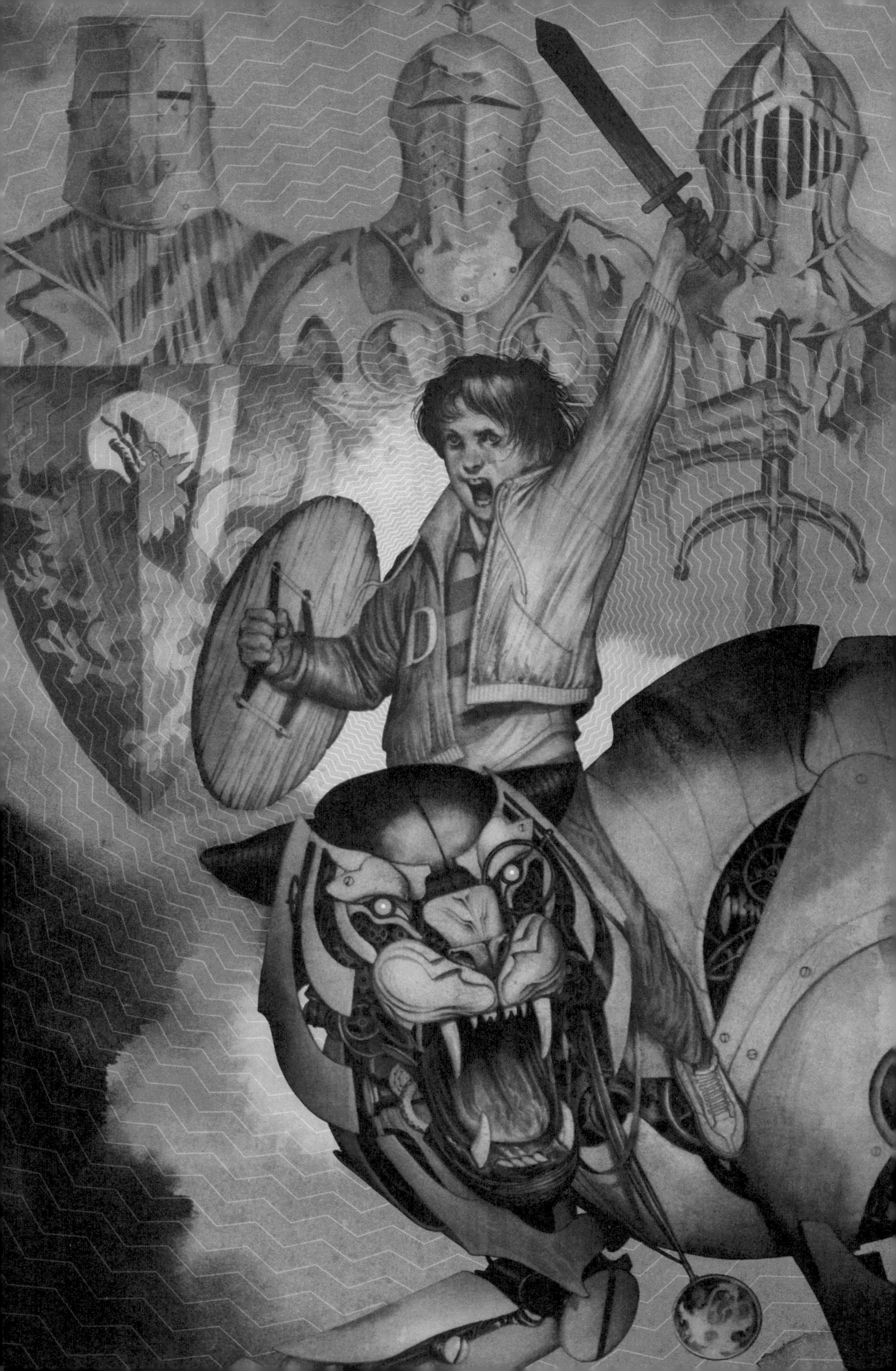

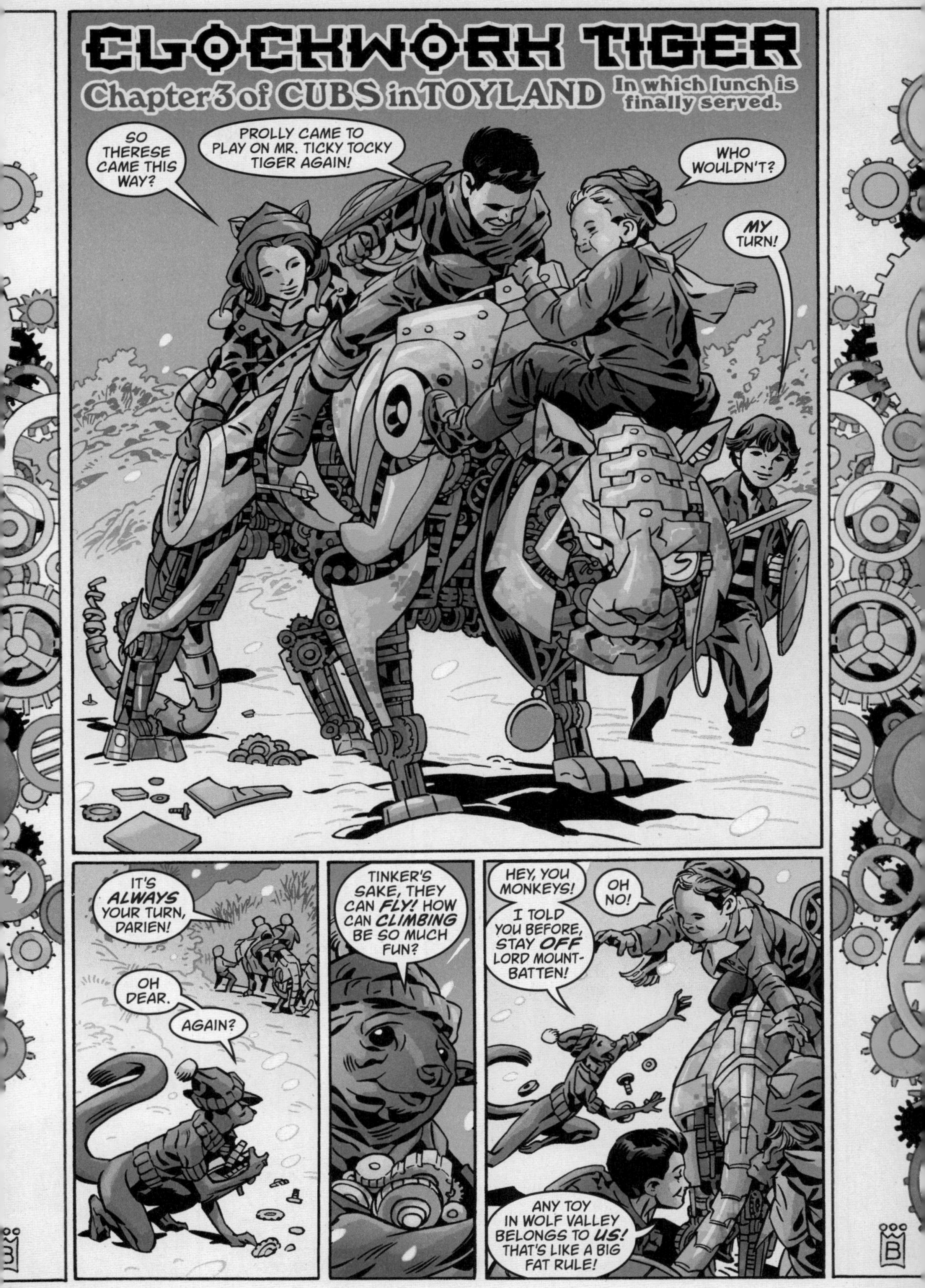
CLOCKWORK TIGER
Chapter 3 of CUBS in TOYLAND
In which lunch is finally served.
SO THERESE CAME THIS WAY?
PROLLY CAME TO PLAY ON MR. TICKY TOCKY TIGER AGAIN!
WHO WOULDN'T?
MY TURN!
IT'S ALWAYS YOUR TURN, DARIEN!
OH DEAR.
AGAIN?
TINKER'S SAKE, THEY CAN FLY! HOW CAN CLIMBING BE SO MUCH FUN?
HEY, YOU MONKEYS!
OH NO!
I TOLD YOU BEFORE, STAY OFF LORD MOUNT-BATTEN!
ANY TOY IN WOLF VALLEY BELONGS TO US! THAT'S LIKE A BIG FAT RULE!

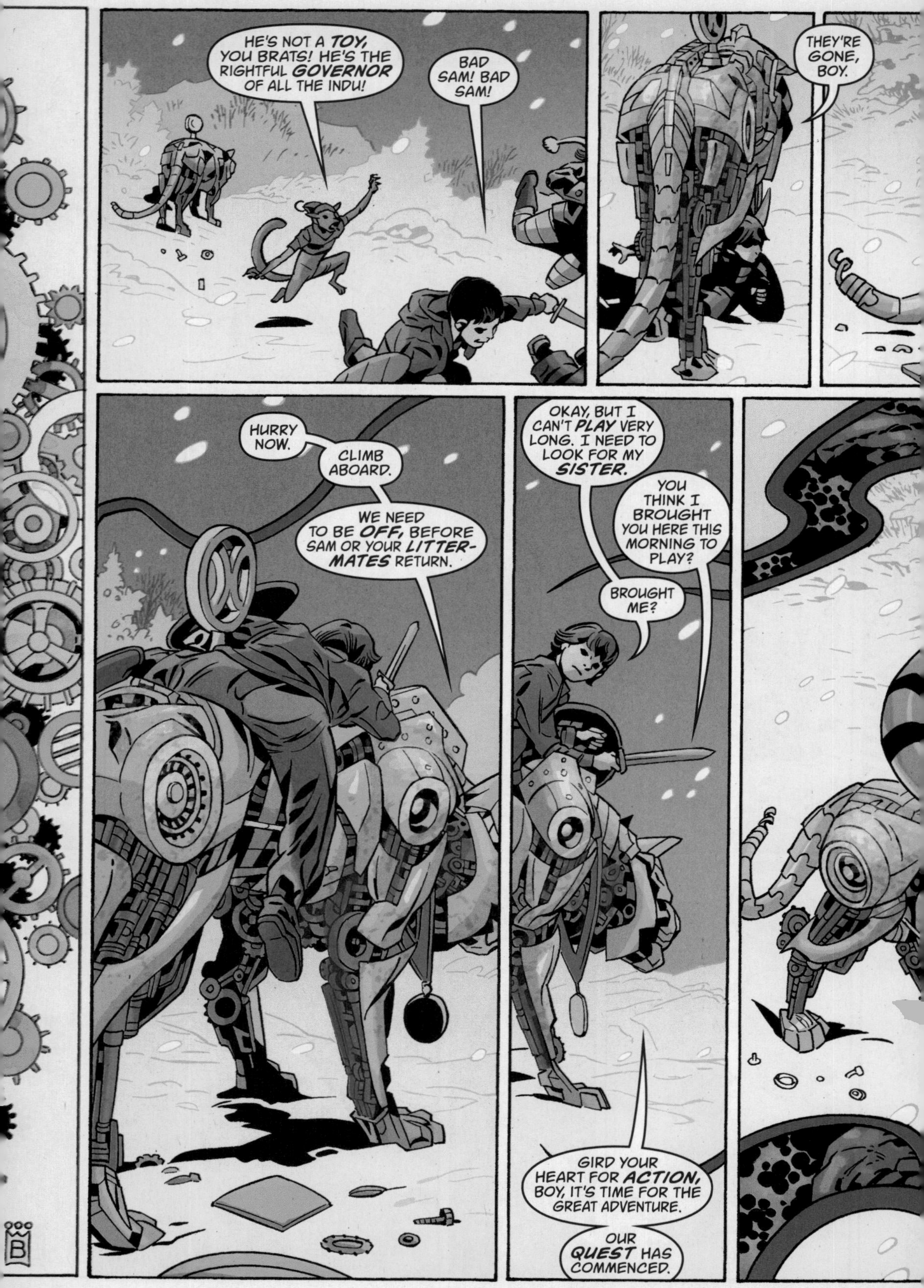
HE'S NOT A TOY, YOU BRATS! HE'S THE RIGHTFUL GOVERNOR OF ALL THE INDU!
BAD SAM! BAD SAM!
THEY'RE GONE, BOY.
HURRY NOW.
CLIMB ABOARD.
WE NEED TO BE OFF, BEFORE SAM OR YOUR LITTER-MATES RETURN.
OKAY, BUT I CAN'T PLAY VERY LONG. I NEED TO LOOK FOR MY SISTER.
YOU THINK I BROUGHT YOU HERE THIS MORNING TO PLAY?
BROUGHT ME?
GIRD YOUR HEART FOR ACTION, BOY, IT'S TIME FOR THE GREAT ADVENTURE.
OUR QUEST HAS COMMENCED.

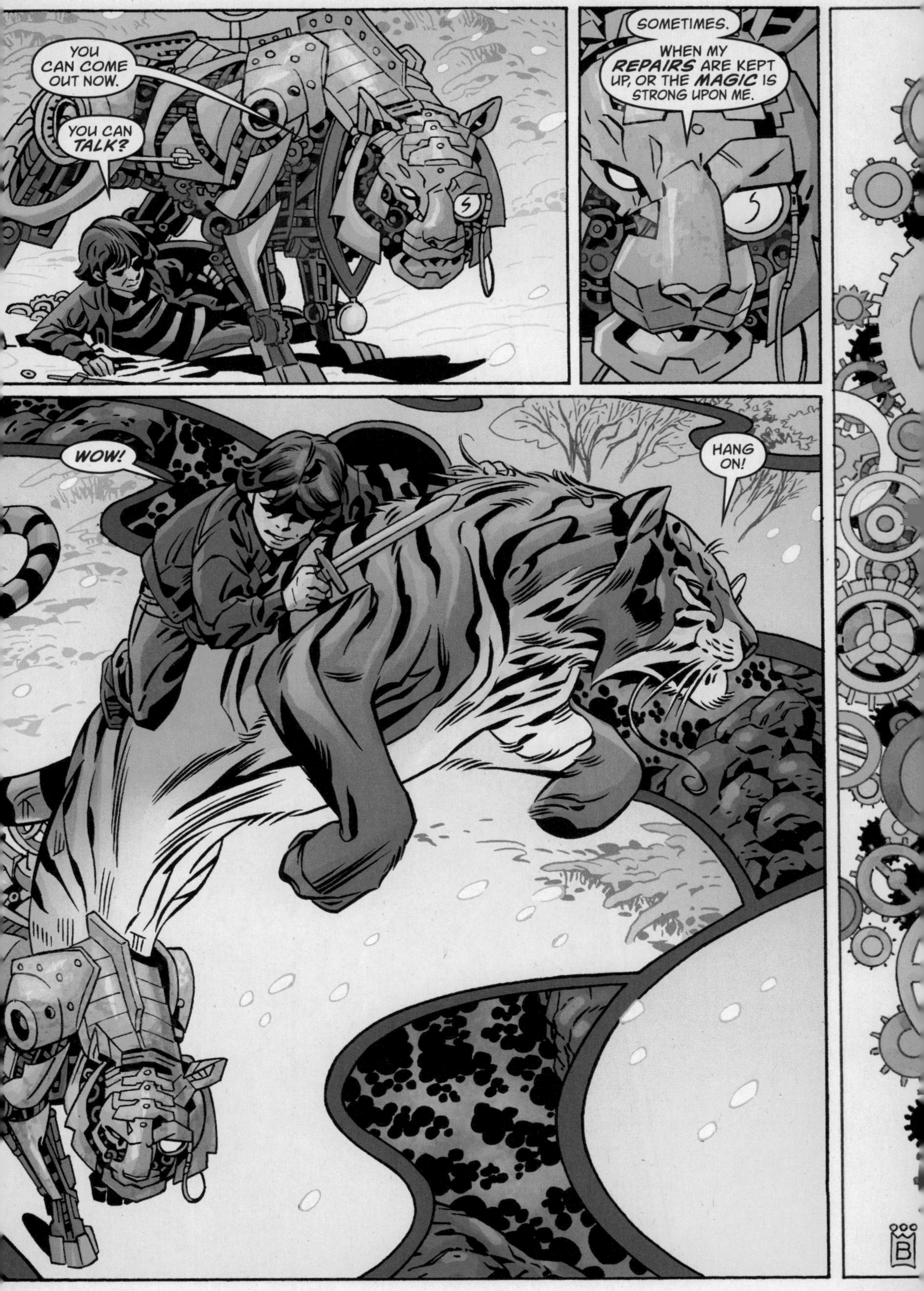
YOU CAN COME OUT NOW.
YOU CAN TALK?
SOMETIMES.
WHEN MY REPAIRS ARE KEPT UP, OR THE MAGIC IS STRONG UPON ME.
WOW!
HANG ON!

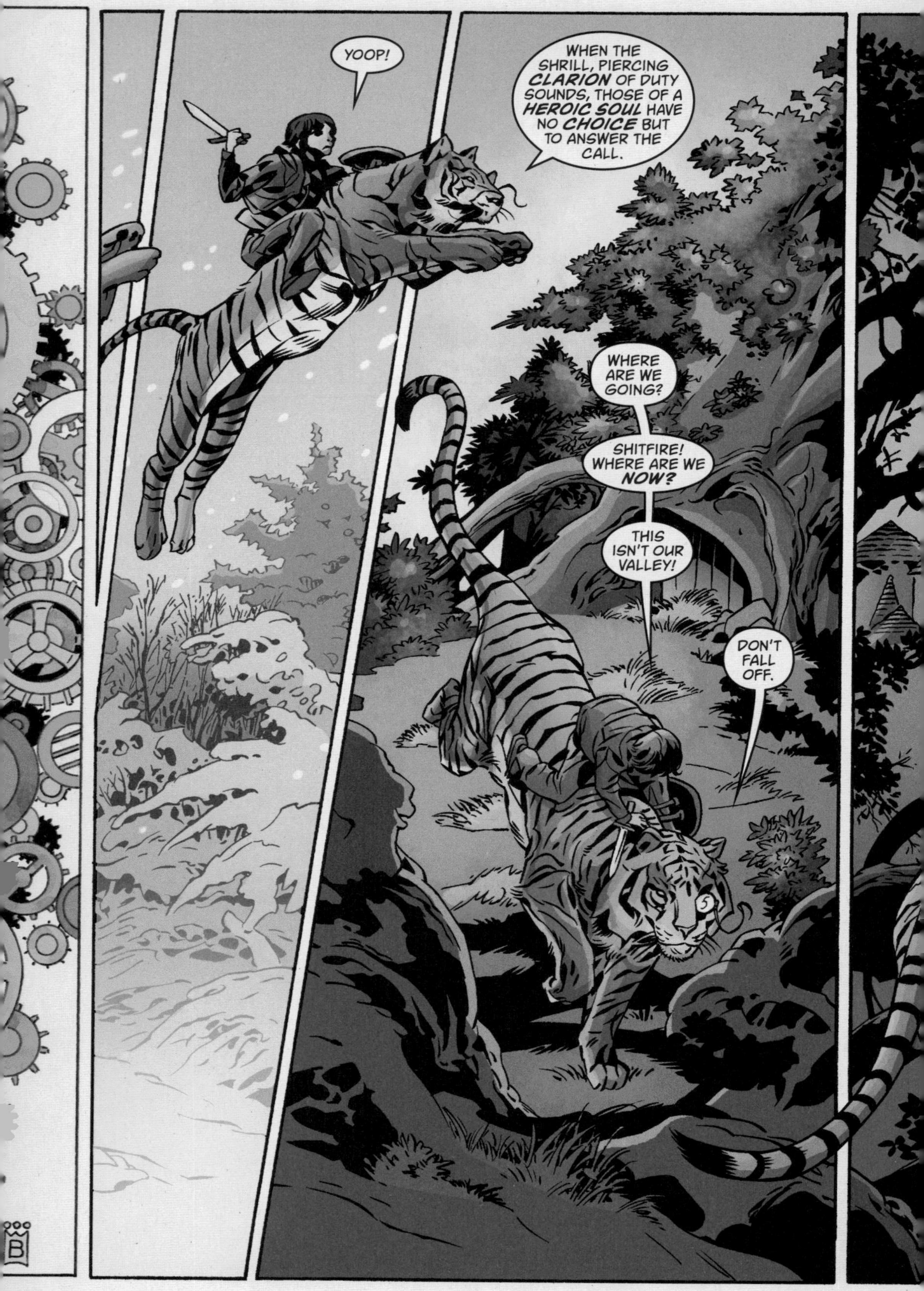

YOOP!
WHEN THE SHRILL, PIERCING CLARION OF DUTY SOUNDS, THOSE OF A HEROIC SOUL HAVE NO CHOICE BUT TO ANSWER THE CALL.
WHERE ARE WE GOING?
SHITFIRE! WHERE ARE WE NOW?
THIS ISN'T OUR VALLEY!
DON'T FALL OFF.

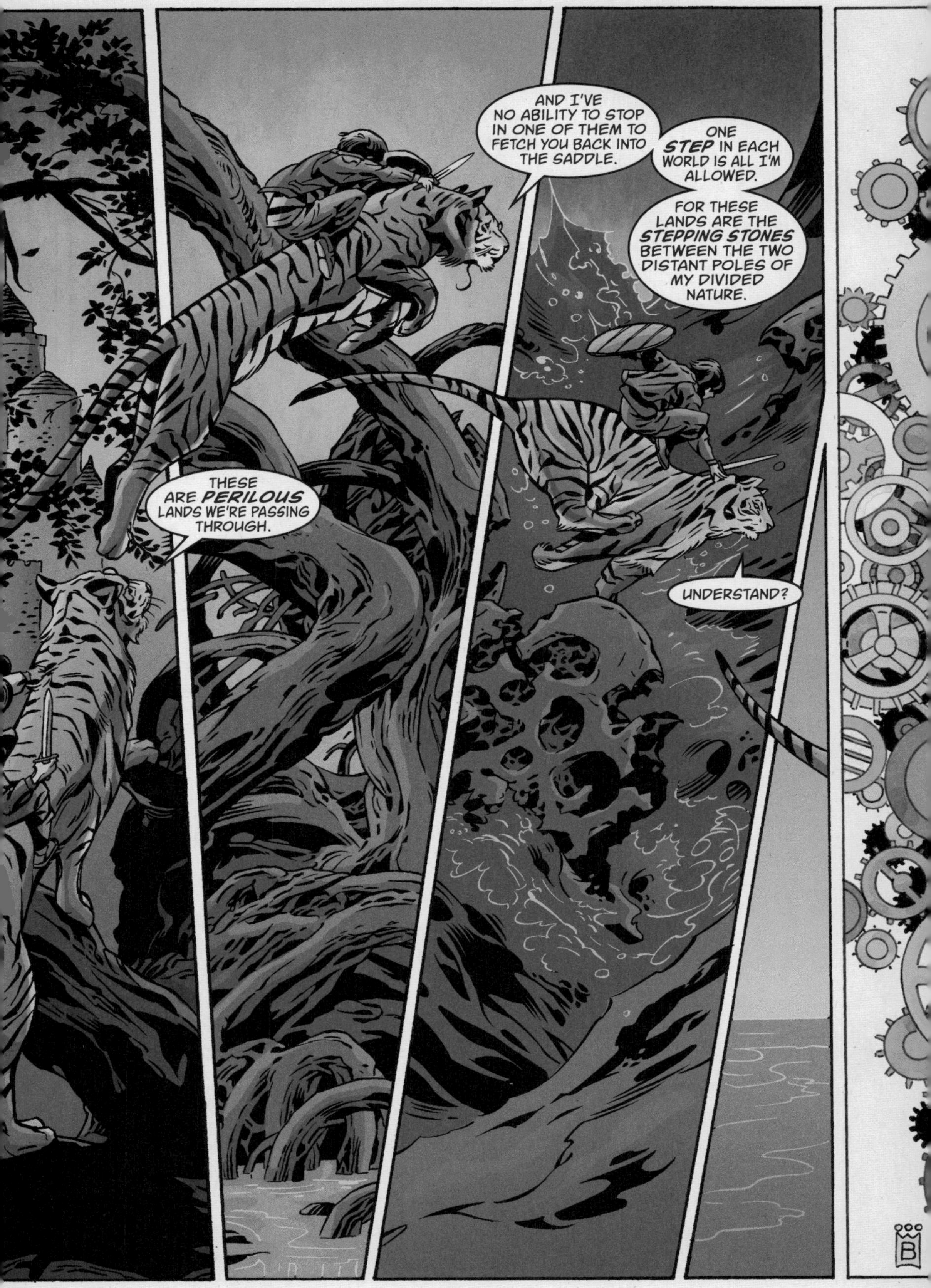
THESE ARE PERILOUS LANDS WE'RE PASSING THROUGH.
AND I'VE NO ABILITY TO STOP IN ONE OF THEM TO FETCH YOU BACK INTO THE SADDLE.
ONE STEP IN EACH WORLD IS ALL I'M ALLOWED.
FOR THESE LANDS ARE THE STEPPING STONES BETWEEN THE TWO DISTANT POLES OF MY DIVIDED NATURE.
UNDERSTAND?

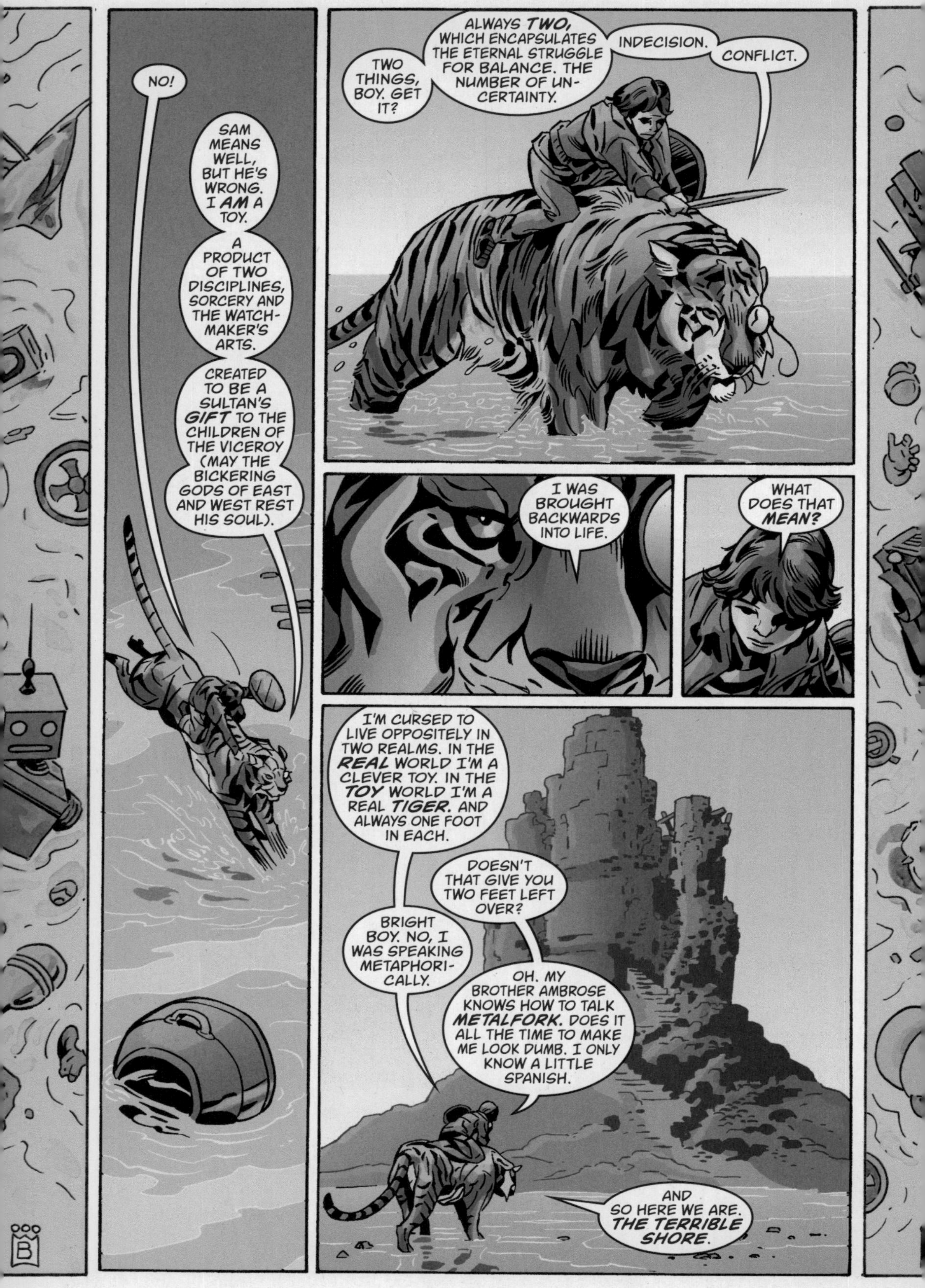
NO!
SAM MEANS WELL, BUT HE'S WRONG. I AM A TOY.
A PRODUCT OF TWO DISCIPLINES, SORCERY AND THE WATCH-MAKER'S ARTS.
CREATED TO BE A SULTAN'S GIFT TO THE CHILDREN OF THE VICEROY (MAY THE BICKERING GODS OF EAST AND WEST REST HIS SOUL).
TWO THINGS, BOY. GET IT?
ALWAYS TWO, WHICH ENCAPSULATES THE ETERNAL STRUGGLE FOR BALANCE. THE NUMBER OF UN-CERTAINTY.
INDECISION.
CONFLICT.
I WAS BROUGHT BACKWARDS INTO LIFE.
WHAT DOES THAT MEAN?
I'M CURSED TO LIVE OPPOSITELY IN TWO REALMS. IN THE REAL WORLD I'M A CLEVER TOY. IN THE TOY WORLD I'M A REAL TIGER. AND ALWAYS ONE FOOT IN EACH.
DOESN'T THAT GIVE YOU TWO FEET LEFT OVER?
BRIGHT BOY. NO, I WAS SPEAKING METAPHORI-CALLY.
OH. MY BROTHER AMBROSE KNOWS HOW TO TALK METALFORK. DOES IT ALL THE TIME TO MAKE ME LOOK DUMB. I ONLY KNOW A LITTLE SPANISH.
AND SO HERE WE ARE. THE TERRIBLE SHORE.

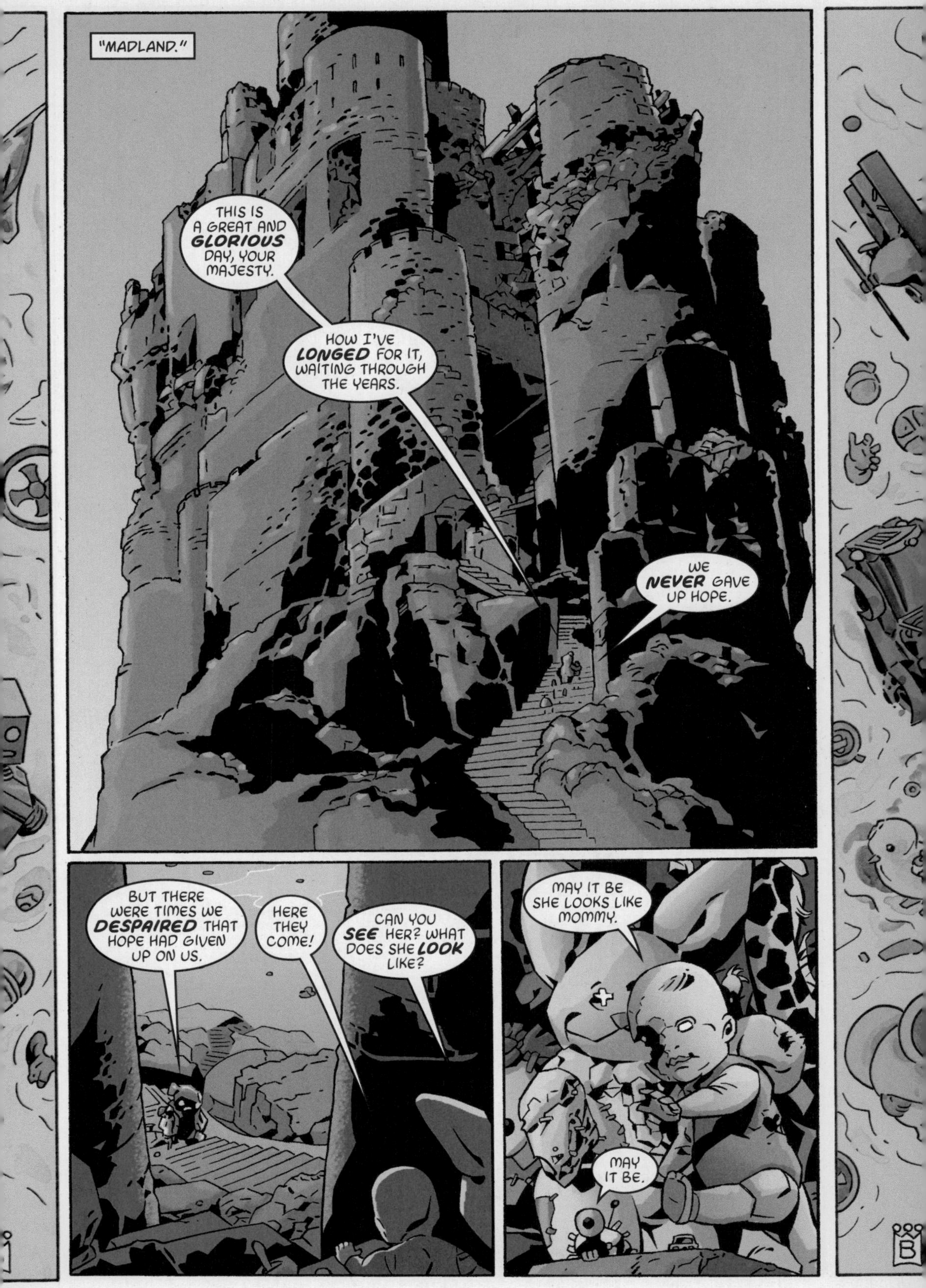

"MADLAND."
THIS IS A GREAT AND GLORIOUS DAY, YOUR MAJESTY.
HOW I'VE LONGED FOR IT, WAITING THROUGH THE YEARS.
WE NEVER GAVE UP HOPE.
BUT THERE WERE TIMES WE DESPAIRED THAT HOPE HAD GIVEN UP ON US.
HERE THEY COME!
CAN YOU SEE HER? WHAT DOES SHE LOOK LIKE?
MAY IT BE SHE LOOKS LIKE MOMMY.
MAY IT BE.

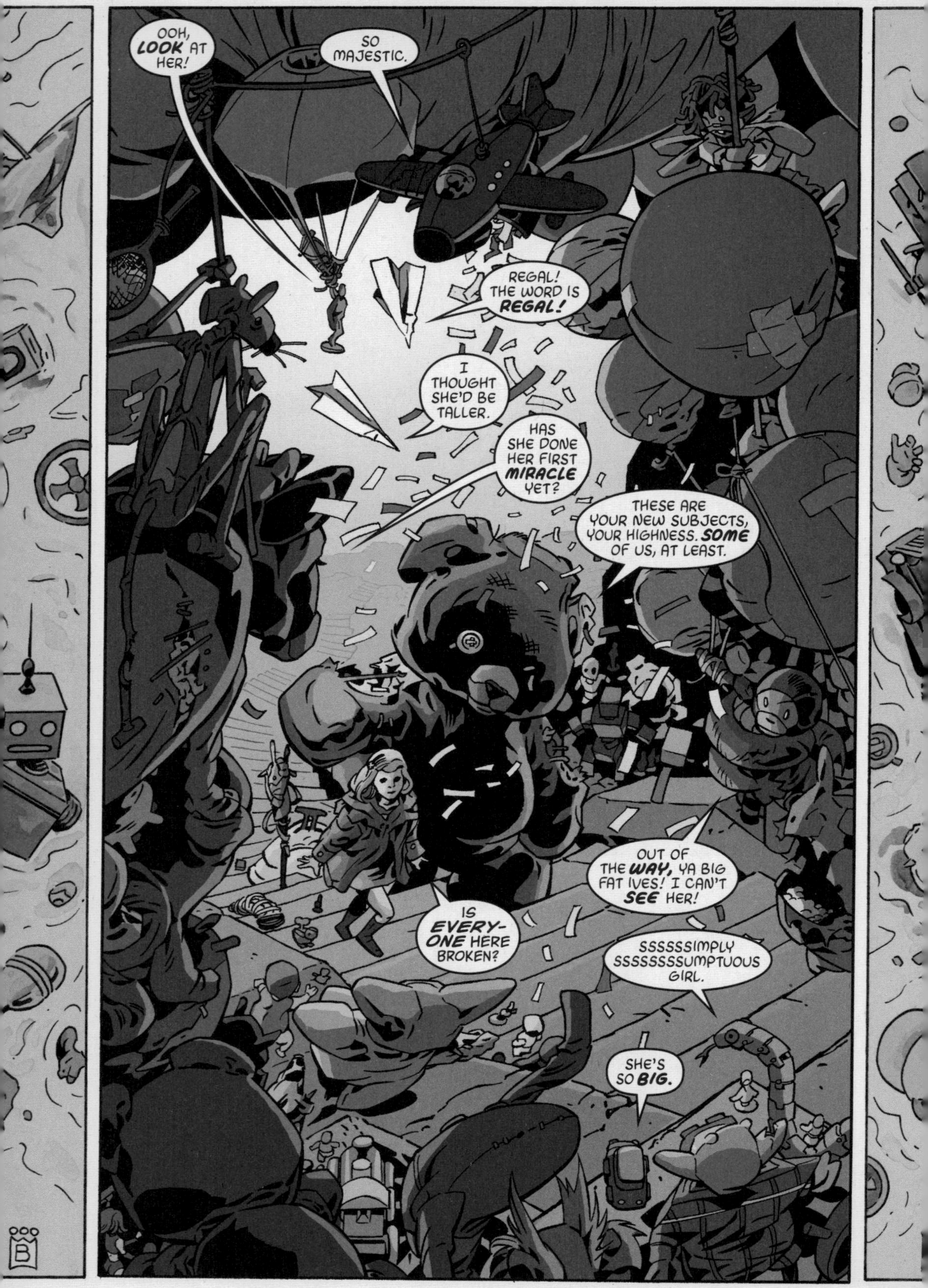
OOH, LOOK AT HER!
SO MAJESTIC.
REGAL! THE WORD IS REGAL!
I THOUGHT SHE'D BE TALLER.
HAS SHE DONE HER FIRST MIRACLE YET?
THESE ARE YOUR NEW SUBJECTS, YOUR HIGHNESS. SOME OF US, AT LEAST.
OUT OF THE WAY, YA BIG FAT IVES! I CAN'T SEE HER!
IS EVERY-ONE HERE BROKEN?
SSSSSIMPLY SSSSSSSUMPTUOUS GIRL.
SHE'S SO BIG.

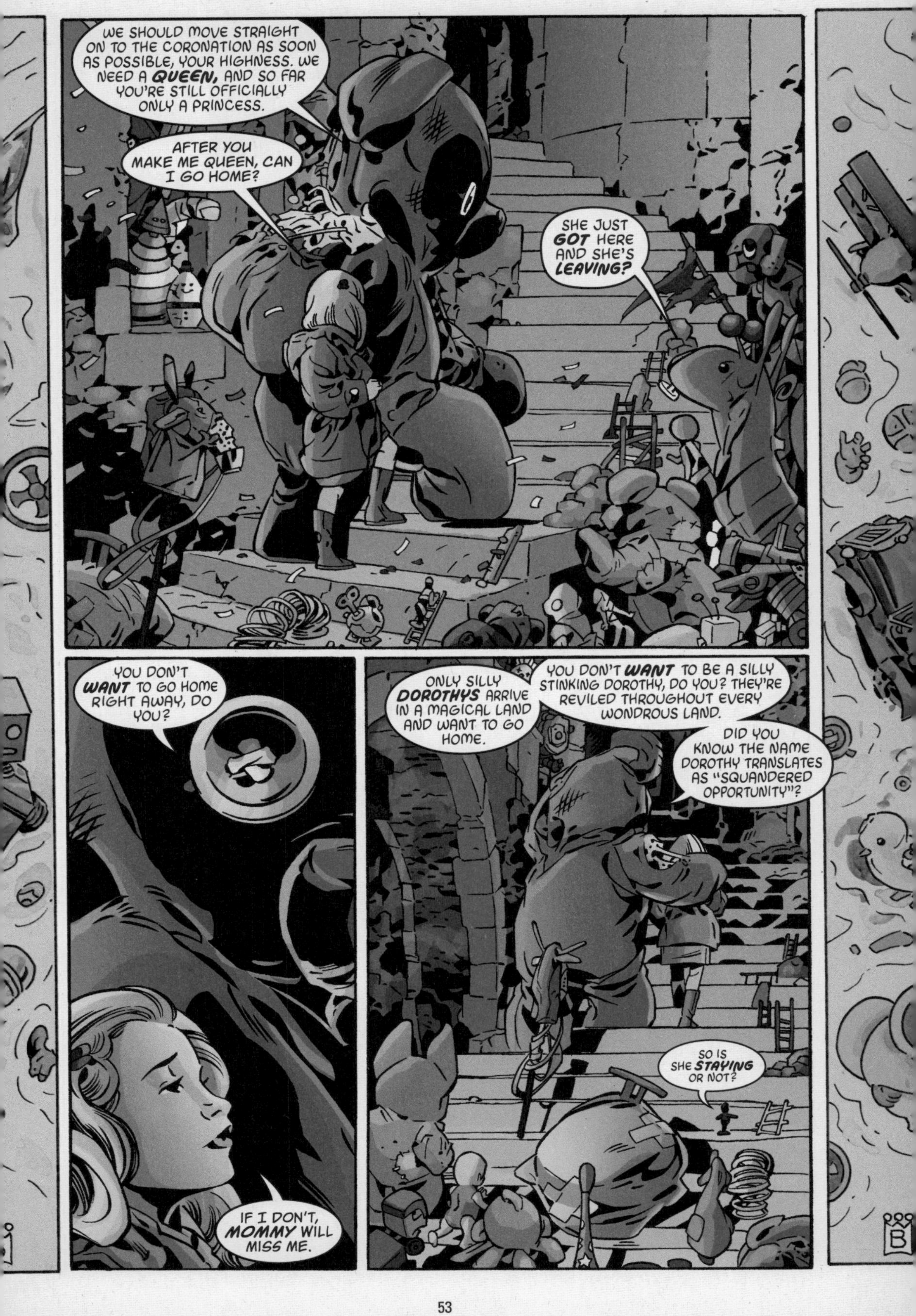
WE SHOULD MOVE STRAIGHT ON TO THE CORONATION AS SOON AS POSSIBLE, YOUR HIGHNESS. WE NEED A QUEEN, AND SO FAR YOU'RE STILL OFFICIALLY ONLY A PRINCESS.
AFTER YOU MAKE ME QUEEN, CAN I GO HOME?
SHE JUST GOT HERE AND SHE'S LEAVING?
YOU DON'T WANT TO GO HOME RIGHT AWAY, DO YOU?
IF I DON'T, MOMMY WILL MISS ME.
ONLY SILLY DOROTHYS ARRIVE IN A MAGICAL LAND AND WANT TO GO HOME.
YOU DON'T WANT TO BE A SILLY STINKING DOROTHY, DO YOU? THEY'RE REVILED THROUGHOUT EVERY WONDROUS LAND.
DID YOU KNOW THE NAME DOROTHY TRANSLATES AS "SQUANDERED OPPORTUNITY"?
SO IS SHE STAYING OR NOT?

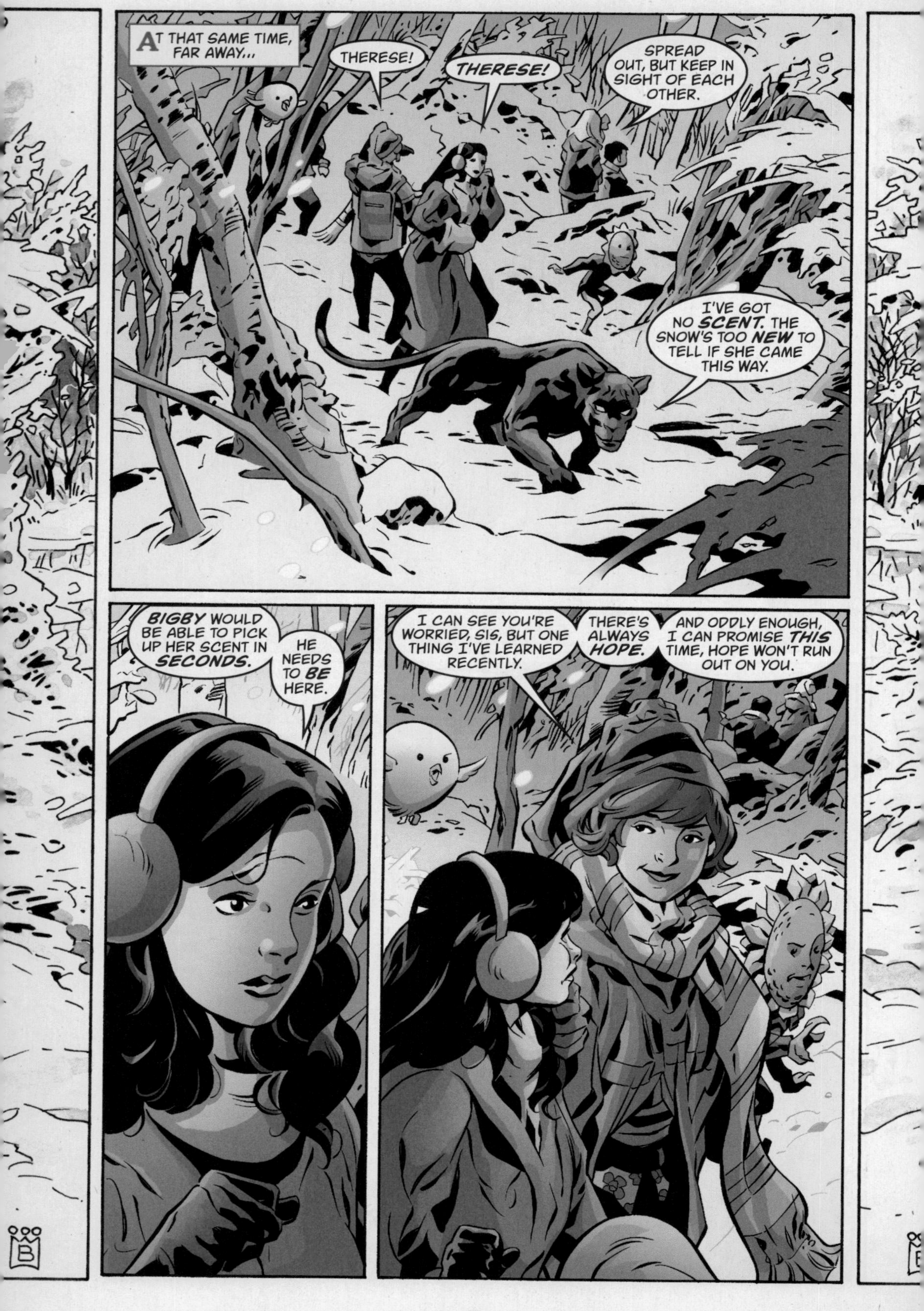
AT THAT SAME TIME, FAR AWAY...
THERESE!
THERESE!
SPREAD OUT, BUT KEEP IN SIGHT OF EACH OTHER.
I'VE GOT NO SCENT. THE SNOW'S TOO NEW TO TELL IF SHE CAME THIS WAY.
BIGBY WOULD BE ABLE TO PICK UP HER SCENT IN SECONDS.
HE NEEDS TO BE HERE.
I CAN SEE YOU'RE WORRIED, SIS, BUT ONE THING I'VE LEARNED RECENTLY.
THERE'S ALWAYS HOPE.
AND ODDLY ENOUGH, I CAN PROMISE THIS TIME, HOPE WON'T RUN OUT ON YOU.

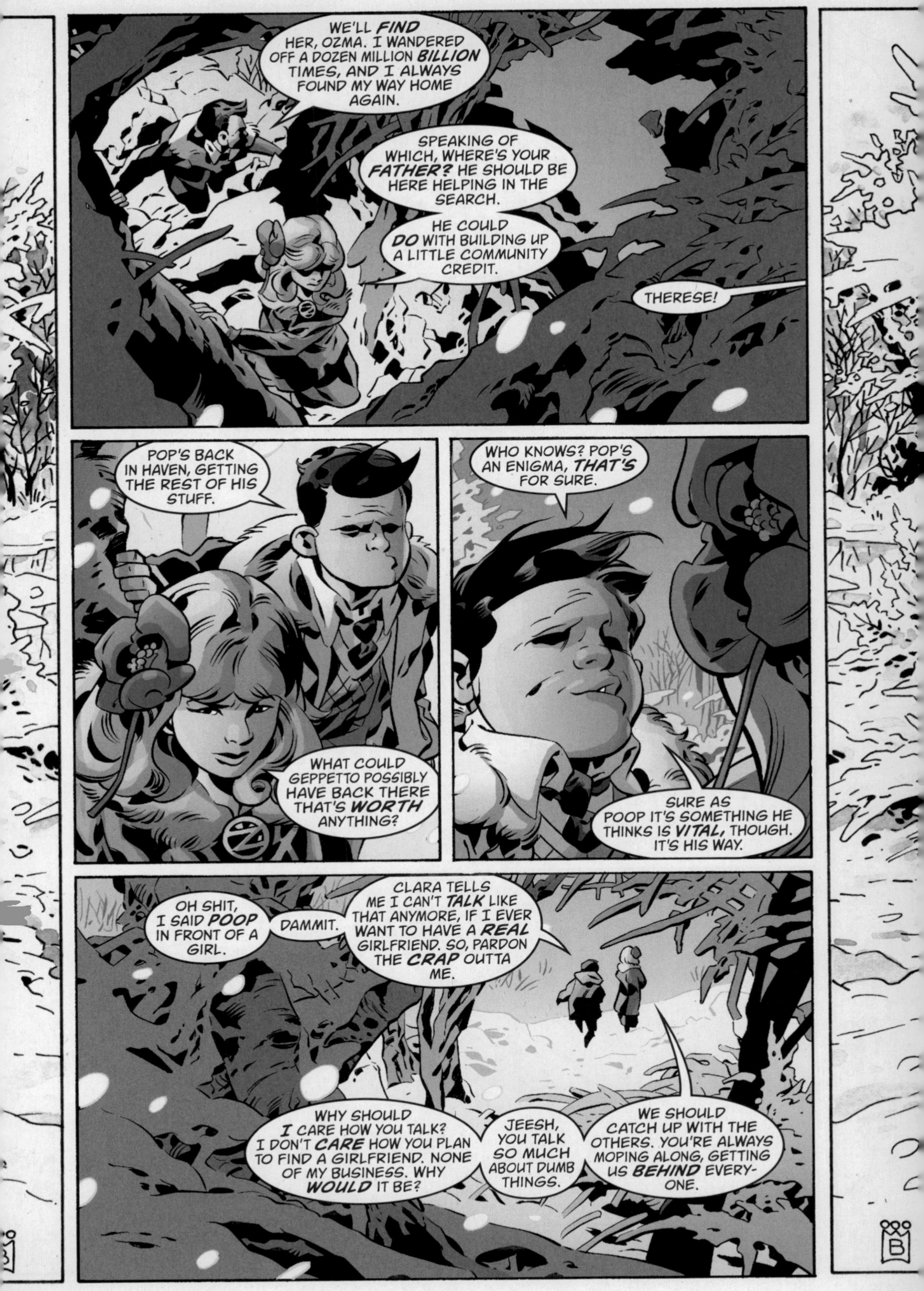
WE'LL FIND HER, OZMA. I WANDERED OFF A DOZEN MILLION BILLION TIMES, AND I ALWAYS FOUND MY WAY HOME AGAIN.
SPEAKING OF WHICH, WHERE'S YOUR FATHER? HE SHOULD BE HERE HELPING IN THE SEARCH.
HE COULD DO WITH BUILDING UP A LITTLE COMMUNITY CREDIT.
THERESE!
POP'S BACK IN HAVEN, GETTING THE REST OF HIS STUFF.
WHAT COULD GEPPETTO POSSIBLY HAVE BACK THERE THAT'S WORTH ANYTHING?
WHO KNOWS? POP'S AN ENIGMA, THAT'S FOR SURE.
SURE AS POOP IT'S SOMETHING HE THINKS IS VITAL, THOUGH. IT'S HIS WAY.
OH SHIT, I SAID POOP IN FRONT OF A GIRL.
DAMMIT.
CLARA TELLS ME I CAN'T TALK LIKE THAT ANYMORE, IF I EVER WANT TO HAVE A REAL GIRLFRIEND. SO, PARDON THE CRAP OUTTA ME.
WHY SHOULD I CARE HOW YOU TALK? I DON'T CARE HOW YOU PLAN TO FIND A GIRLFRIEND. NONE OF MY BUSINESS. WHY WOULD IT BE?
JEESH, YOU TALK SO MUCH ABOUT DUMB THINGS.
WE SHOULD CATCH UP WITH THE OTHERS. YOU'RE ALWAYS MOPING ALONG, GETTING US BEHIND EVERY-ONE.

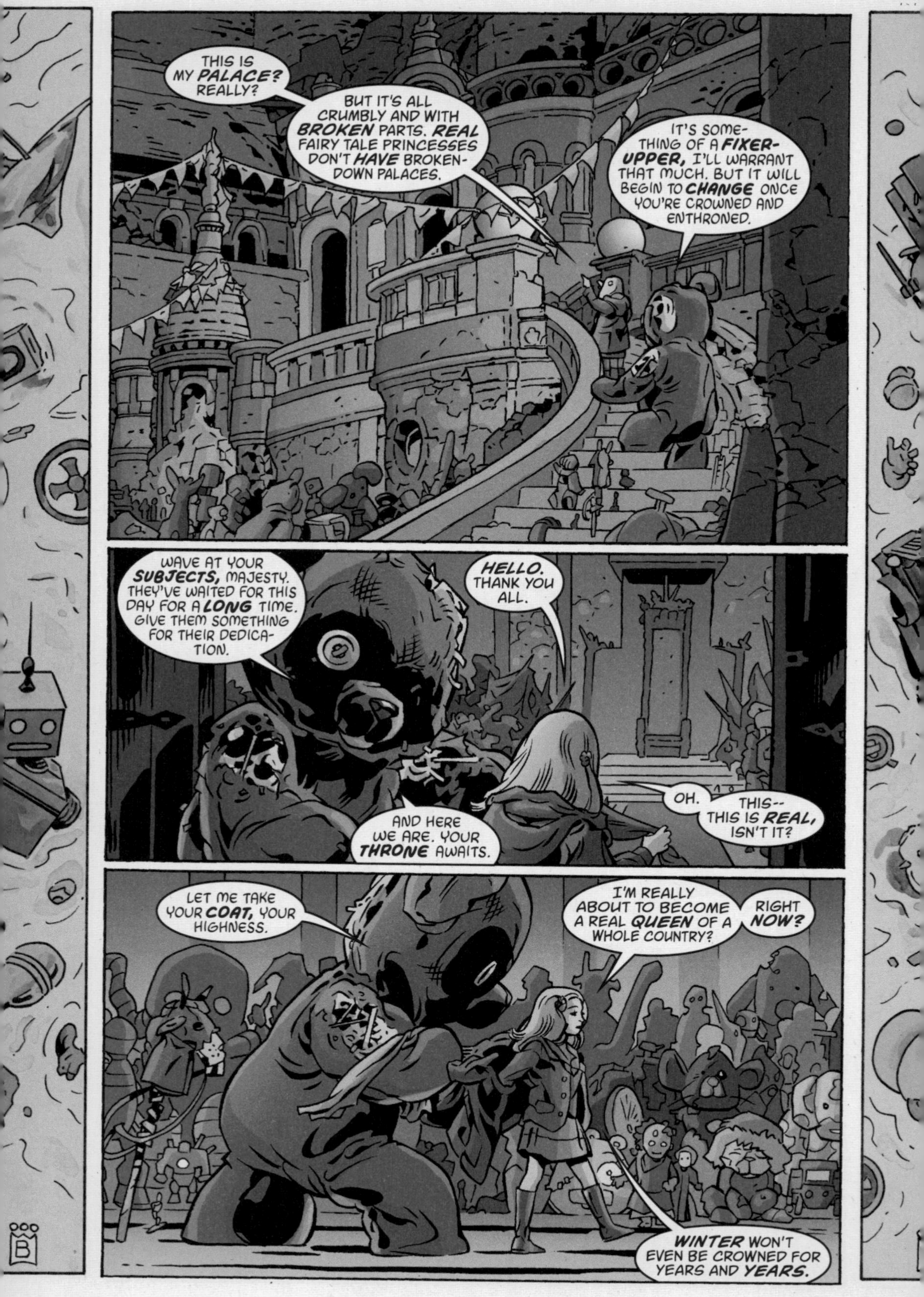

THIS IS MY PALACE? REALLY?
BUT IT'S ALL CRUMBLY AND WITH BROKEN PARTS. REAL FAIRY TALE PRINCESSES DON'T HAVE BROKEN-DOWN PALACES.
IT'S SOMETHING OF A FIXER-UPPER, I'LL WARRANT THAT MUCH. BUT IT WILL BEGIN TO CHANGE ONCE YOU'RE CROWNED AND ENTHRONED.
WAVE AT YOUR SUBJECTS, MAJESTY. THEY'VE WAITED FOR THIS DAY FOR A LONG TIME. GIVE THEM SOMETHING FOR THEIR DEDICATION.
HELLO. THANK YOU ALL.
AND HERE WE ARE. YOUR THRONE AWAITS.
OH.
THIS-- THIS IS REAL, ISN'T IT?
LET ME TAKE YOUR COAT, YOUR HIGHNESS.
I'M REALLY ABOUT TO BECOME A REAL QUEEN OF A WHOLE COUNTRY?
RIGHT NOW?
WINTER WON'T EVEN BE CROWNED FOR YEARS AND YEARS.

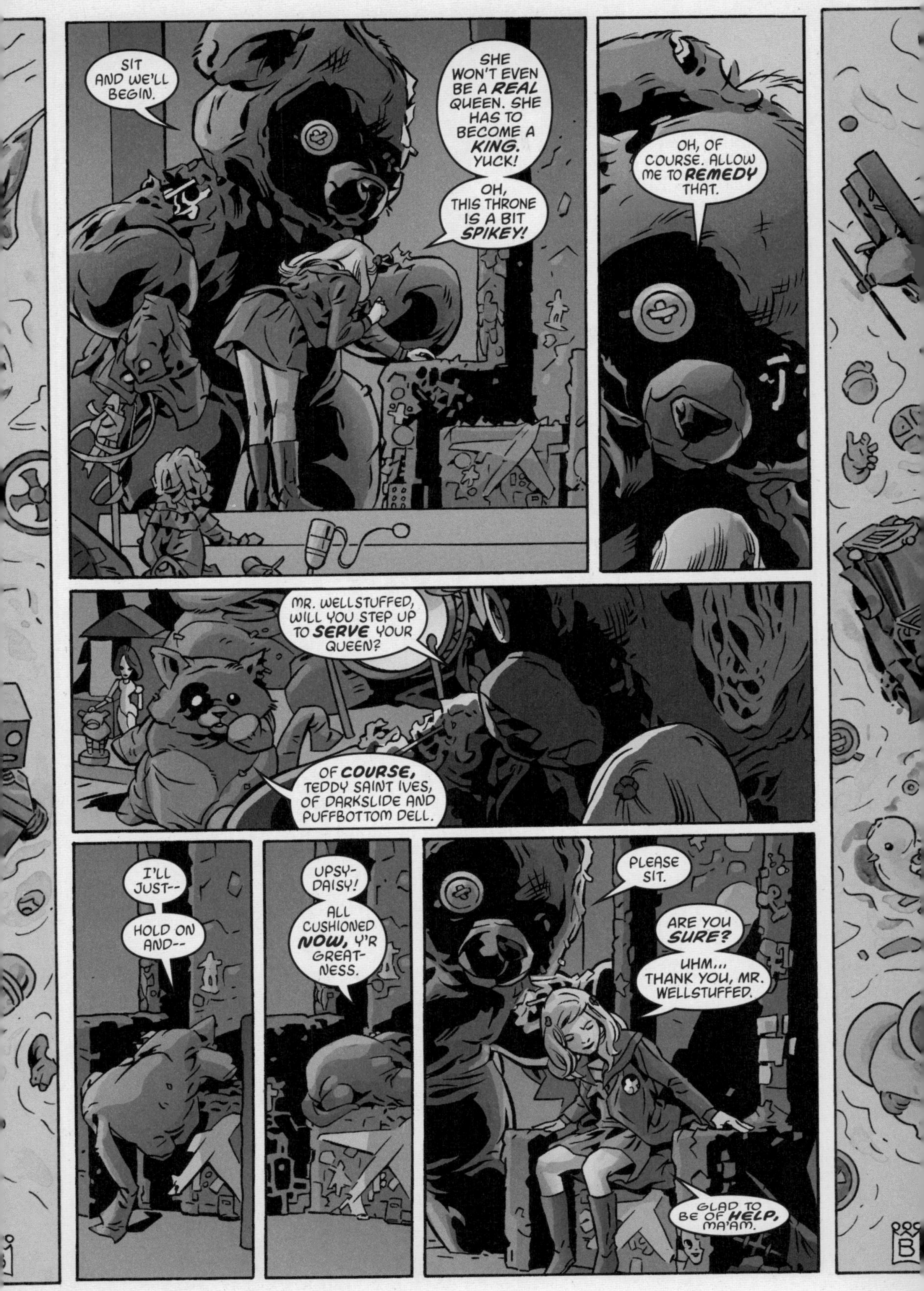
SIT AND WE'LL BEGIN.
SHE WON'T EVEN BE A REAL QUEEN. SHE HAS TO BECOME A KING. YUCK!
OH, THIS THRONE IS A BIT SPIKEY!
OH, OF COURSE. ALLOW ME TO REMEDY THAT.
MR. WELLSTUFFED, WILL YOU STEP UP TO SERVE YOUR QUEEN?
OF COURSE, TEDDY SAINT IVES, OF DARKSLIDE AND PUFFBOTTOM DELL.
I'LL JUST--
HOLD ON AND--
UPSY-DAISY!
ALL CUSHIONED NOW, Y'R GREAT-NESS.
PLEASE SIT.
ARE YOU SURE?
UHM... THANK YOU, MR. WELLSTUFFED.
GLAD TO BE OF HELP, MA'AM.

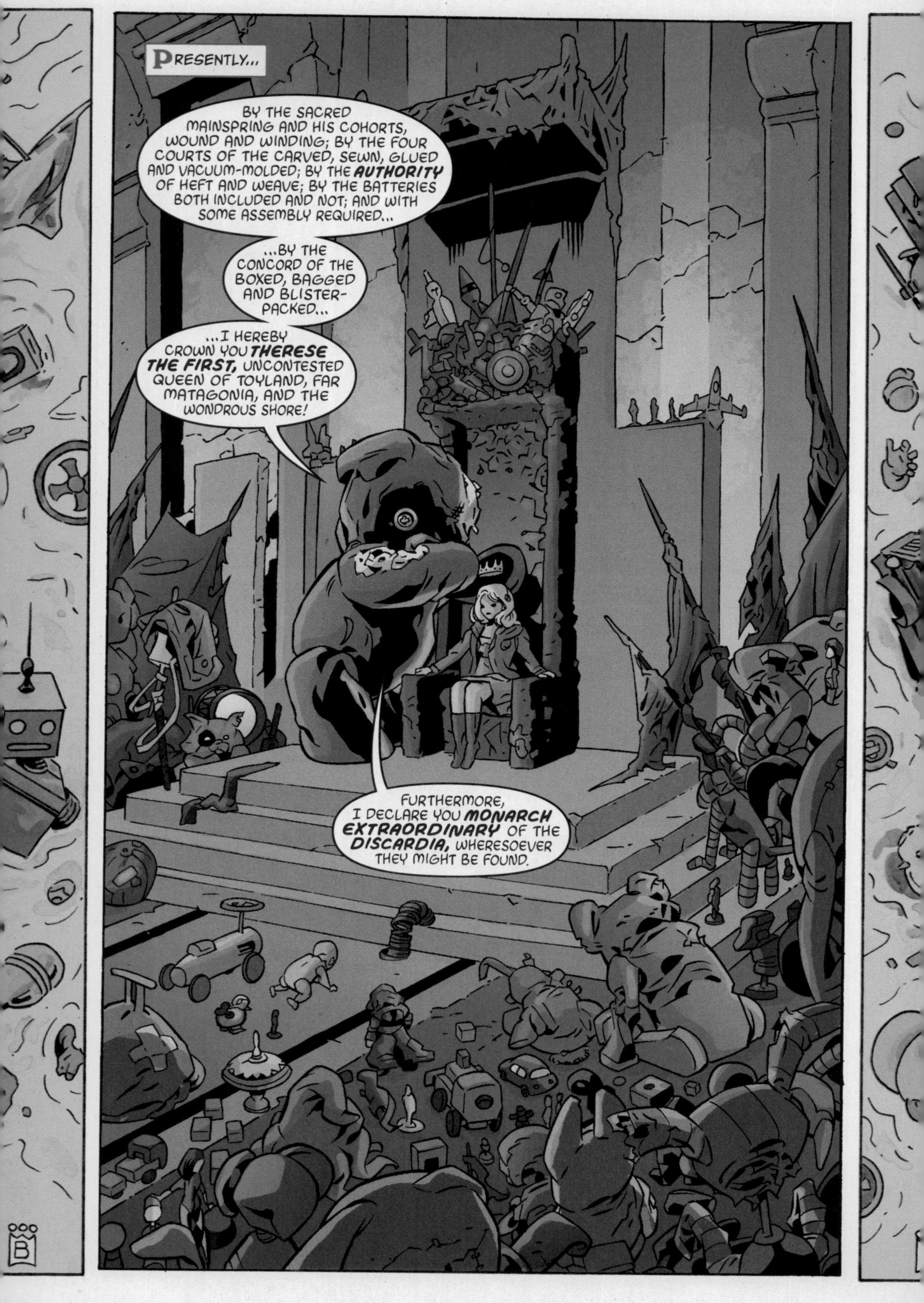
PRESENTLY...
BY THE SACRED MAINSPRING AND HIS COHORTS, WOUND AND WINDING; BY THE FOUR COURTS OF THE CARVED, SEWN, GLUED AND VACUUM-MOLDED; BY THE AUTHORITY OF HEFT AND WEAVE; BY THE BATTERIES BOTH INCLUDED AND NOT; AND WITH SOME ASSEMBLY REQUIRED...
...BY THE CONCORD OF THE BOXED, BAGGED AND BLISTER-PACKED...
...I HEREBY CROWN YOU THERESE THE FIRST, UNCONTESTED QUEEN OF TOYLAND, FAR MATAGONIA, AND THE WONDROUS SHORE!
FURTHERMORE, I DECLARE YOU MONARCH EXTRAORDINARY OF THE DISCARDIA, WHERESOEVER THEY MIGHT BE FOUND.

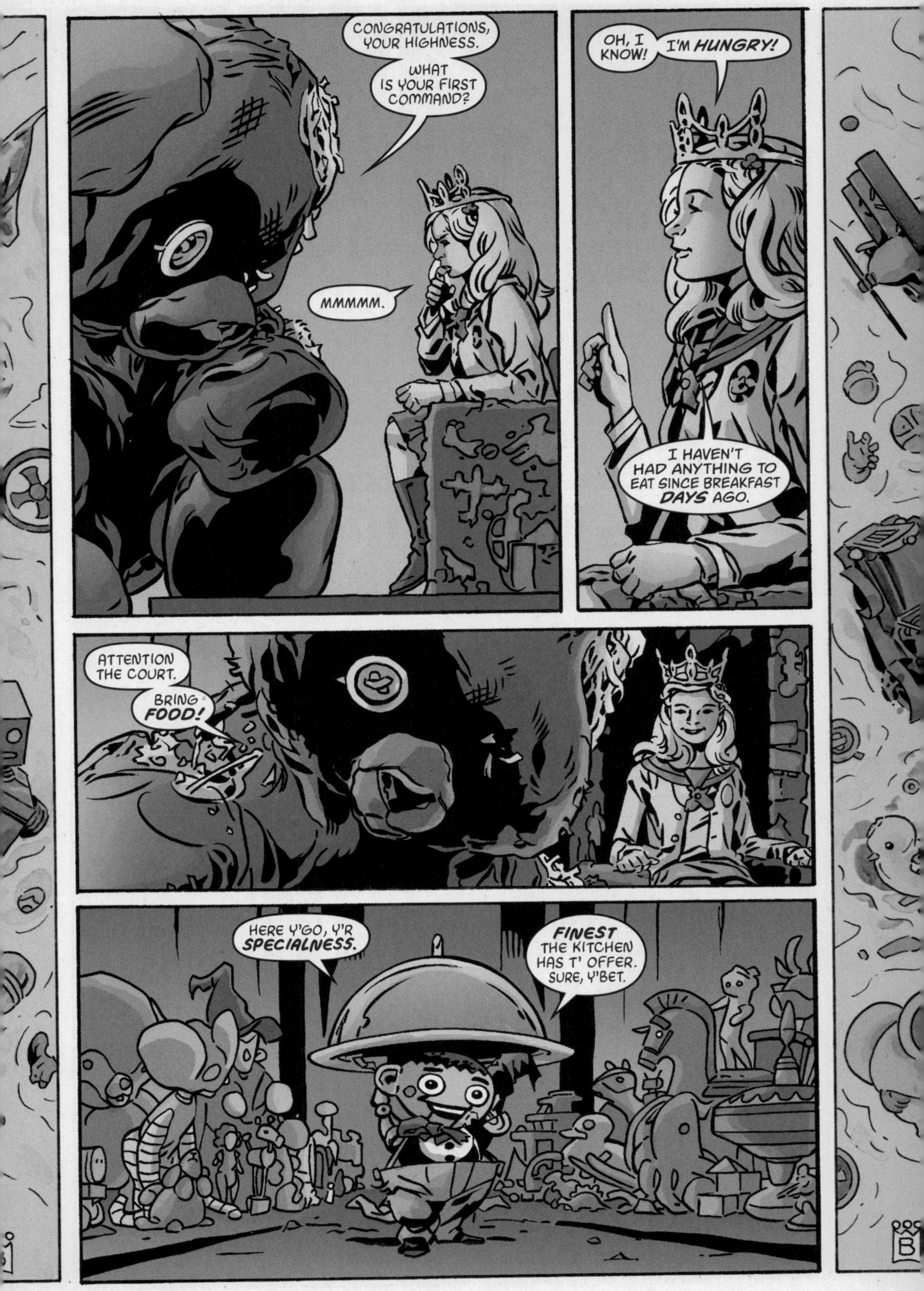
CONGRATULATIONS, YOUR HIGHNESS.
WHAT IS YOUR FIRST COMMAND?
MMMMM.
OH, I KNOW!
I'M HUNGRY!
I HAVEN'T HAD ANYTHING TO EAT SINCE BREAKFAST DAYS AGO.
ATTENTION THE COURT.
BRING FOOD!
HERE Y'GO, Y'R SPECIALNESS.
FINEST THE KITCHEN HAS T' OFFER. SURE, Y'BET.

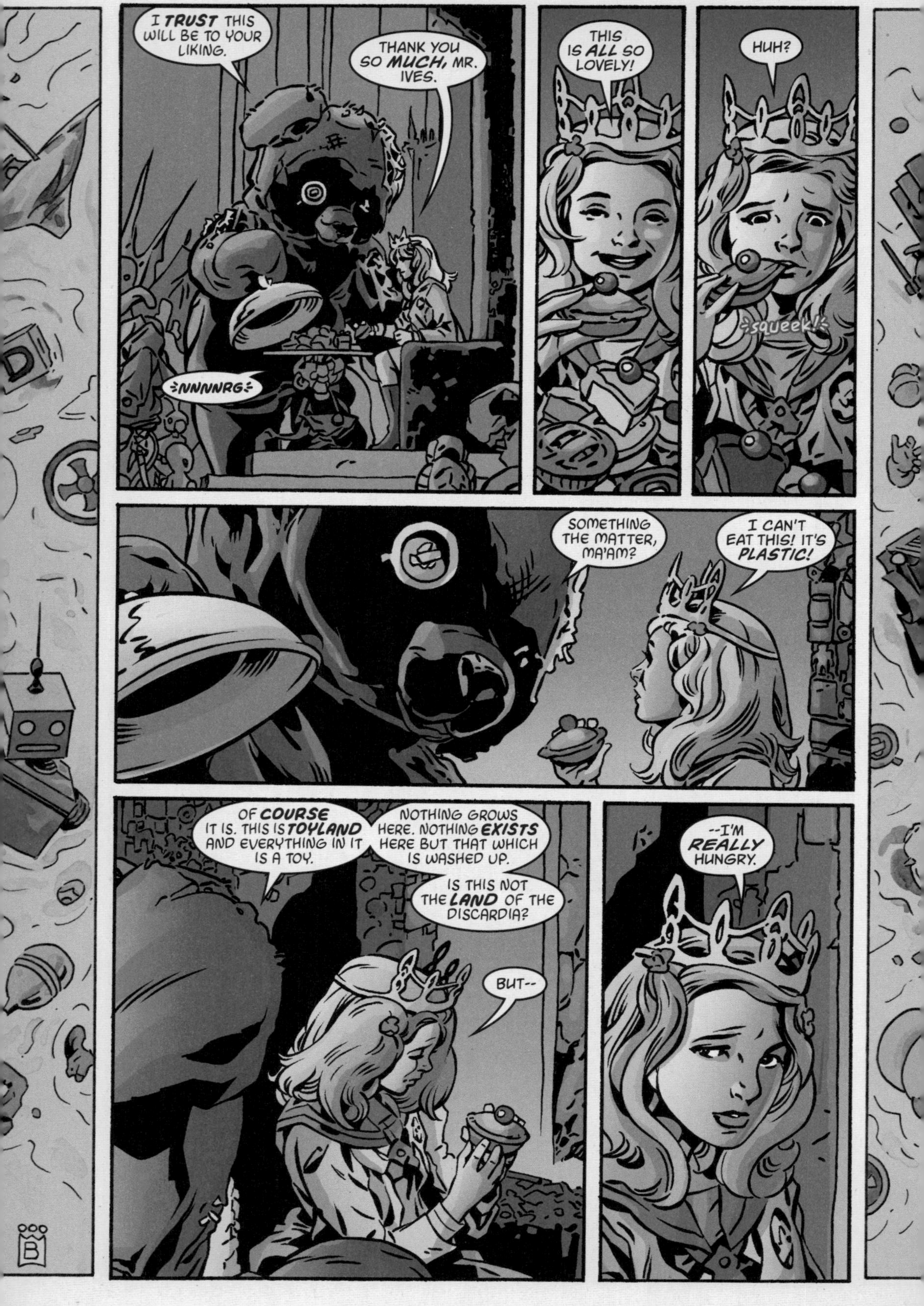

I TRUST THIS WILL BE TO YOUR LIKING.
THANK YOU SO MUCH, MR. IVES.
NNNNRG
THIS IS ALL SO LOVELY!
HUH?
squeek!
SOMETHING THE MATTER, MA'AM?
I CAN'T EAT THIS! IT'S PLASTIC!
OF COURSE IT IS. THIS IS TOYLAND AND EVERYTHING IN IT IS A TOY.
NOTHING GROWS HERE. NOTHING EXISTS HERE BUT THAT WHICH IS WASHED UP.
IS THIS NOT THE LAND OF THE DISCARDIA?
BUT--
--I'M REALLY HUNGRY.

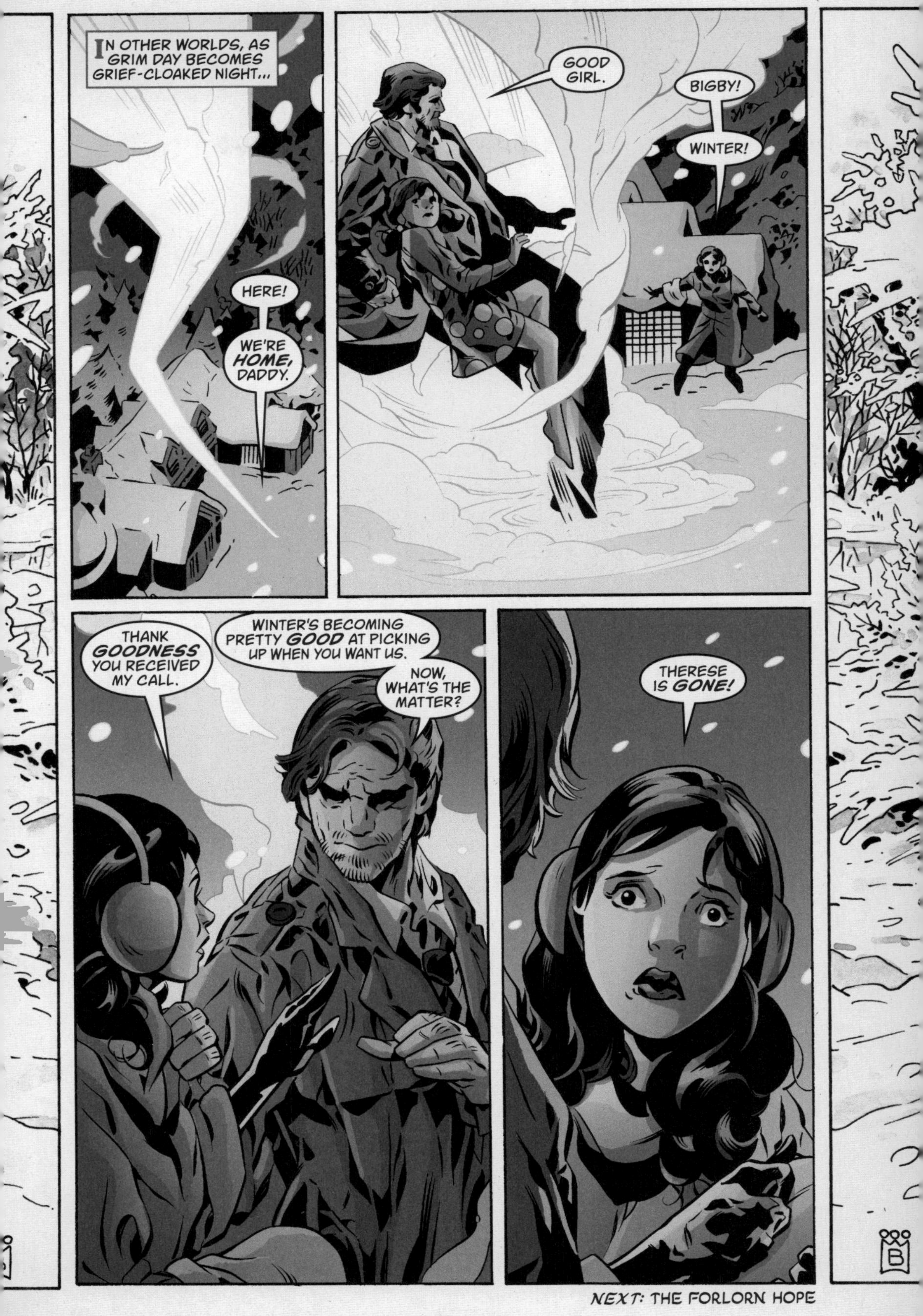

IN OTHER WORLDS, AS GRIM DAY BECOMES GRIEF-CLOAKED NIGHT...
HERE!
WE'RE HOME, DADDY.
GOOD GIRL.
BIGBY!
WINTER!
THANK GOODNESS YOU RECEIVED MY CALL.
WINTER'S BECOMING PRETTY GOOD AT PICKING UP WHEN YOU WANT US.
NOW, WHAT'S THE MATTER?
THERESE IS GONE!

NEXT: THE FORLORN HOPE

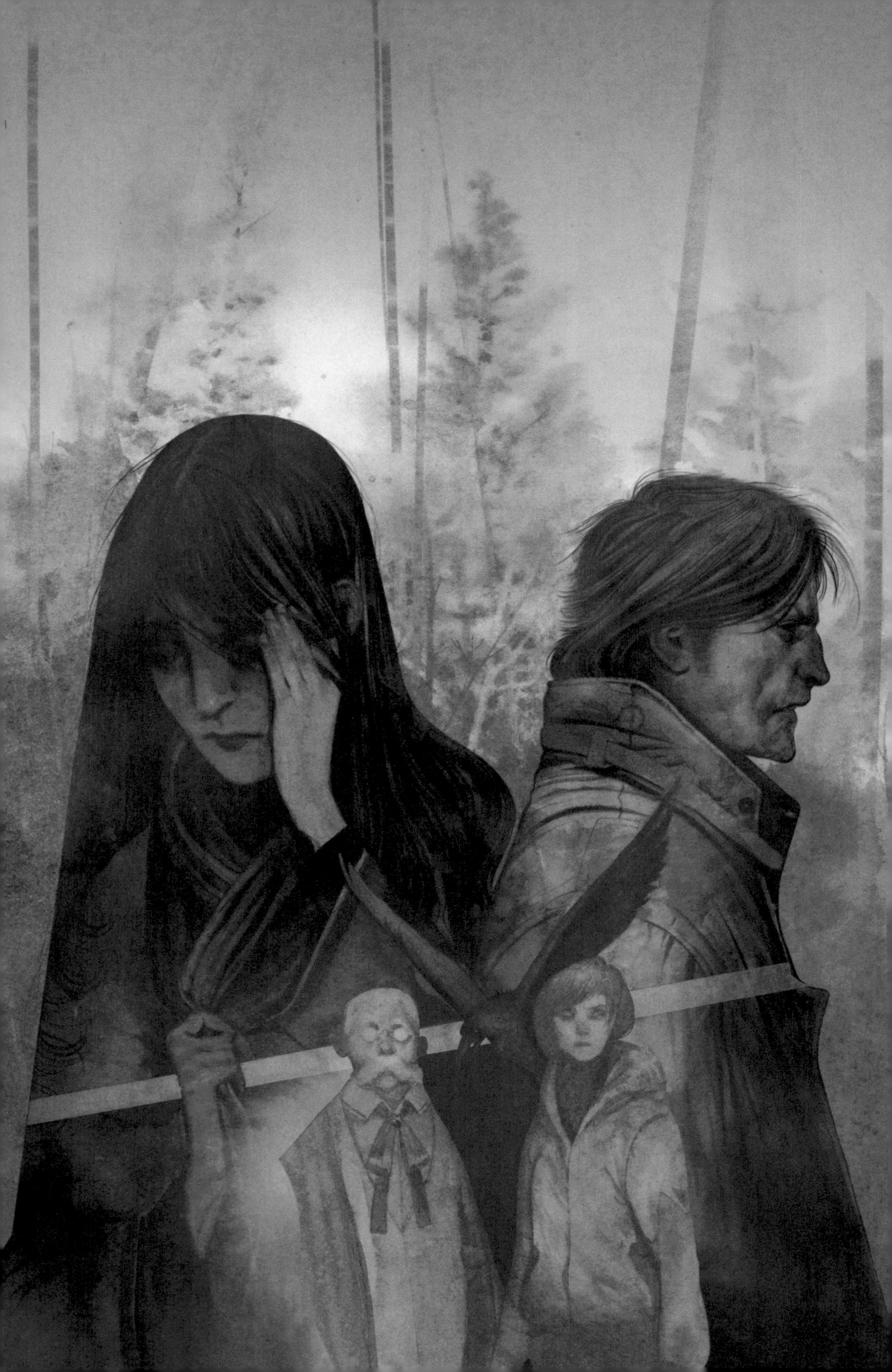

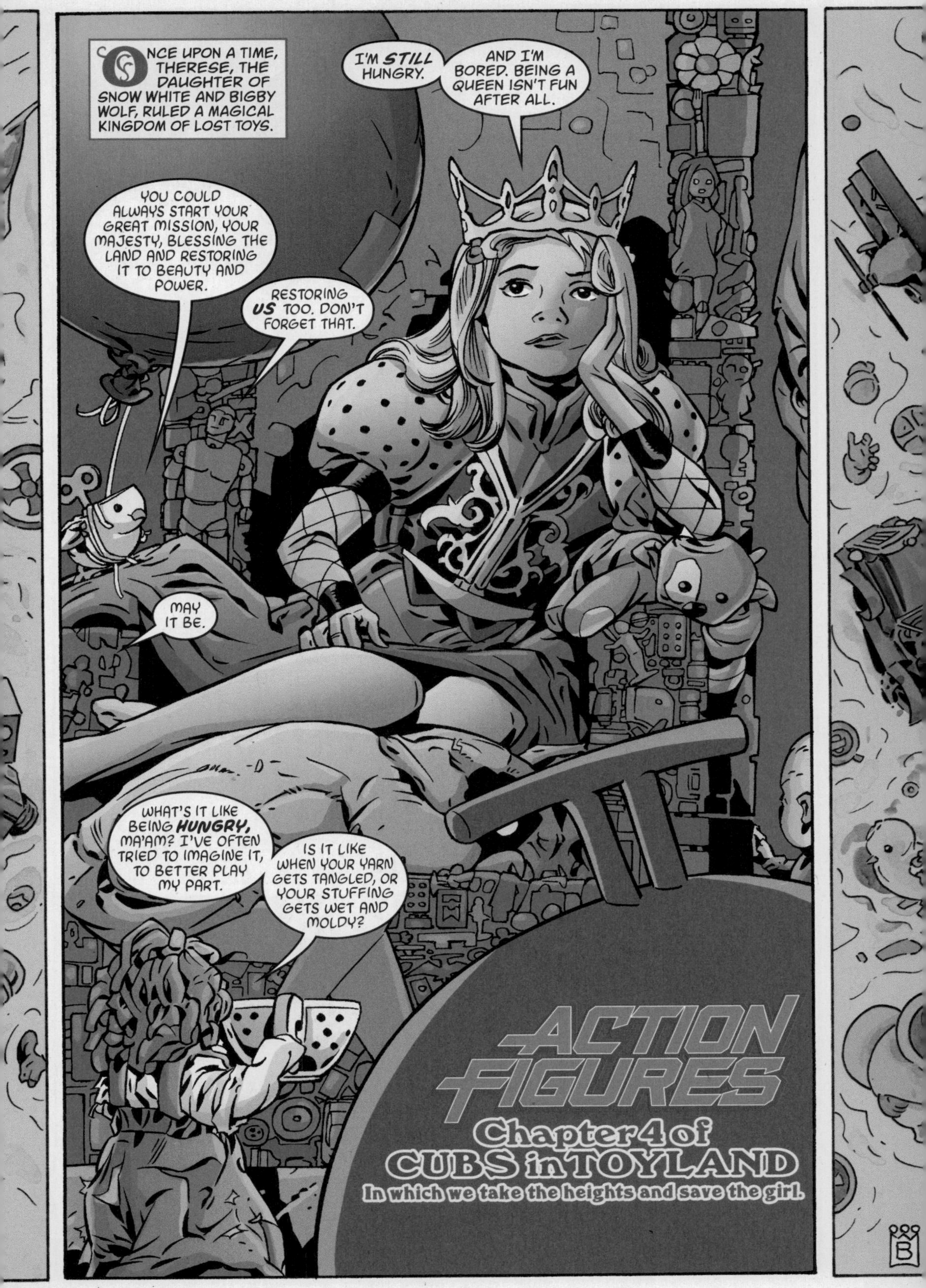
ONCE UPON A TIME, THERESE, THE DAUGHTER OF SNOW WHITE AND BIGBY WOLF, RULED A MAGICAL KINGDOM OF LOST TOYS.
I'M STILL HUNGRY.
AND I'M BORED. BEING A QUEEN ISN'T FUN AFTER ALL.
YOU COULD ALWAYS START YOUR GREAT MISSION, YOUR MAJESTY, BLESSING THE LAND AND RESTORING IT TO BEAUTY AND POWER.
RESTORING US TOO. DON'T FORGET THAT.
MAY IT BE.
WHAT'S IT LIKE BEING HUNGRY, MA'AM? I'VE OFTEN TRIED TO IMAGINE IT, TO BETTER PLAY MY PART.
IS IT LIKE WHEN YOUR YARN GETS TANGLED, OR YOUR STUFFING GETS WET AND MOLDY?
ACTION FIGURES
Chapter 4 of CUBS in TOYLAND
In which we take the heights and save the girl.

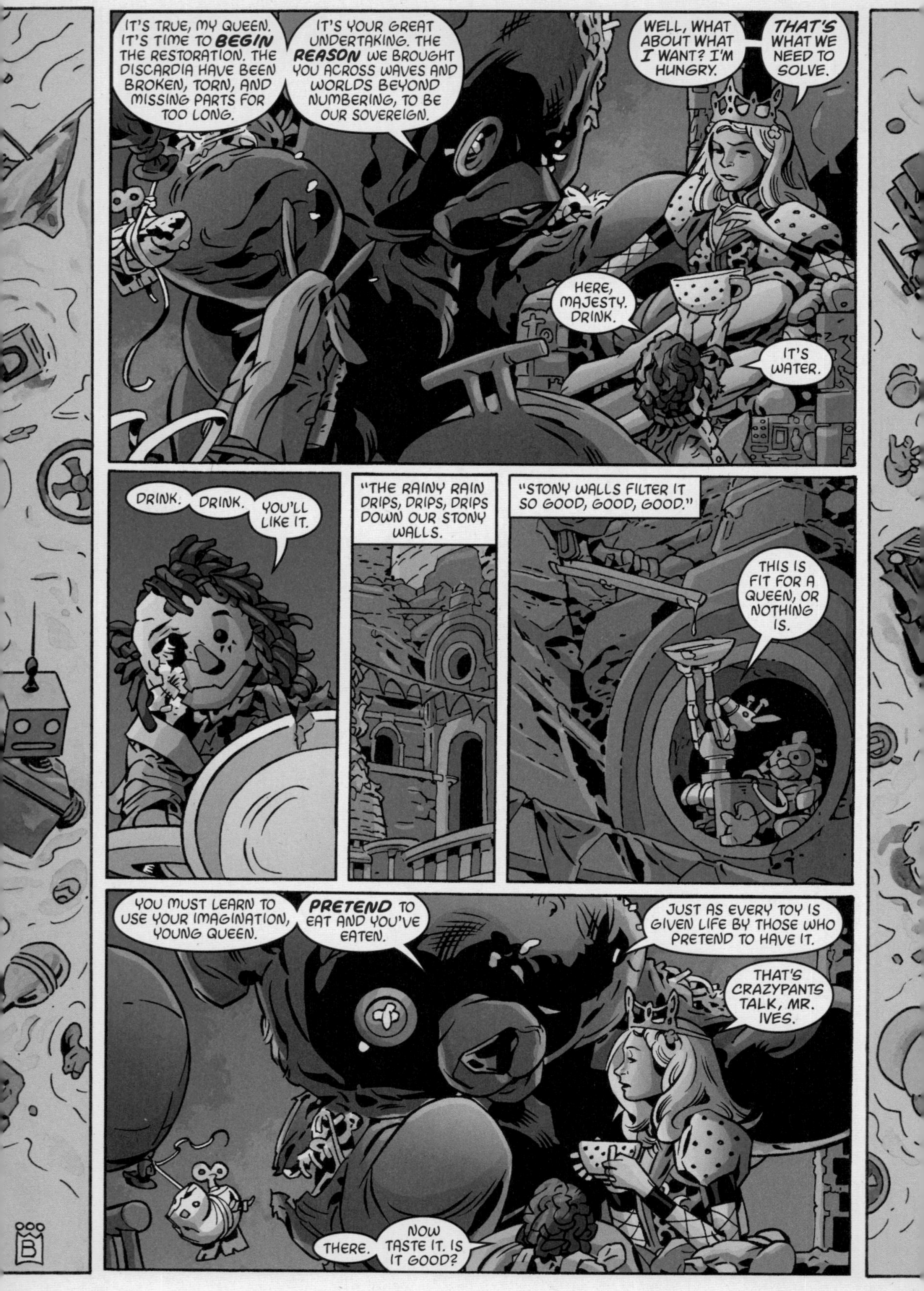
IT'S TRUE, MY QUEEN. IT'S TIME TO BEGIN THE RESTORATION. THE DISCARDIA HAVE BEEN BROKEN, TORN, AND MISSING PARTS FOR TOO LONG.
IT'S YOUR GREAT UNDERTAKING. THE REASON WE BROUGHT YOU ACROSS WAVES AND WORLDS BEYOND NUMBERING, TO BE OUR SOVEREIGN.
WELL, WHAT ABOUT WHAT I WANT? I'M HUNGRY.
THAT'S WHAT WE NEED TO SOLVE.
HERE, MAJESTY. DRINK.
IT'S WATER.
DRINK.
DRINK.
YOU'LL LIKE IT.
"THE RAINY RAIN DRIPS, DRIPS, DRIPS DOWN OUR STONY WALLS.
"STONY WALLS FILTER IT SO GOOD, GOOD, GOOD."
THIS IS FIT FOR A QUEEN, OR NOTHING IS.
YOU MUST LEARN TO USE YOUR IMAGINATION, YOUNG QUEEN.
PRETEND TO EAT AND YOU'VE EATEN.
JUST AS EVERY TOY IS GIVEN LIFE BY THOSE WHO PRETEND TO HAVE IT.
THAT'S CRAZYPANTS TALK, MR. IVES.
THERE.
NOW TASTE IT. IS IT GOOD?

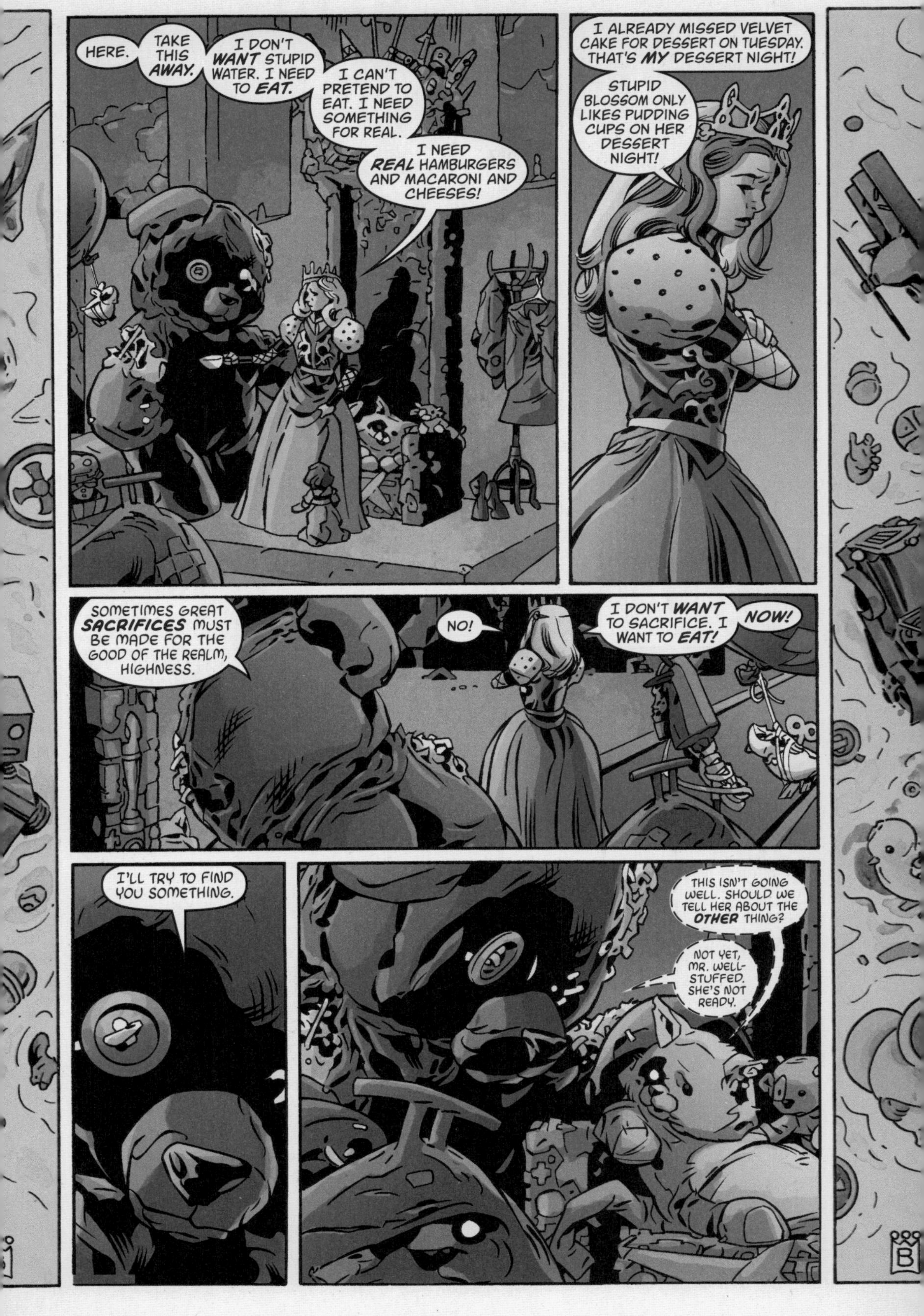
HERE.
TAKE THIS AWAY.
I DON'T WANT STUPID WATER. I NEED TO EAT.
I CAN'T PRETEND TO EAT. I NEED SOMETHING FOR REAL.
I NEED REAL HAMBURGERS AND MACARONI AND CHEESES!
I ALREADY MISSED VELVET CAKE FOR DESSERT ON TUESDAY. THAT'S MY DESSERT NIGHT!
STUPID BLOSSOM ONLY LIKES PUDDING CUPS ON HER DESSERT NIGHT!
SOMETIMES GREAT SACRIFICES MUST BE MADE FOR THE GOOD OF THE REALM, HIGHNESS.
NO!
I DON'T WANT TO SACRIFICE. I WANT TO EAT!
NOW!
I'LL TRY TO FIND YOU SOMETHING.
THIS ISN'T GOING WELL. SHOULD WE TELL HER ABOUT THE OTHER THING?
NOT YET, MR. WELL-STUFFED. SHE'S NOT READY.

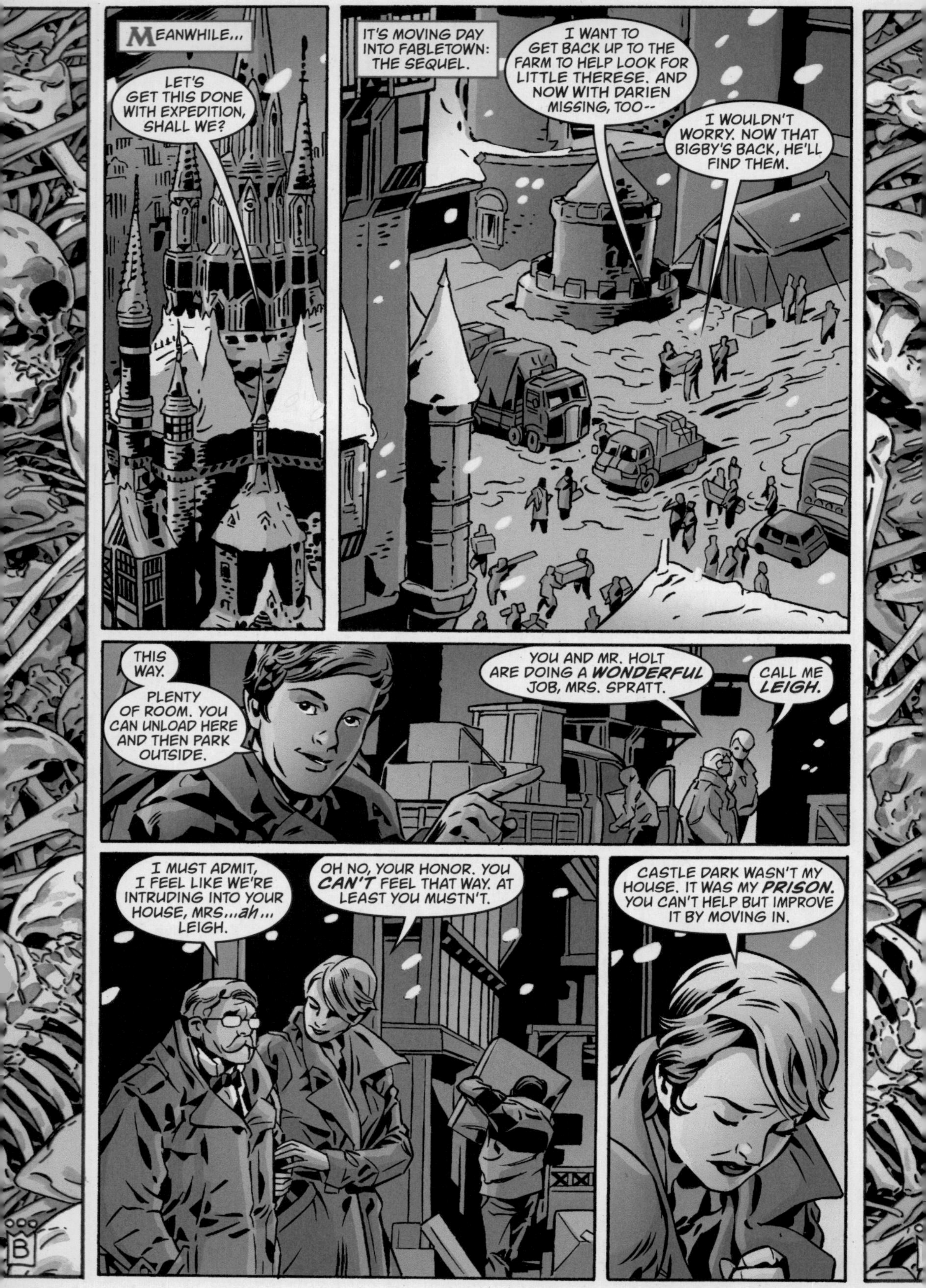
MEANWHILE...
LET'S GET THIS DONE WITH EXPEDITION, SHALL WE?
IT'S MOVING DAY INTO FABLETOWN: THE SEQUEL.
I WANT TO GET BACK UP TO THE FARM TO HELP LOOK FOR LITTLE THERESE. AND NOW WITH DARIEN MISSING, TOO--
I WOULDN'T WORRY. NOW THAT BIGBY'S BACK, HE'LL FIND THEM.
THIS WAY.
PLENTY OF ROOM. YOU CAN UNLOAD HERE AND THEN PARK OUTSIDE.
YOU AND MR. HOLT ARE DOING A WONDERFUL JOB, MRS. SPRATT.
CALL ME LEIGH.
I MUST ADMIT, I FEEL LIKE WE'RE INTRUDING INTO YOUR HOUSE, MRS...ah... LEIGH.
OH NO, YOUR HONOR. YOU CAN'T FEEL THAT WAY. AT LEAST YOU MUSTN'T.
CASTLE DARK WASN'T MY HOUSE. IT WAS MY PRISON. YOU CAN'T HELP BUT IMPROVE IT BY MOVING IN.

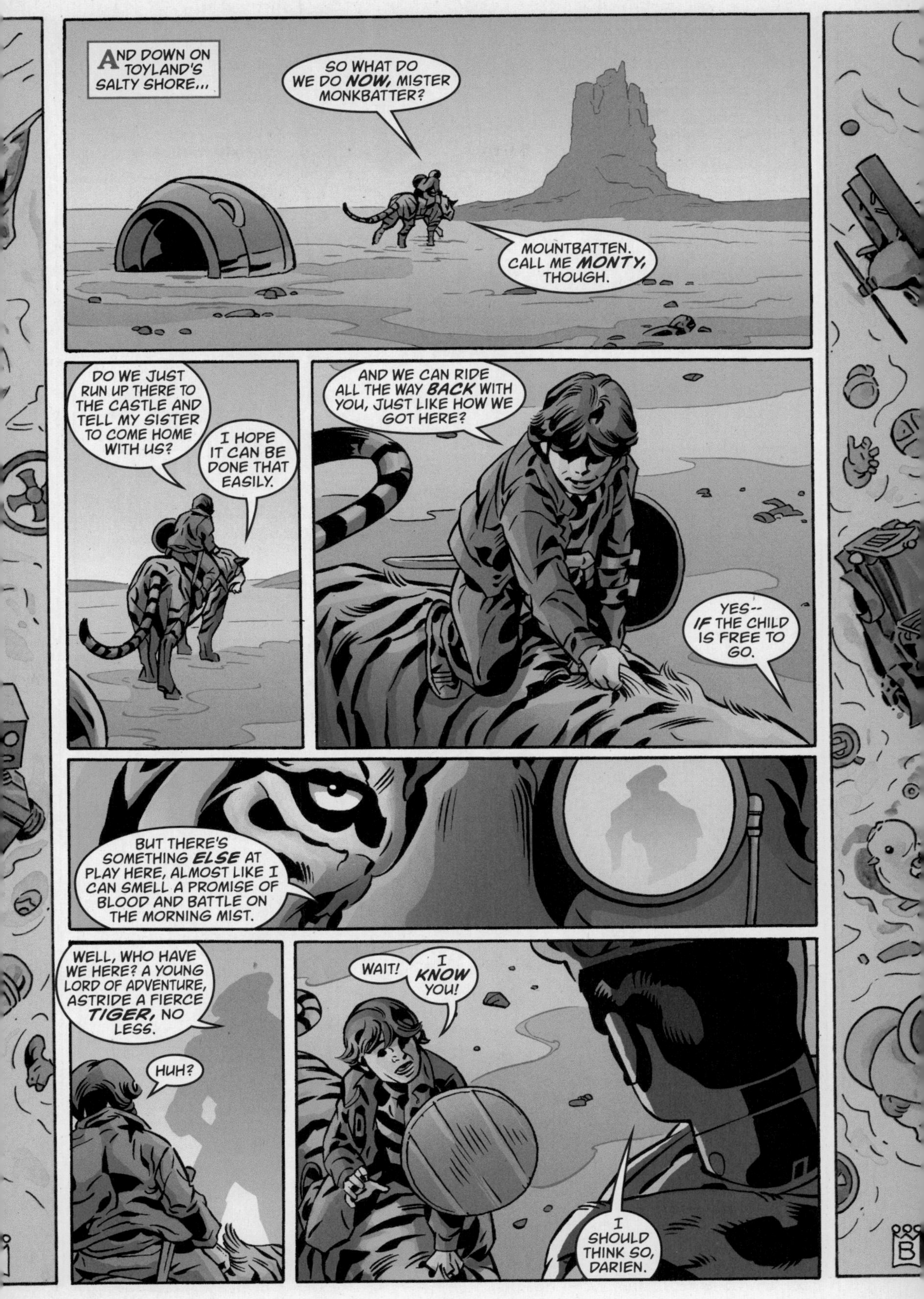
AND DOWN ON TOYLAND'S SALTY SHORE...
SO WHAT DO WE DO NOW, MISTER MONKBATTER?
MOUNTBATTEN. CALL ME MONTY, THOUGH.
DO WE JUST RUN UP THERE TO THE CASTLE AND TELL MY SISTER TO COME HOME WITH US?
I HOPE IT CAN BE DONE THAT EASILY.
AND WE CAN RIDE ALL THE WAY BACK WITH YOU, JUST LIKE HOW WE GOT HERE?
YES-- IF THE CHILD IS FREE TO GO.
BUT THERE'S SOMETHING ELSE AT PLAY HERE, ALMOST LIKE I CAN SMELL A PROMISE OF BLOOD AND BATTLE ON THE MORNING MIST.
WELL, WHO HAVE WE HERE? A YOUNG LORD OF ADVENTURE, ASTRIDE A FIERCE TIGER, NO LESS.
HUH?
WAIT!
I KNOW YOU!
I SHOULD THINK SO, DARIEN.

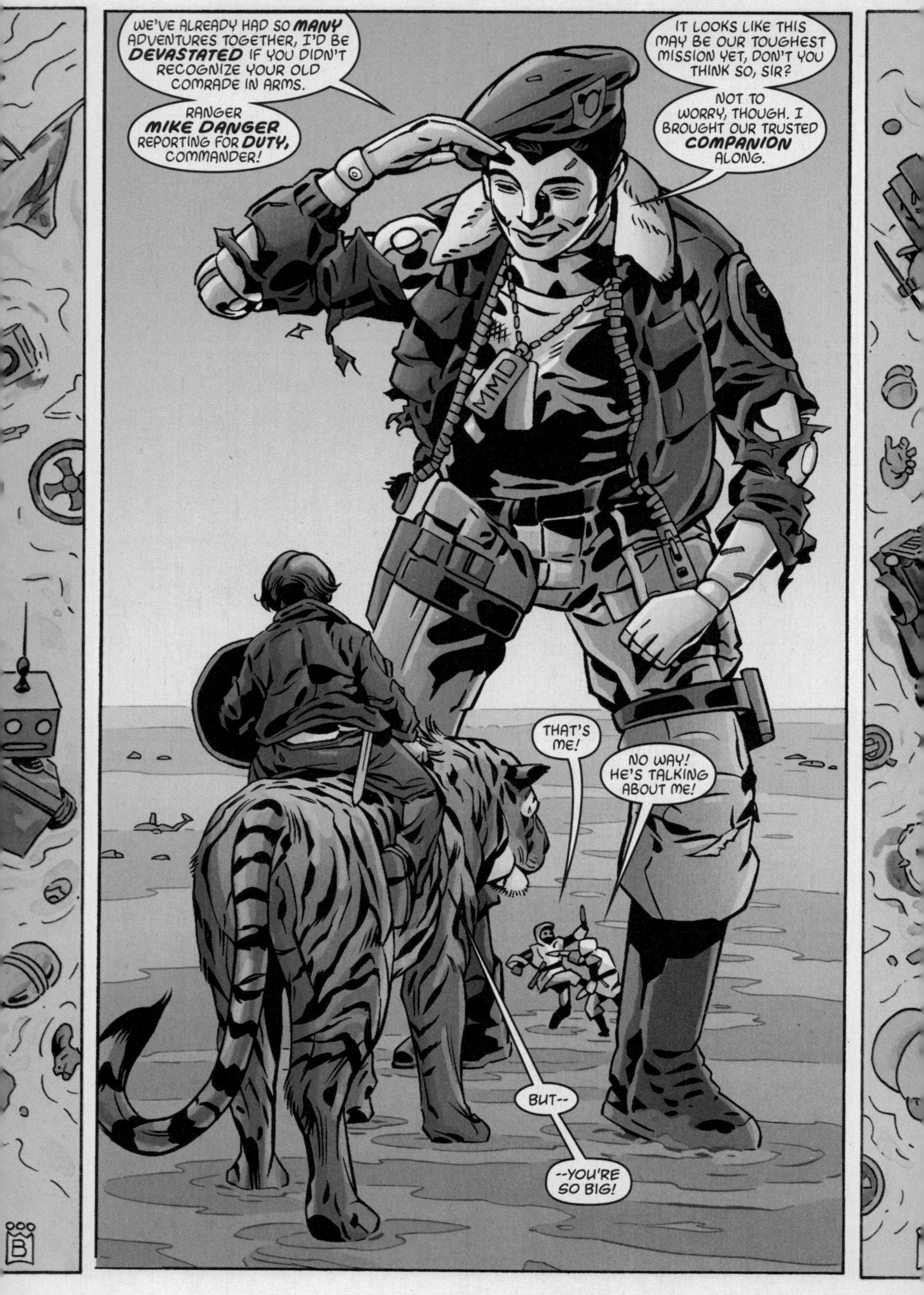
WE'VE ALREADY HAD SO MANY ADVENTURES TOGETHER, I'D BE DEVASTATED IF YOU DIDN'T RECOGNIZE YOUR OLD COMRADE IN ARMS.
RANGER MIKE DANGER REPORTING FOR DUTY, COMMANDER!
IT LOOKS LIKE THIS MAY BE OUR TOUGHEST MISSION YET, DON'T YOU THINK SO, SIR?
NOT TO WORRY, THOUGH. I BROUGHT OUR TRUSTED COMPANION ALONG.
MMD
THAT'S ME!
NO WAY! HE'S TALKING ABOUT ME!
BUT--
--YOU'RE SO BIG!

Panel 1:
If I've increased in **STATURE** over the years, it's because of the trust and responsibility you've **PLACED** in me, sir!

WOW! You're like the **COOLEST** toy ever!

And who are these two?

Panel 2:
As I said: my faithful companion and man friday, **KARATE NINJA NOBU.**

BOTH versions.

Panel 3:
I'm the real NOBU! Original series!

Panel 4:
NO! I'm the real one!

Panel 5:
The newer version with **KUNG FU ACTION** fist!

Panel 6:
UHM... **SPRING'S** a bit worn. Can someone help me push this back in?

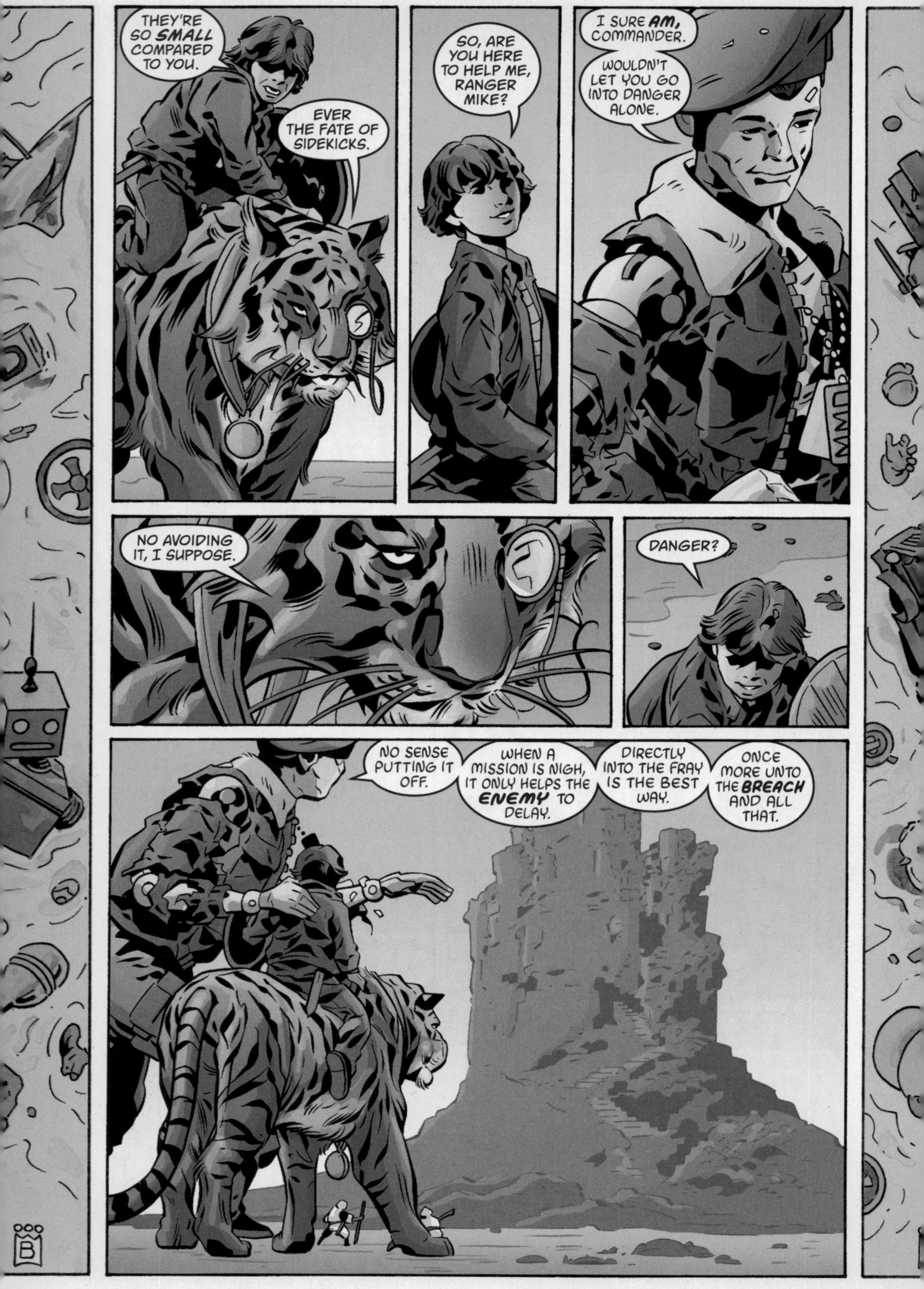
THEY'RE SO SMALL COMPARED TO YOU.
EVER THE FATE OF SIDEKICKS.
SO, ARE YOU HERE TO HELP ME, RANGER MIKE?
I SURE AM, COMMANDER.
WOULDN'T LET YOU GO INTO DANGER ALONE.
NO AVOIDING IT, I SUPPOSE.
DANGER?
NO SENSE PUTTING IT OFF.
WHEN A MISSION IS NIGH, IT ONLY HELPS THE ENEMY TO DELAY.
DIRECTLY INTO THE FRAY IS THE BEST WAY.
ONCE MORE UNTO THE BREACH AND ALL THAT.

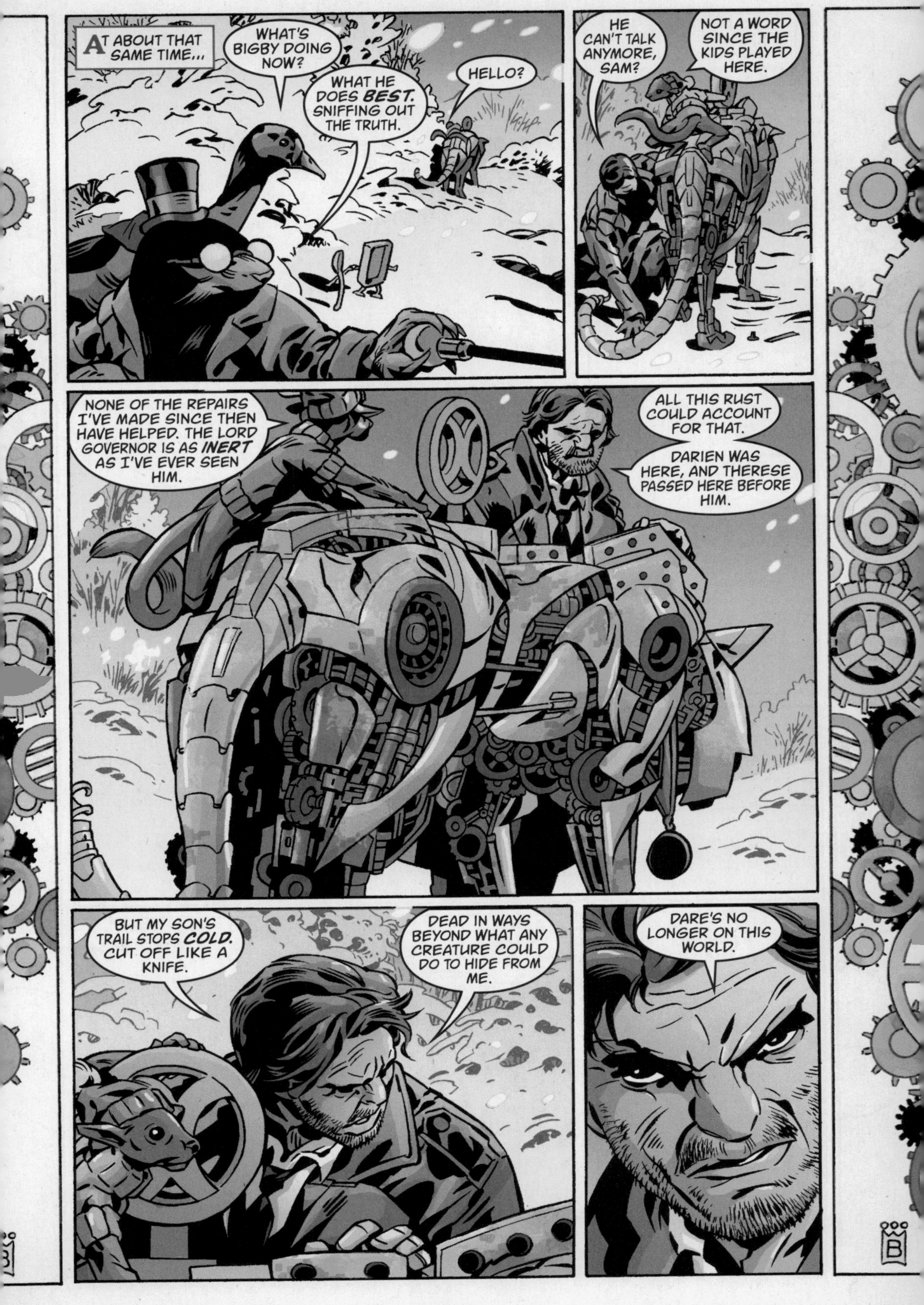
AT ABOUT THAT SAME TIME...
WHAT'S BIGBY DOING NOW?
WHAT HE DOES BEST. SNIFFING OUT THE TRUTH.
HELLO?
HE CAN'T TALK ANYMORE, SAM?
NOT A WORD SINCE THE KIDS PLAYED HERE.
NONE OF THE REPAIRS I'VE MADE SINCE THEN HAVE HELPED. THE LORD GOVERNOR IS AS INERT AS I'VE EVER SEEN HIM.
ALL THIS RUST COULD ACCOUNT FOR THAT.
DARIEN WAS HERE, AND THERESE PASSED HERE BEFORE HIM.
BUT MY SON'S TRAIL STOPS COLD. CUT OFF LIKE A KNIFE.
DEAD IN WAYS BEYOND WHAT ANY CREATURE COULD DO TO HIDE FROM ME.
DARE'S NO LONGER ON THIS WORLD.

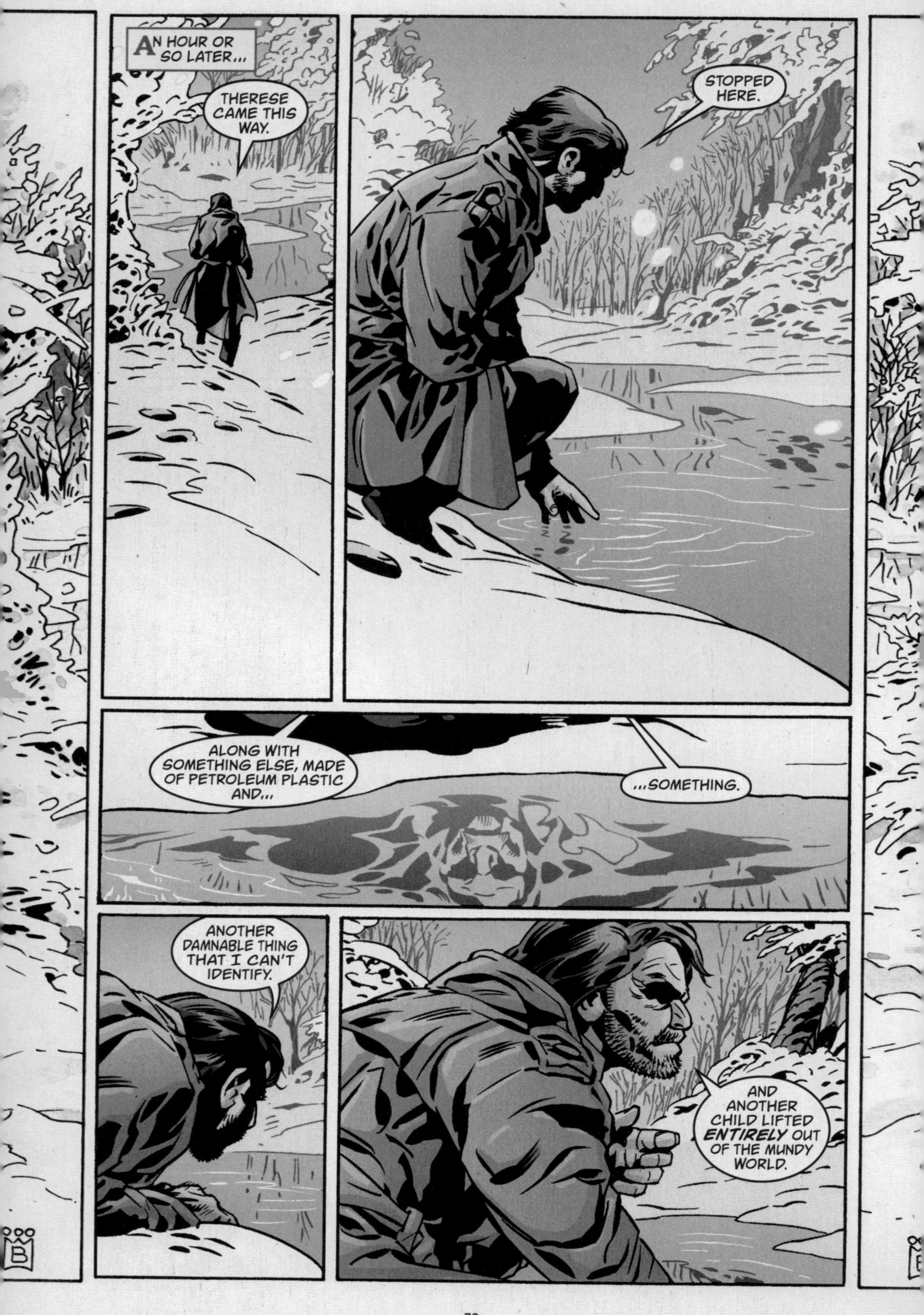
AN HOUR OR SO LATER...
THERESE CAME THIS WAY.
STOPPED HERE.
ALONG WITH SOMETHING ELSE, MADE OF PETROLEUM PLASTIC AND...
...SOMETHING.
ANOTHER DAMNABLE THING THAT I CAN'T IDENTIFY.
AND ANOTHER CHILD LIFTED ENTIRELY OUT OF THE MUNDY WORLD.

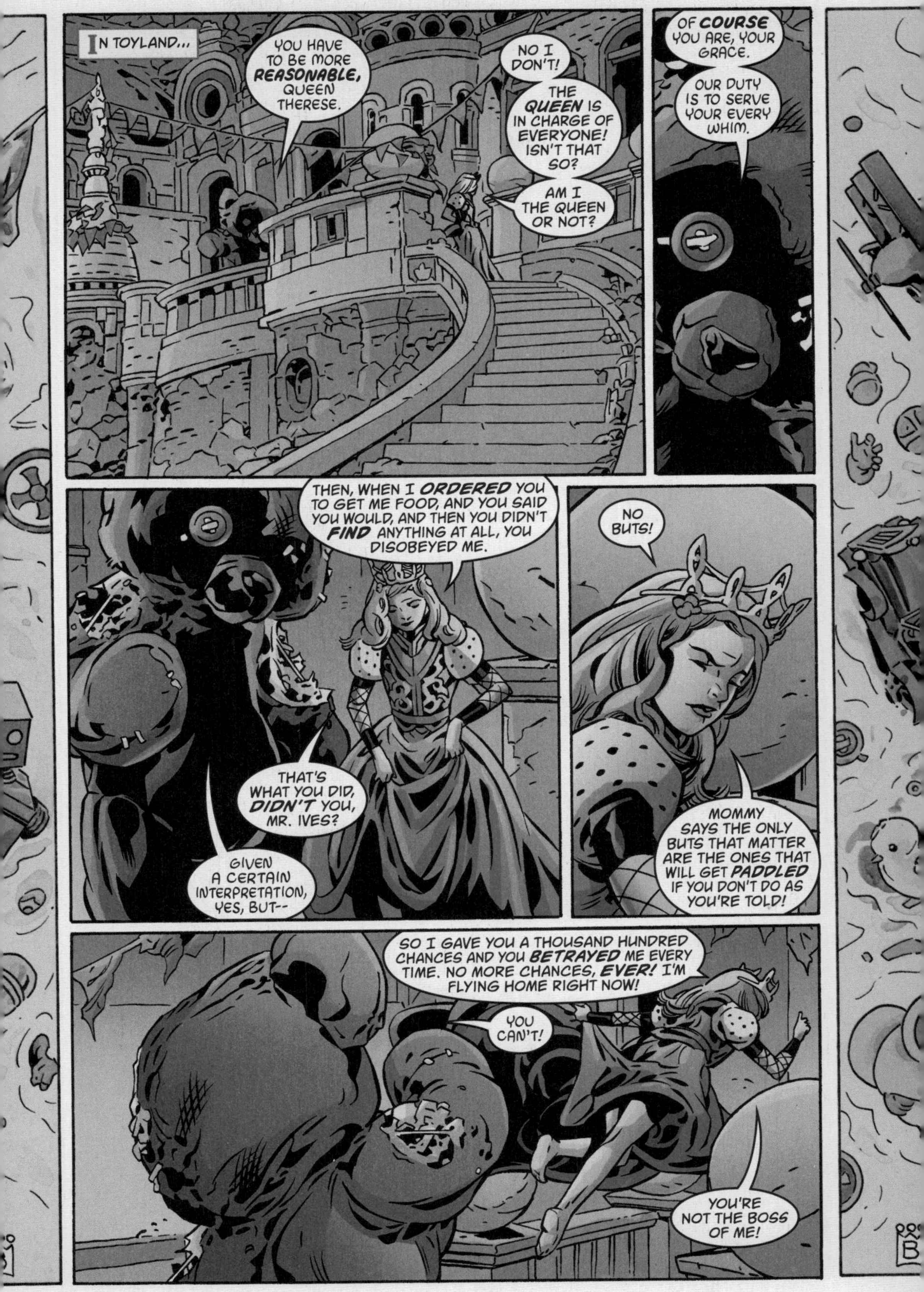
IN TOYLAND...
YOU HAVE TO BE MORE REASONABLE, QUEEN THERESE.
NO I DON'T!
THE QUEEN IS IN CHARGE OF EVERYONE! ISN'T THAT SO?
AM I THE QUEEN OR NOT?
OF COURSE YOU ARE, YOUR GRACE.
OUR DUTY IS TO SERVE YOUR EVERY WHIM.
THEN, WHEN I ORDERED YOU TO GET ME FOOD, AND YOU SAID YOU WOULD, AND THEN YOU DIDN'T FIND ANYTHING AT ALL, YOU DISOBEYED ME.
THAT'S WHAT YOU DID, DIDN'T YOU, MR. IVES?
GIVEN A CERTAIN INTERPRETATION, YES, BUT--
NO BUTS!
MOMMY SAYS THE ONLY BUTS THAT MATTER ARE THE ONES THAT WILL GET PADDLED IF YOU DON'T DO AS YOU'RE TOLD!
SO I GAVE YOU A THOUSAND HUNDRED CHANCES AND YOU BETRAYED ME EVERY TIME. NO MORE CHANCES, EVER! I'M FLYING HOME RIGHT NOW!
YOU CAN'T!
YOU'RE NOT THE BOSS OF ME!

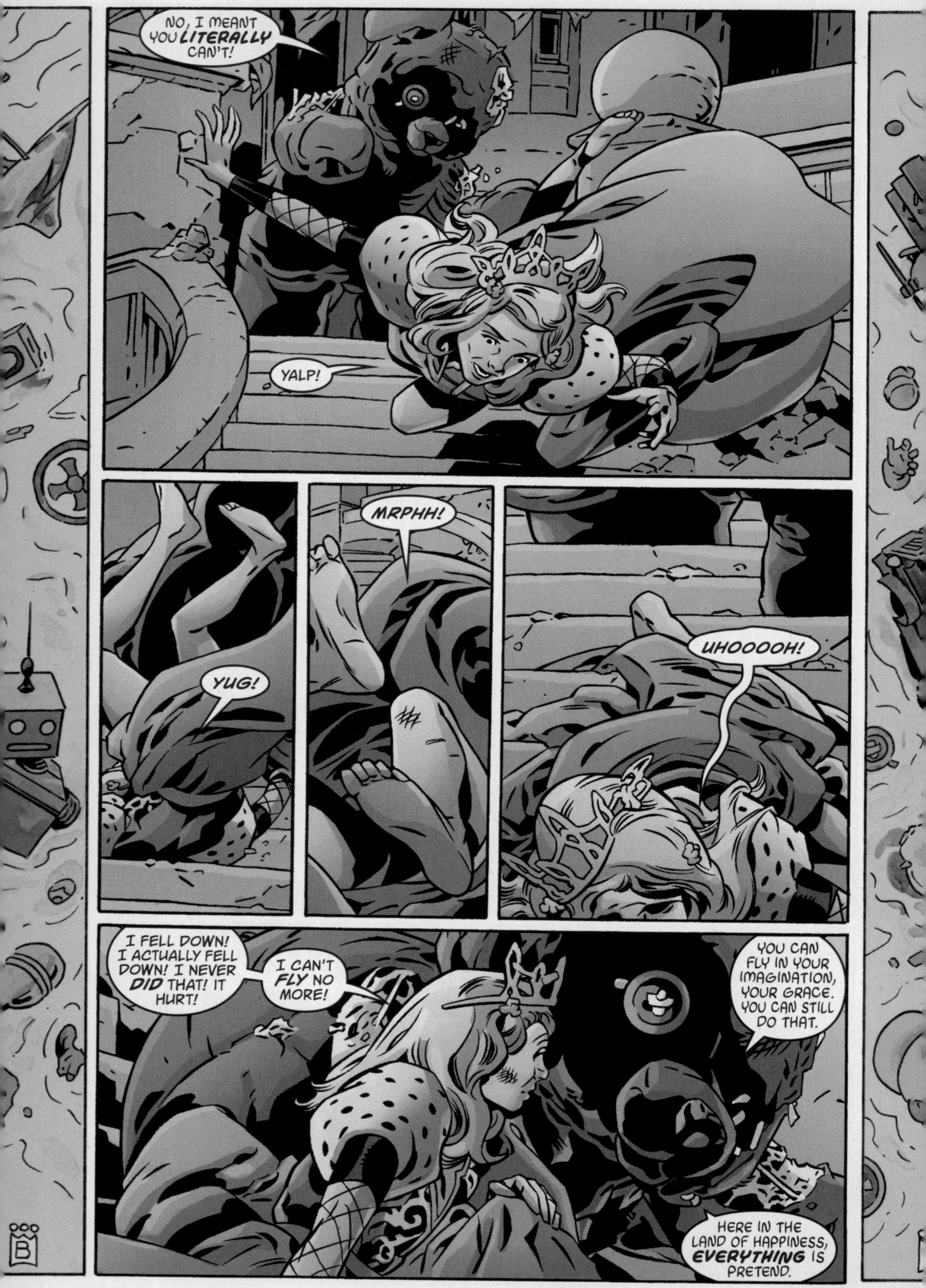

NO, I MEANT YOU LITERALLY CAN'T!
YALP!
YUG!
MRPHH!
UHOOOOH!
I FELL DOWN! I ACTUALLY FELL DOWN! I NEVER DID THAT! IT HURT!
I CAN'T FLY NO MORE!
YOU CAN FLY IN YOUR IMAGINATION, YOUR GRACE. YOU CAN STILL DO THAT.
HERE IN THE LAND OF HAPPINESS, EVERYTHING IS PRETEND.

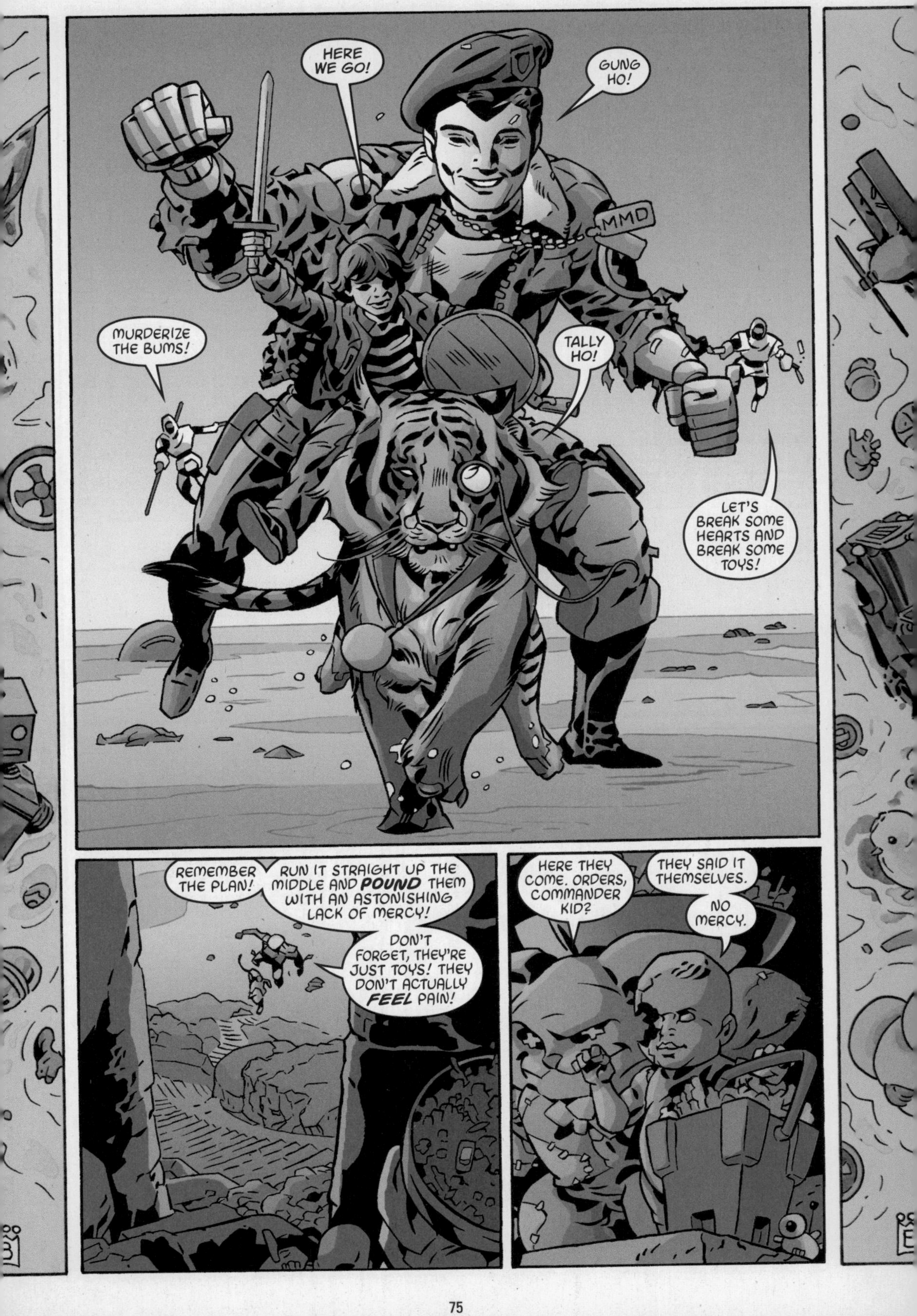
HERE WE GO!
GUNG HO!
MURDERIZE THE BUMS!
TALLY HO!
LET'S BREAK SOME HEARTS AND BREAK SOME TOYS!
REMEMBER THE PLAN!
RUN IT STRAIGHT UP THE MIDDLE AND POUND THEM WITH AN ASTONISHING LACK OF MERCY!
DON'T FORGET, THEY'RE JUST TOYS! THEY DON'T ACTUALLY FEEL PAIN!
HERE THEY COME. ORDERS, COMMANDER KID?
THEY SAID IT THEMSELVES.
NO MERCY.

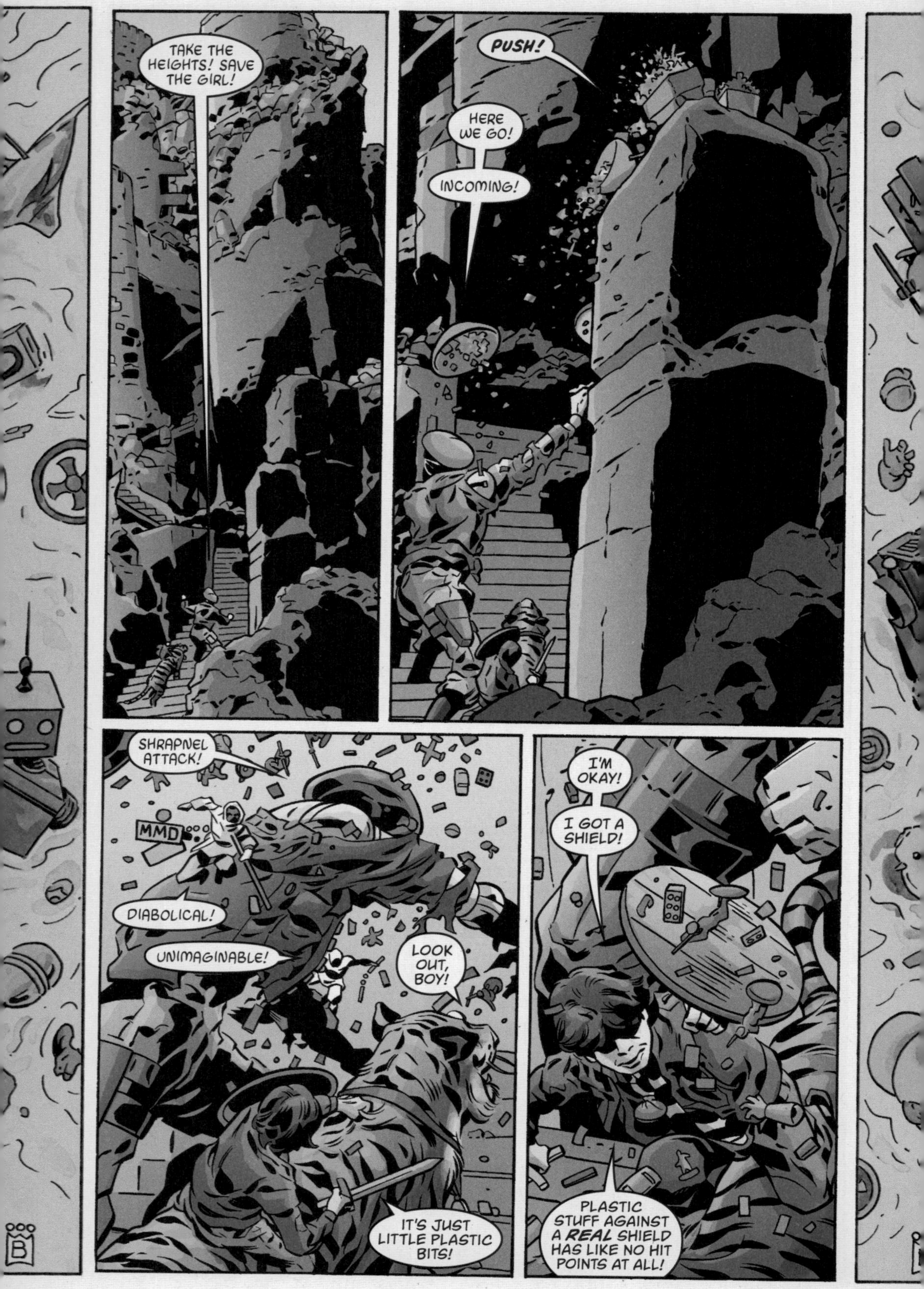
TAKE THE HEIGHTS! SAVE THE GIRL!
PUSH!
HERE WE GO!
INCOMING!
SHRAPNEL ATTACK!
MMD
DIABOLICAL!
UNIMAGINABLE!
LOOK OUT, BOY!
IT'S JUST LITTLE PLASTIC BITS!
I'M OKAY!
I GOT A SHIELD!
PLASTIC STUFF AGAINST A REAL SHIELD HAS LIKE NO HIT POINTS AT ALL!

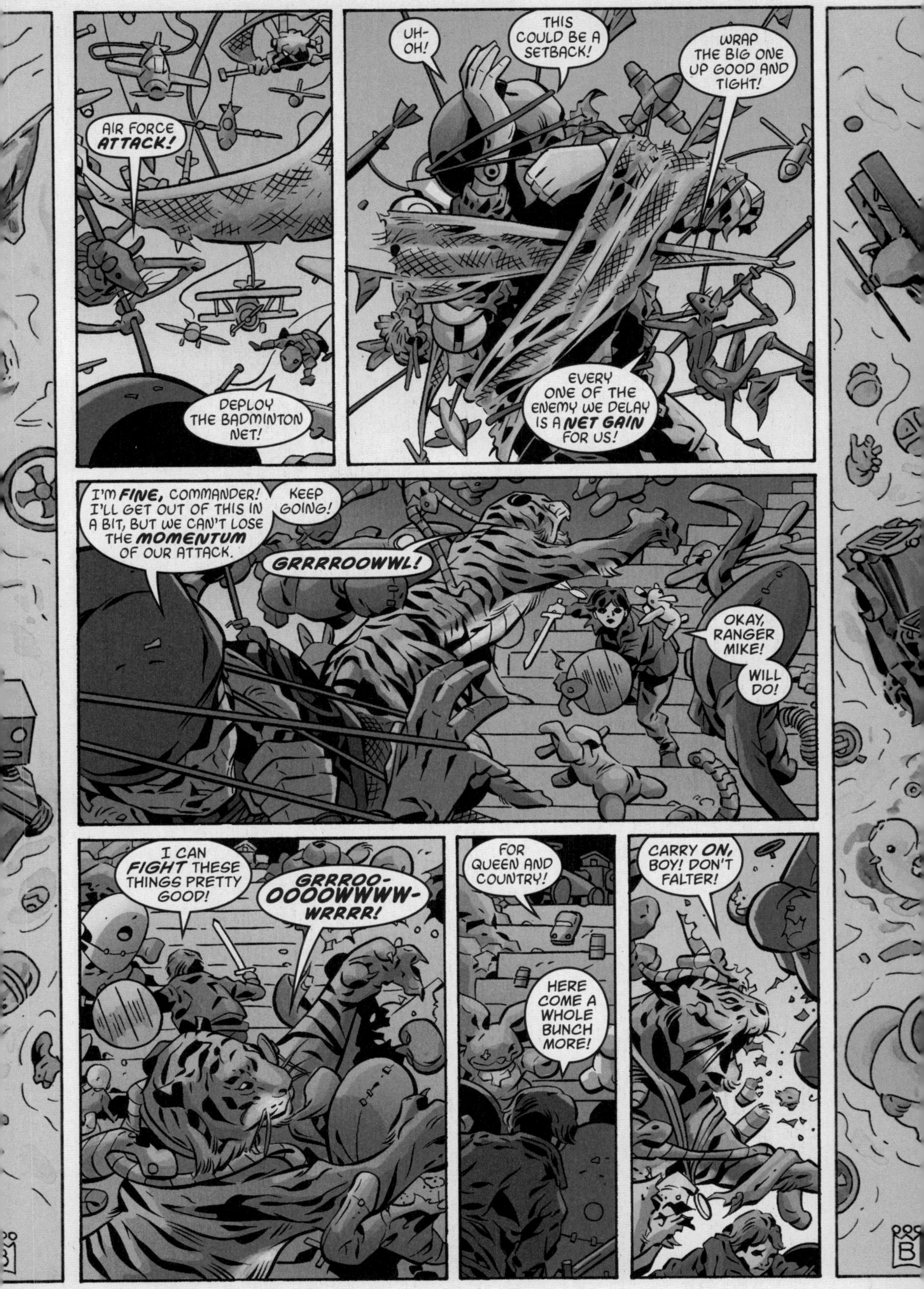
AIR FORCE ATTACK!
DEPLOY THE BADMINTON NET!
UH-OH!
THIS COULD BE A SETBACK!
WRAP THE BIG ONE UP GOOD AND TIGHT!
EVERY ONE OF THE ENEMY WE DELAY IS A NET GAIN FOR US!
I'M FINE, COMMANDER! I'LL GET OUT OF THIS IN A BIT, BUT WE CAN'T LOSE THE MOMENTUM OF OUR ATTACK.
KEEP GOING!
GRRRROOWWL!
OKAY, RANGER MIKE!
WILL DO!
I CAN FIGHT THESE THINGS PRETTY GOOD!
GRRROO-OOOOWWWW-WRRRR!
FOR QUEEN AND COUNTRY!
HERE COME A WHOLE BUNCH MORE!
CARRY ON, BOY! DON'T FALTER!

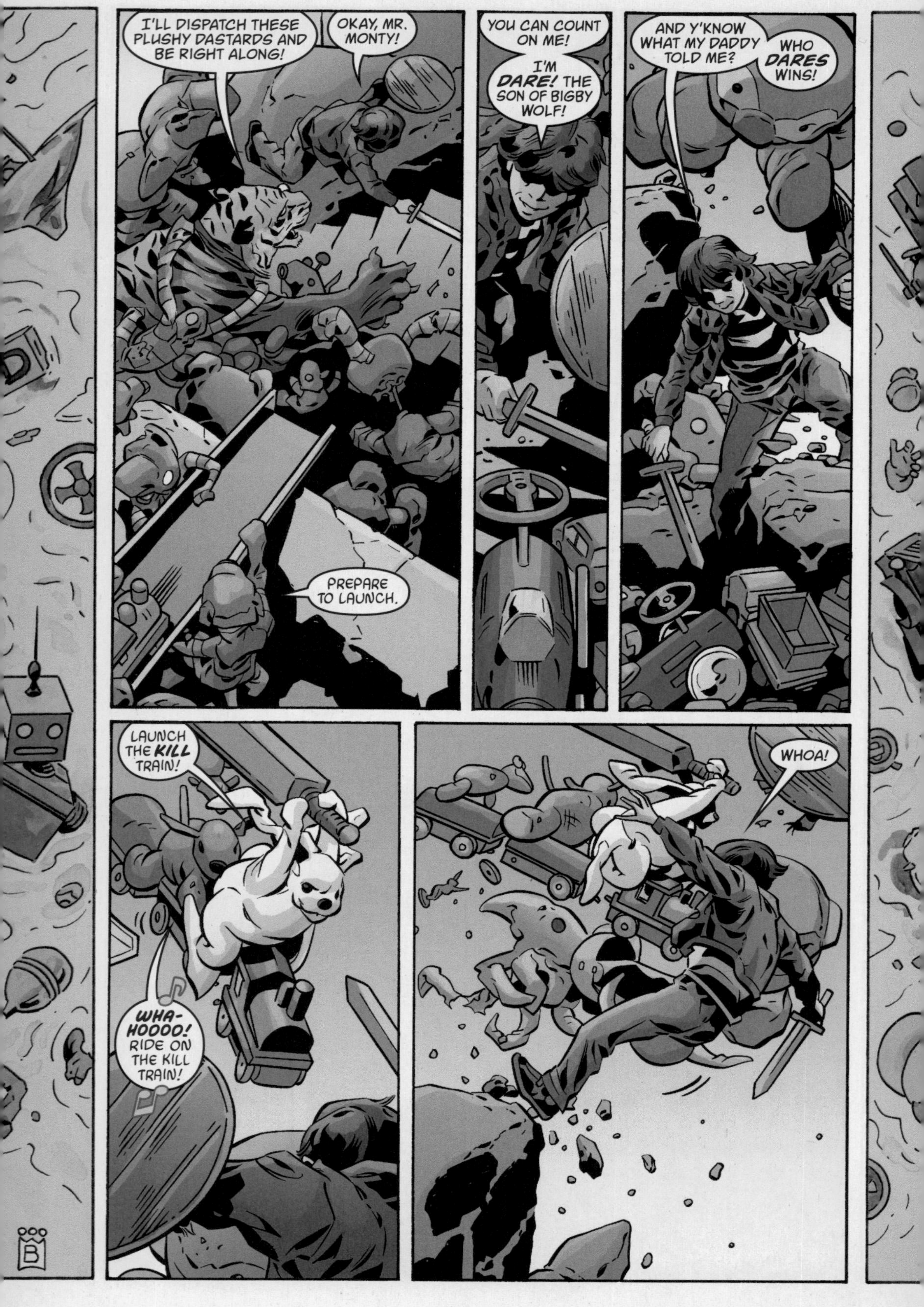
I'LL DISPATCH THESE PLUSHY DASTARDS AND BE RIGHT ALONG!
OKAY, MR. MONTY!
PREPARE TO LAUNCH.
YOU CAN COUNT ON ME!
I'M DARE! THE SON OF BIGBY WOLF!
AND Y'KNOW WHAT MY DADDY TOLD ME?
WHO DARES WINS!
LAUNCH THE KILL TRAIN!
WHA-HOOOO! RIDE ON THE KILL TRAIN!
WHOA!

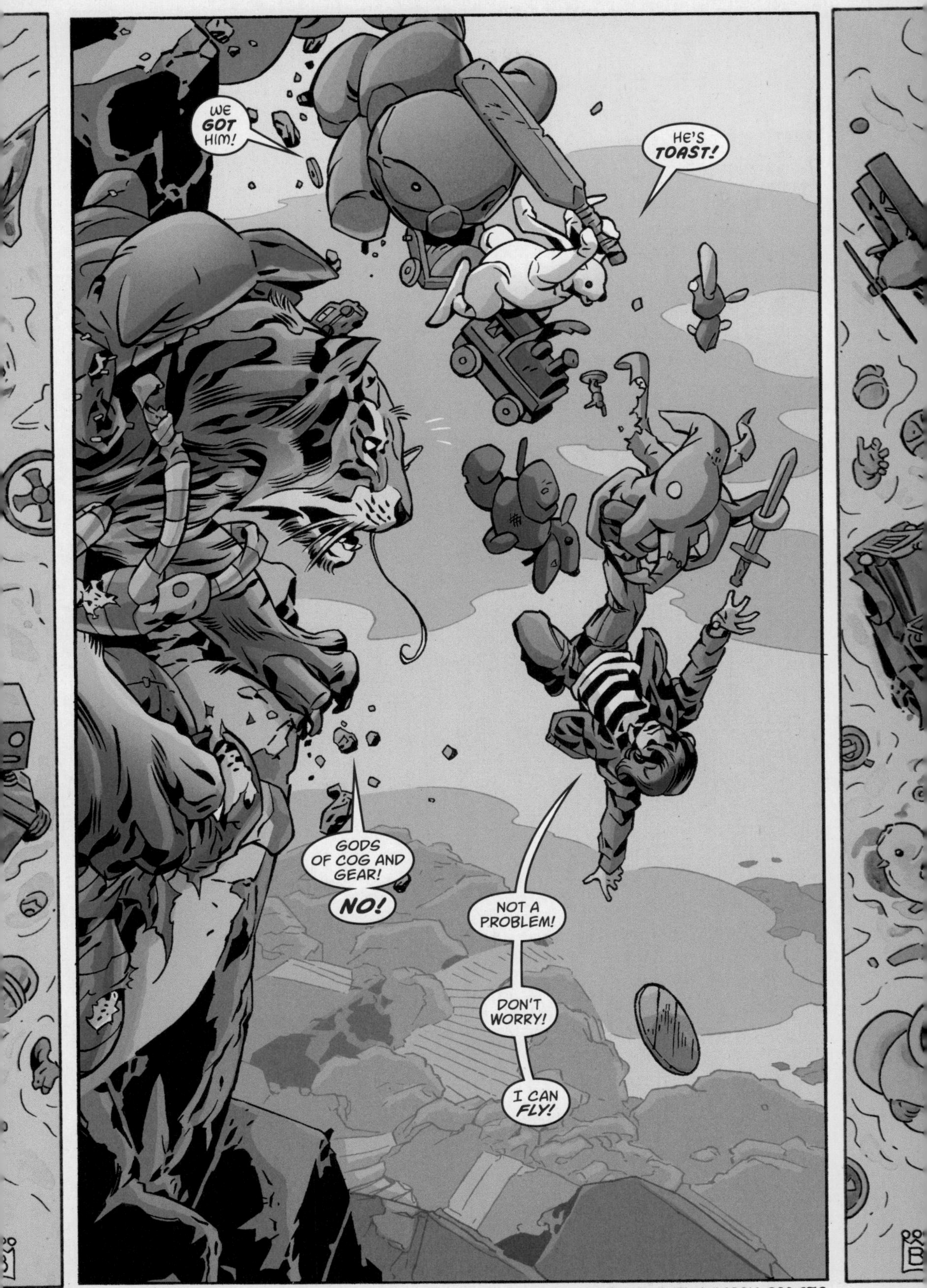
WE GOT HIM!
HE'S TOAST!
GODS OF COG AND GEAR!
NO!
NOT A PROBLEM!
DON'T WORRY!
I CAN FLY!

NEXT: THE HUNGRY GAMES

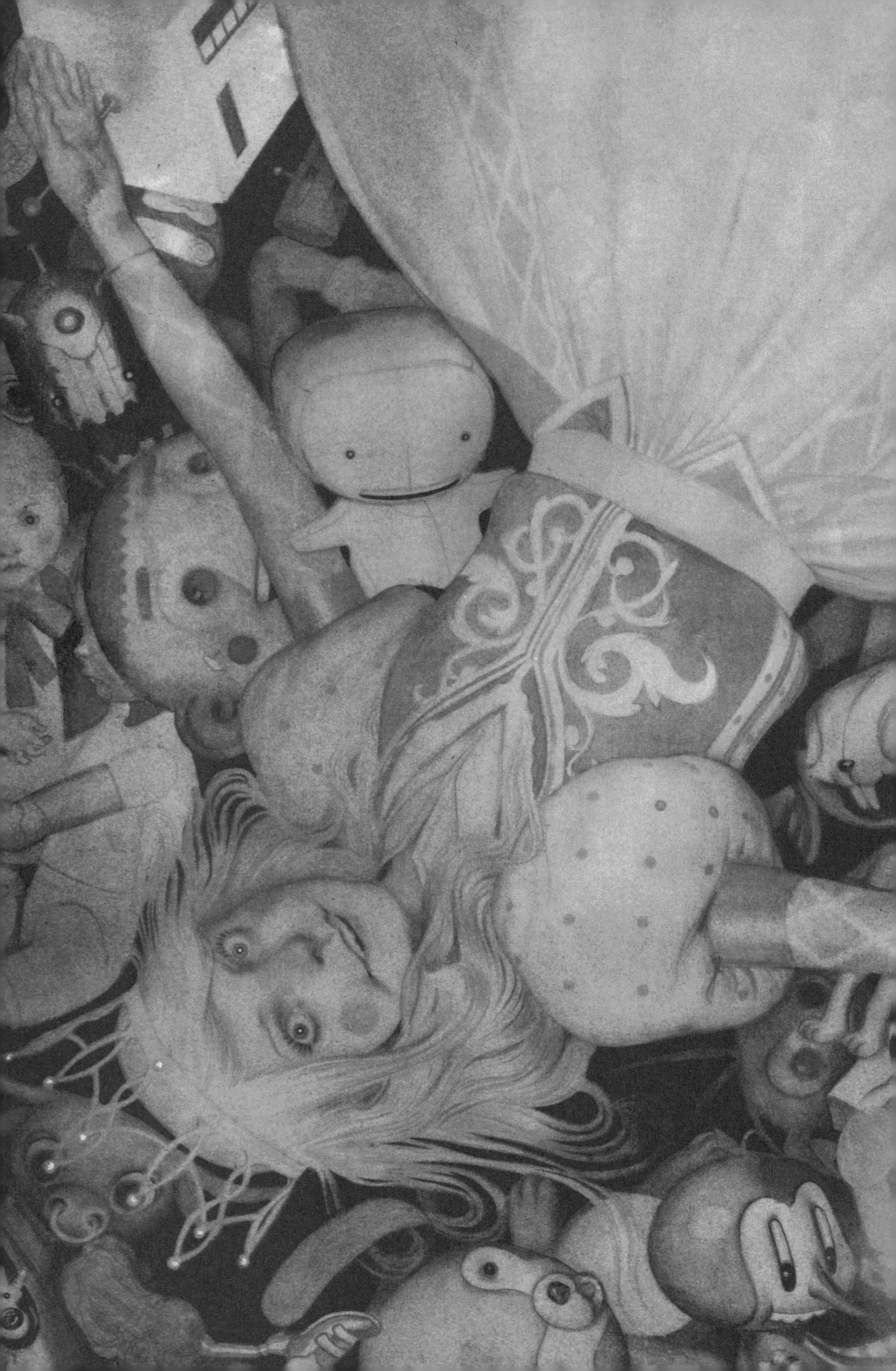

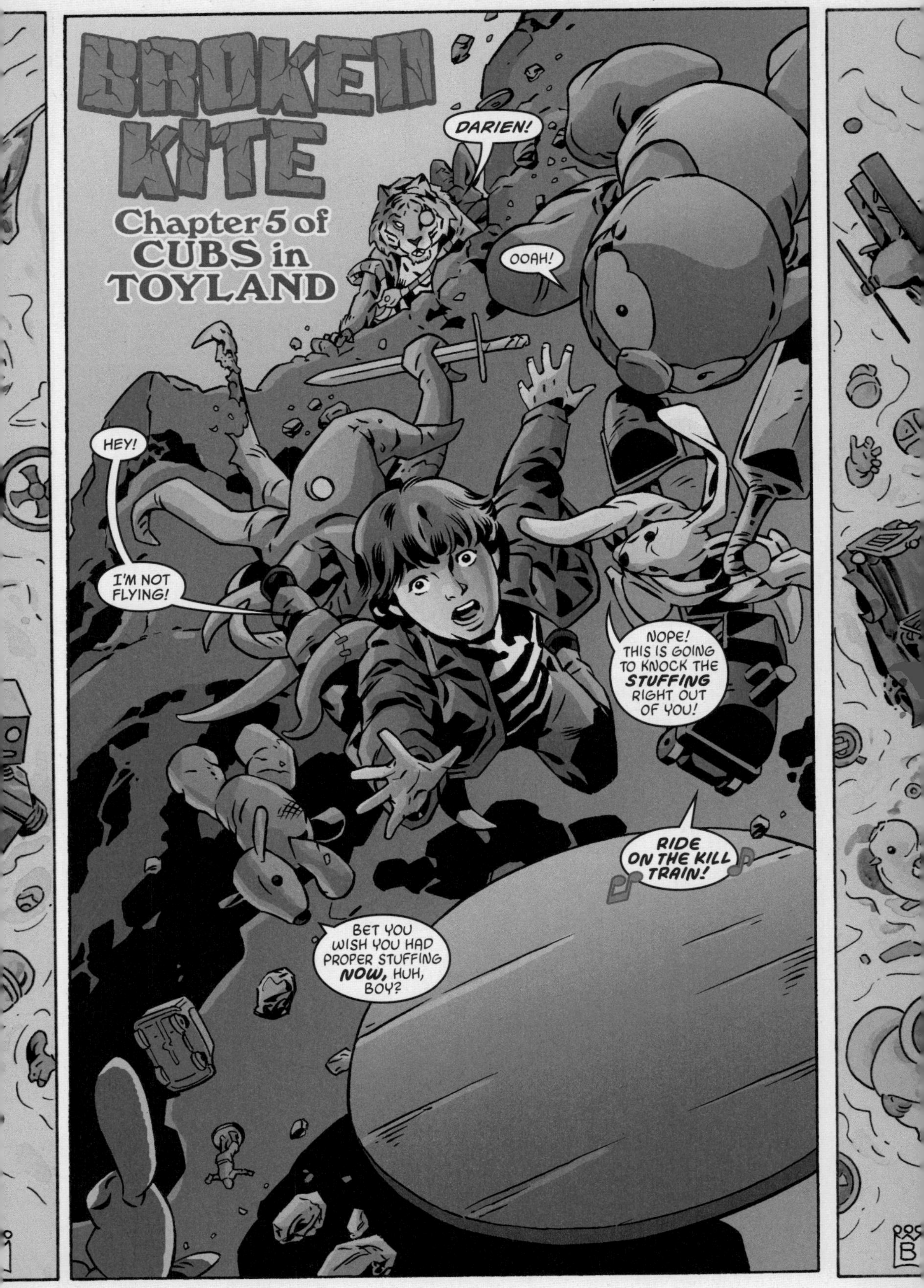
BROKEN KITE
Chapter 5 of CUBS in TOYLAND
DARIEN!
OOAH!
HEY!
I'M NOT FLYING!
NOPE! THIS IS GOING TO KNOCK THE STUFFING RIGHT OUT OF YOU!
RIDE ON THE KILL TRAIN!
BET YOU WISH YOU HAD PROPER STUFFING NOW, HUH, BOY?

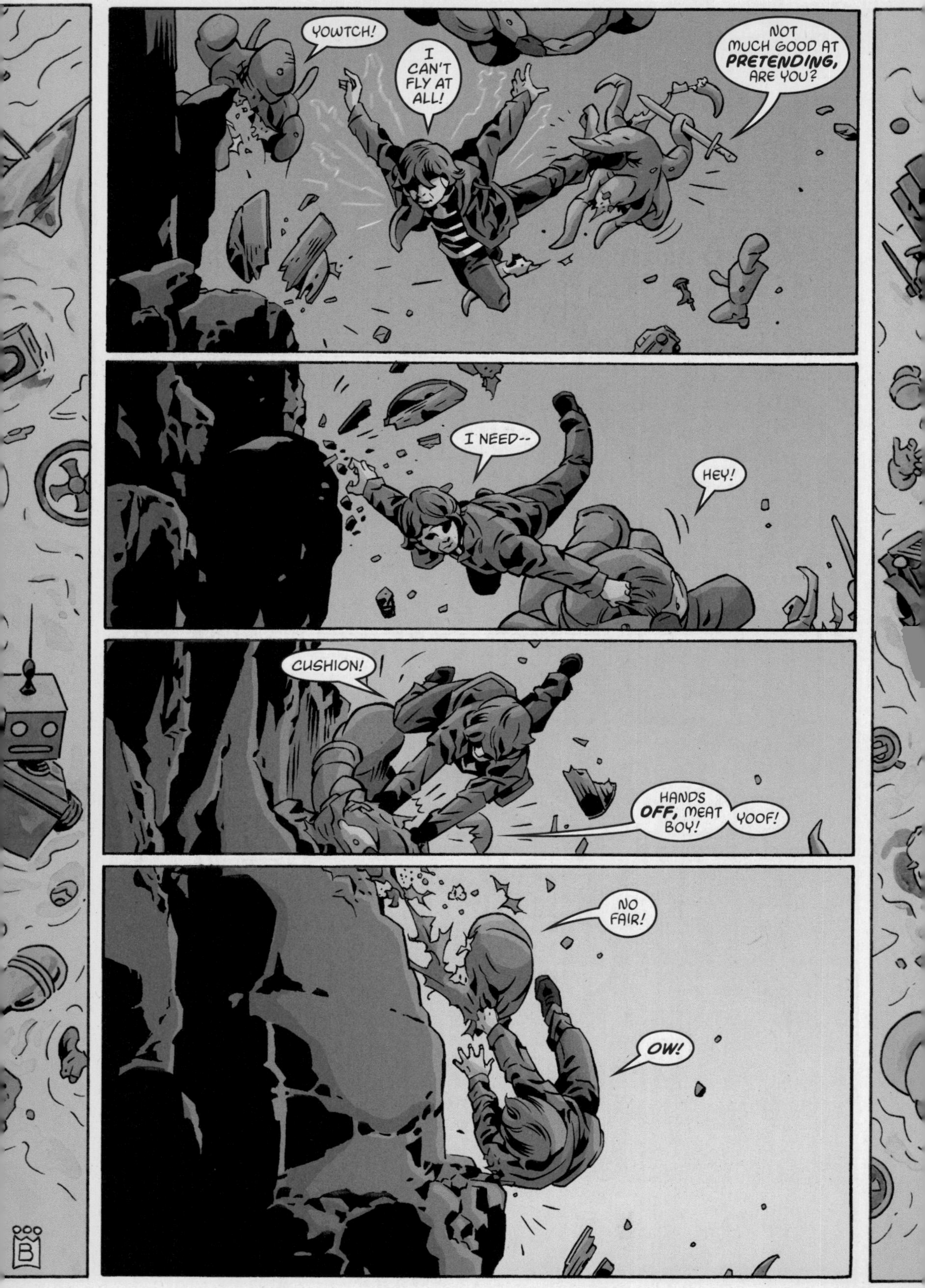
YOWTCH!
I CAN'T FLY AT ALL!
NOT MUCH GOOD AT PRETENDING, ARE YOU?
I NEED--
HEY!
CUSHION!
HANDS OFF, MEAT BOY!
YOOF!
NO FAIR!
OW!

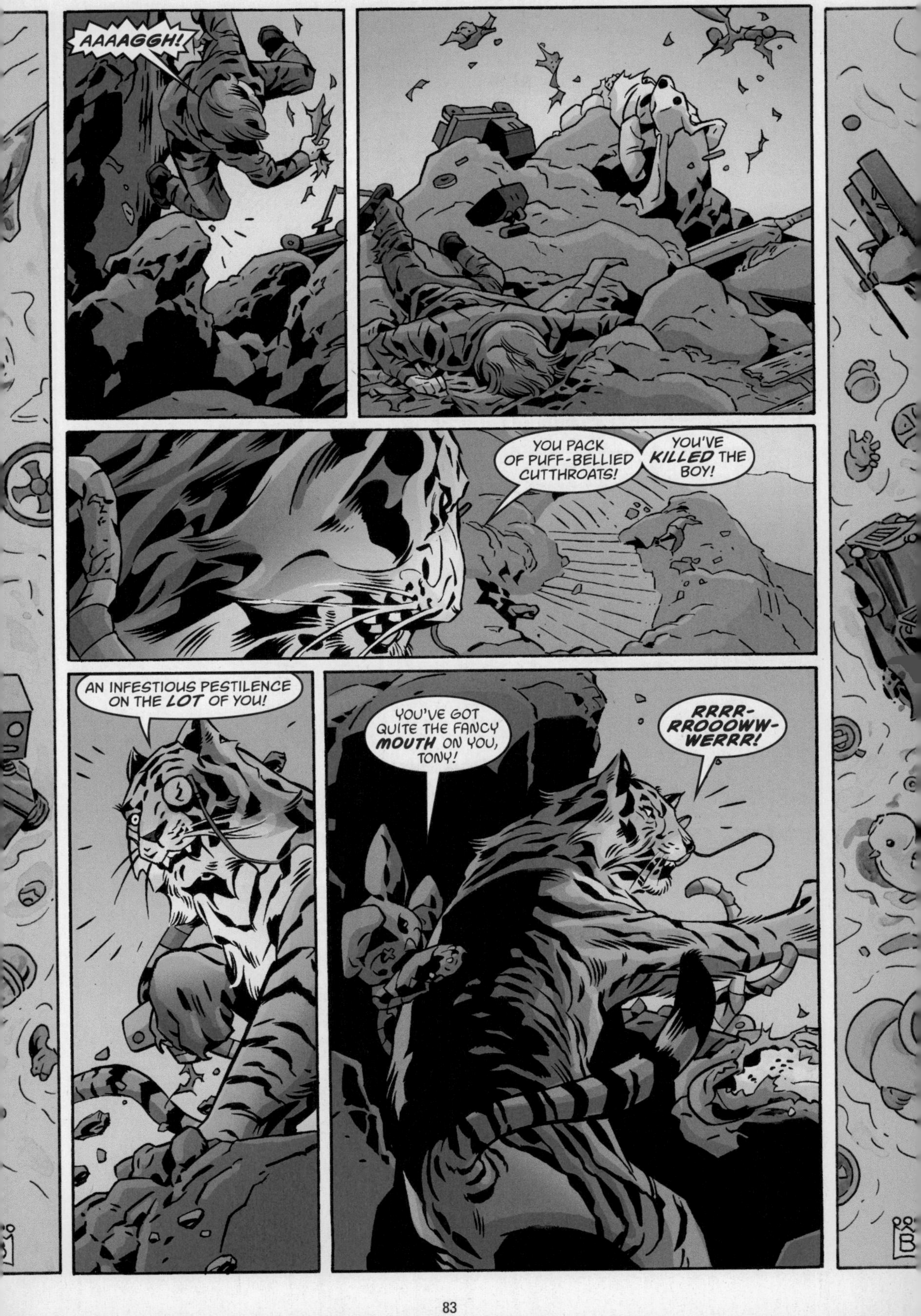
AAAAGGH!
YOU PACK OF PUFF-BELLIED CUTTHROATS!
YOU'VE KILLED THE BOY!
AN INFESTIOUS PESTILENCE ON THE LOT OF YOU!
YOU'VE GOT QUITE THE FANCY MOUTH ON YOU, TONY!
RRRR-RROOOWW-WERRR!

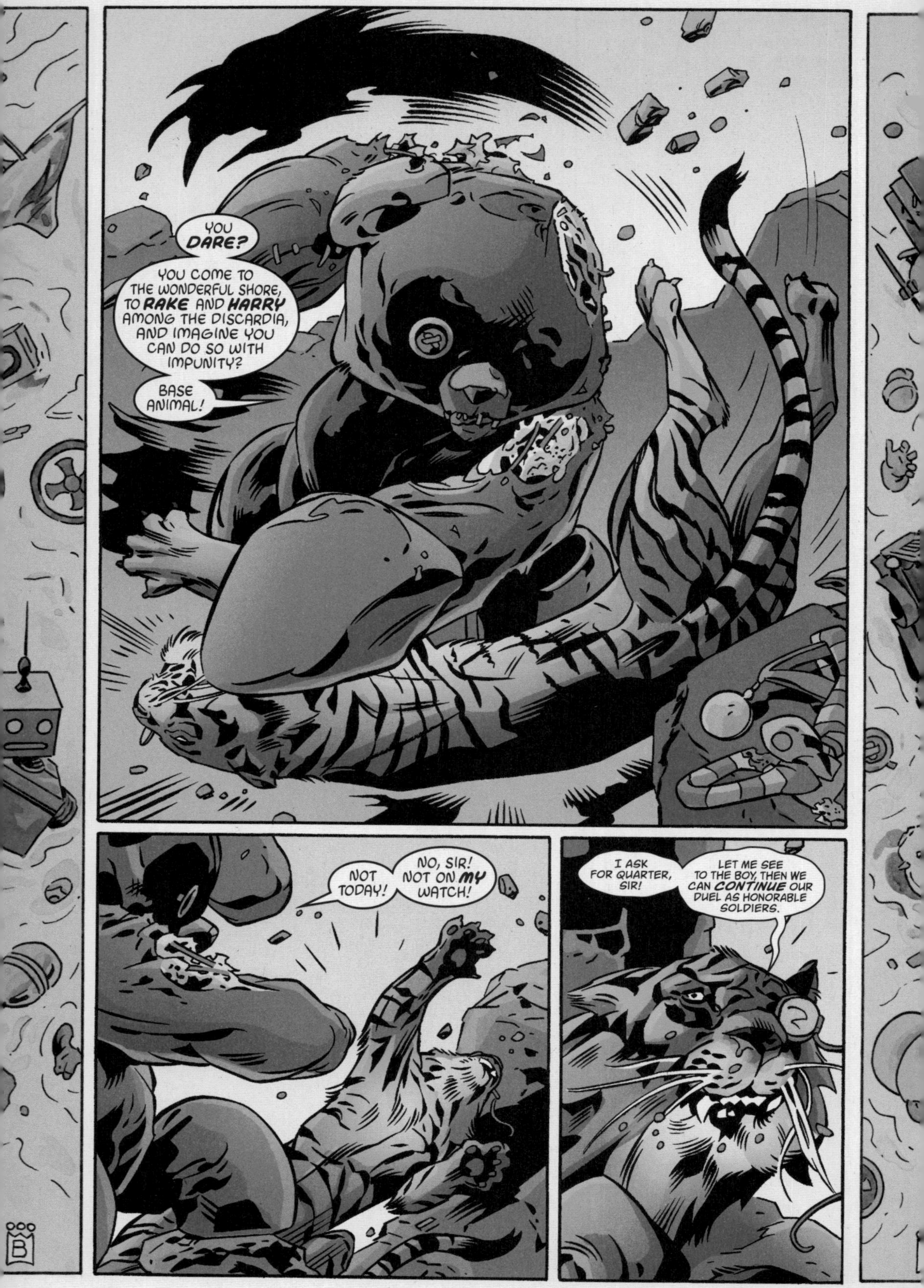
YOU DARE?
YOU COME TO THE WONDERFUL SHORE, TO RAKE AND HARRY AMONG THE DISCARDIA, AND IMAGINE YOU CAN DO SO WITH IMPUNITY?
BASE ANIMAL!
NOT TODAY!
NO, SIR! NOT ON MY WATCH!
I ASK FOR QUARTER, SIR!
LET ME SEE TO THE BOY, THEN WE CAN CONTINUE OUR DUEL AS HONORABLE SOLDIERS.

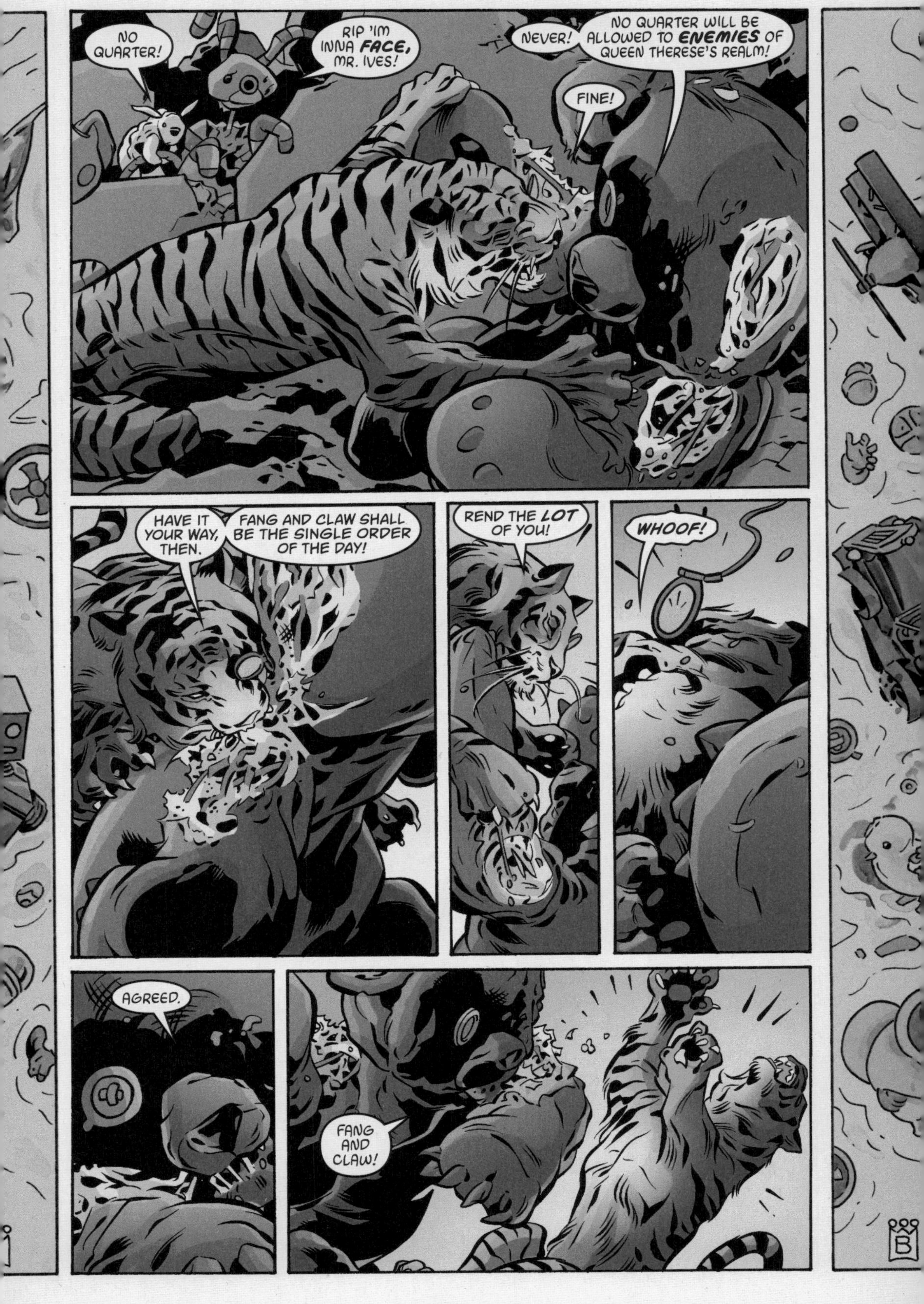
NO QUARTER!
RIP 'IM INNA FACE, MR. IVES!
NEVER!
NO QUARTER WILL BE ALLOWED TO ENEMIES OF QUEEN THERESE'S REALM!
FINE!
HAVE IT YOUR WAY, THEN.
FANG AND CLAW SHALL BE THE SINGLE ORDER OF THE DAY!
REND THE LOT OF YOU!
WHOOF!
AGREED.
FANG AND CLAW!

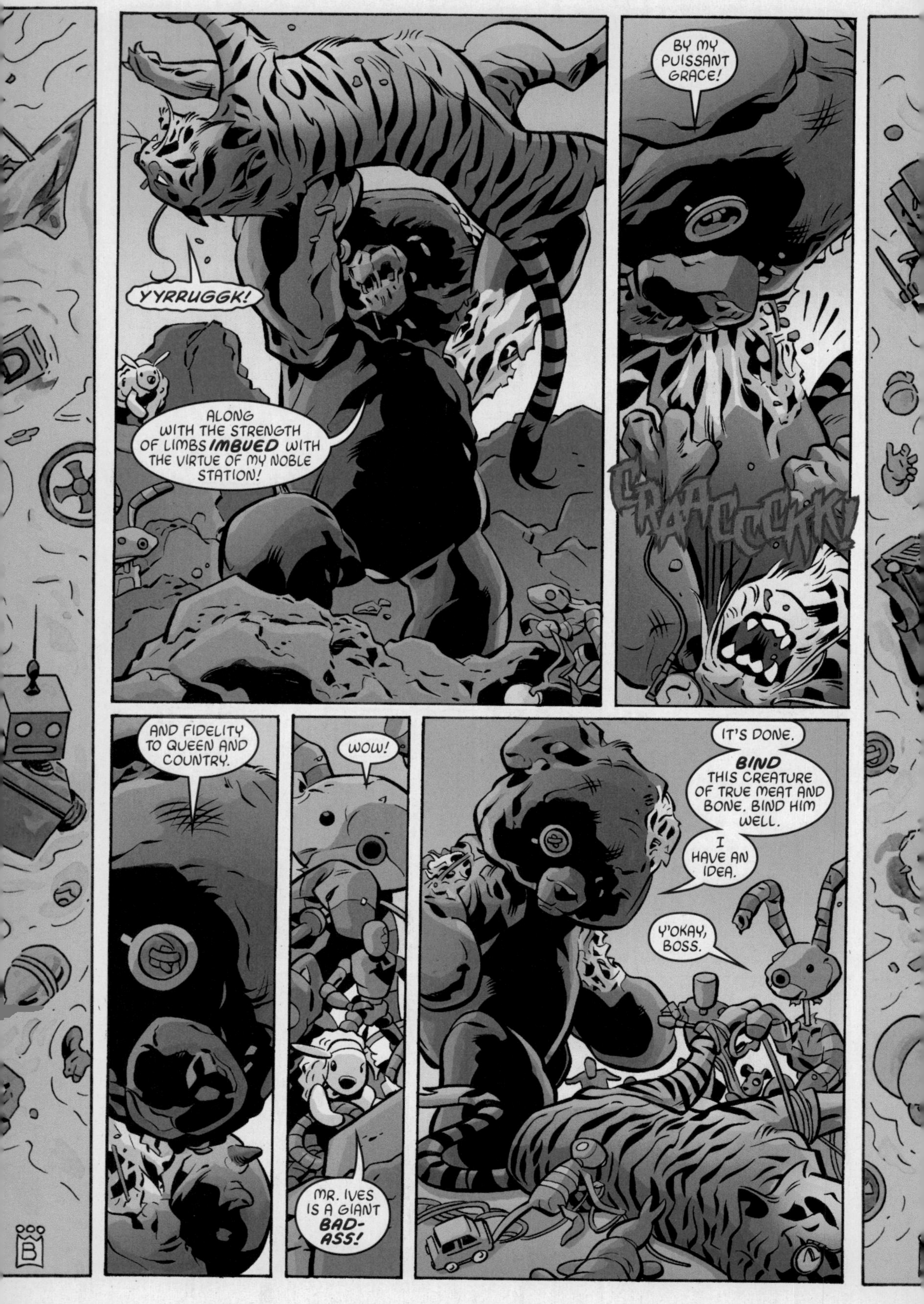
YYRRUGGK!
ALONG WITH THE STRENGTH OF LIMBS IMBUED WITH THE VIRTUE OF MY NOBLE STATION!
BY MY PUISSANT GRACE!
CRAAACCKK!
AND FIDELITY TO QUEEN AND COUNTRY.
WOW!
MR. IVES IS A GIANT BAD-ASS!
IT'S DONE.
BIND THIS CREATURE OF TRUE MEAT AND BONE. BIND HIM WELL.
I HAVE AN IDEA.
Y'OKAY, BOSS.

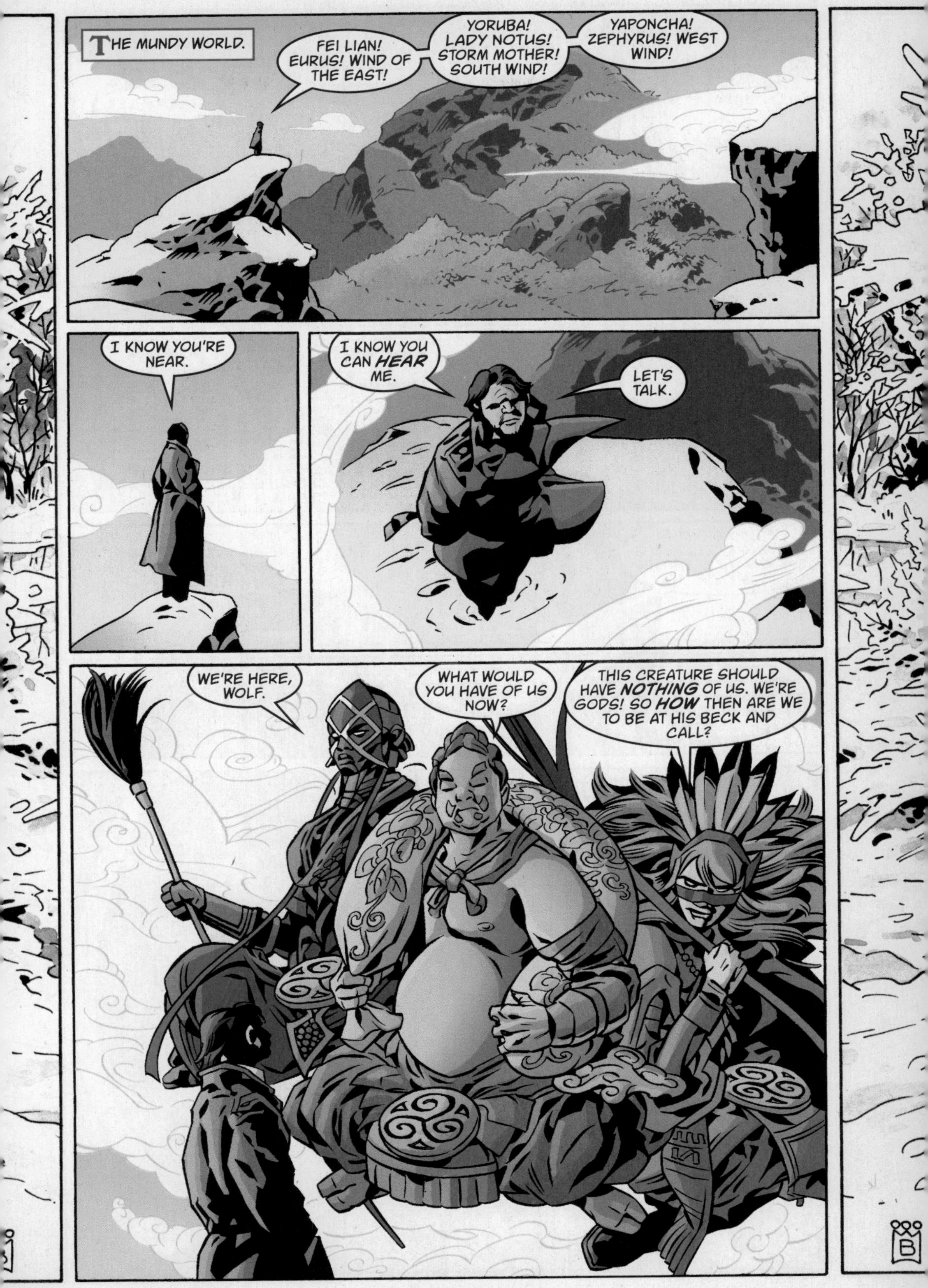
THE MUNDY WORLD.
FEI LIAN! EURUS! WIND OF THE EAST!
YORUBA! LADY NOTUS! STORM MOTHER! SOUTH WIND!
YAPONCHA! ZEPHYRUS! WEST WIND!
I KNOW YOU'RE NEAR.
I KNOW YOU CAN HEAR ME.
LET'S TALK.
WE'RE HERE, WOLF.
WHAT WOULD YOU HAVE OF US NOW?
THIS CREATURE SHOULD HAVE NOTHING OF US. WE'RE GODS! SO HOW THEN ARE WE TO BE AT HIS BECK AND CALL?

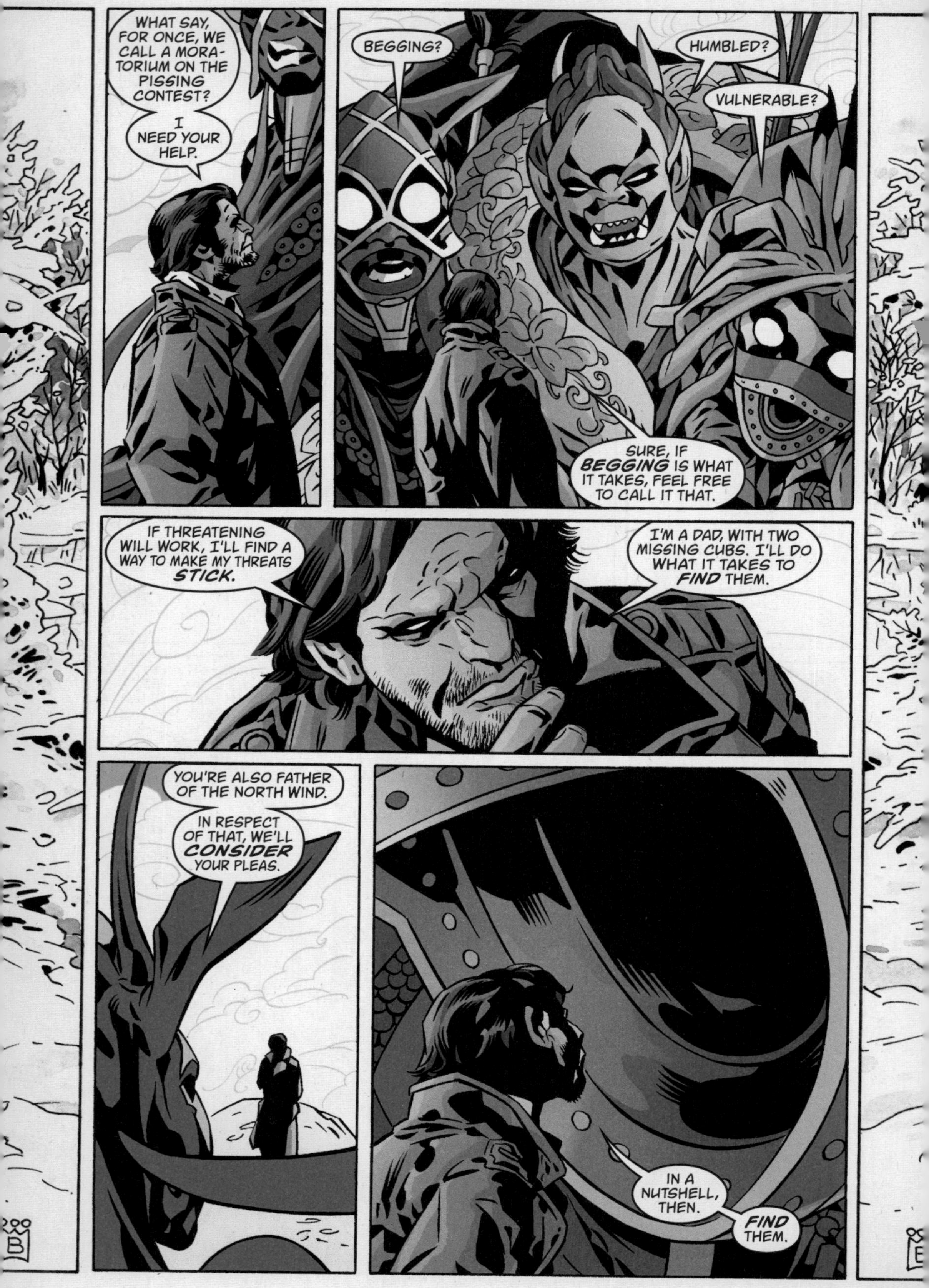
WHAT SAY, FOR ONCE, WE CALL A MORATORIUM ON THE PISSING CONTEST?
I NEED YOUR HELP.
BEGGING?
HUMBLED?
VULNERABLE?
SURE, IF BEGGING IS WHAT IT TAKES, FEEL FREE TO CALL IT THAT.
IF THREATENING WILL WORK, I'LL FIND A WAY TO MAKE MY THREATS STICK.
I'M A DAD, WITH TWO MISSING CUBS. I'LL DO WHAT IT TAKES TO FIND THEM.
YOU'RE ALSO FATHER OF THE NORTH WIND.
IN RESPECT OF THAT, WE'LL CONSIDER YOUR PLEAS.
IN A NUTSHELL, THEN.
FIND THEM.

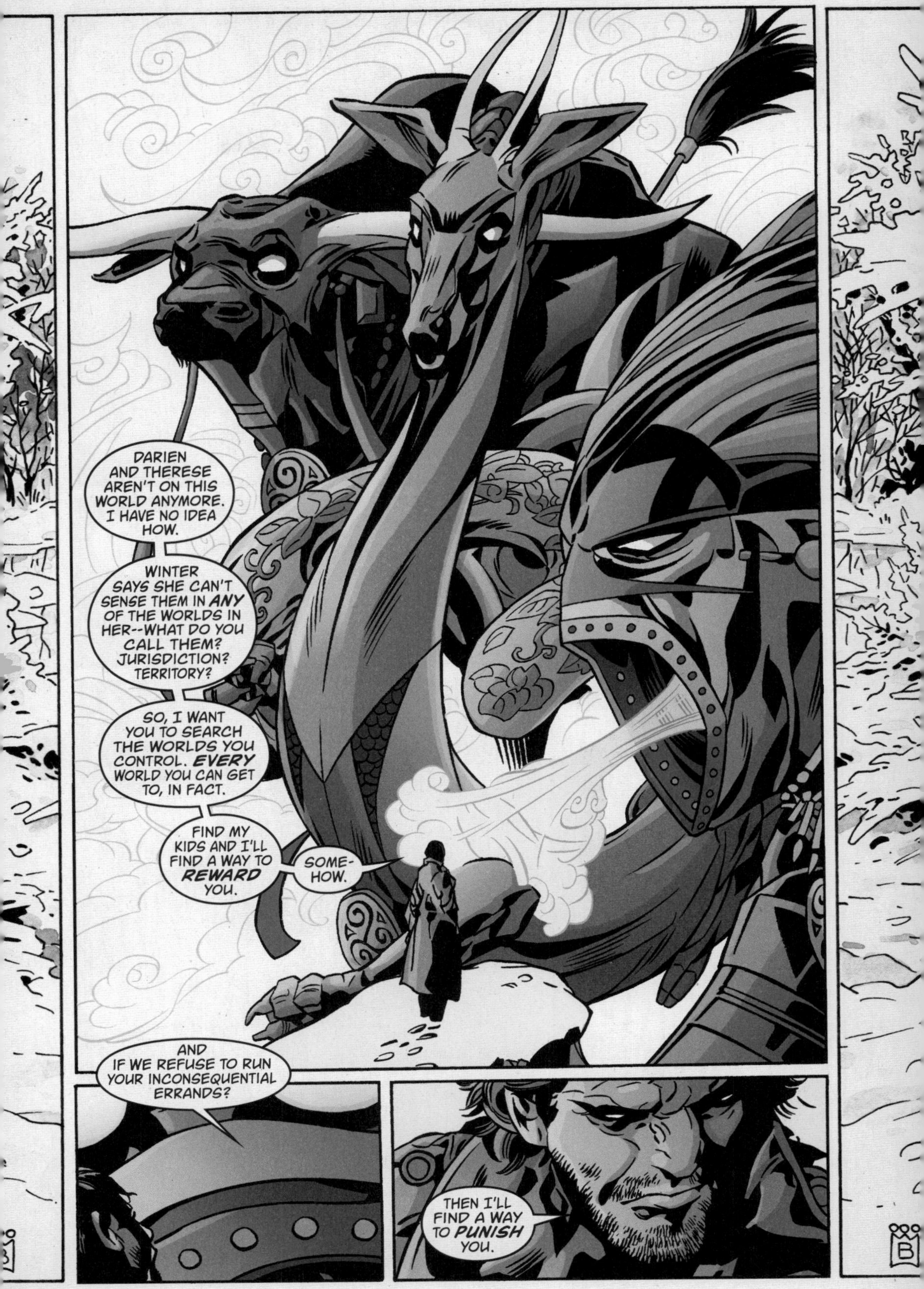
DARIEN AND THERESE AREN'T ON THIS WORLD ANYMORE. I HAVE NO IDEA HOW.
WINTER SAYS SHE CAN'T SENSE THEM IN ANY OF THE WORLDS IN HER--WHAT DO YOU CALL THEM? JURISDICTION? TERRITORY?
SO, I WANT YOU TO SEARCH THE WORLDS YOU CONTROL. EVERY WORLD YOU CAN GET TO, IN FACT.
FIND MY KIDS AND I'LL FIND A WAY TO REWARD YOU.
SOME-HOW.
AND IF WE REFUSE TO RUN YOUR INCONSEQUENTIAL ERRANDS?
THEN I'LL FIND A WAY TO PUNISH YOU.

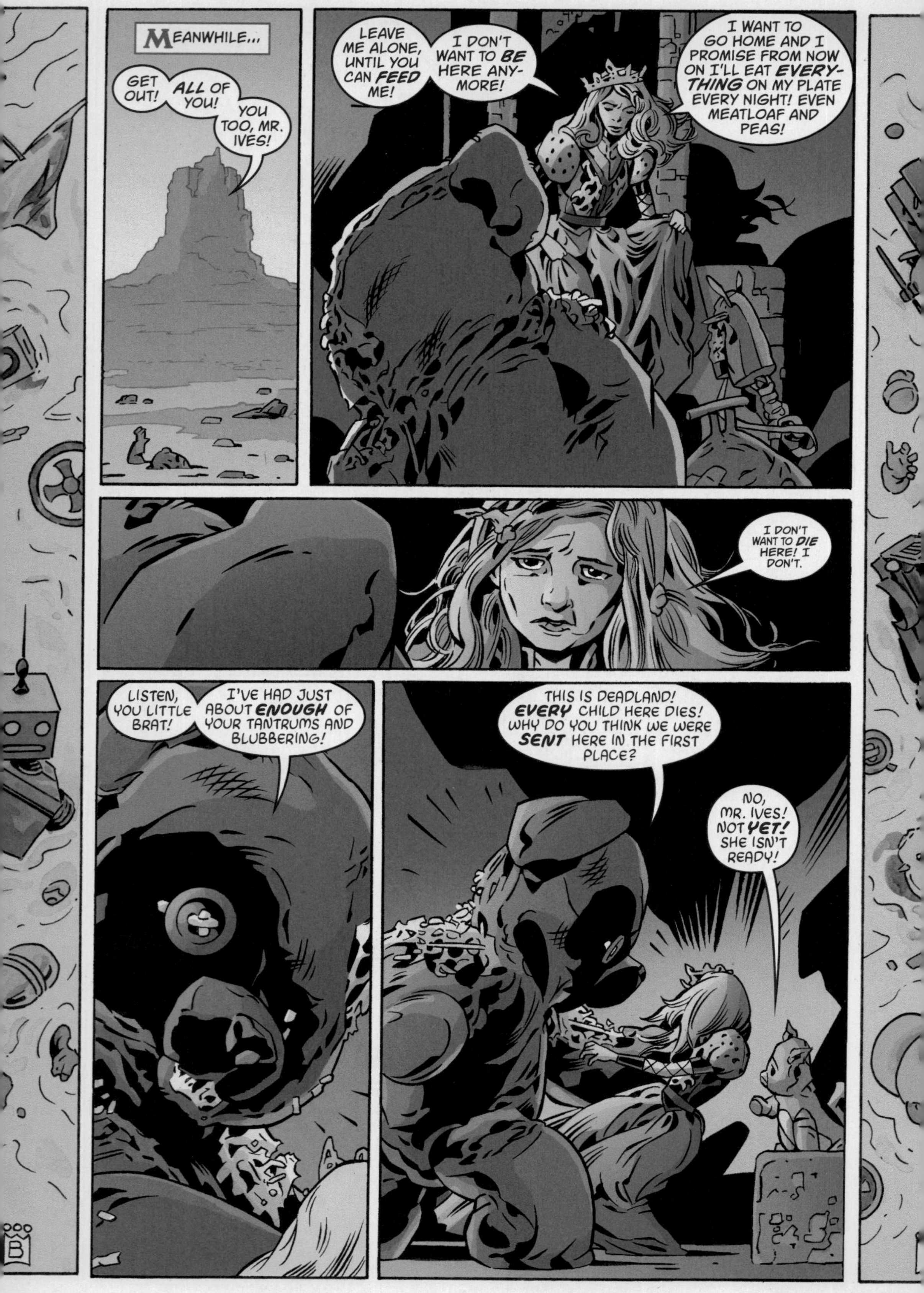
MEANWHILE...
GET OUT!
ALL OF YOU!
YOU TOO, MR. IVES!
LEAVE ME ALONE, UNTIL YOU CAN FEED ME!
I DON'T WANT TO BE HERE ANY-MORE!
I WANT TO GO HOME AND I PROMISE FROM NOW ON I'LL EAT EVERY-THING ON MY PLATE EVERY NIGHT! EVEN MEATLOAF AND PEAS!
I DON'T WANT TO DIE HERE! I DON'T.
LISTEN, YOU LITTLE BRAT!
I'VE HAD JUST ABOUT ENOUGH OF YOUR TANTRUMS AND BLUBBERING!
THIS IS DEADLAND! EVERY CHILD HERE DIES! WHY DO YOU THINK WE WERE SENT HERE IN THE FIRST PLACE?
NO, MR. IVES! NOT YET! SHE ISN'T READY!

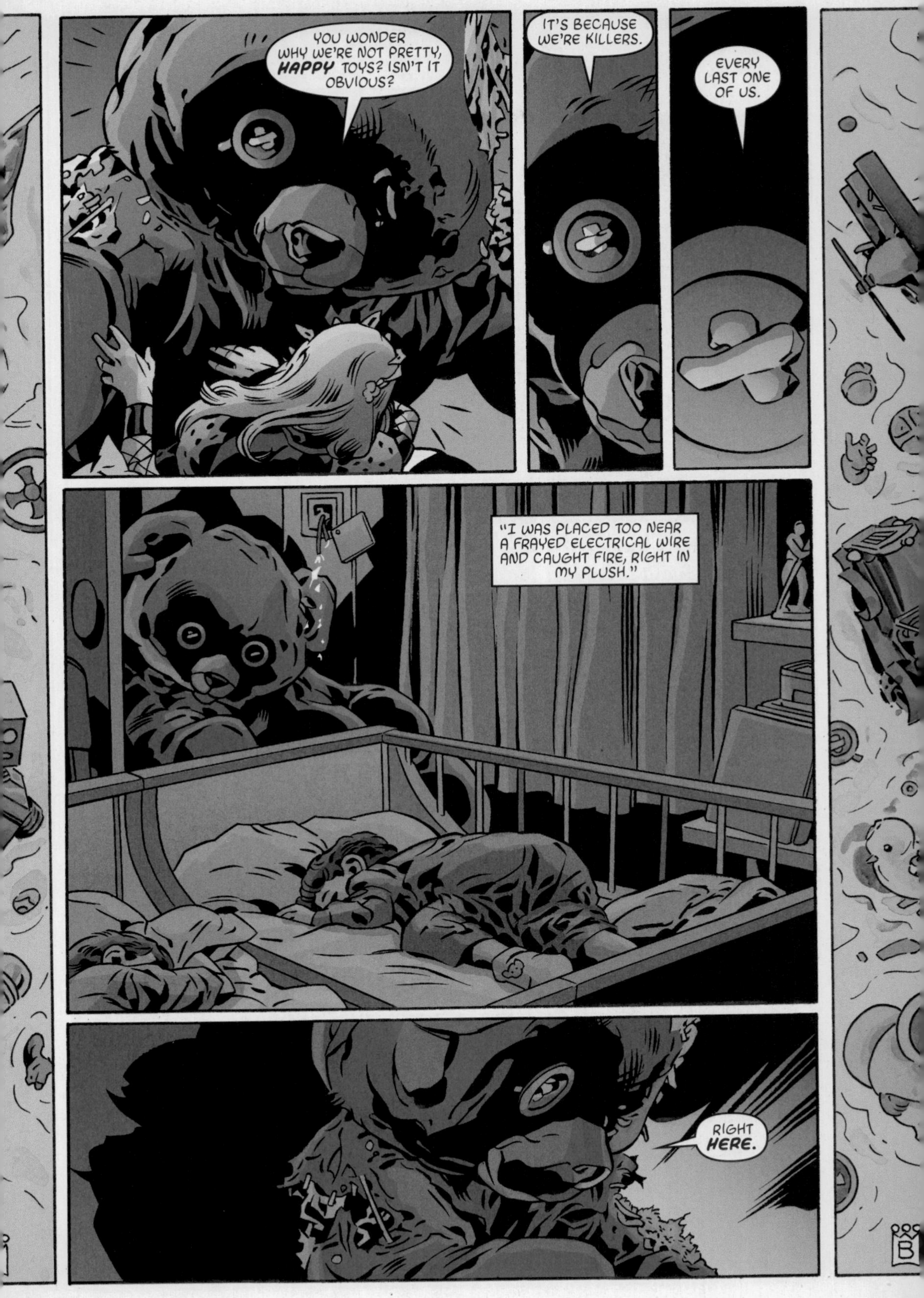
YOU WONDER WHY WE'RE NOT PRETTY, HAPPY TOYS? ISN'T IT OBVIOUS?
IT'S BECAUSE WE'RE KILLERS.
EVERY LAST ONE OF US.
"I WAS PLACED TOO NEAR A FRAYED ELECTRICAL WIRE AND CAUGHT FIRE, RIGHT IN MY PLUSH."
RIGHT HERE.

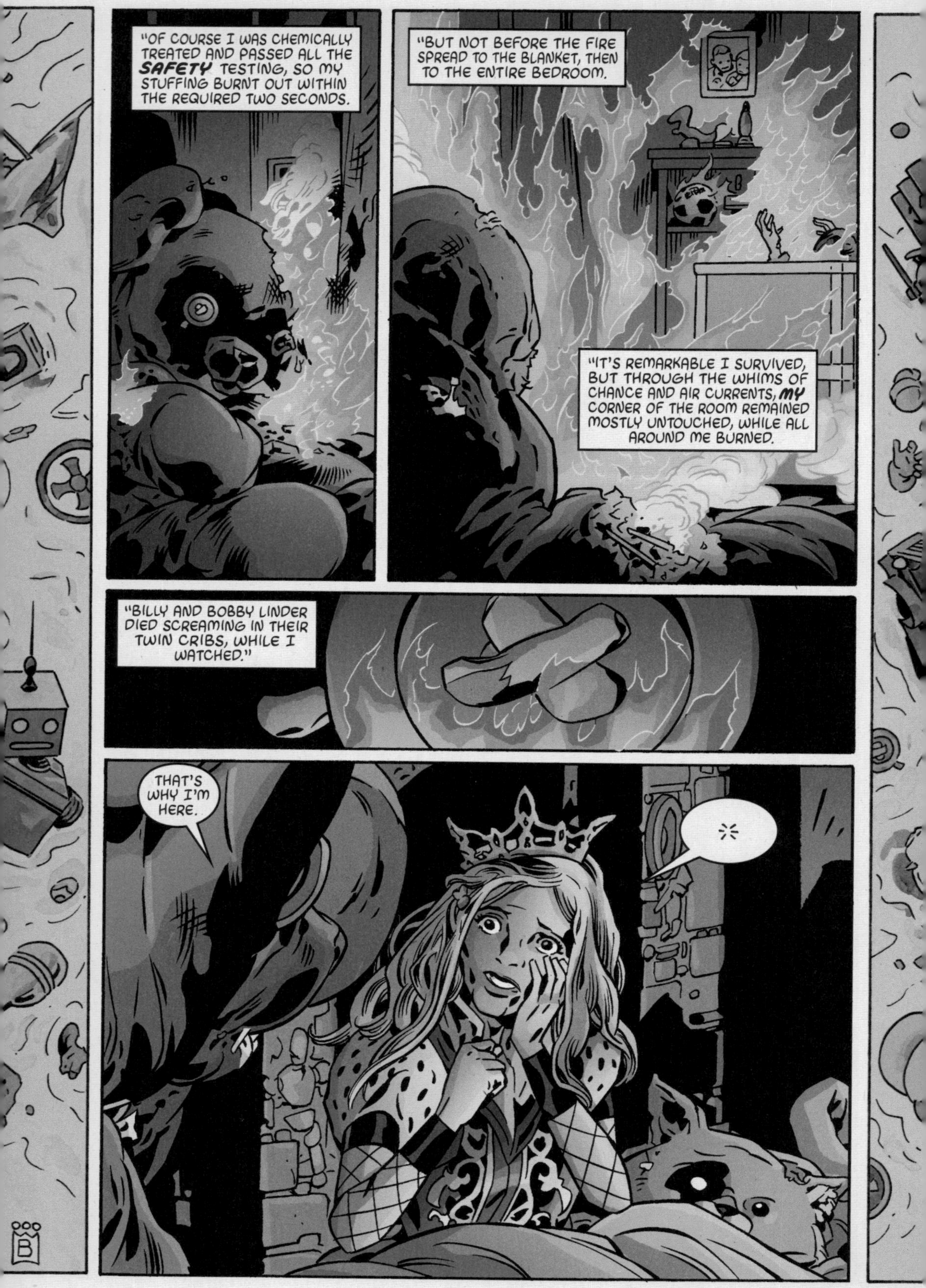
"OF COURSE I WAS CHEMICALLY TREATED AND PASSED ALL THE SAFETY TESTING, SO MY STUFFING BURNT OUT WITHIN THE REQUIRED TWO SECONDS.
"BUT NOT BEFORE THE FIRE SPREAD TO THE BLANKET, THEN TO THE ENTIRE BEDROOM.
"IT'S REMARKABLE I SURVIVED, BUT THROUGH THE WHIMS OF CHANCE AND AIR CURRENTS, MY CORNER OF THE ROOM REMAINED MOSTLY UNTOUCHED, WHILE ALL AROUND ME BURNED.
"BILLY AND BOBBY LINDER DIED SCREAMING IN THEIR TWIN CRIBS, WHILE I WATCHED."
THAT'S WHY I'M HERE.

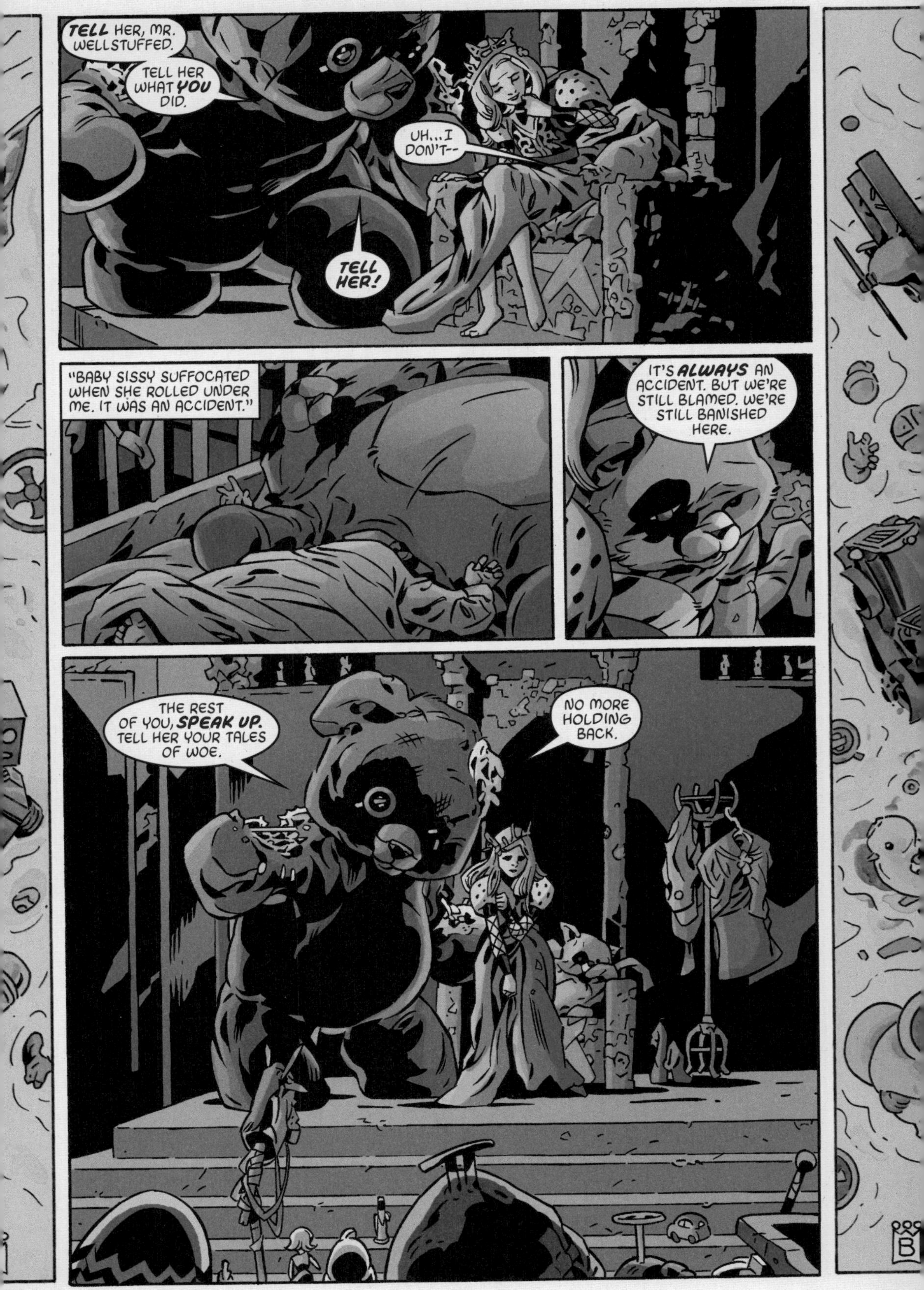
TELL HER, MR. WELLSTUFFED.
TELL HER WHAT YOU DID.
UH...I DON'T--
TELL HER!
"BABY SISSY SUFFOCATED WHEN SHE ROLLED UNDER ME. IT WAS AN ACCIDENT."
IT'S ALWAYS AN ACCIDENT. BUT WE'RE STILL BLAMED. WE'RE STILL BANISHED HERE.
THE REST OF YOU, SPEAK UP. TELL HER YOUR TALES OF WOE.
NO MORE HOLDING BACK.

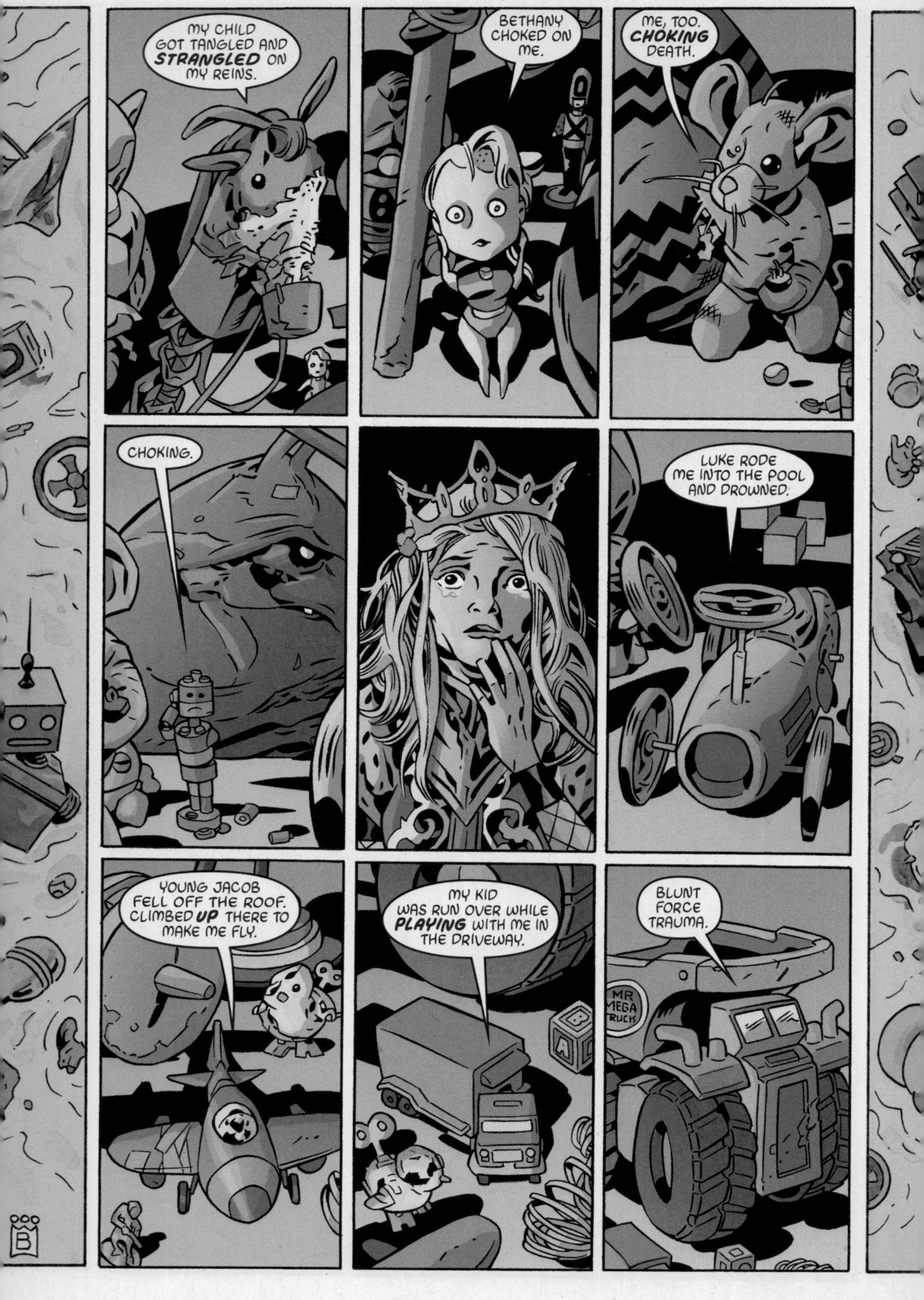
MY CHILD GOT TANGLED AND STRANGLED ON MY REINS.
BETHANY CHOKED ON ME.
ME, TOO. CHOKING DEATH.
CHOKING.
LUKE RODE ME INTO THE POOL AND DROWNED.
YOUNG JACOB FELL OFF THE ROOF. CLIMBED UP THERE TO MAKE ME FLY.
MY KID WAS RUN OVER WHILE PLAYING WITH ME IN THE DRIVEWAY.
BLUNT FORCE TRAUMA.
MR MEGA TRUCK

MONICA SKATED TOO NEAR THE PINE PARK STAIRS.

WE FELL TOGETHER, BUMPITY, BUMPITY, **BUMPITY,** ALL THE WAY DOWN.

I WAS PAINTED WITH LEAD-BASED PAINT.

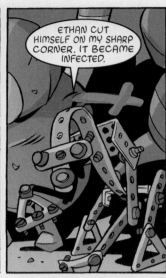

ETHAN CUT HIMSELF ON MY SHARP CORNER. IT BECAME INFECTED.

THIS--

I CAN'T--

I HAVE TO GO!

WAS IT **ENTIRELY** NECESSARY TO DO THAT, MR. IVES?

SHE NEEDED A SHARP DOSE OF REALITY.

A **SLAP** TO WAKE HER UP.

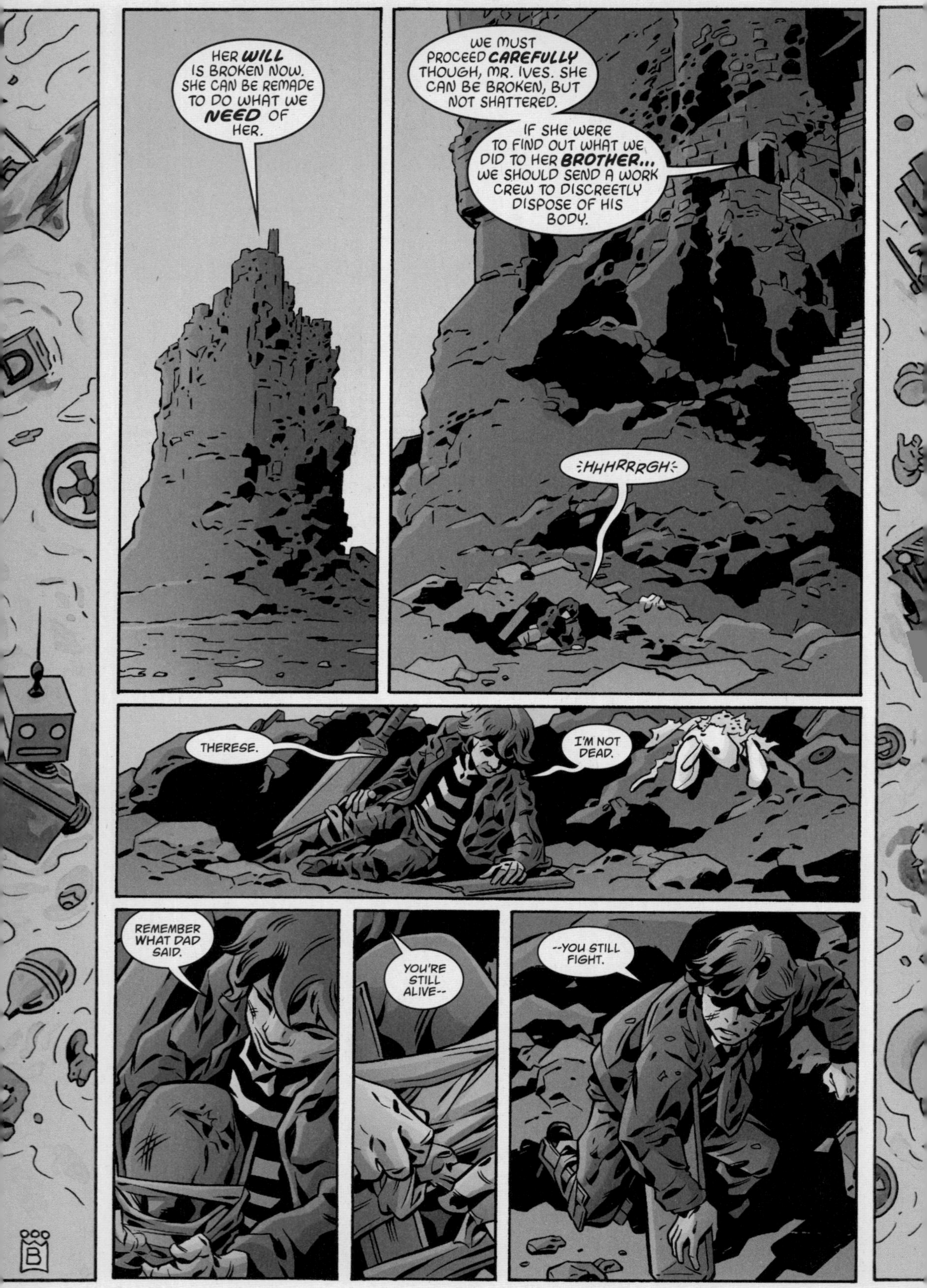
HER WILL IS BROKEN NOW. SHE CAN BE REMADE TO DO WHAT WE NEED OF HER.
WE MUST PROCEED CAREFULLY THOUGH, MR. IVES. SHE CAN BE BROKEN, BUT NOT SHATTERED.
IF SHE WERE TO FIND OUT WHAT WE DID TO HER BROTHER... WE SHOULD SEND A WORK CREW TO DISCREETLY DISPOSE OF HIS BODY.
HHHRRRGH
THERESE.
I'M NOT DEAD.
REMEMBER WHAT DAD SAID.
YOU'RE STILL ALIVE--
--YOU STILL FIGHT.

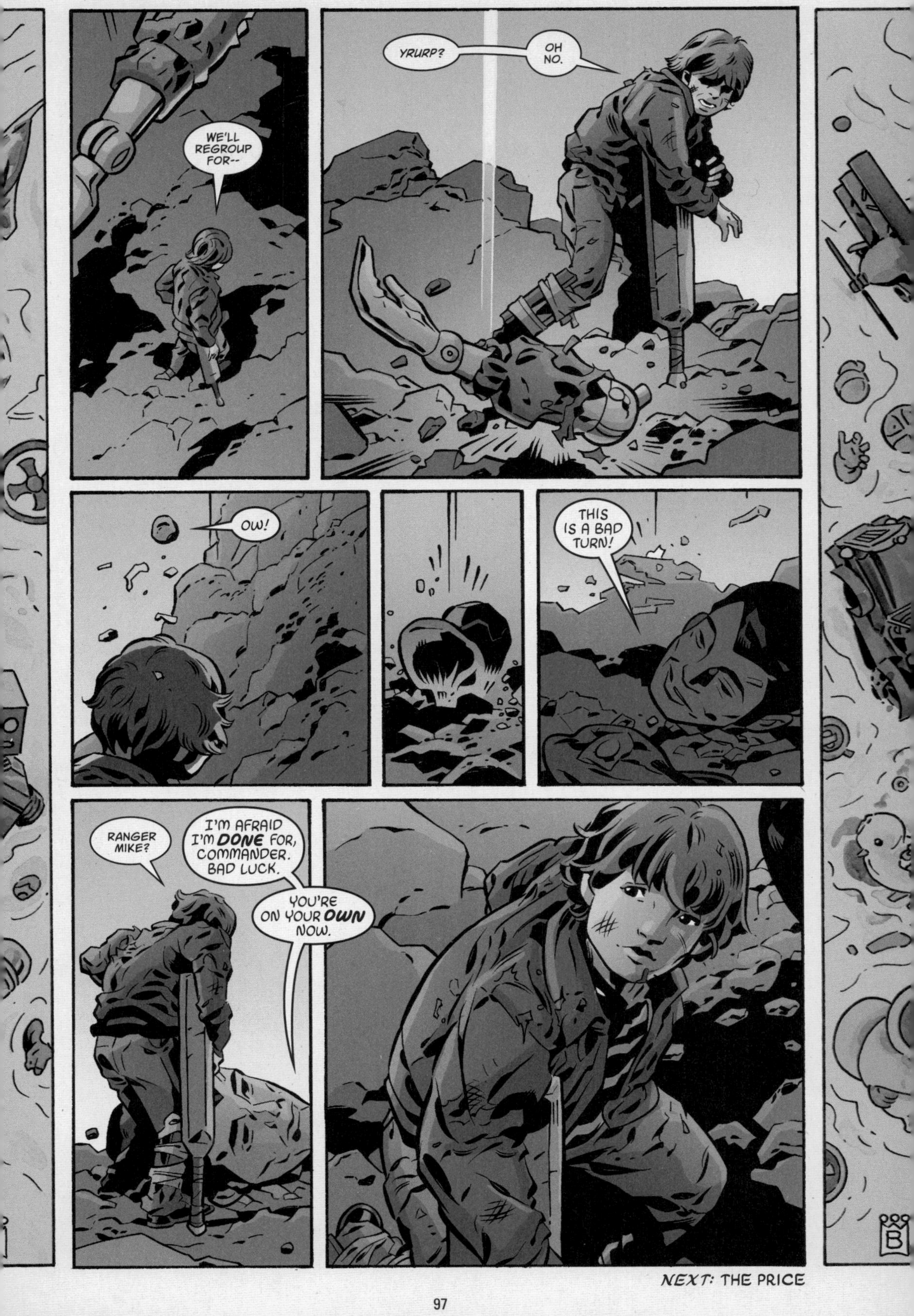
WE'LL REGROUP FOR--
YRURP?
OH NO.
OW!
THIS IS A BAD TURN!
RANGER MIKE?
I'M AFRAID I'M **DONE** FOR, COMMANDER. BAD LUCK.
YOU'RE ON YOUR **OWN** NOW.

NEXT: THE PRICE

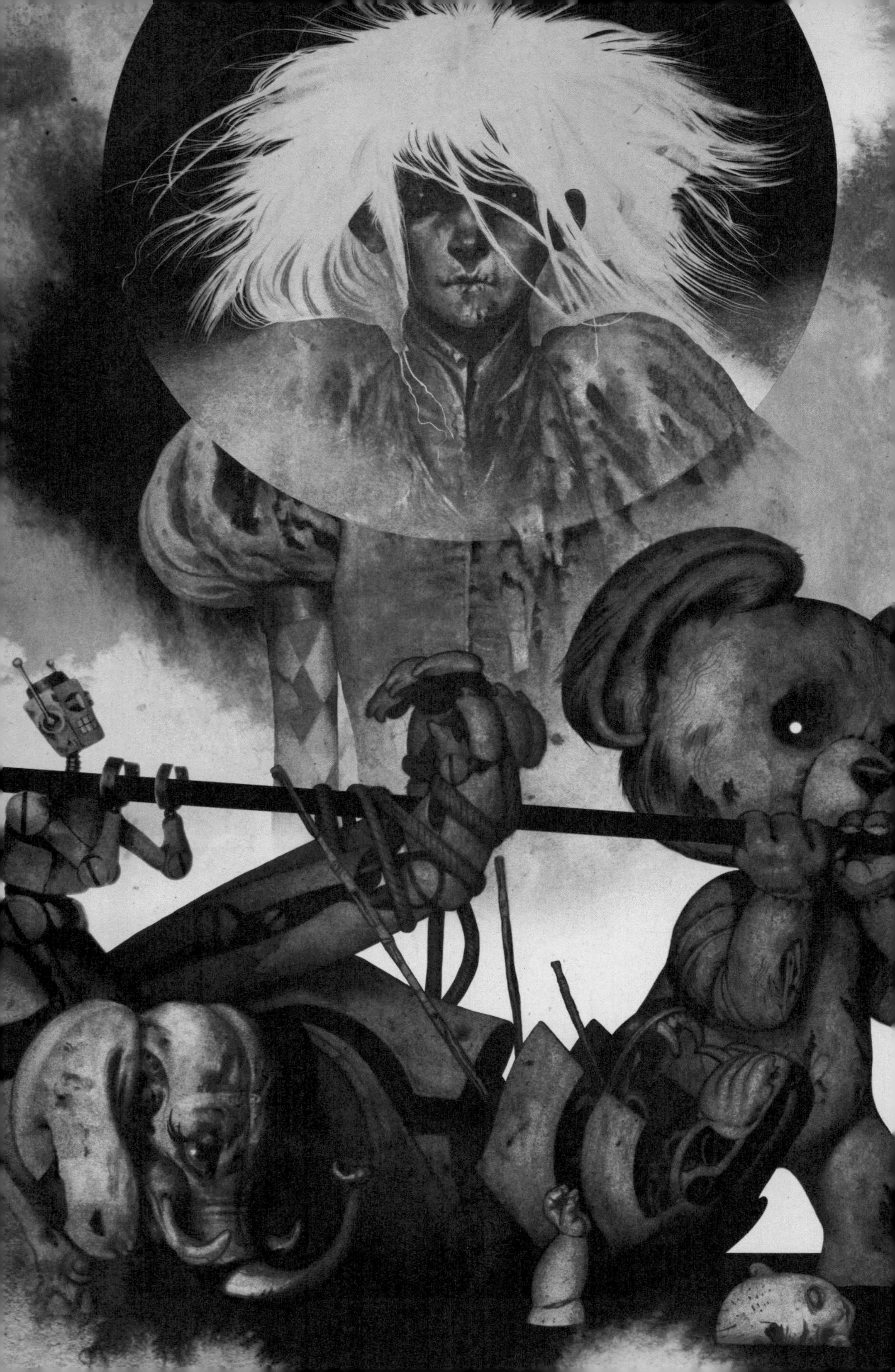

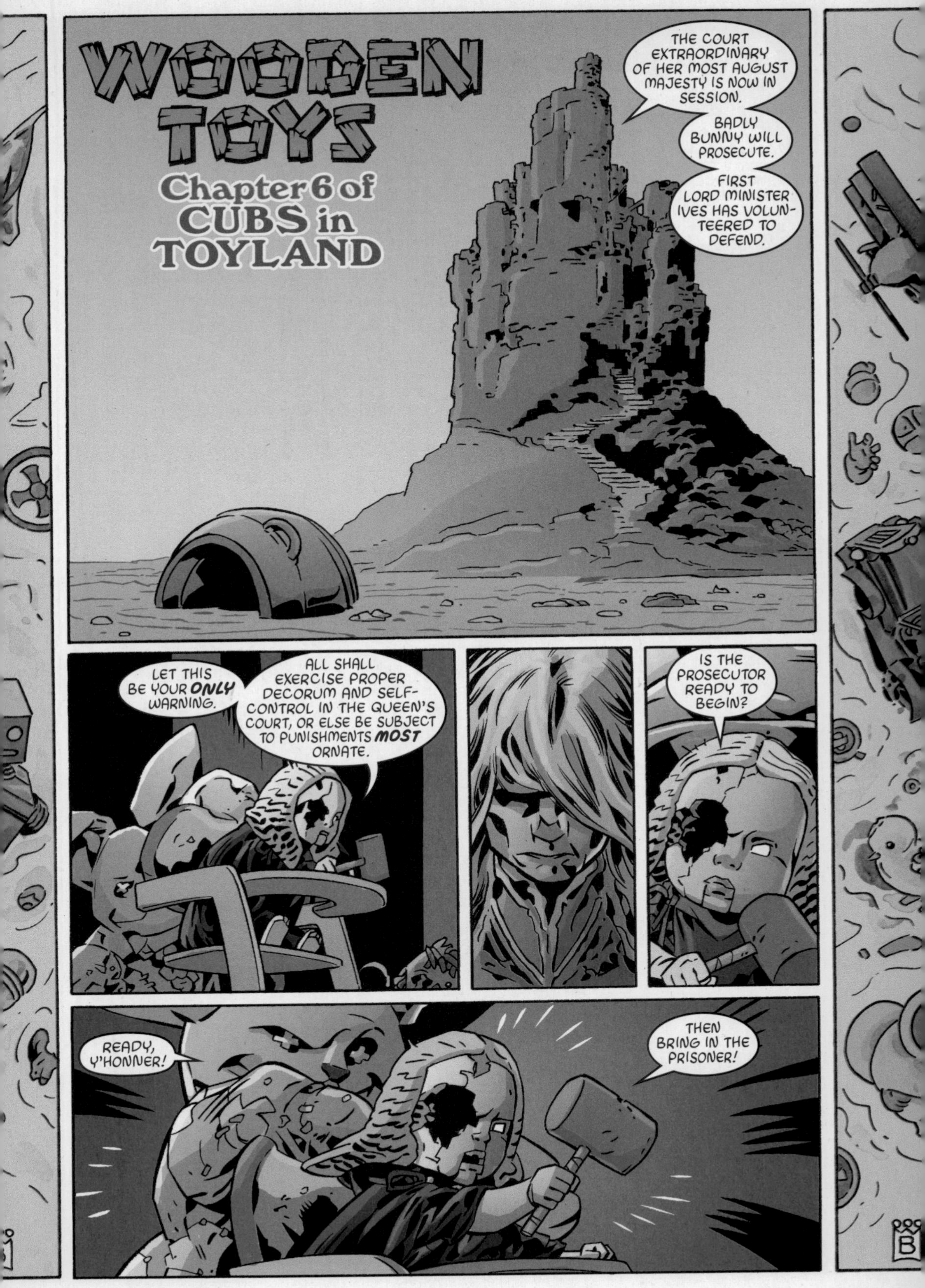

WOODEN TOYS
Chapter 6 of CUBS in TOYLAND
THE COURT EXTRAORDINARY OF HER MOST AUGUST MAJESTY IS NOW IN SESSION.
BADLY BUNNY WILL PROSECUTE.
FIRST LORD MINISTER IVES HAS VOLUNTEERED TO DEFEND.
LET THIS BE YOUR ONLY WARNING.
ALL SHALL EXERCISE PROPER DECORUM AND SELF-CONTROL IN THE QUEEN'S COURT, OR ELSE BE SUBJECT TO PUNISHMENTS MOST ORNATE.
IS THE PROSECUTOR READY TO BEGIN?
READY, Y'HONNER!
THEN BRING IN THE PRISONER!

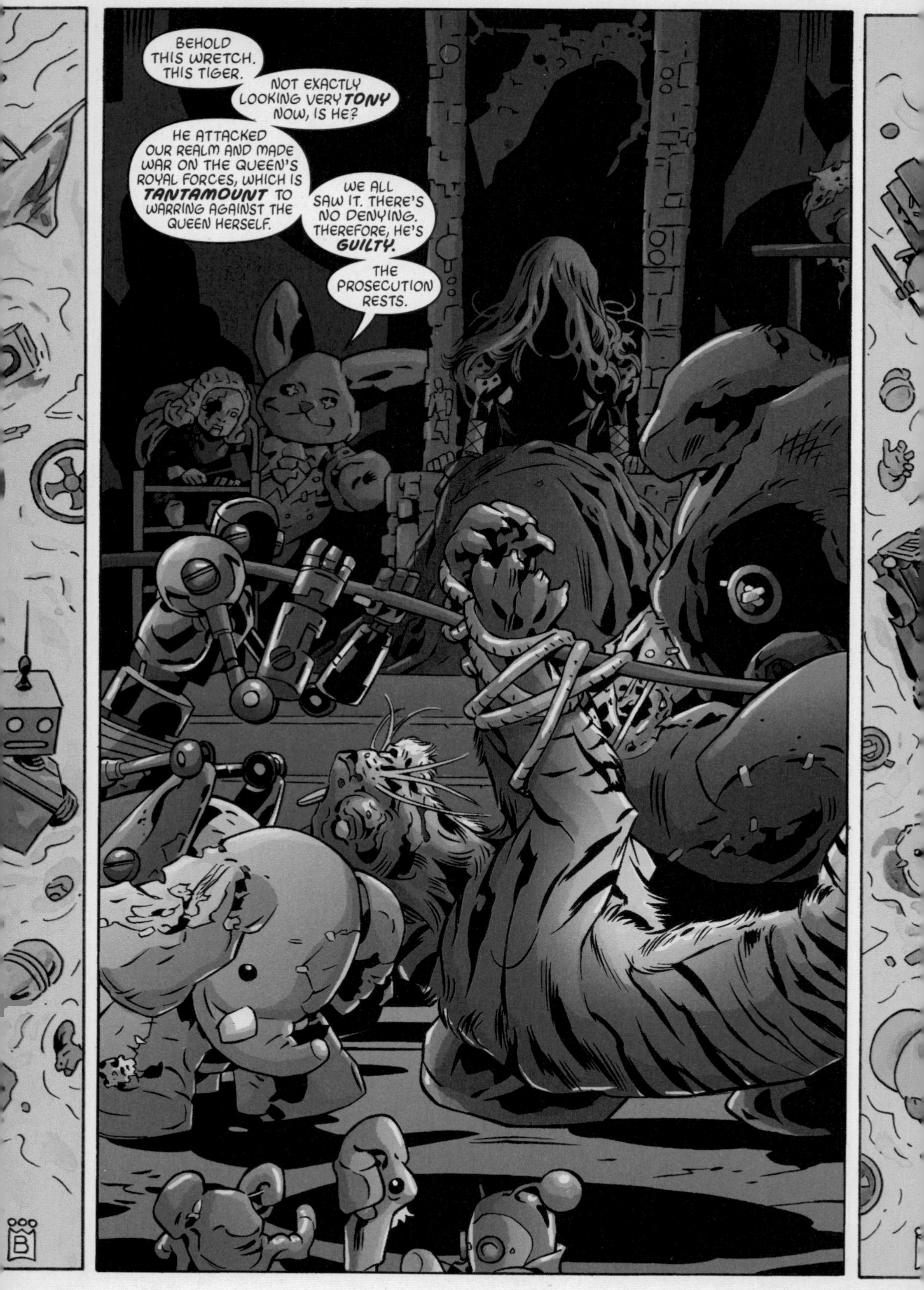
BEHOLD THIS WRETCH. THIS TIGER.
NOT EXACTLY LOOKING VERY TONY NOW, IS HE?
HE ATTACKED OUR REALM AND MADE WAR ON THE QUEEN'S ROYAL FORCES, WHICH IS TANTAMOUNT TO WARRING AGAINST THE QUEEN HERSELF.
WE ALL SAW IT. THERE'S NO DENYING. THEREFORE, HE'S GUILTY.
THE PROSECUTION RESTS.

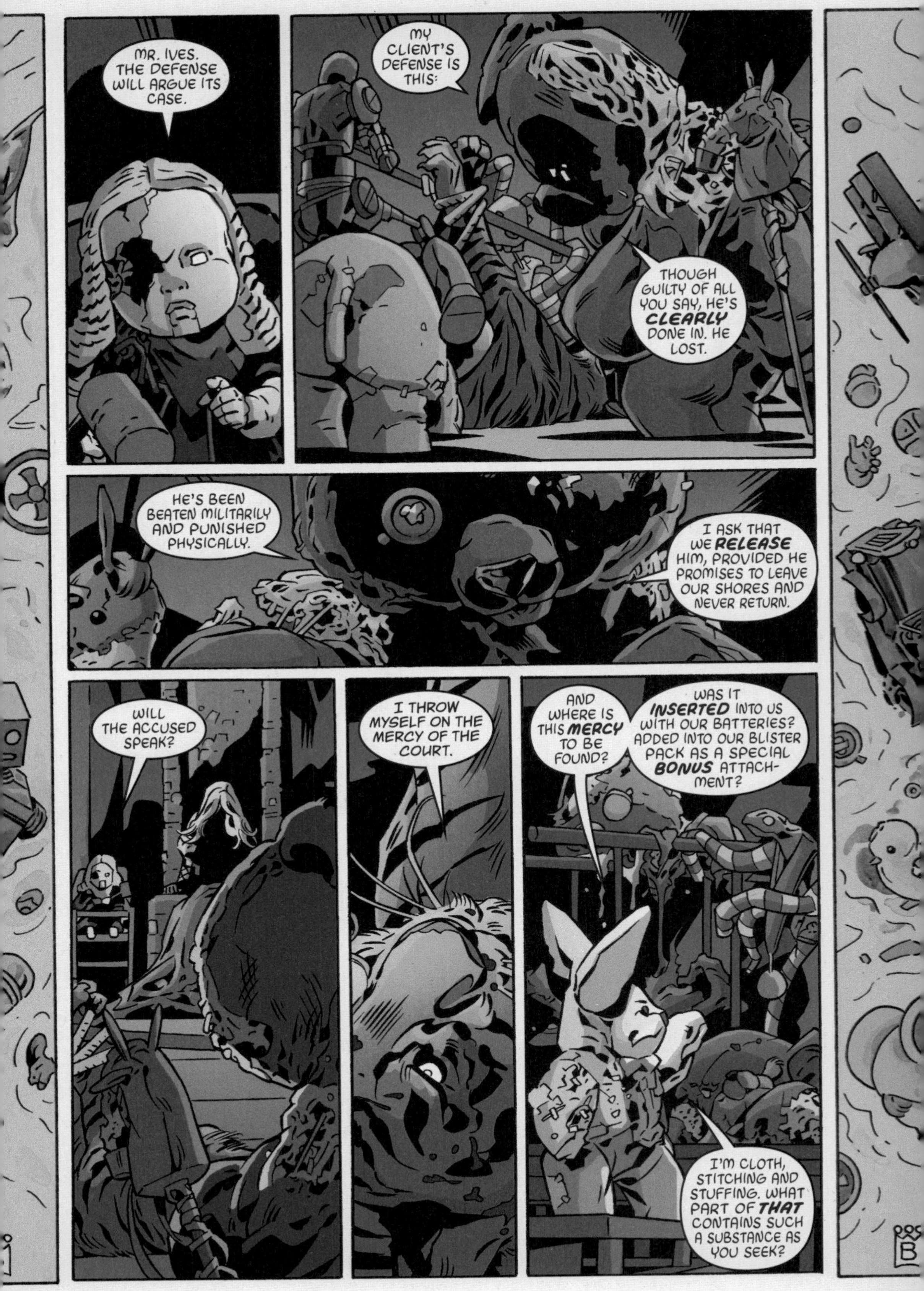

MR. IVES. THE DEFENSE WILL ARGUE ITS CASE.
MY CLIENT'S DEFENSE IS THIS:
THOUGH GUILTY OF ALL YOU SAY, HE'S **CLEARLY** DONE IN. HE LOST.
HE'S BEEN BEATEN MILITARILY AND PUNISHED PHYSICALLY.
I ASK THAT WE **RELEASE** HIM, PROVIDED HE PROMISES TO LEAVE OUR SHORES AND NEVER RETURN.
WILL THE ACCUSED SPEAK?
I THROW MYSELF ON THE MERCY OF THE COURT.
AND WHERE IS THIS **MERCY** TO BE FOUND?
WAS IT **INSERTED** INTO US WITH OUR BATTERIES? ADDED INTO OUR BLISTER PACK AS A SPECIAL **BONUS** ATTACHMENT?
I'M CLOTH, STITCHING AND STUFFING. WHAT PART OF **THAT** CONTAINS SUCH A SUBSTANCE AS YOU SEEK?

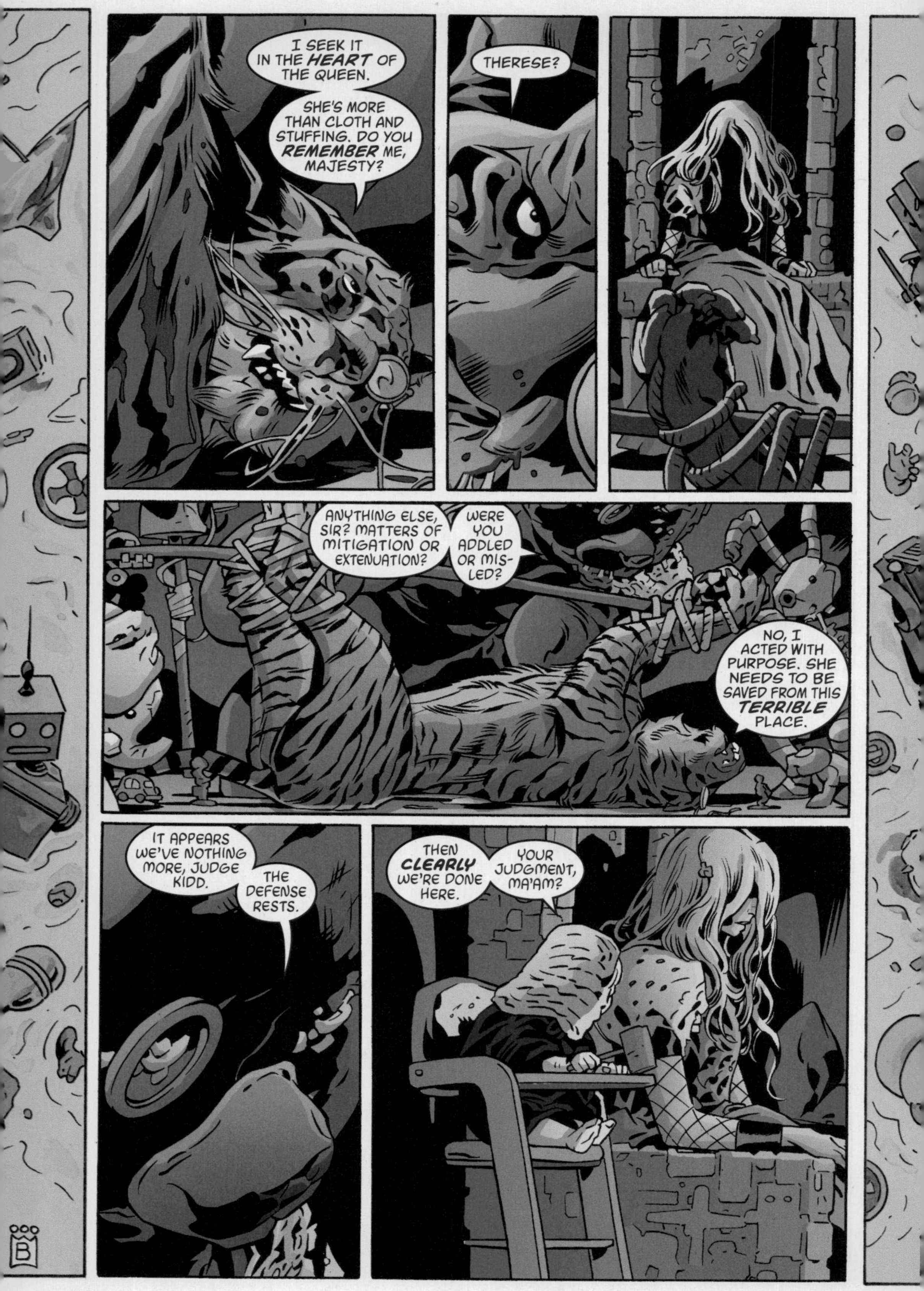
I SEEK IT IN THE HEART OF THE QUEEN.
SHE'S MORE THAN CLOTH AND STUFFING. DO YOU REMEMBER ME, MAJESTY?
THERESE?
ANYTHING ELSE, SIR? MATTERS OF MITIGATION OR EXTENUATION?
WERE YOU ADDLED OR MIS-LED?
NO, I ACTED WITH PURPOSE. SHE NEEDS TO BE SAVED FROM THIS TERRIBLE PLACE.
IT APPEARS WE'VE NOTHING MORE, JUDGE KIDD.
THE DEFENSE RESTS.
THEN CLEARLY WE'RE DONE HERE.
YOUR JUDGMENT, MA'AM?

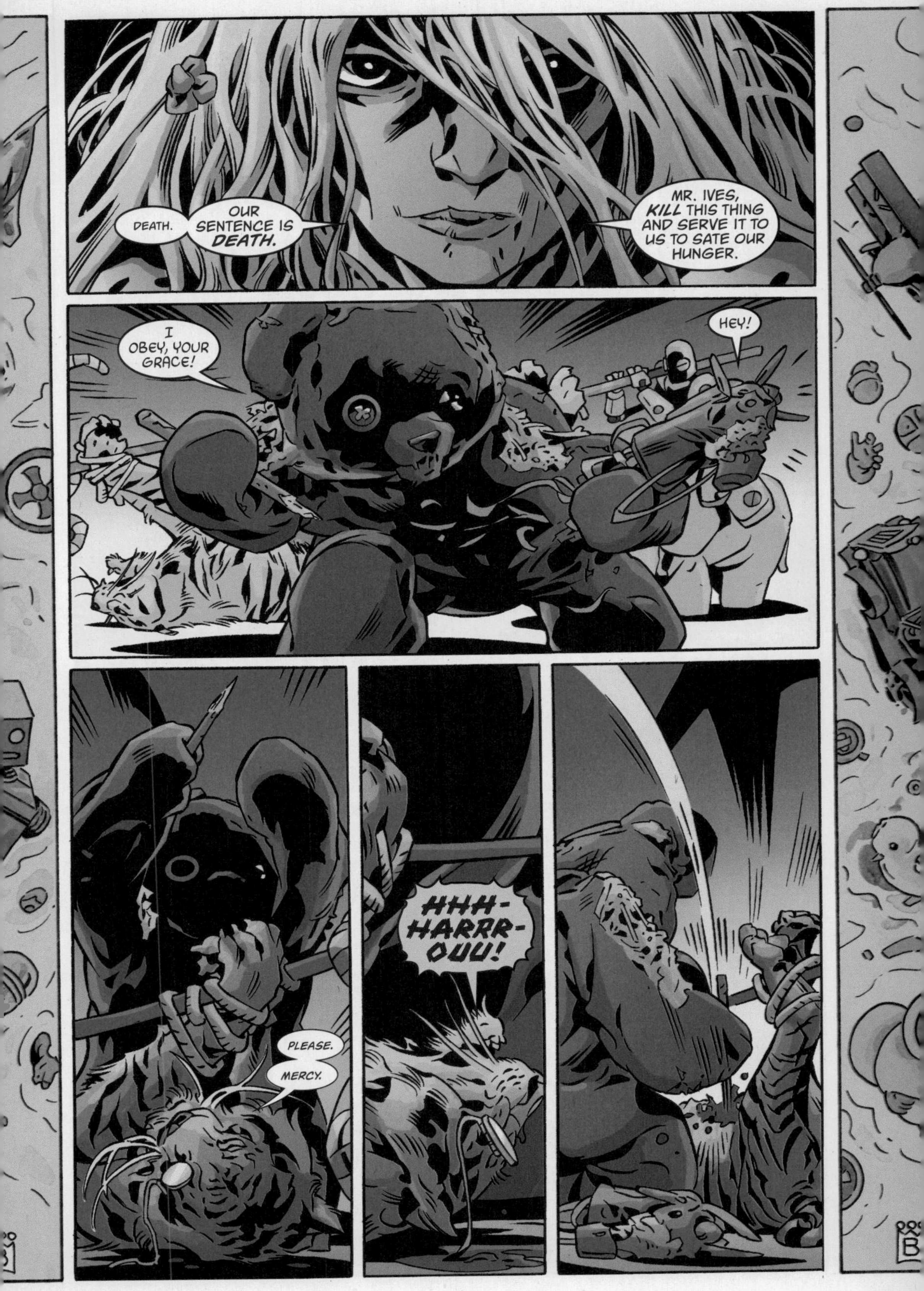
DEATH.
OUR SENTENCE IS DEATH.
MR. IVES, KILL THIS THING AND SERVE IT TO US TO SATE OUR HUNGER.
I OBEY, YOUR GRACE!
HEY!
PLEASE.
MERCY.
HHH-HARRR-OUU!

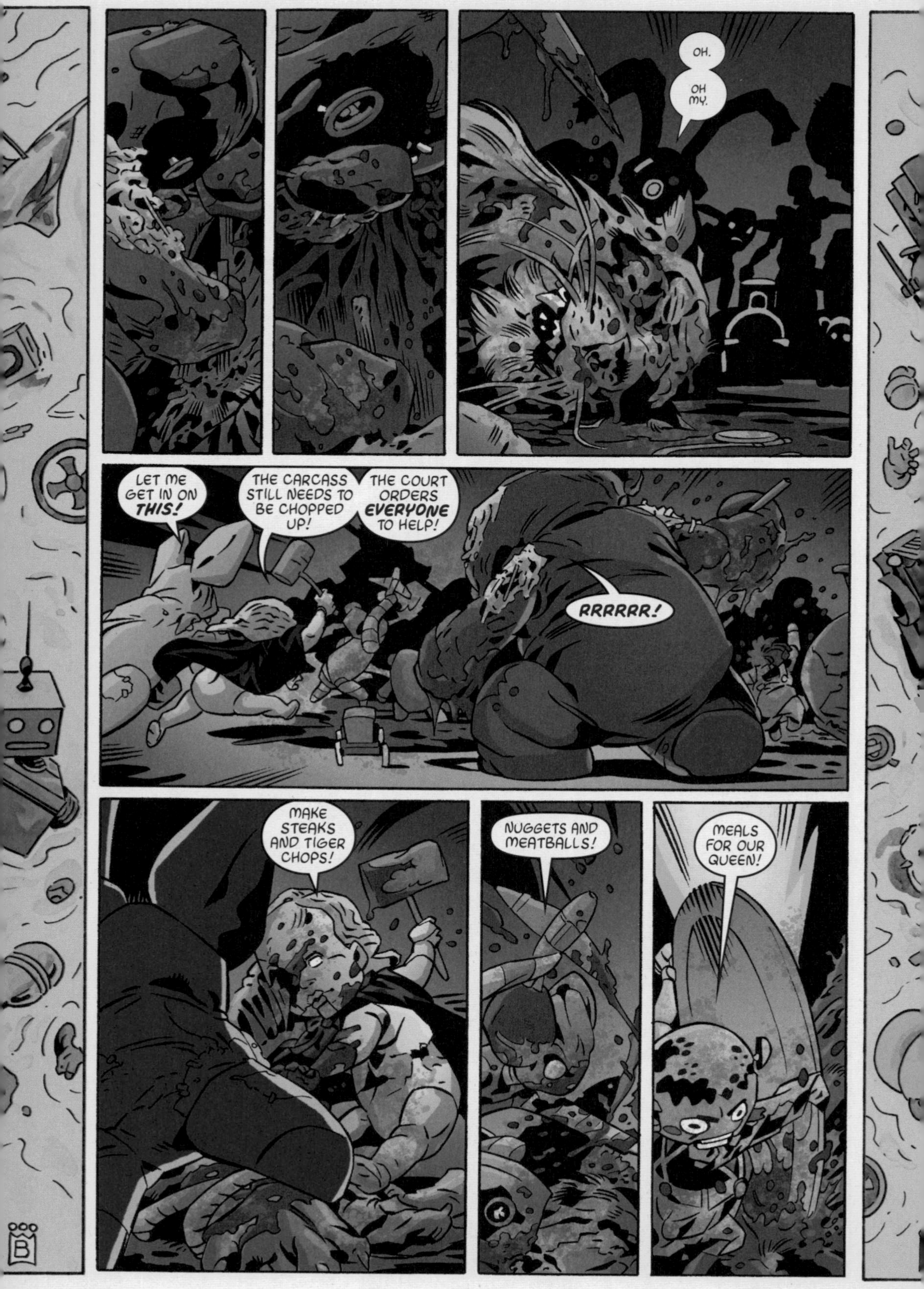
OH.
OH MY.
LET ME GET IN ON THIS!
THE CARCASS STILL NEEDS TO BE CHOPPED UP!
THE COURT ORDERS EVERYONE TO HELP!
RRRRRR!
MAKE STEAKS AND TIGER CHOPS!
NUGGETS AND MEATBALLS!
MEALS FOR OUR QUEEN!

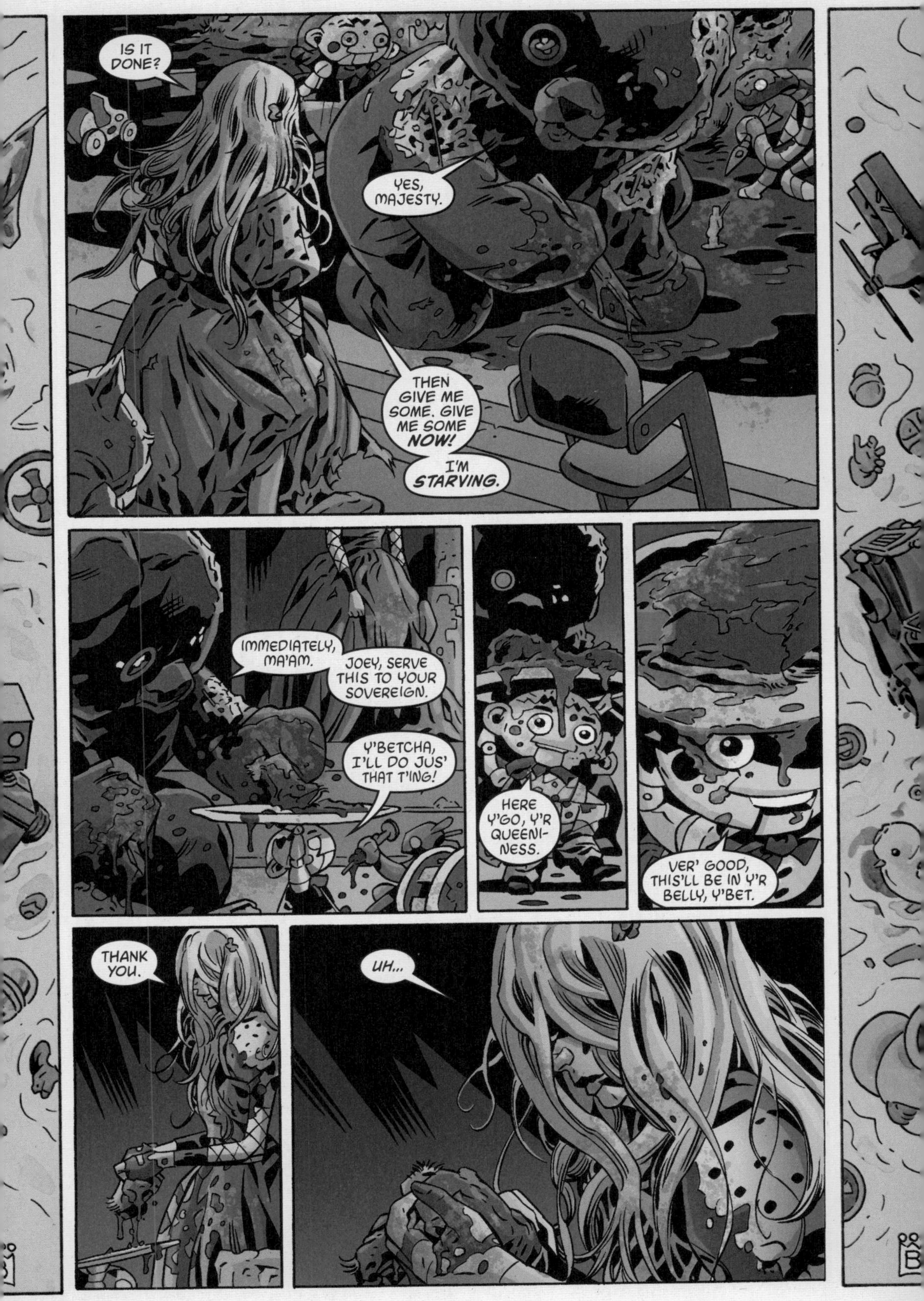
IS IT DONE?
YES, MAJESTY.
THEN GIVE ME SOME. GIVE ME SOME NOW!
I'M STARVING.
IMMEDIATELY, MA'AM.
JOEY, SERVE THIS TO YOUR SOVEREIGN.
Y'BETCHA, I'LL DO JUS' THAT T'ING!
HERE Y'GO, Y'R QUEENI-NESS.
VER' GOOD, THIS'LL BE IN Y'R BELLY, Y'BET.
THANK YOU.
UH...

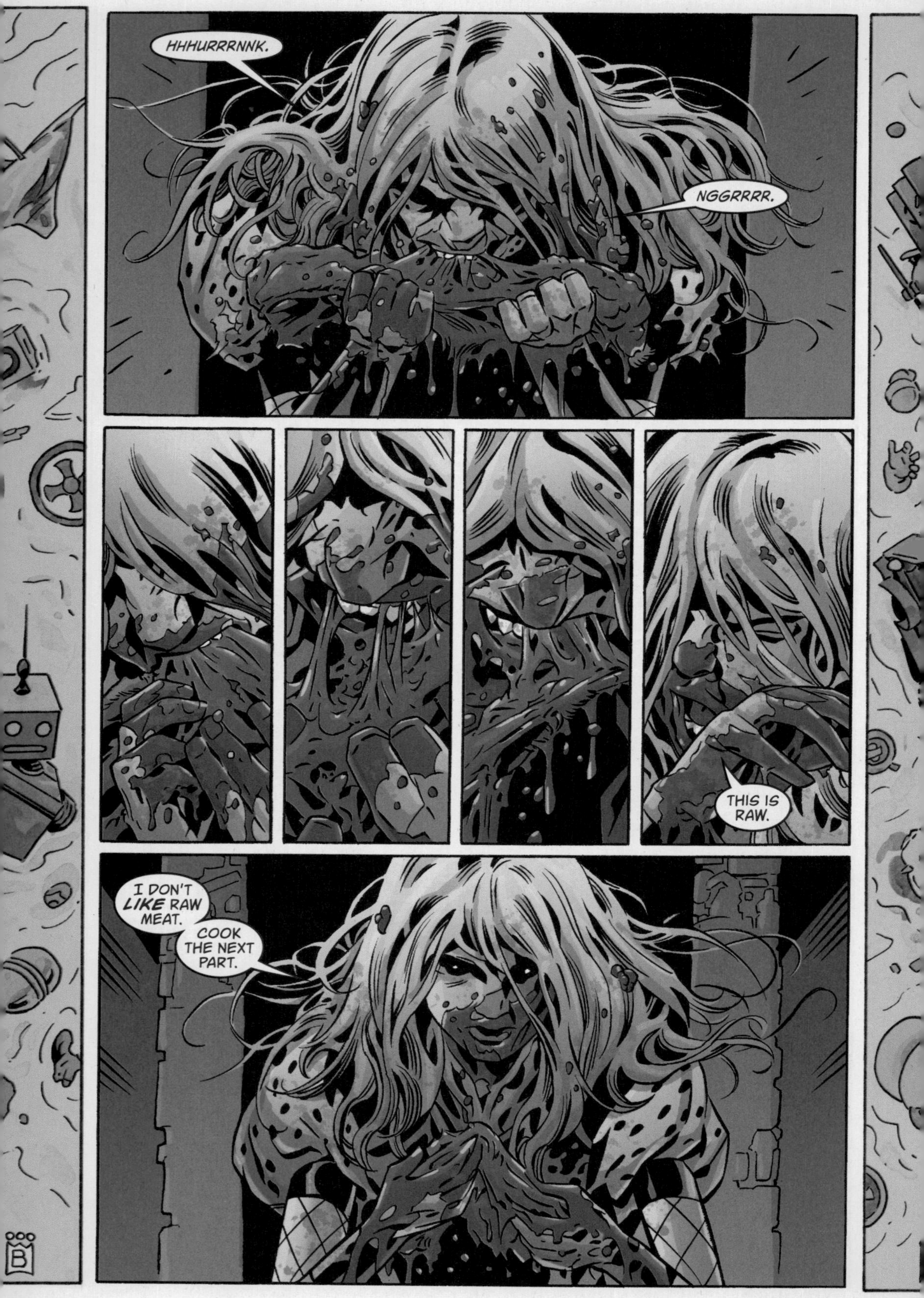
HHHURRRNNK.
NGGRRRR.
THIS IS RAW.
I DON'T LIKE RAW MEAT.
COOK THE NEXT PART.

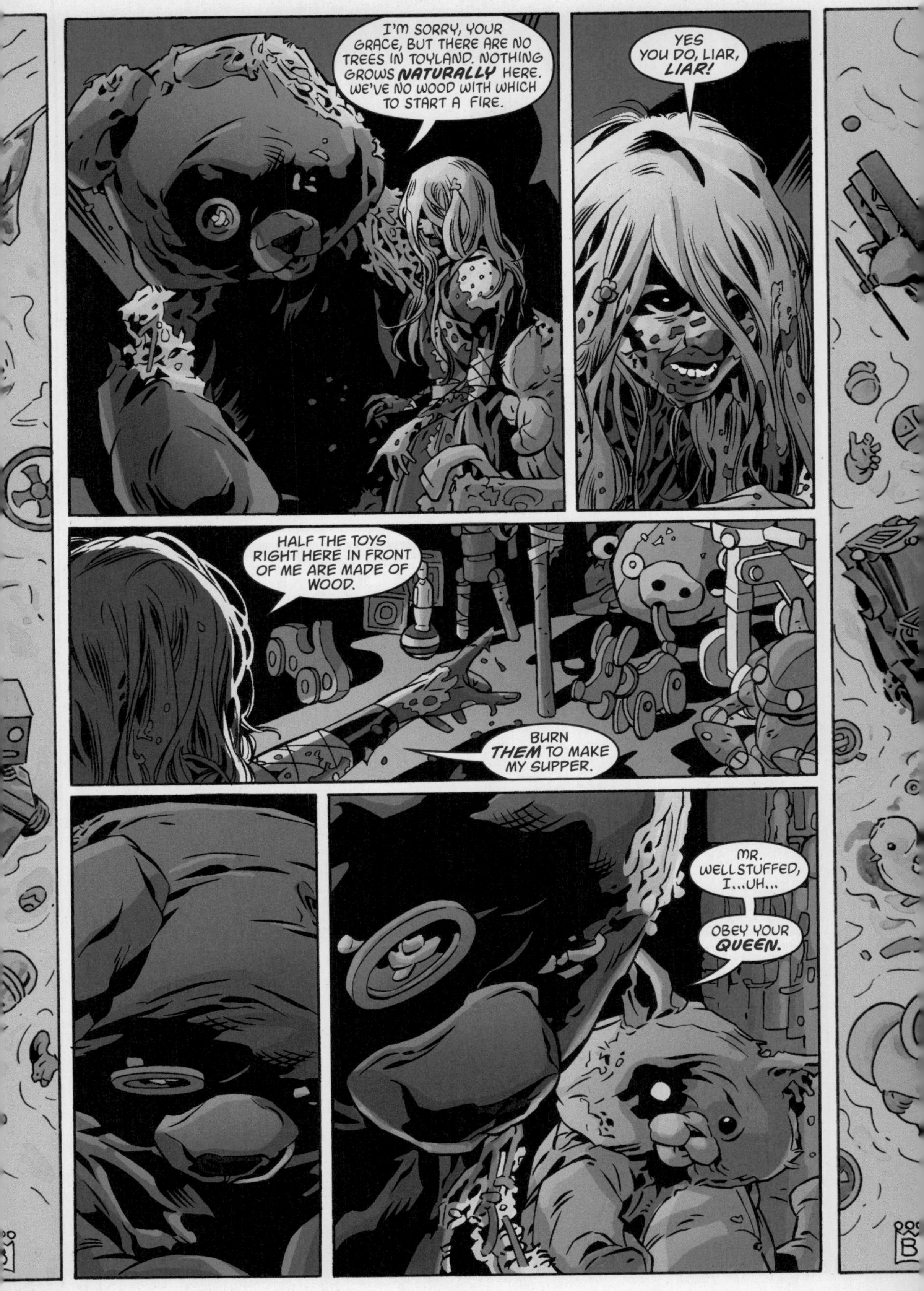

I'M SORRY, YOUR GRACE, BUT THERE ARE NO TREES IN TOYLAND. NOTHING GROWS NATURALLY HERE. WE'VE NO WOOD WITH WHICH TO START A FIRE.
YES YOU DO, LIAR, LIAR!
HALF THE TOYS RIGHT HERE IN FRONT OF ME ARE MADE OF WOOD.
BURN THEM TO MAKE MY SUPPER.
MR. WELLSTUFFED, I...UH...
OBEY YOUR QUEEN.

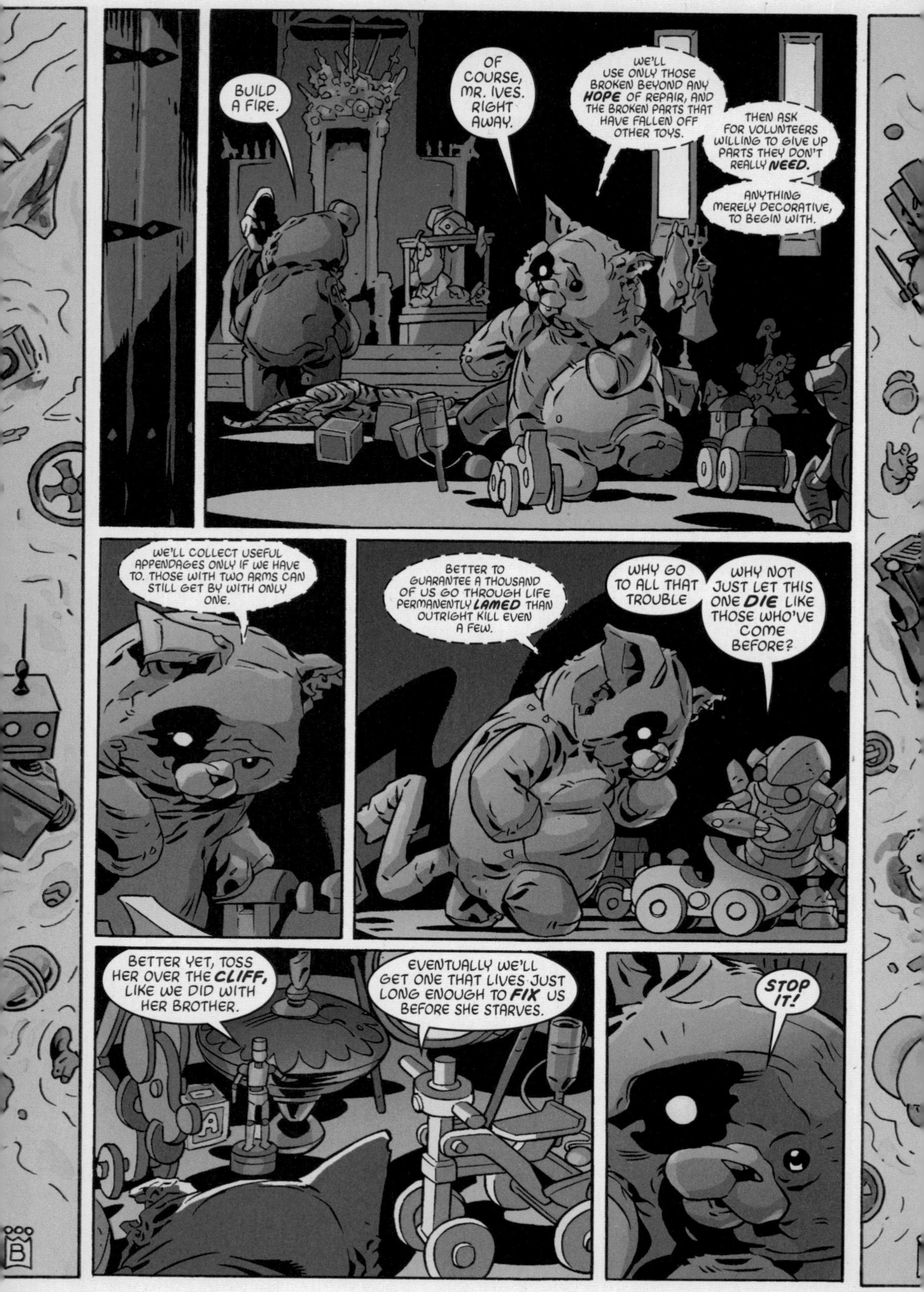
BUILD A FIRE.
OF COURSE, MR. IVES. RIGHT AWAY.
WE'LL USE ONLY THOSE BROKEN BEYOND ANY HOPE OF REPAIR, AND THE BROKEN PARTS THAT HAVE FALLEN OFF OTHER TOYS.
THEN ASK FOR VOLUNTEERS WILLING TO GIVE UP PARTS THEY DON'T REALLY NEED.
ANYTHING MERELY DECORATIVE, TO BEGIN WITH.
WE'LL COLLECT USEFUL APPENDAGES ONLY IF WE HAVE TO. THOSE WITH TWO ARMS CAN STILL GET BY WITH ONLY ONE.
BETTER TO GUARANTEE A THOUSAND OF US GO THROUGH LIFE PERMANENTLY LAMED THAN OUTRIGHT KILL EVEN A FEW.
WHY GO TO ALL THAT TROUBLE
WHY NOT JUST LET THIS ONE DIE LIKE THOSE WHO'VE COME BEFORE?
BETTER YET, TOSS HER OVER THE CLIFF, LIKE WE DID WITH HER BROTHER.
EVENTUALLY WE'LL GET ONE THAT LIVES JUST LONG ENOUGH TO FIX US BEFORE SHE STARVES.
STOP IT!

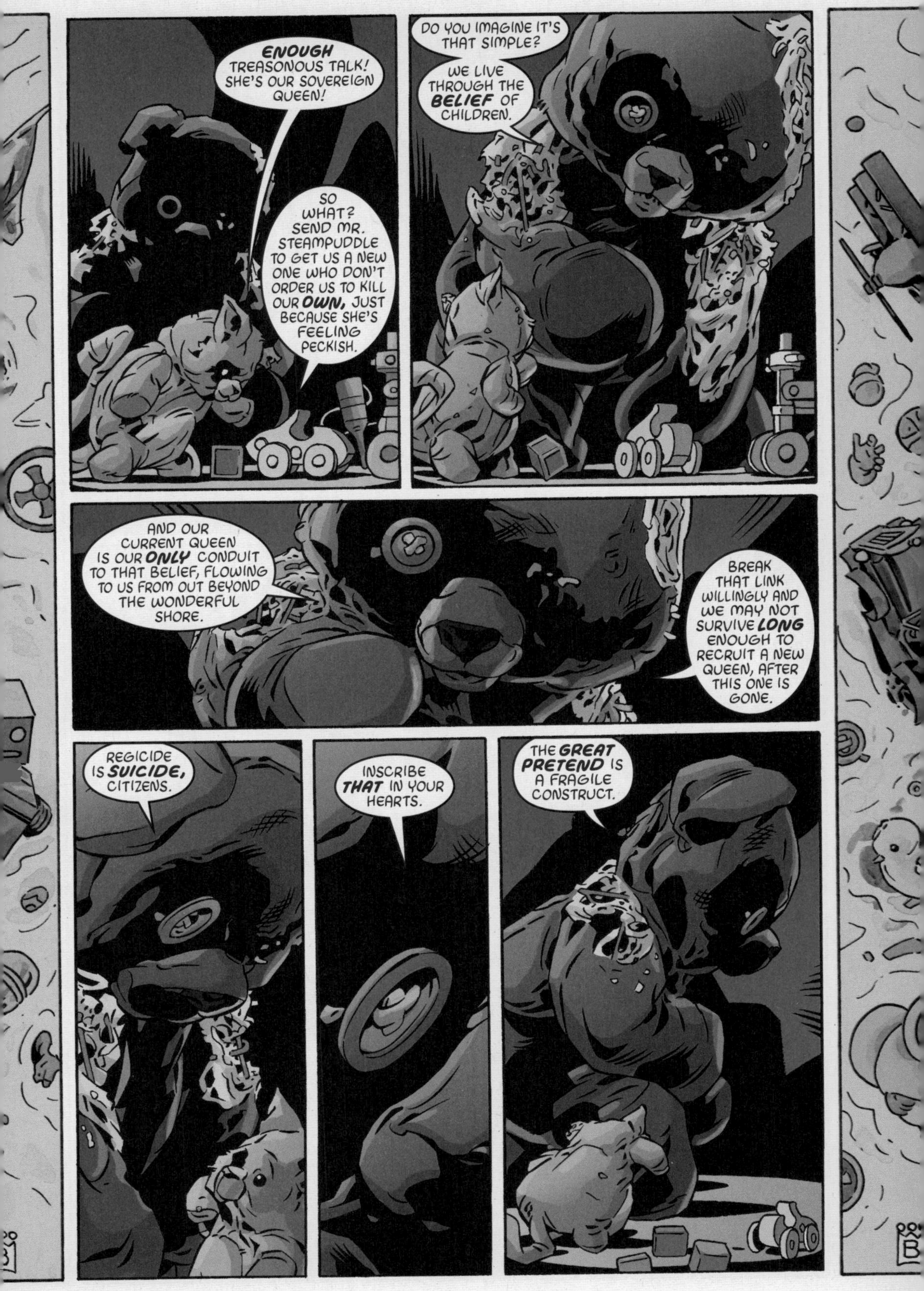
ENOUGH TREASONOUS TALK! SHE'S OUR SOVEREIGN QUEEN!
SO WHAT? SEND MR. STEAMPUDDLE TO GET US A NEW ONE WHO DON'T ORDER US TO KILL OUR OWN, JUST BECAUSE SHE'S FEELING PECKISH.
DO YOU IMAGINE IT'S THAT SIMPLE?
WE LIVE THROUGH THE BELIEF OF CHILDREN.
AND OUR CURRENT QUEEN IS OUR ONLY CONDUIT TO THAT BELIEF, FLOWING TO US FROM OUT BEYOND THE WONDERFUL SHORE.
BREAK THAT LINK WILLINGLY AND WE MAY NOT SURVIVE LONG ENOUGH TO RECRUIT A NEW QUEEN, AFTER THIS ONE IS GONE.
REGICIDE IS SUICIDE, CITIZENS.
INSCRIBE THAT IN YOUR HEARTS.
THE GREAT PRETEND IS A FRAGILE CONSTRUCT.

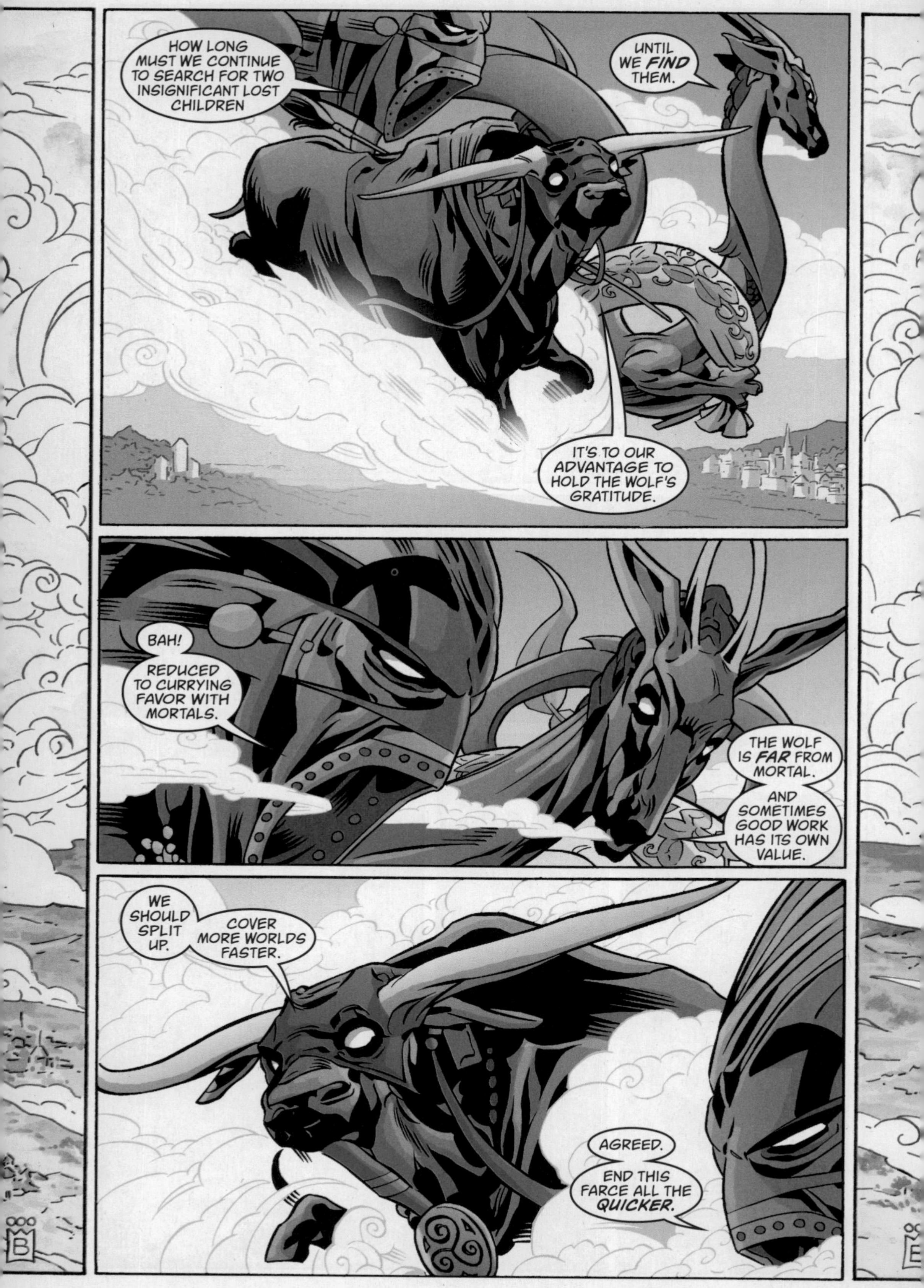
HOW LONG MUST WE CONTINUE TO SEARCH FOR TWO INSIGNIFICANT LOST CHILDREN
UNTIL WE *FIND* THEM.
IT'S TO OUR ADVANTAGE TO HOLD THE WOLF'S GRATITUDE.
BAH!
REDUCED TO CURRYING FAVOR WITH MORTALS.
THE WOLF IS *FAR* FROM MORTAL.
AND SOMETIMES GOOD WORK HAS ITS OWN VALUE.
WE SHOULD SPLIT UP.
COVER MORE WORLDS FASTER.
AGREED.
END THIS FARCE ALL THE *QUICKER*.

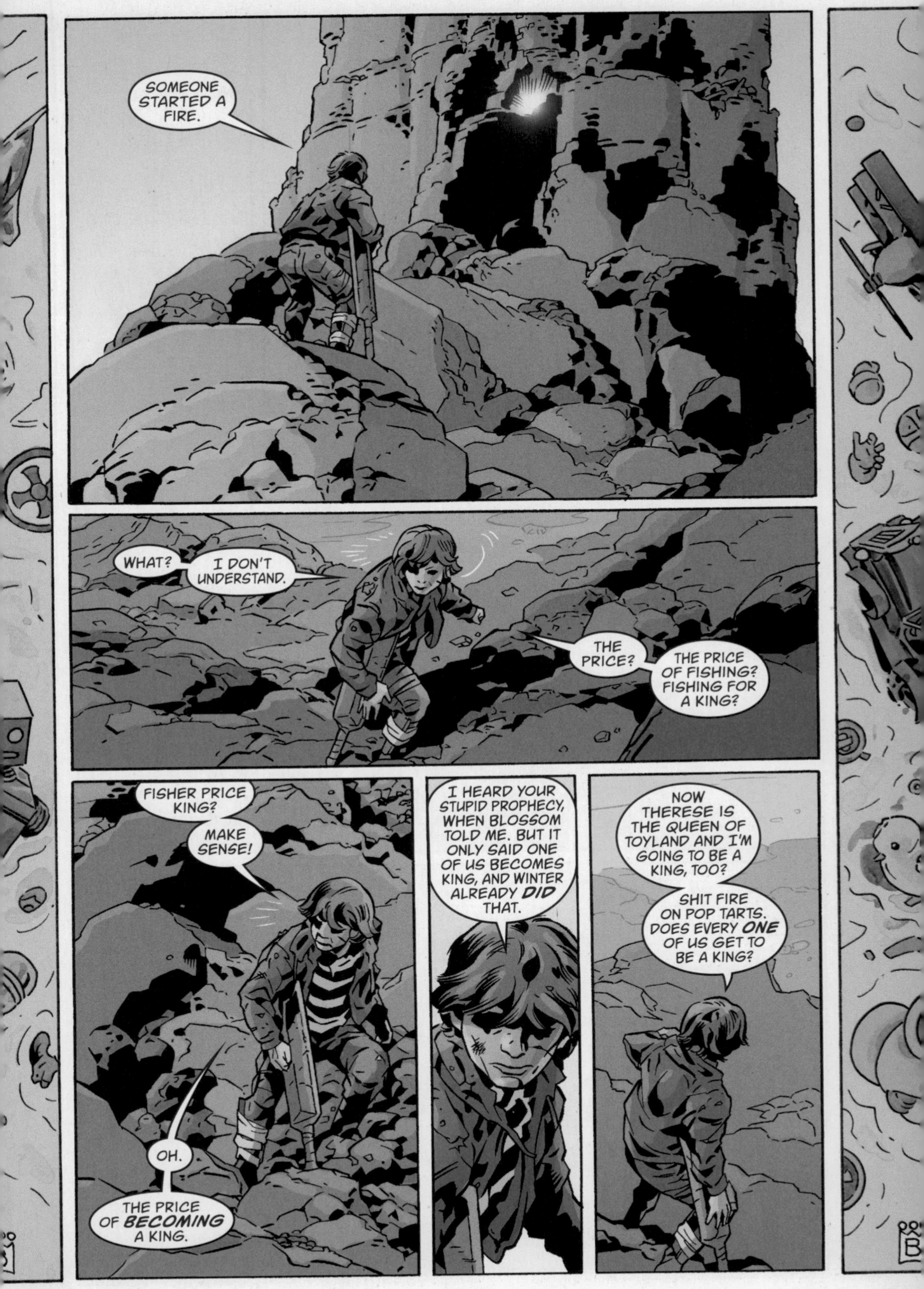
SOMEONE STARTED A FIRE.
WHAT?
I DON'T UNDERSTAND.
THE PRICE?
THE PRICE OF FISHING? FISHING FOR A KING?
FISHER PRICE KING?
MAKE SENSE!
OH.
THE PRICE OF BECOMING A KING.
I HEARD YOUR STUPID PROPHECY, WHEN BLOSSOM TOLD ME. BUT IT ONLY SAID ONE OF US BECOMES KING, AND WINTER ALREADY DID THAT.
NOW THERESE IS THE QUEEN OF TOYLAND AND I'M GOING TO BE A KING, TOO?
SHIT FIRE ON POP TARTS. DOES EVERY ONE OF US GET TO BE A KING?

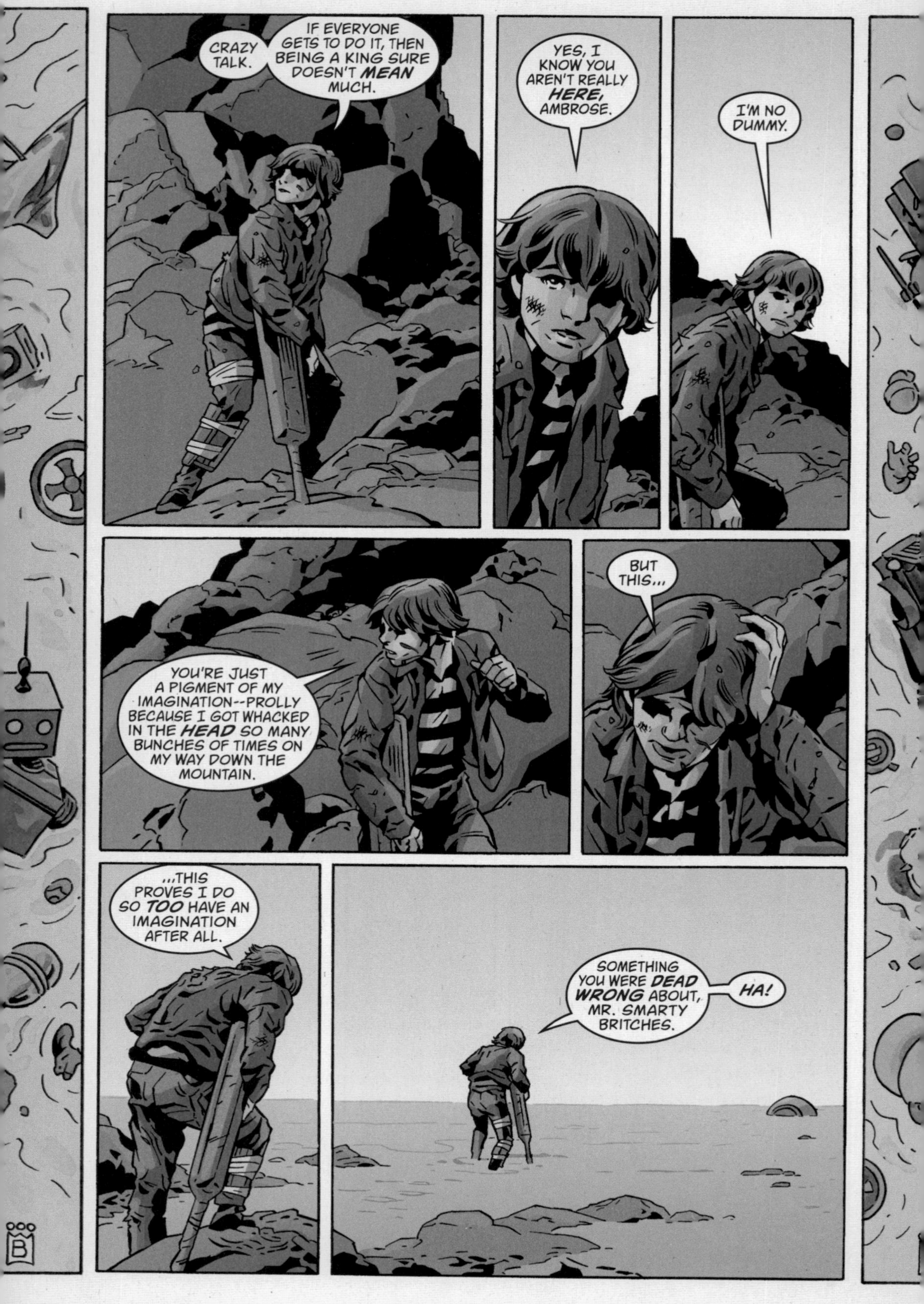
CRAZY TALK.
IF EVERYONE GETS TO DO IT, THEN BEING A KING SURE DOESN'T MEAN MUCH.
YES, I KNOW YOU AREN'T REALLY HERE, AMBROSE.
I'M NO DUMMY.
YOU'RE JUST A PIGMENT OF MY IMAGINATION--PROLLY BECAUSE I GOT WHACKED IN THE HEAD SO MANY BUNCHES OF TIMES ON MY WAY DOWN THE MOUNTAIN.
BUT THIS...
...THIS PROVES I DO SO TOO HAVE AN IMAGINATION AFTER ALL.
SOMETHING YOU WERE DEAD WRONG ABOUT, MR. SMARTY BRITCHES.
HA!

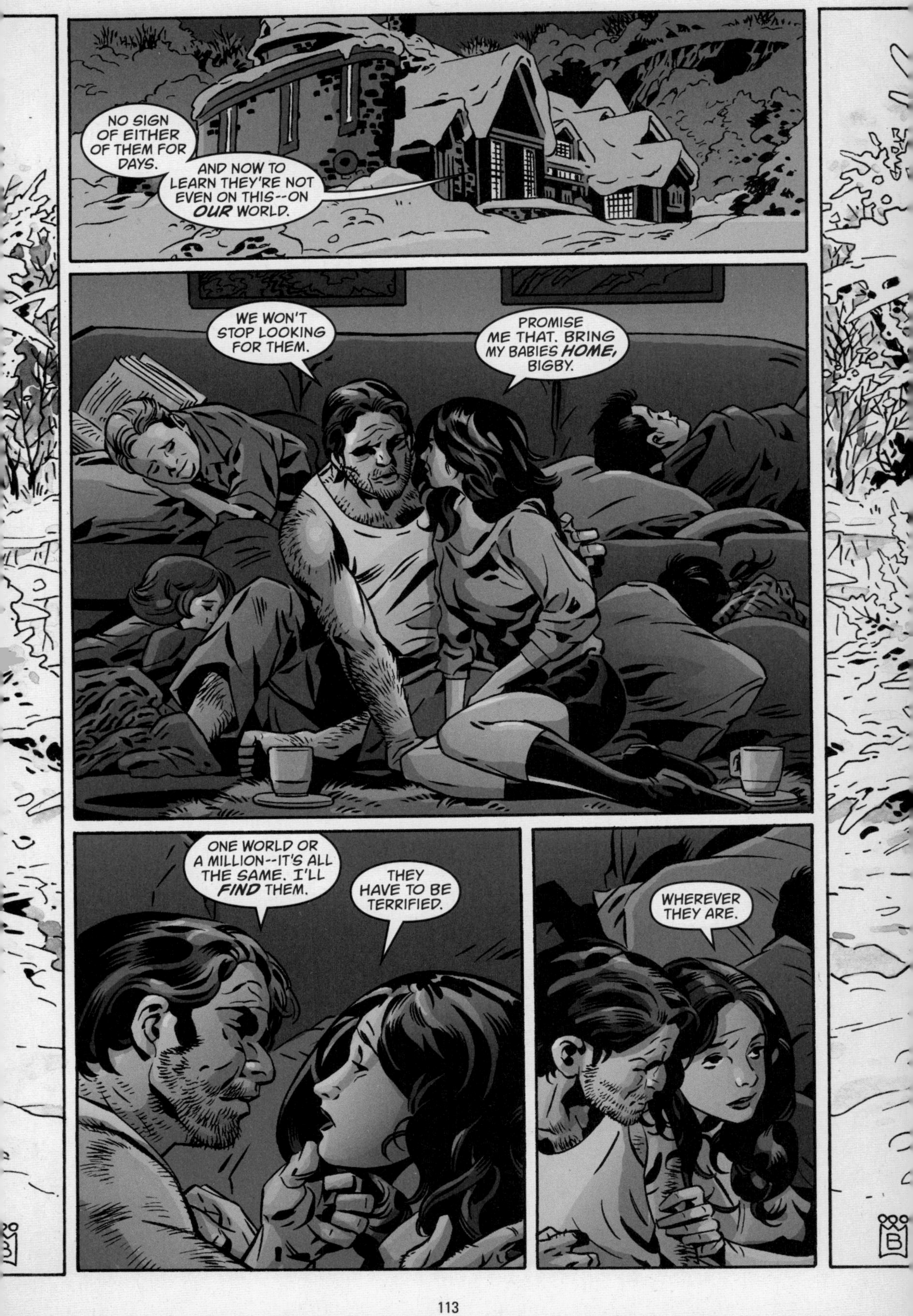
NO SIGN OF EITHER OF THEM FOR DAYS.
AND NOW TO LEARN THEY'RE NOT EVEN ON THIS--ON OUR WORLD.
WE WON'T STOP LOOKING FOR THEM.
PROMISE ME THAT. BRING MY BABIES HOME, BIGBY.
ONE WORLD OR A MILLION--IT'S ALL THE SAME. I'LL FIND THEM.
THEY HAVE TO BE TERRIFIED.
WHEREVER THEY ARE.

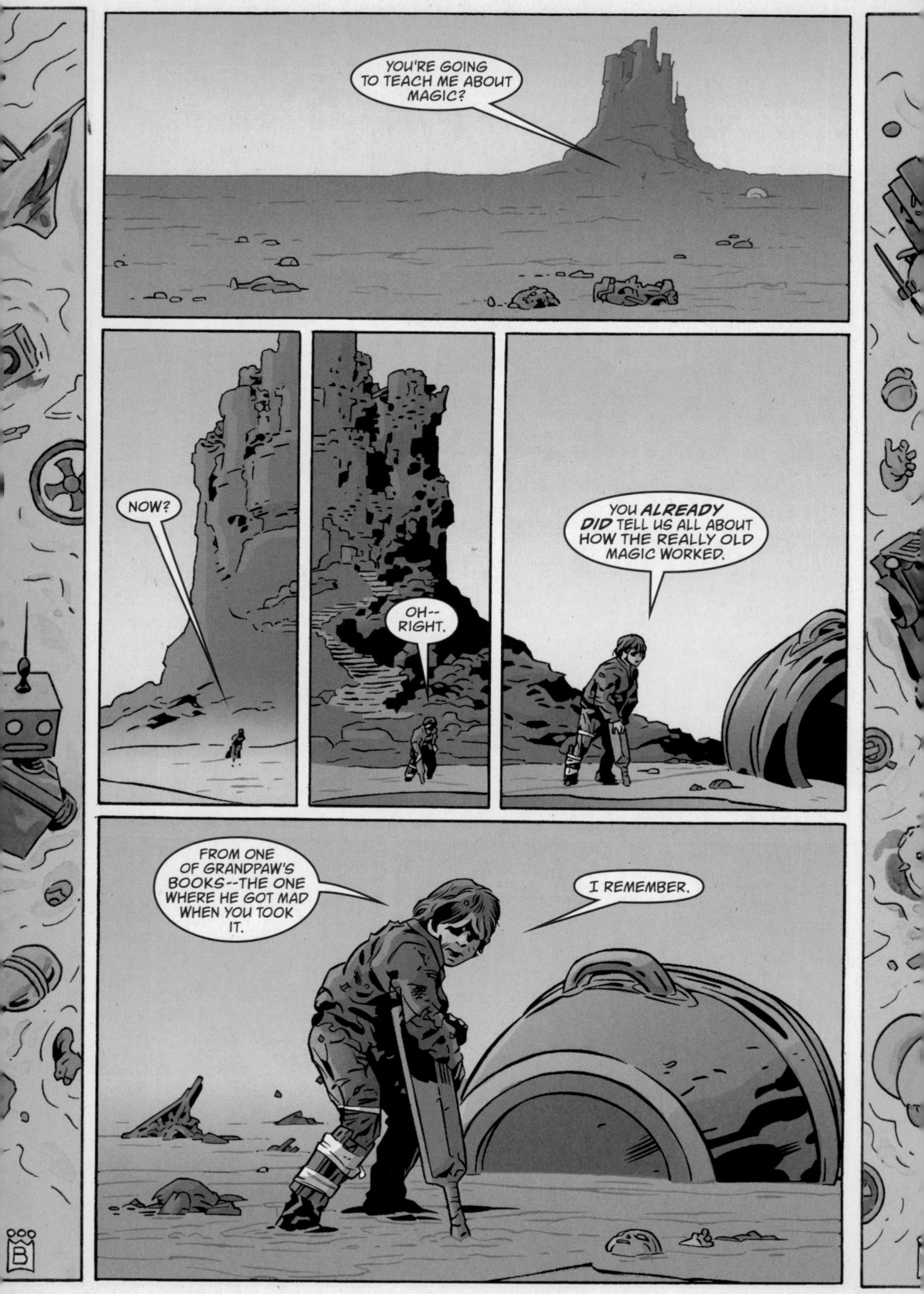
YOU'RE GOING TO TEACH ME ABOUT MAGIC?
NOW?
OH-- RIGHT.
YOU ALREADY DID TELL US ALL ABOUT HOW THE REALLY OLD MAGIC WORKED.
FROM ONE OF GRANDPAW'S BOOKS--THE ONE WHERE HE GOT MAD WHEN YOU TOOK IT.
I REMEMBER.

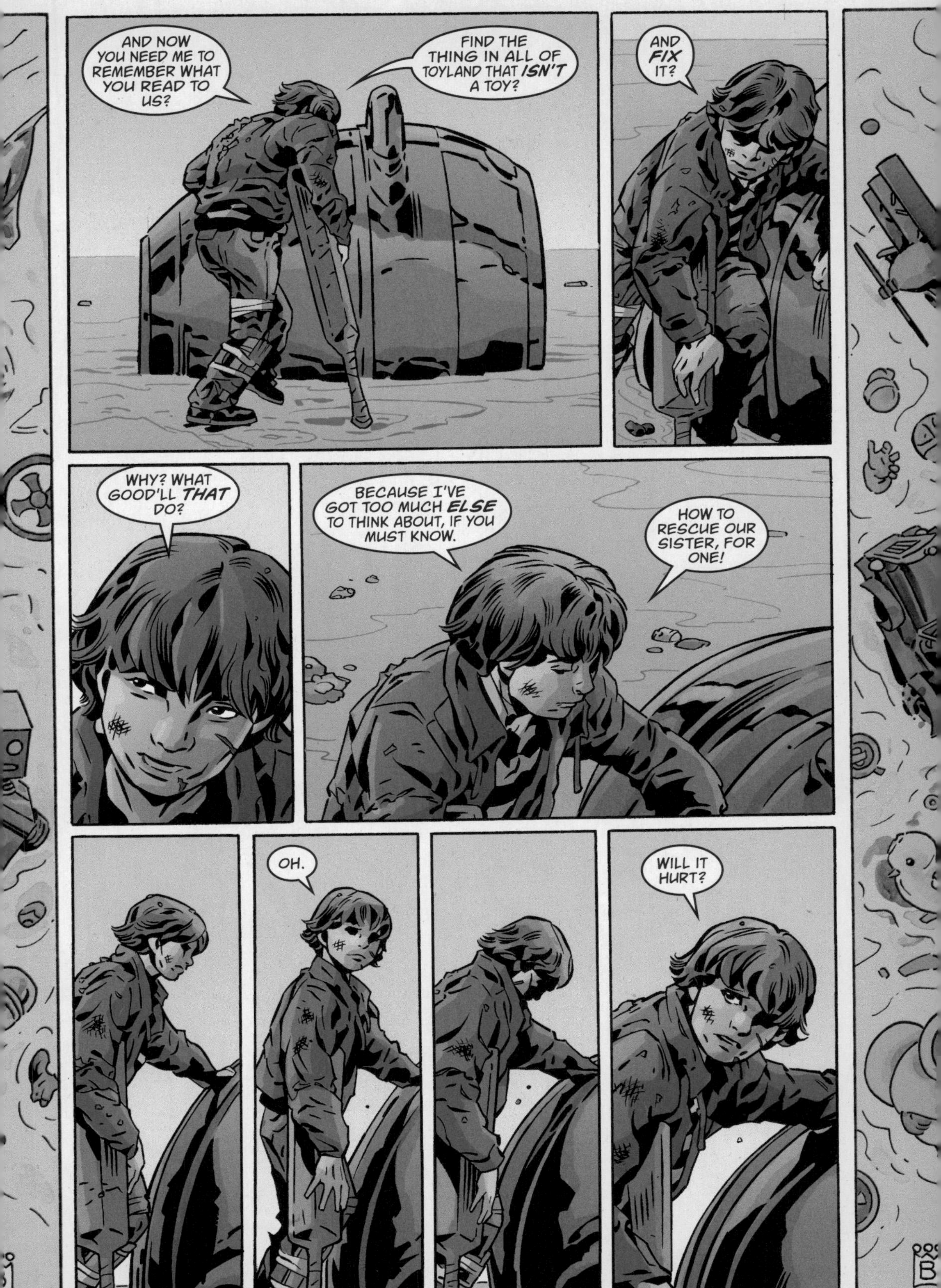
AND NOW YOU NEED ME TO REMEMBER WHAT YOU READ TO US?
FIND THE THING IN ALL OF TOYLAND THAT ISN'T A TOY?
AND FIX IT?
WHY? WHAT GOOD'LL THAT DO?
BECAUSE I'VE GOT TOO MUCH ELSE TO THINK ABOUT, IF YOU MUST KNOW.
HOW TO RESCUE OUR SISTER, FOR ONE!
OH.
WILL IT HURT?

NEXT: THE FISHER KING

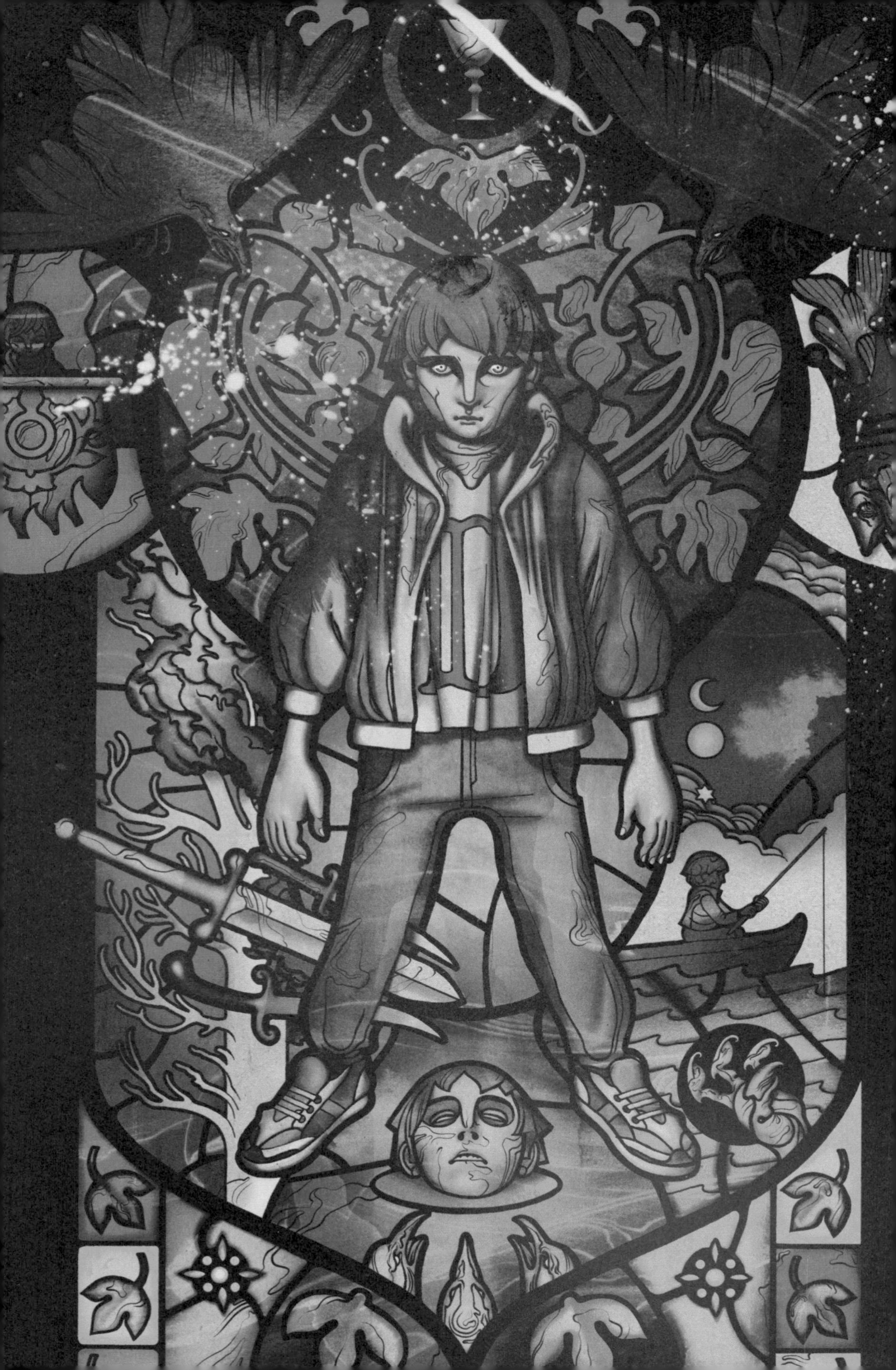

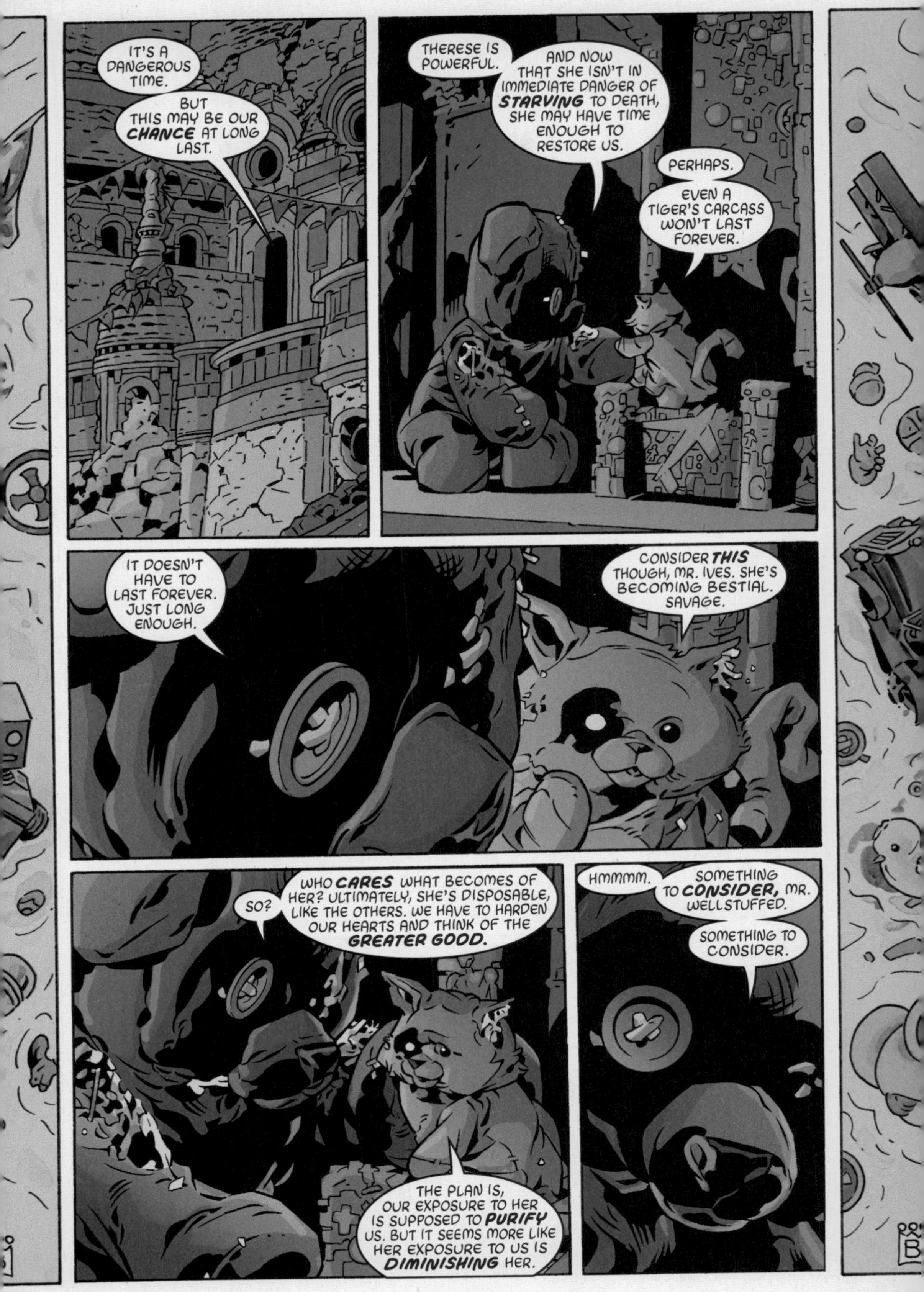
IT'S A DANGEROUS TIME.
BUT THIS MAY BE OUR CHANCE AT LONG LAST.
THERESE IS POWERFUL.
AND NOW THAT SHE ISN'T IN IMMEDIATE DANGER OF STARVING TO DEATH, SHE MAY HAVE TIME ENOUGH TO RESTORE US.
PERHAPS.
EVEN A TIGER'S CARCASS WON'T LAST FOREVER.
IT DOESN'T HAVE TO LAST FOREVER. JUST LONG ENOUGH.
CONSIDER THIS THOUGH, MR. IVES. SHE'S BECOMING BESTIAL. SAVAGE.
SO?
WHO CARES WHAT BECOMES OF HER? ULTIMATELY, SHE'S DISPOSABLE, LIKE THE OTHERS. WE HAVE TO HARDEN OUR HEARTS AND THINK OF THE GREATER GOOD.
THE PLAN IS, OUR EXPOSURE TO HER IS SUPPOSED TO PURIFY US. BUT IT SEEMS MORE LIKE HER EXPOSURE TO US IS DIMINISHING HER.
HMMMM.
SOMETHING TO CONSIDER, MR. WELLSTUFFED.
SOMETHING TO CONSIDER.

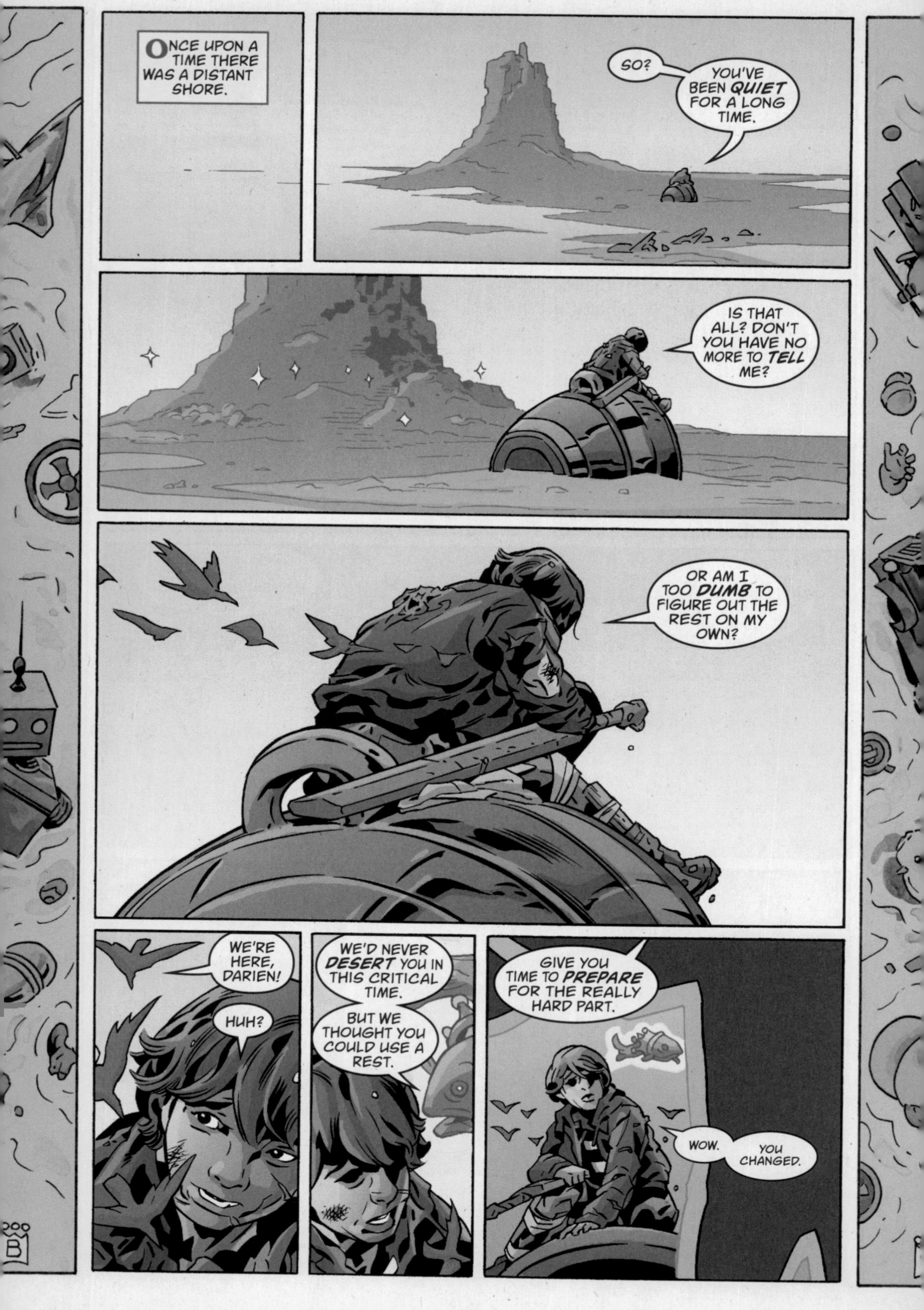
ONCE UPON A TIME THERE WAS A DISTANT SHORE.
SO?
YOU'VE BEEN QUIET FOR A LONG TIME.
IS THAT ALL? DON'T YOU HAVE NO MORE TO TELL ME?
OR AM I TOO DUMB TO FIGURE OUT THE REST ON MY OWN?
WE'RE HERE, DARIEN!
HUH?
WE'D NEVER DESERT YOU IN THIS CRITICAL TIME.
BUT WE THOUGHT YOU COULD USE A REST.
GIVE YOU TIME TO PREPARE FOR THE REALLY HARD PART.
WOW.
YOU CHANGED.

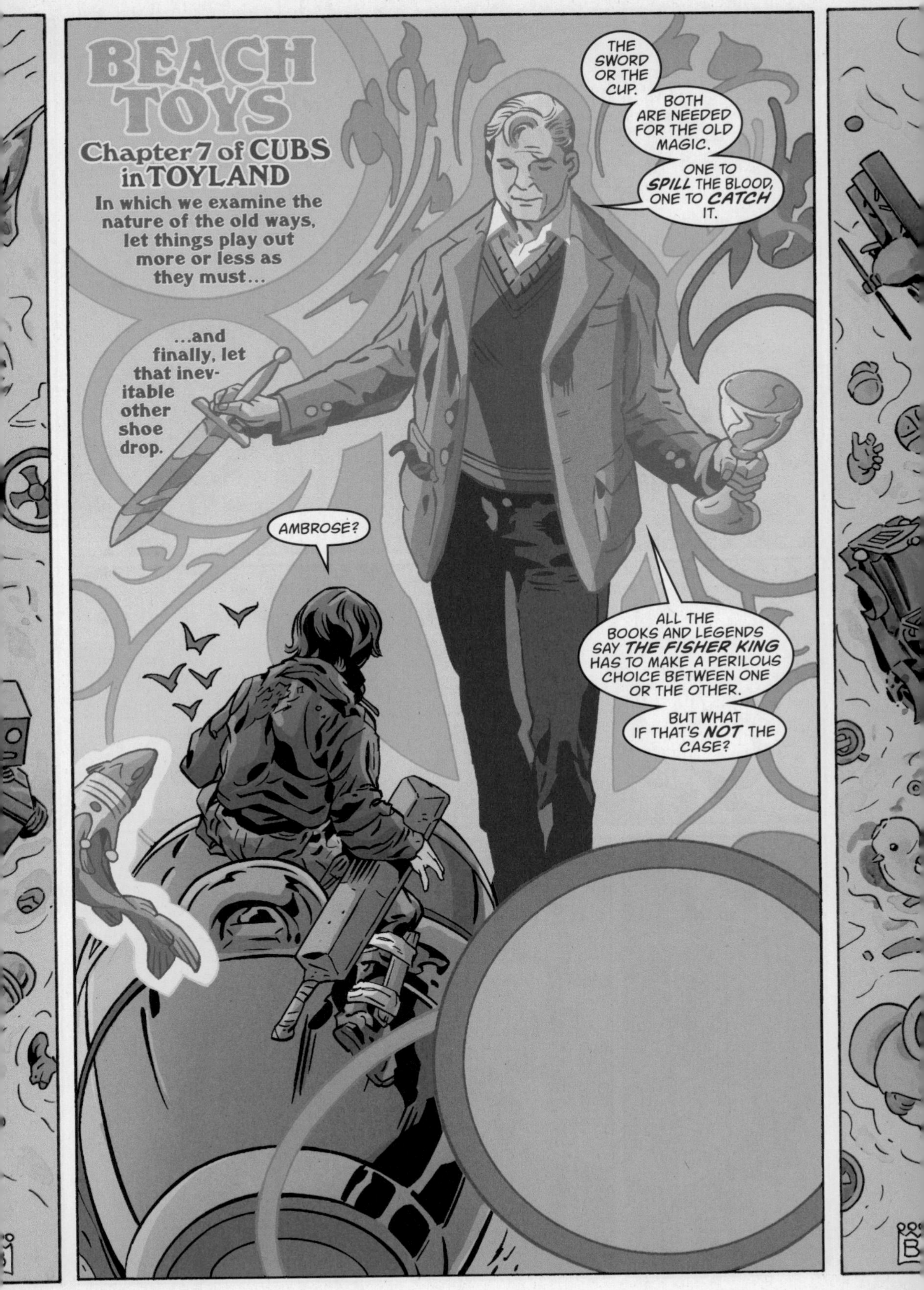

BEACH TOYS
Chapter 7 of CUBS in TOYLAND
In which we examine the nature of the old ways, let things play out more or less as they must...
...and finally, let that inev-itable other shoe drop.
THE SWORD OR THE CUP.
BOTH ARE NEEDED FOR THE OLD MAGIC.
ONE TO SPILL THE BLOOD, ONE TO CATCH IT.
AMBROSE?
ALL THE BOOKS AND LEGENDS SAY THE FISHER KING HAS TO MAKE A PERILOUS CHOICE BETWEEN ONE OR THE OTHER.
BUT WHAT IF THAT'S NOT THE CASE?

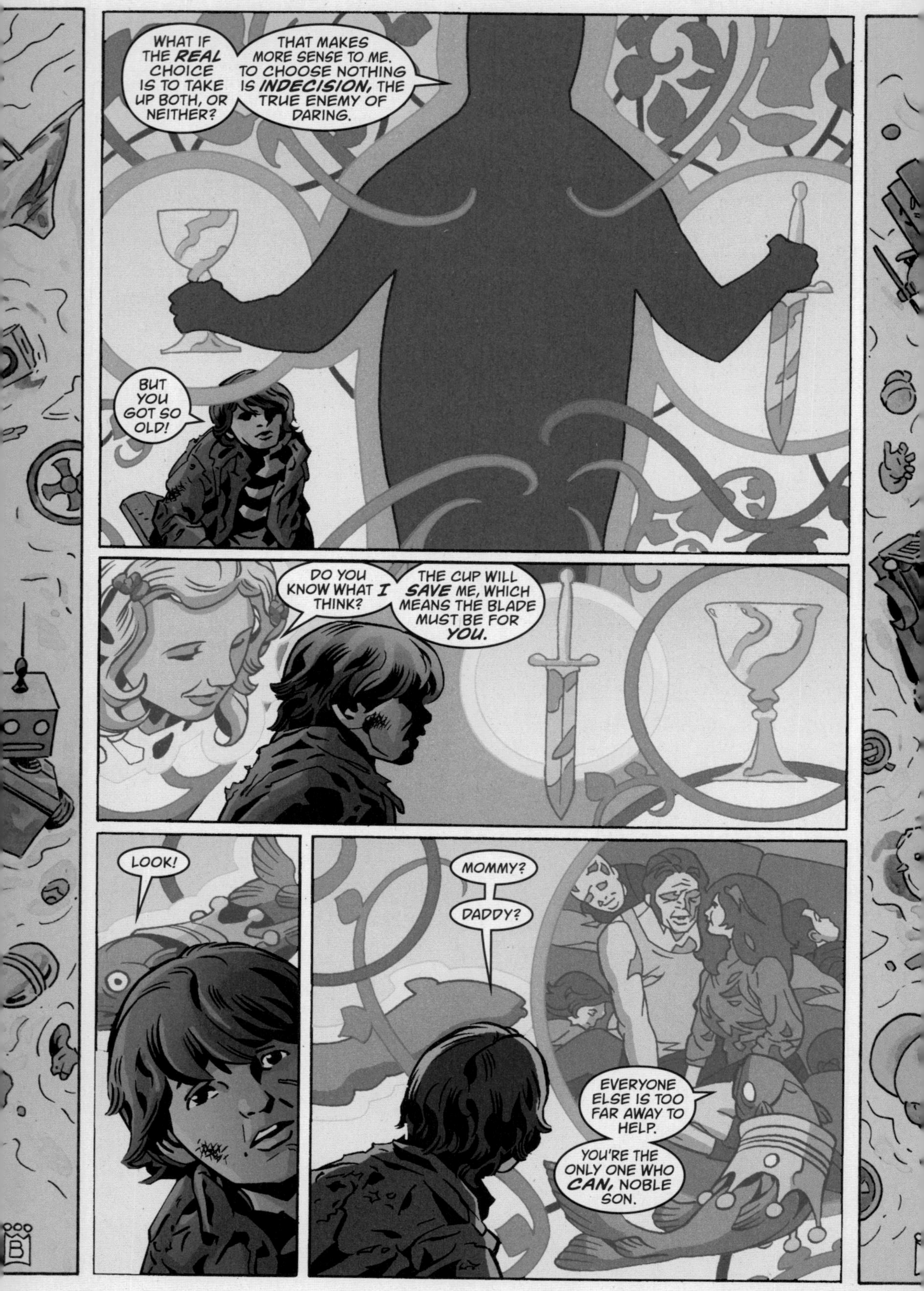

WHAT IF THE REAL CHOICE IS TO TAKE UP BOTH, OR NEITHER?
THAT MAKES MORE SENSE TO ME. TO CHOOSE NOTHING IS INDECISION, THE TRUE ENEMY OF DARING.
BUT YOU GOT SO OLD!
DO YOU KNOW WHAT I THINK?
THE CUP WILL SAVE ME, WHICH MEANS THE BLADE MUST BE FOR YOU.
LOOK!
MOMMY?
DADDY?
EVERYONE ELSE IS TOO FAR AWAY TO HELP.
YOU'RE THE ONLY ONE WHO CAN, NOBLE SON.

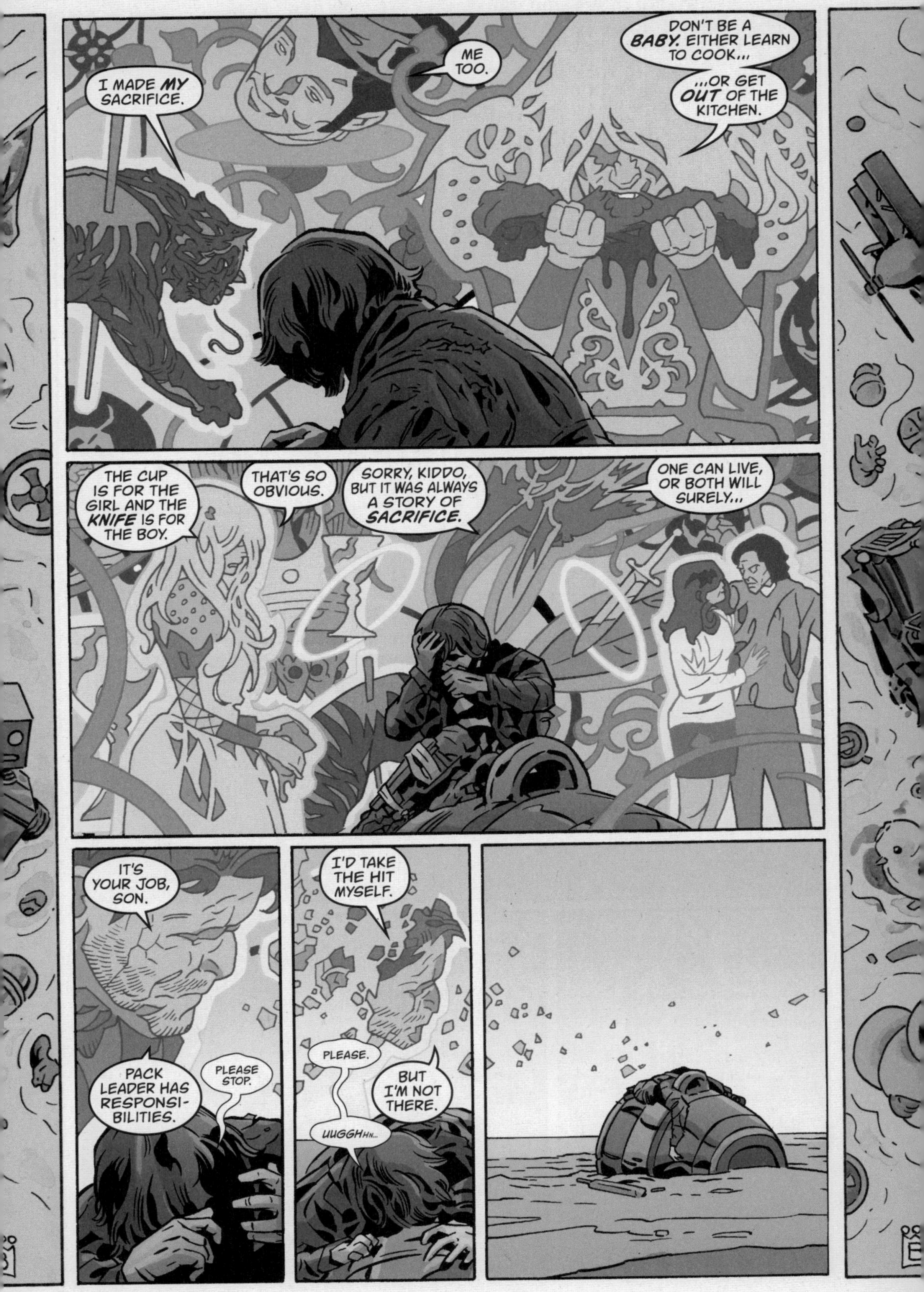
I MADE MY SACRIFICE.
ME TOO.
DON'T BE A BABY. EITHER LEARN TO COOK...
...OR GET OUT OF THE KITCHEN.
THE CUP IS FOR THE GIRL AND THE KNIFE IS FOR THE BOY.
THAT'S SO OBVIOUS.
SORRY, KIDDO, BUT IT WAS ALWAYS A STORY OF SACRIFICE.
ONE CAN LIVE, OR BOTH WILL SURELY...
IT'S YOUR JOB, SON.
PACK LEADER HAS RESPONSI-BILITIES.
PLEASE STOP.
I'D TAKE THE HIT MYSELF.
PLEASE.
BUT I'M NOT THERE.
UUGGHHN...

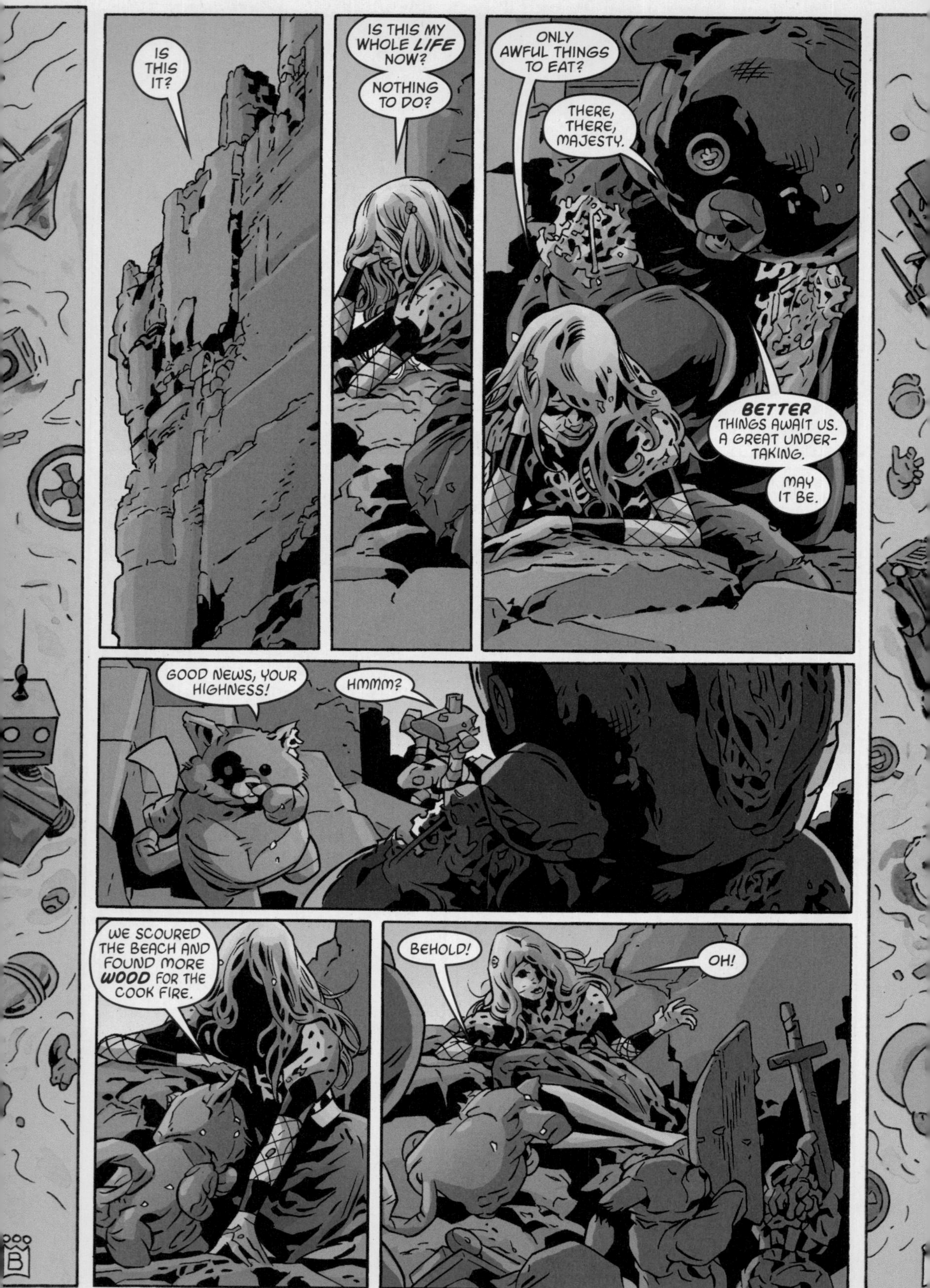
IS THIS IT?
IS THIS MY WHOLE LIFE NOW?
NOTHING TO DO?
ONLY AWFUL THINGS TO EAT?
THERE, THERE, MAJESTY.
BETTER THINGS AWAIT US. A GREAT UNDER-TAKING.
MAY IT BE.
GOOD NEWS, YOUR HIGHNESS!
HMMM?
WE SCOURED THE BEACH AND FOUND MORE WOOD FOR THE COOK FIRE.
BEHOLD!
OH!

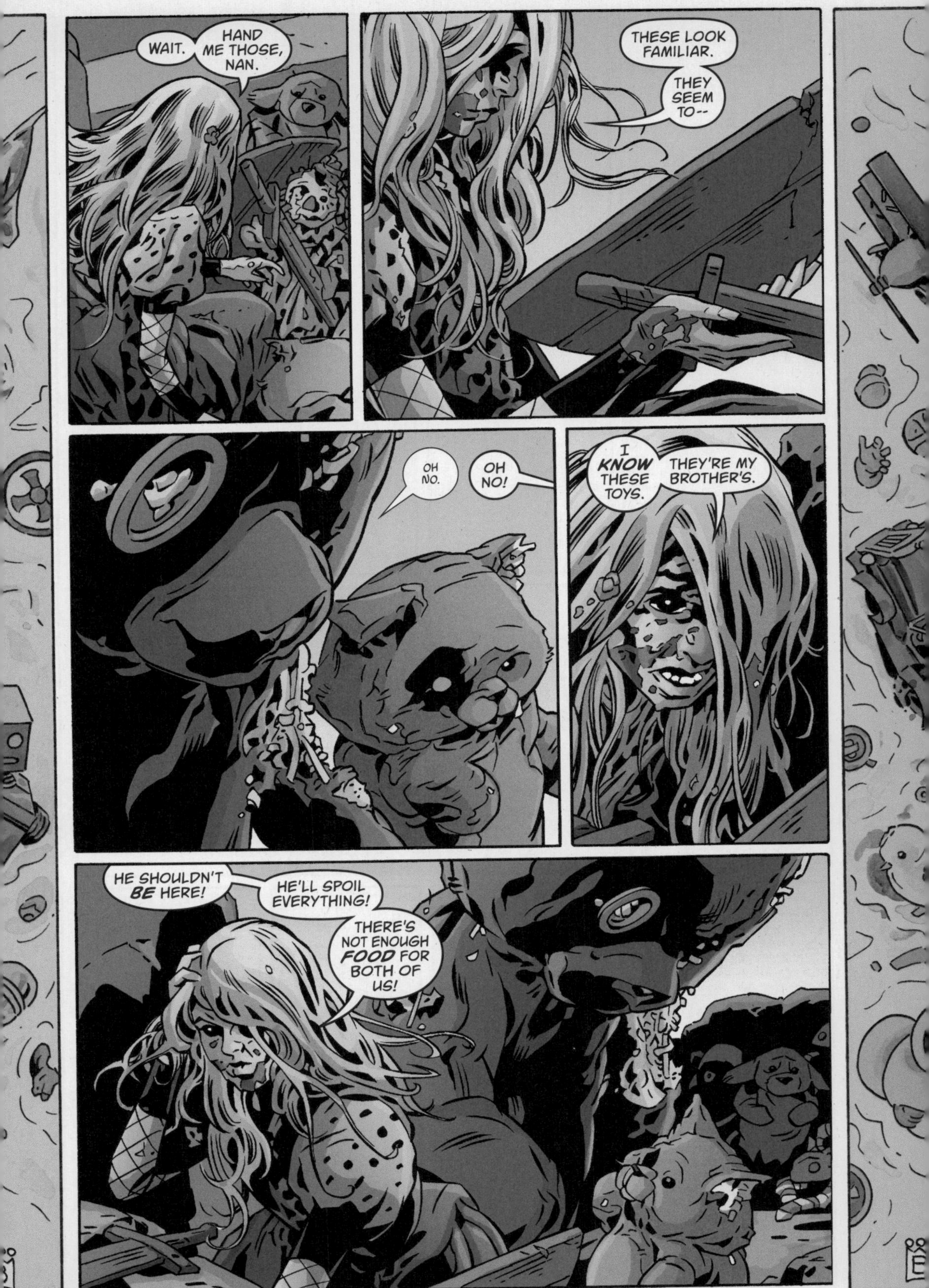
WAIT.
HAND ME THOSE, NAN.
THESE LOOK FAMILIAR.
THEY SEEM TO--
OH NO.
OH NO!
I KNOW THESE TOYS.
THEY'RE MY BROTHER'S.
HE SHOULDN'T BE HERE!
HE'LL SPOIL EVERYTHING!
THERE'S NOT ENOUGH FOOD FOR BOTH OF US!

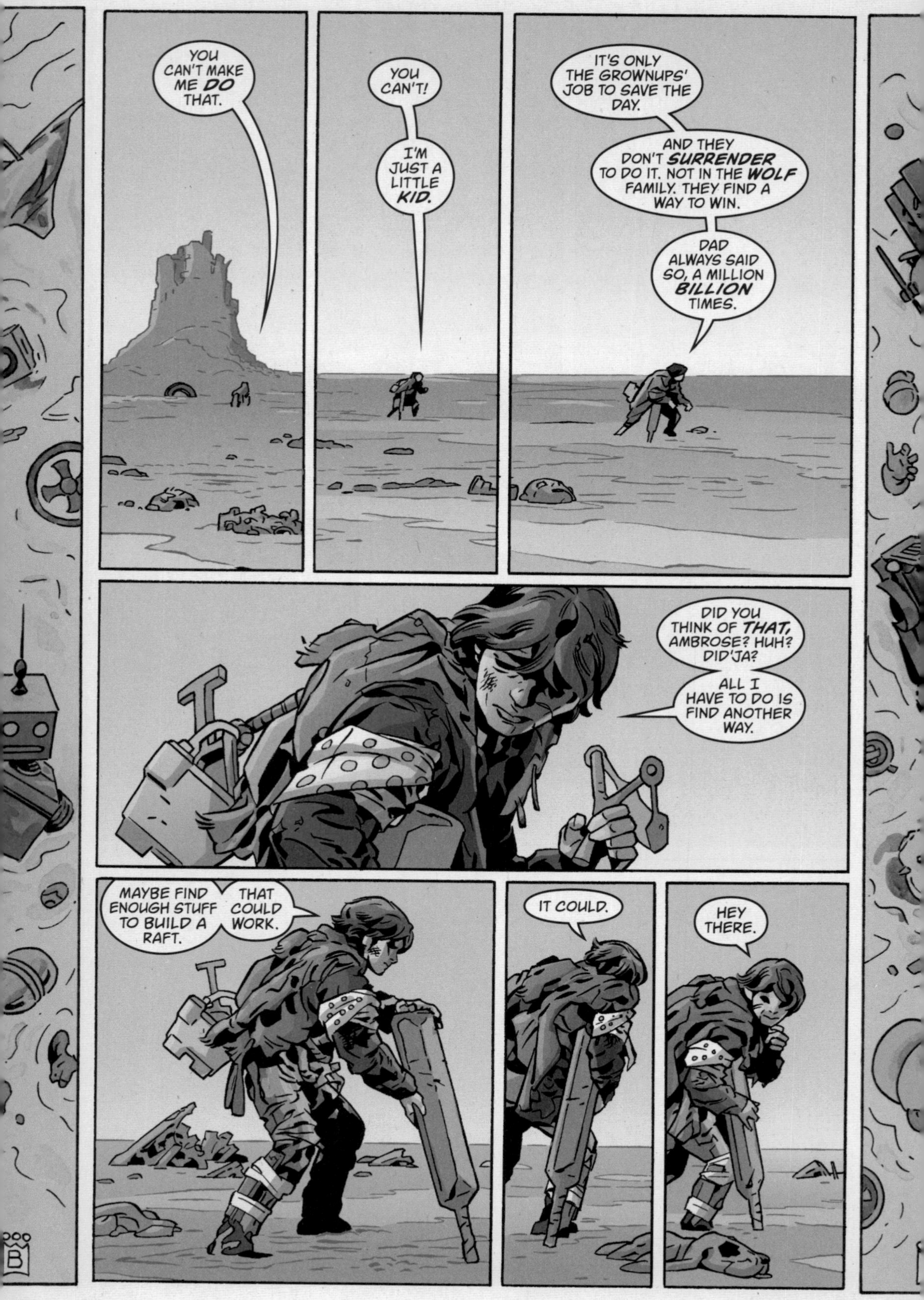
YOU CAN'T MAKE ME DO THAT.
YOU CAN'T!
I'M JUST A LITTLE KID.
IT'S ONLY THE GROWNUPS' JOB TO SAVE THE DAY.
AND THEY DON'T SURRENDER TO DO IT. NOT IN THE WOLF FAMILY. THEY FIND A WAY TO WIN.
DAD ALWAYS SAID SO, A MILLION BILLION TIMES.
DID YOU THINK OF THAT, AMBROSE? HUH? DID'JA?
ALL I HAVE TO DO IS FIND ANOTHER WAY.
MAYBE FIND ENOUGH STUFF TO BUILD A RAFT.
THAT COULD WORK.
IT COULD.
HEY THERE.

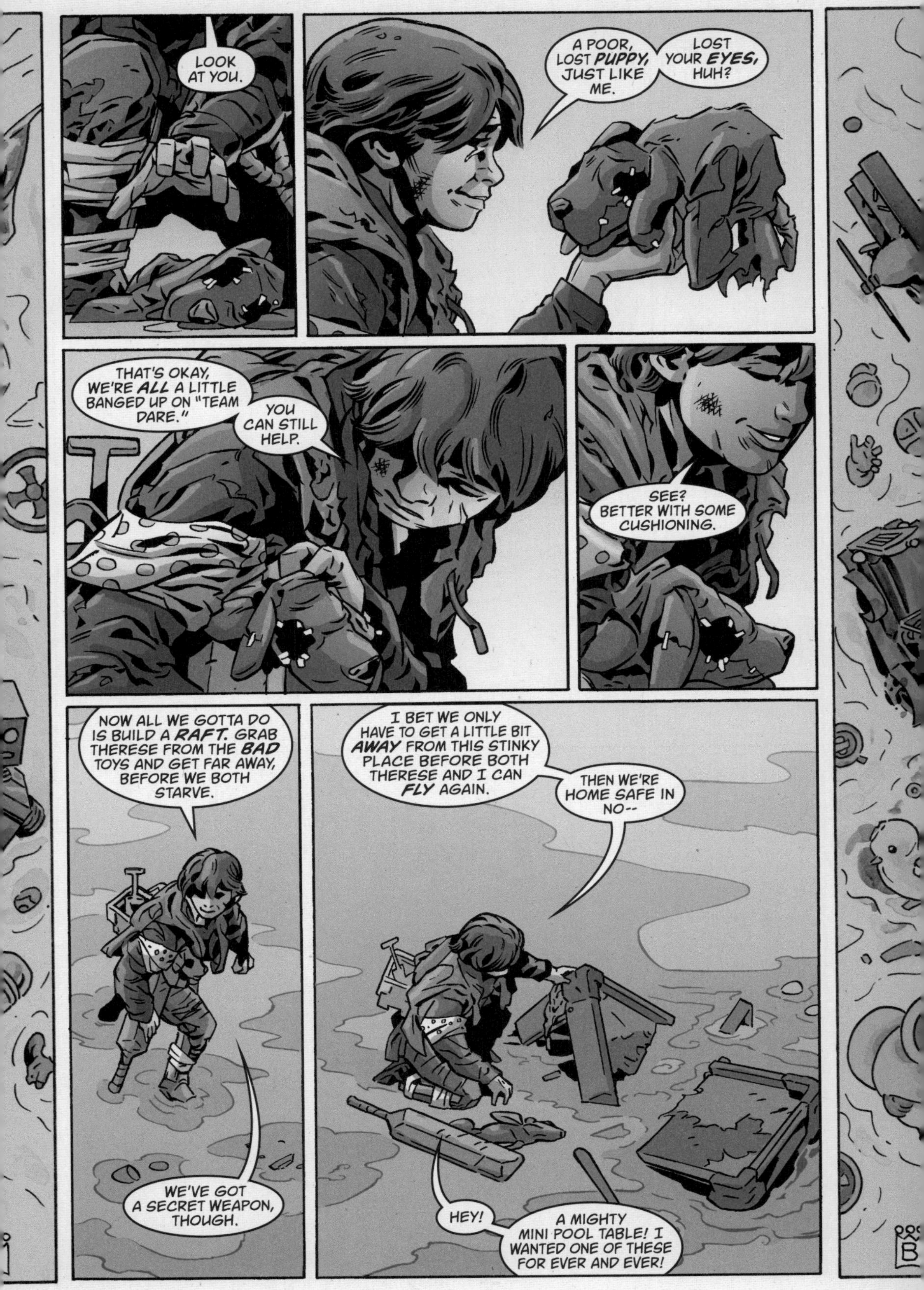
LOOK AT YOU.
A POOR, LOST PUPPY, JUST LIKE ME.
LOST YOUR EYES, HUH?
THAT'S OKAY, WE'RE ALL A LITTLE BANGED UP ON "TEAM DARE."
YOU CAN STILL HELP.
SEE? BETTER WITH SOME CUSHIONING.
NOW ALL WE GOTTA DO IS BUILD A RAFT. GRAB THERESE FROM THE BAD TOYS AND GET FAR AWAY, BEFORE WE BOTH STARVE.
WE'VE GOT A SECRET WEAPON, THOUGH.
I BET WE ONLY HAVE TO GET A LITTLE BIT AWAY FROM THIS STINKY PLACE BEFORE BOTH THERESE AND I CAN FLY AGAIN.
THEN WE'RE HOME SAFE IN NO--
HEY!
A MIGHTY MINI POOL TABLE! I WANTED ONE OF THESE FOR EVER AND EVER!

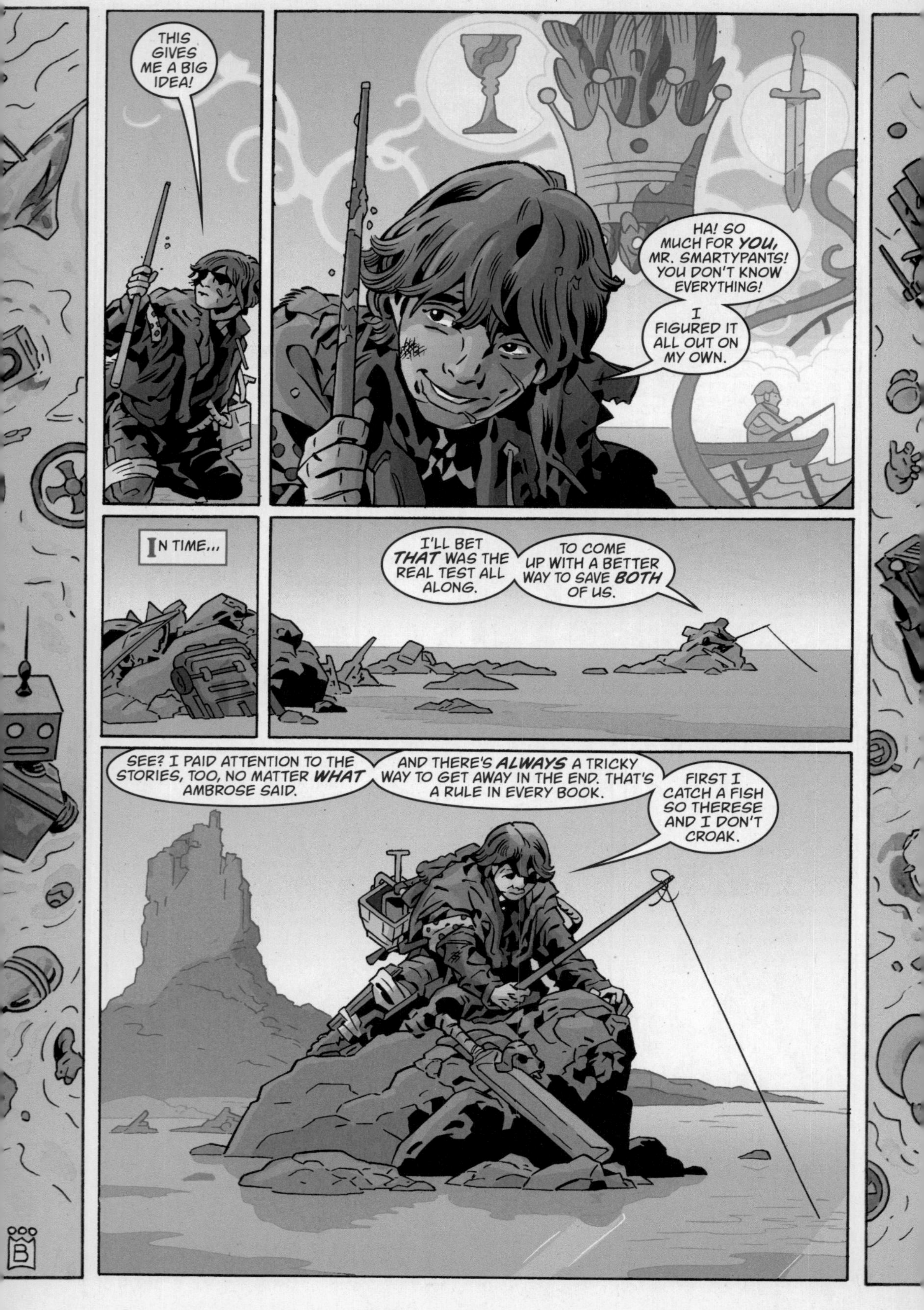
THIS GIVES ME A BIG IDEA!
HA! SO MUCH FOR YOU, MR. SMARTYPANTS! YOU DON'T KNOW EVERYTHING!
I FIGURED IT ALL OUT ON MY OWN.
IN TIME...
I'LL BET THAT WAS THE REAL TEST ALL ALONG.
TO COME UP WITH A BETTER WAY TO SAVE BOTH OF US.
SEE? I PAID ATTENTION TO THE STORIES, TOO, NO MATTER WHAT AMBROSE SAID.
AND THERE'S ALWAYS A TRICKY WAY TO GET AWAY IN THE END. THAT'S A RULE IN EVERY BOOK.
FIRST I CATCH A FISH SO THERESE AND I DON'T CROAK.

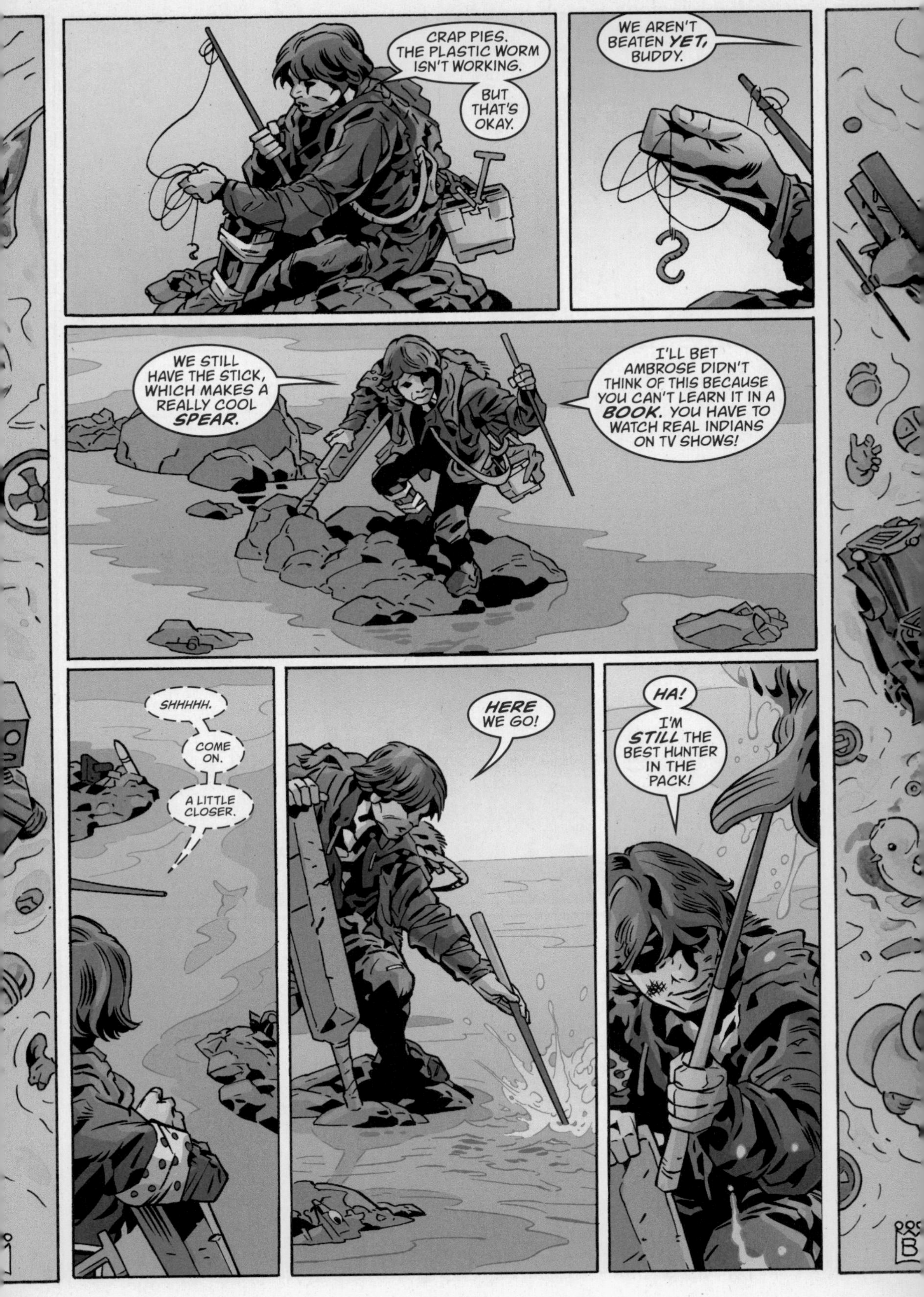
CRAP PIES. THE PLASTIC WORM ISN'T WORKING.
BUT THAT'S OKAY.
WE AREN'T BEATEN YET, BUDDY.
WE STILL HAVE THE STICK, WHICH MAKES A REALLY COOL SPEAR.
I'LL BET AMBROSE DIDN'T THINK OF THIS BECAUSE YOU CAN'T LEARN IT IN A BOOK. YOU HAVE TO WATCH REAL INDIANS ON TV SHOWS!
SHHHHH.
COME ON.
A LITTLE CLOSER.
HERE WE GO!
HA!
I'M STILL THE BEST HUNTER IN THE PACK!

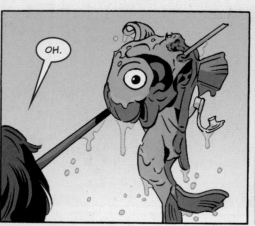

OH.

RUBBER.

VERY FUNNY.

THAT'S JUST *CHEATING!*

I WON! I *DID!*

I FOUND A DIFFERENT WAY, FAIR AND SQUARE, BUT YOU--!

I DON'T *WANT* TO DIE.

PLEASE! NOT YET.

I'M STILL A LITTLE KID.

CAN'T I *GROW UP* JUST A LITTLE MORE, FIRST?

I NEVER EVEN GOT TO *DO* ANYTHING YET.

PLEASE?

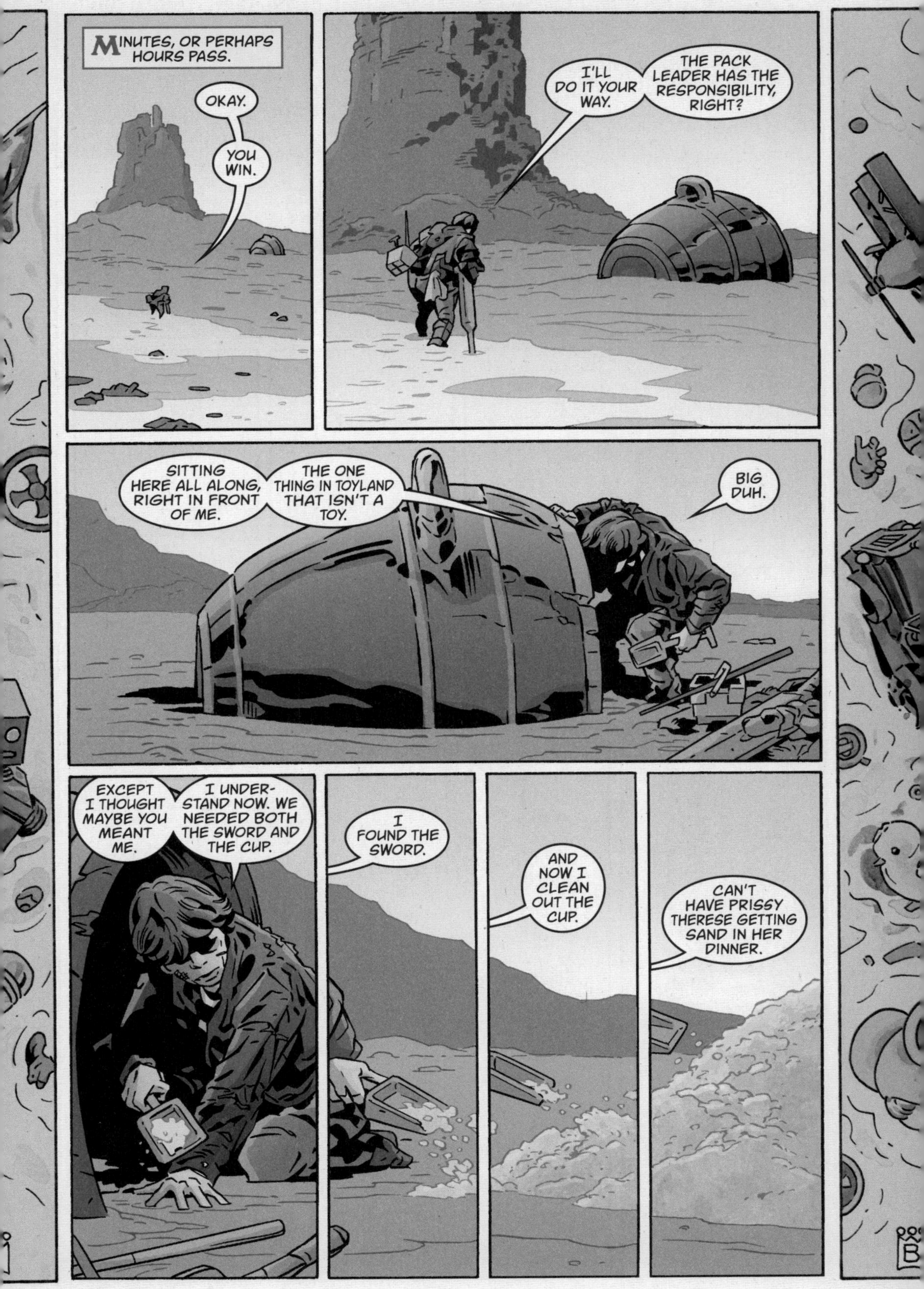
MINUTES, OR PERHAPS HOURS PASS.
OKAY.
YOU WIN.
I'LL DO IT YOUR WAY.
THE PACK LEADER HAS THE RESPONSIBILITY, RIGHT?
SITTING HERE ALL ALONG, RIGHT IN FRONT OF ME.
THE ONE THING IN TOYLAND THAT ISN'T A TOY.
BIG DUH.
EXCEPT I THOUGHT MAYBE YOU MEANT ME.
I UNDERSTAND NOW. WE NEEDED BOTH THE SWORD AND THE CUP.
I FOUND THE SWORD.
AND NOW I CLEAN OUT THE CUP.
CAN'T HAVE PRISSY THERESE GETTING SAND IN HER DINNER.

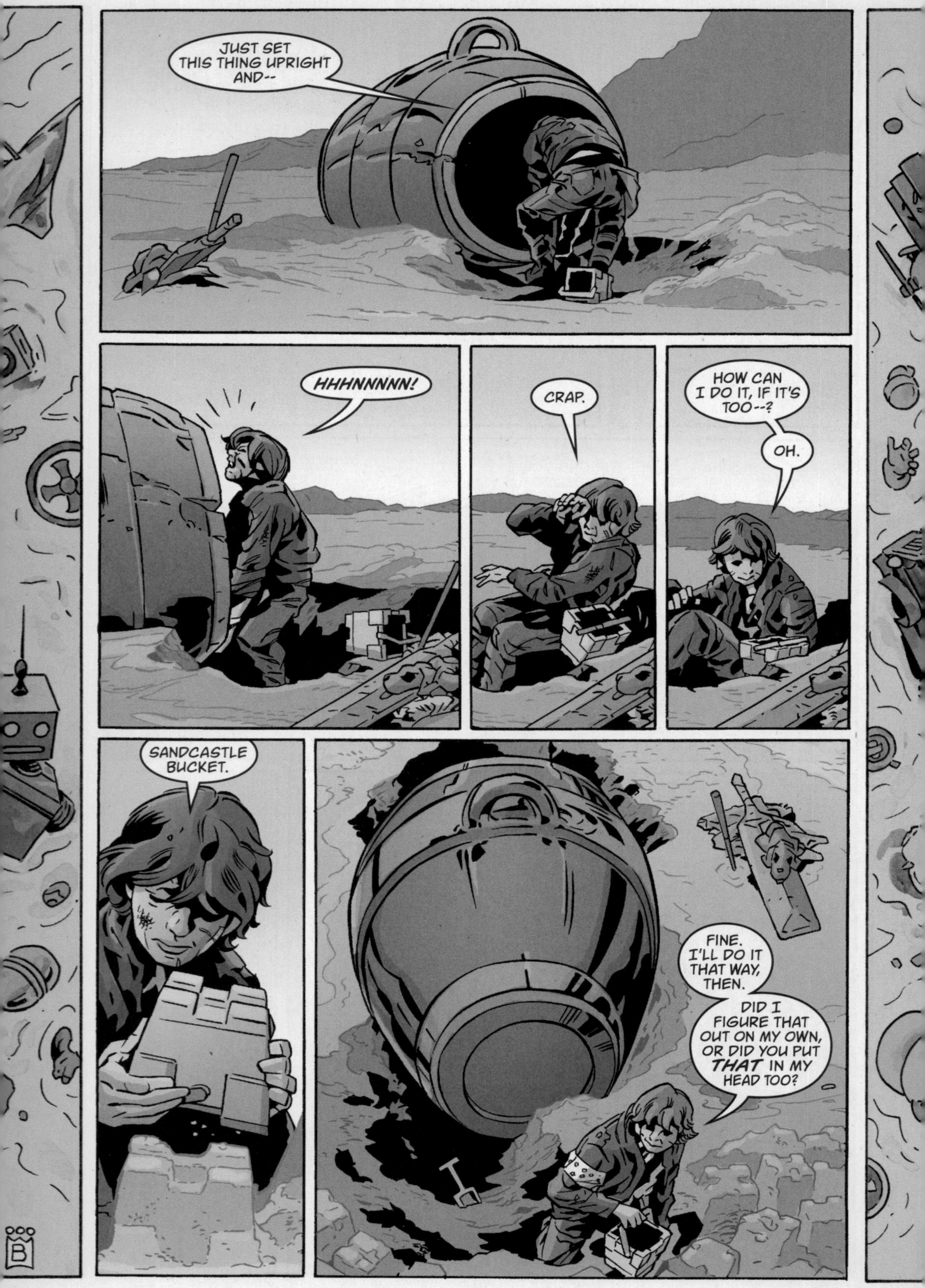
JUST SET THIS THING UPRIGHT AND--
HHHNNNNN!
CRAP.
HOW CAN I DO IT, IF IT'S TOO--?
OH.
SANDCASTLE BUCKET.
FINE. I'LL DO IT THAT WAY, THEN.
DID I FIGURE THAT OUT ON MY OWN, OR DID YOU PUT *THAT* IN MY HEAD TOO?

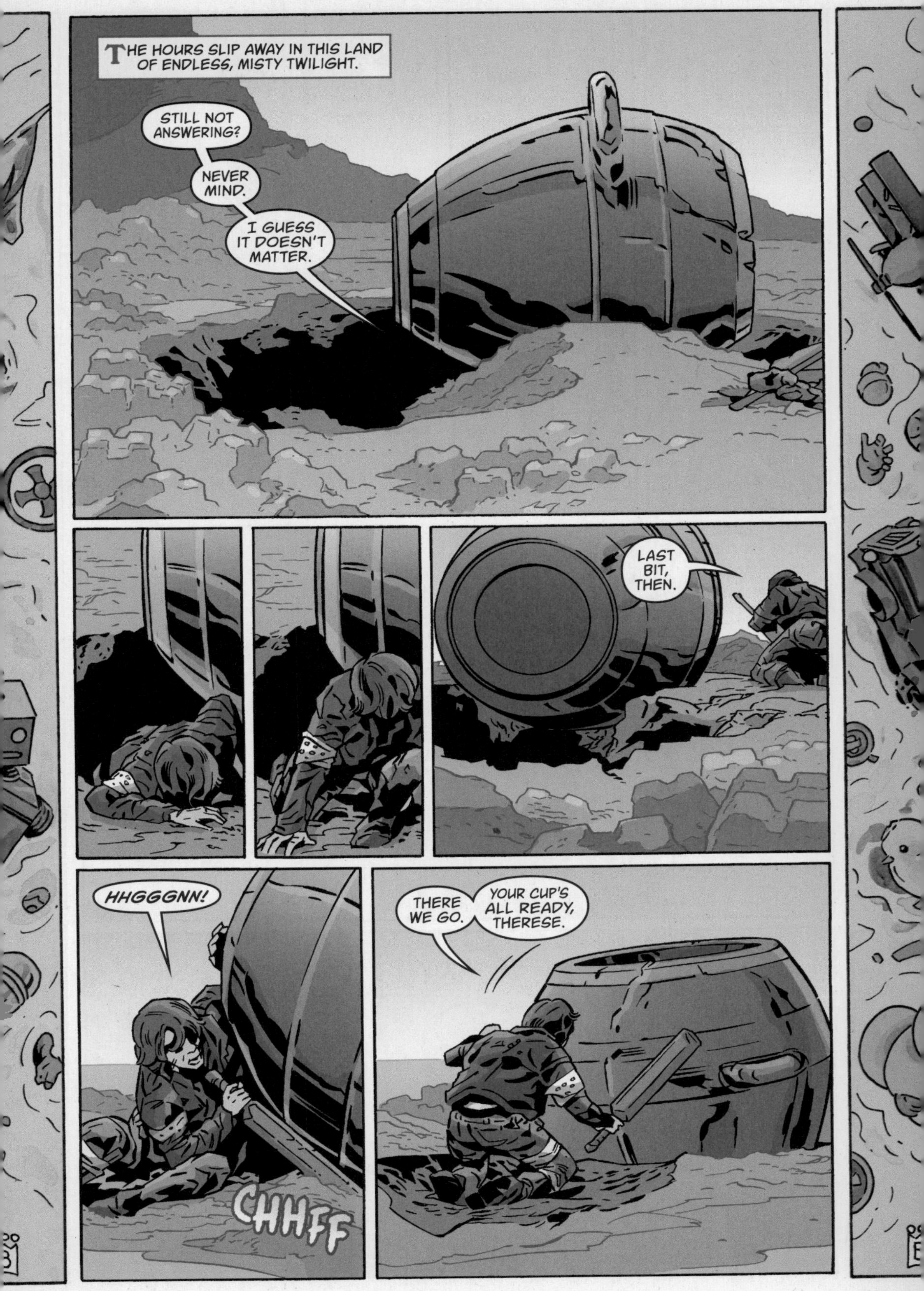
THE HOURS SLIP AWAY IN THIS LAND OF ENDLESS, MISTY TWILIGHT.
STILL NOT ANSWERING?
NEVER MIND.
I GUESS IT DOESN'T MATTER.
LAST BIT, THEN.
HHGGGNN!
CHHFF
THERE WE GO.
YOUR CUP'S ALL READY, THERESE.

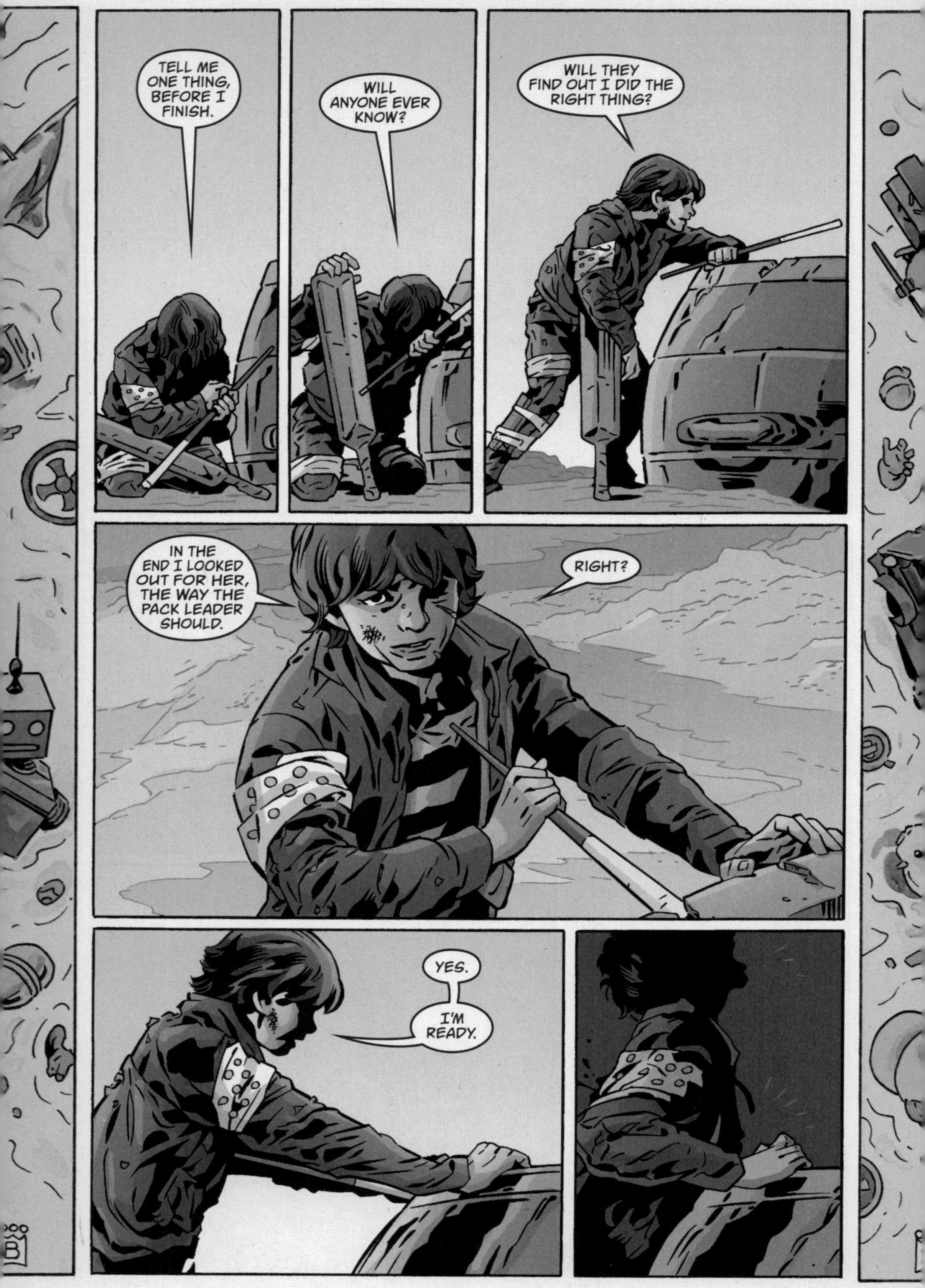

TELL ME ONE THING, BEFORE I FINISH.
WILL ANYONE EVER KNOW?
WILL THEY FIND OUT I DID THE RIGHT THING?
IN THE END I LOOKED OUT FOR HER, THE WAY THE PACK LEADER SHOULD.
RIGHT?
YES.
I'M READY.

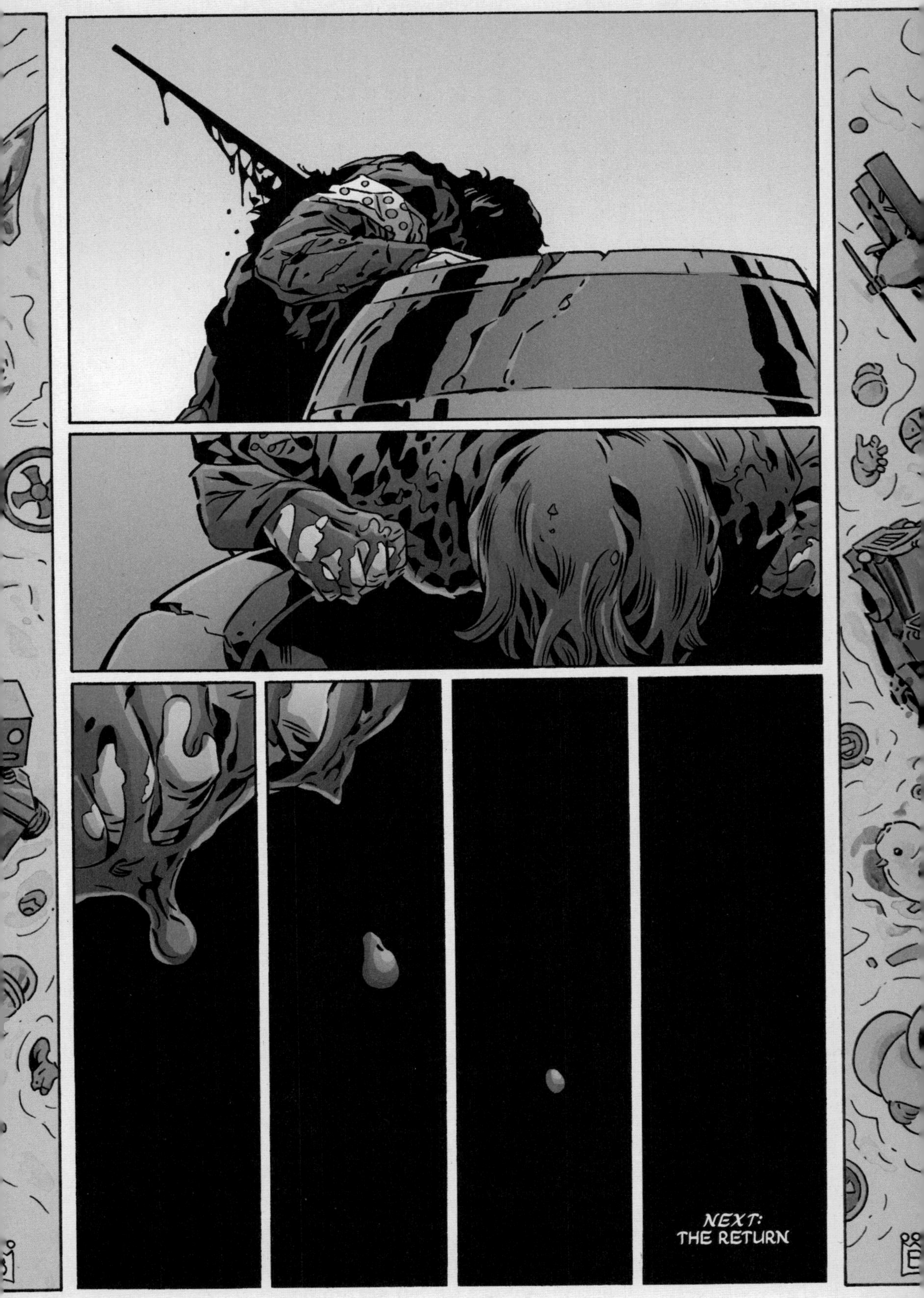
NEXT:
THE RETURN

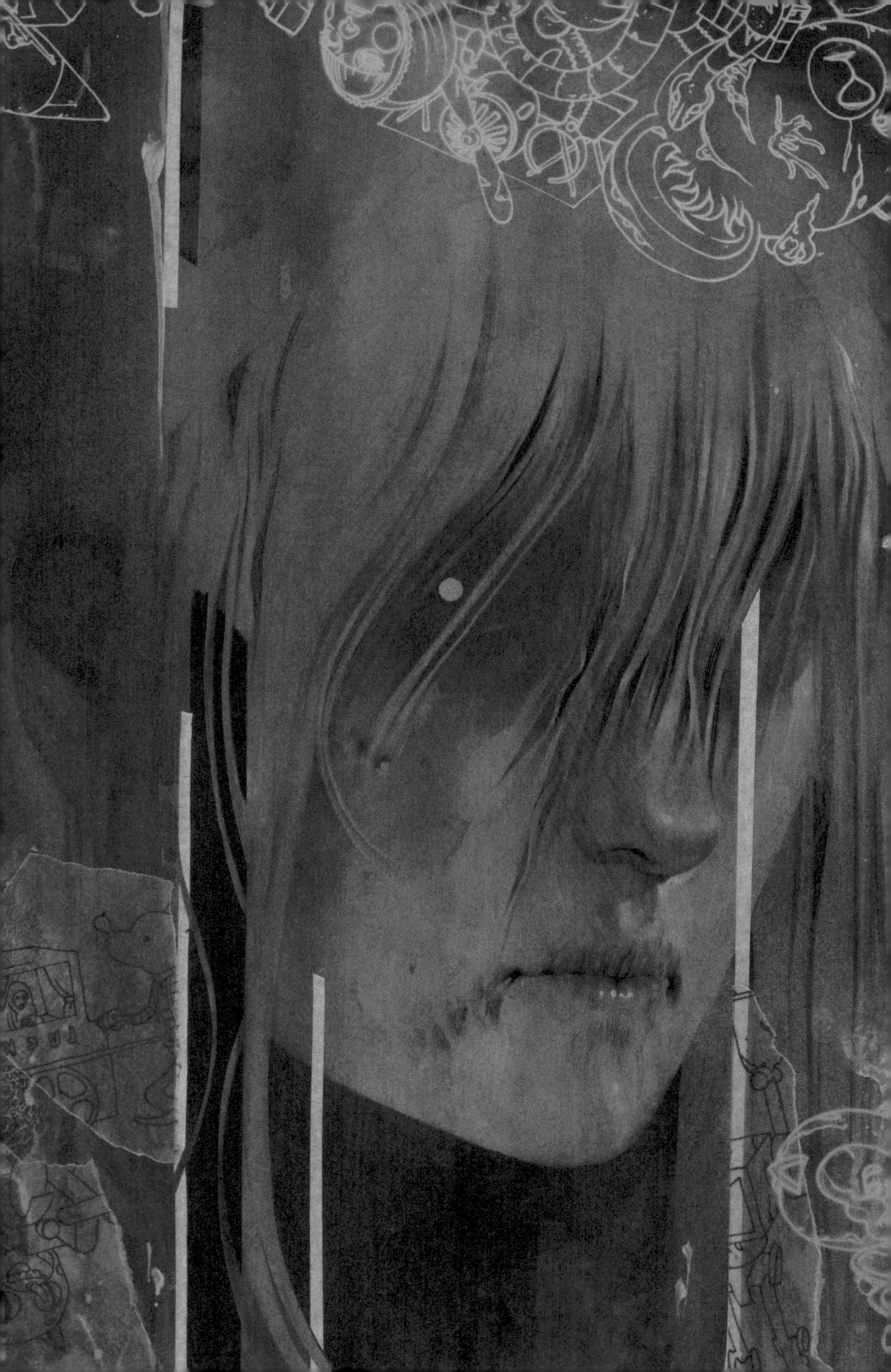

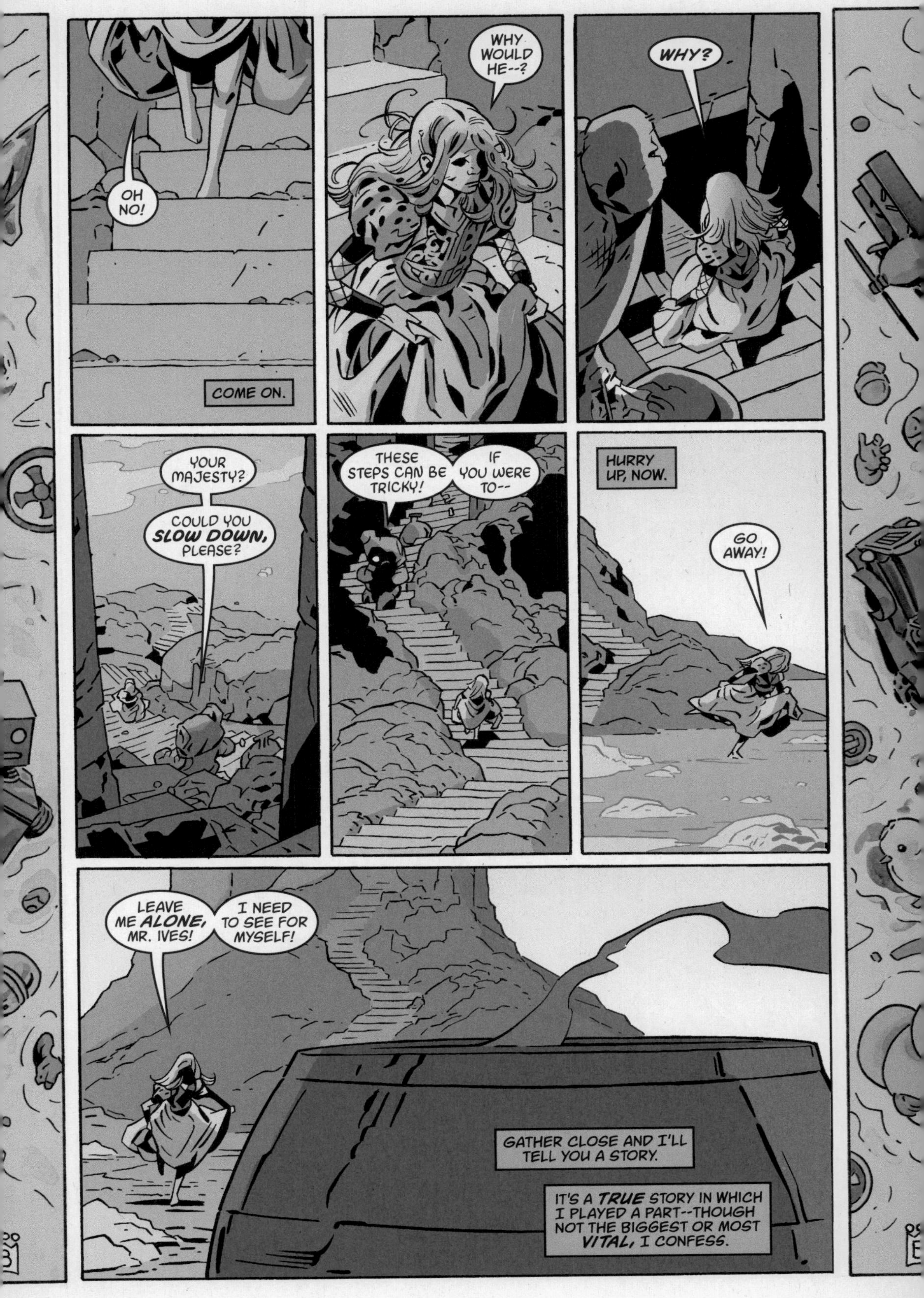
OH NO!
COME ON.
WHY WOULD HE--?
WHY?
YOUR MAJESTY?
COULD YOU SLOW DOWN, PLEASE?
THESE STEPS CAN BE TRICKY!
IF YOU WERE TO--
HURRY UP, NOW.
GO AWAY!
LEAVE ME ALONE, MR. IVES!
I NEED TO SEE FOR MYSELF!
GATHER CLOSE AND I'LL TELL YOU A STORY.
IT'S A TRUE STORY IN WHICH I PLAYED A PART--THOUGH NOT THE BIGGEST OR MOST VITAL, I CONFESS.

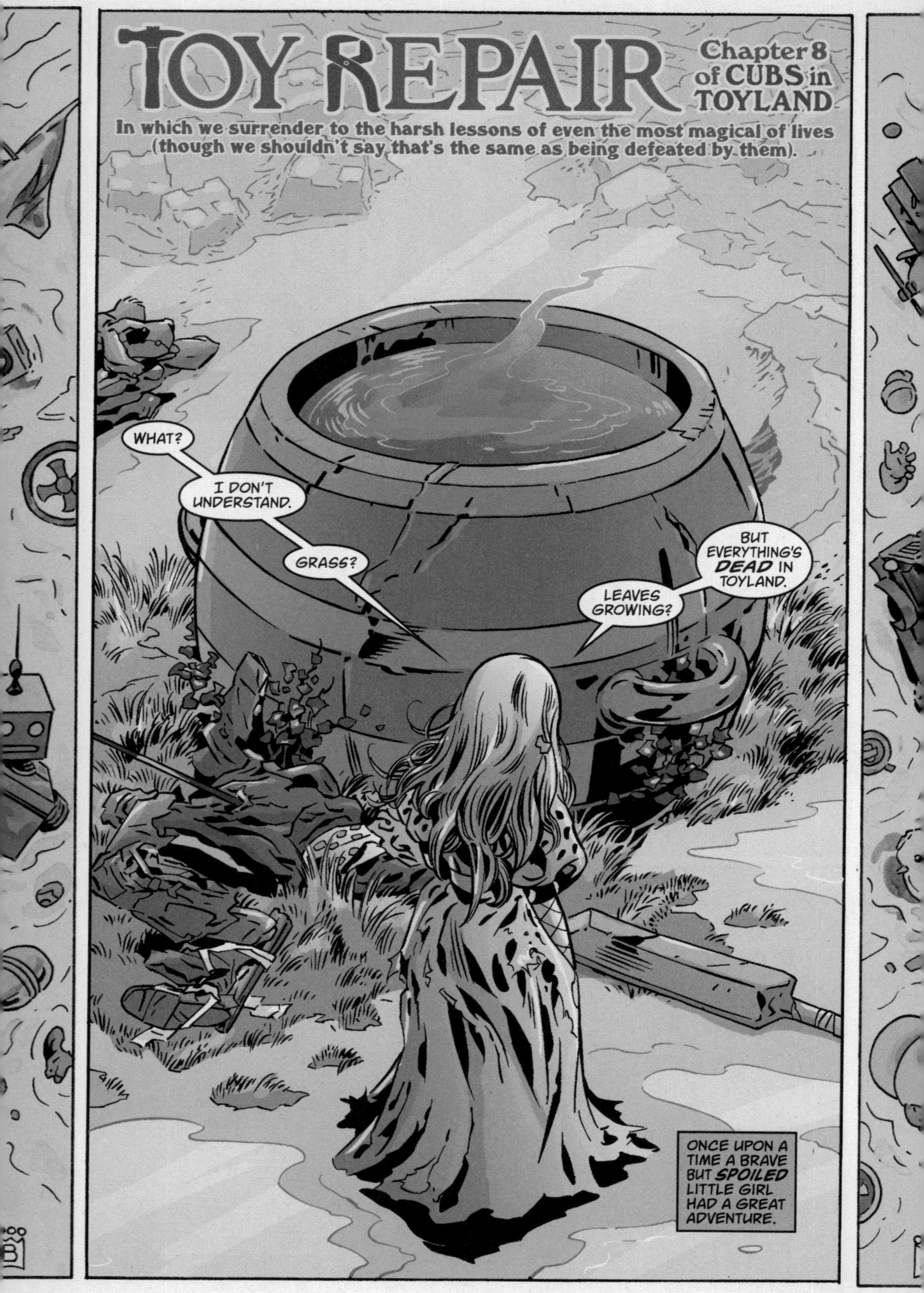
TOY REPAIR
Chapter 8 of CUBS in TOYLAND
In which we surrender to the harsh lessons of even the most magical of lives (though we shouldn't say that's the same as being defeated by them).
WHAT?
I DON'T UNDERSTAND.
GRASS?
LEAVES GROWING?
BUT EVERYTHING'S DEAD IN TOYLAND.
ONCE UPON A TIME A BRAVE BUT SPOILED LITTLE GIRL HAD A GREAT ADVENTURE.

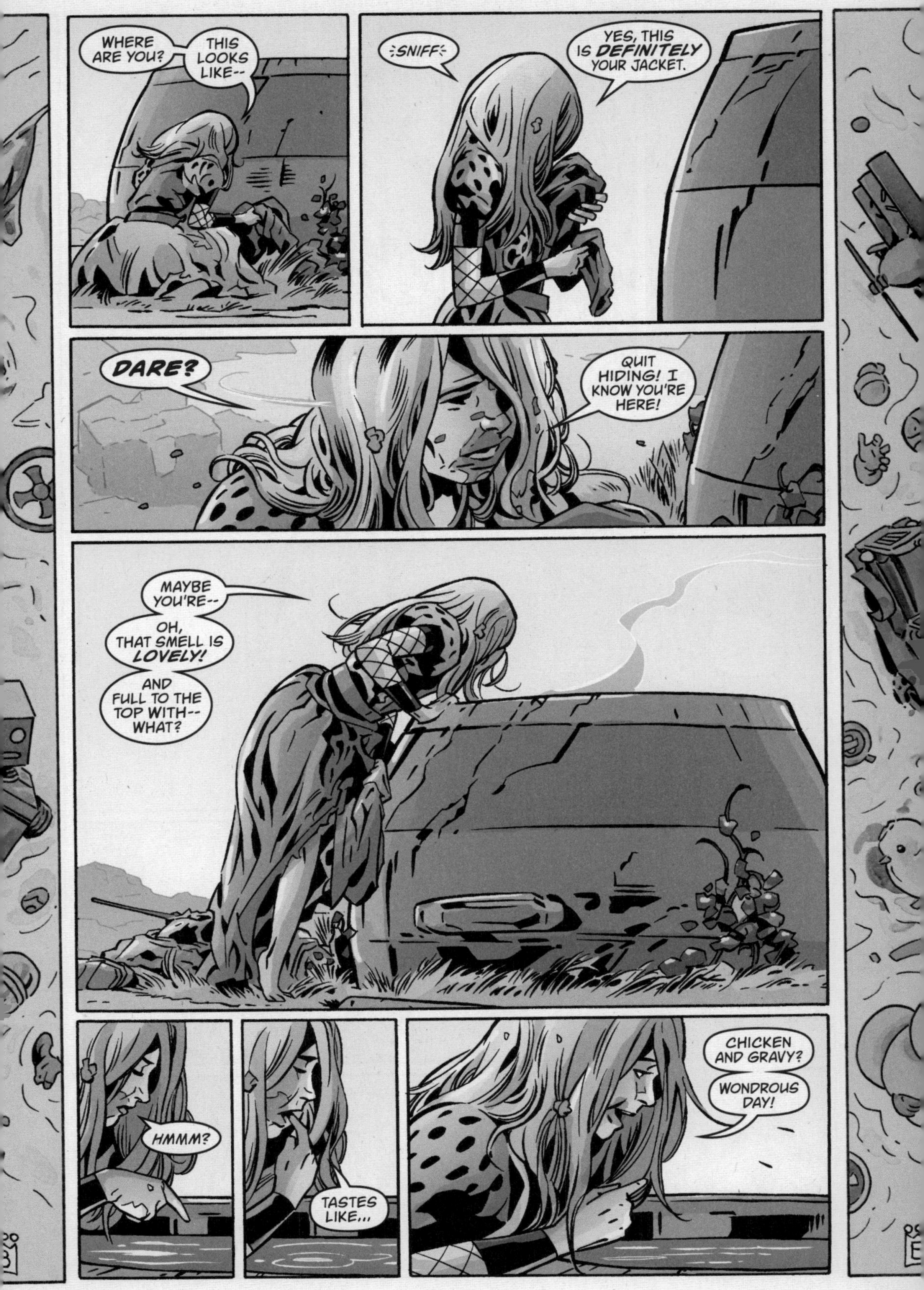

WHERE ARE YOU?
THIS LOOKS LIKE--
:SNIFF:
YES, THIS IS DEFINITELY YOUR JACKET.
DARE?
QUIT HIDING! I KNOW YOU'RE HERE!
MAYBE YOU'RE--
OH, THAT SMELL IS LOVELY!
AND FULL TO THE TOP WITH-- WHAT?
HMMM?
TASTES LIKE...
CHICKEN AND GRAVY?
WONDROUS DAY!

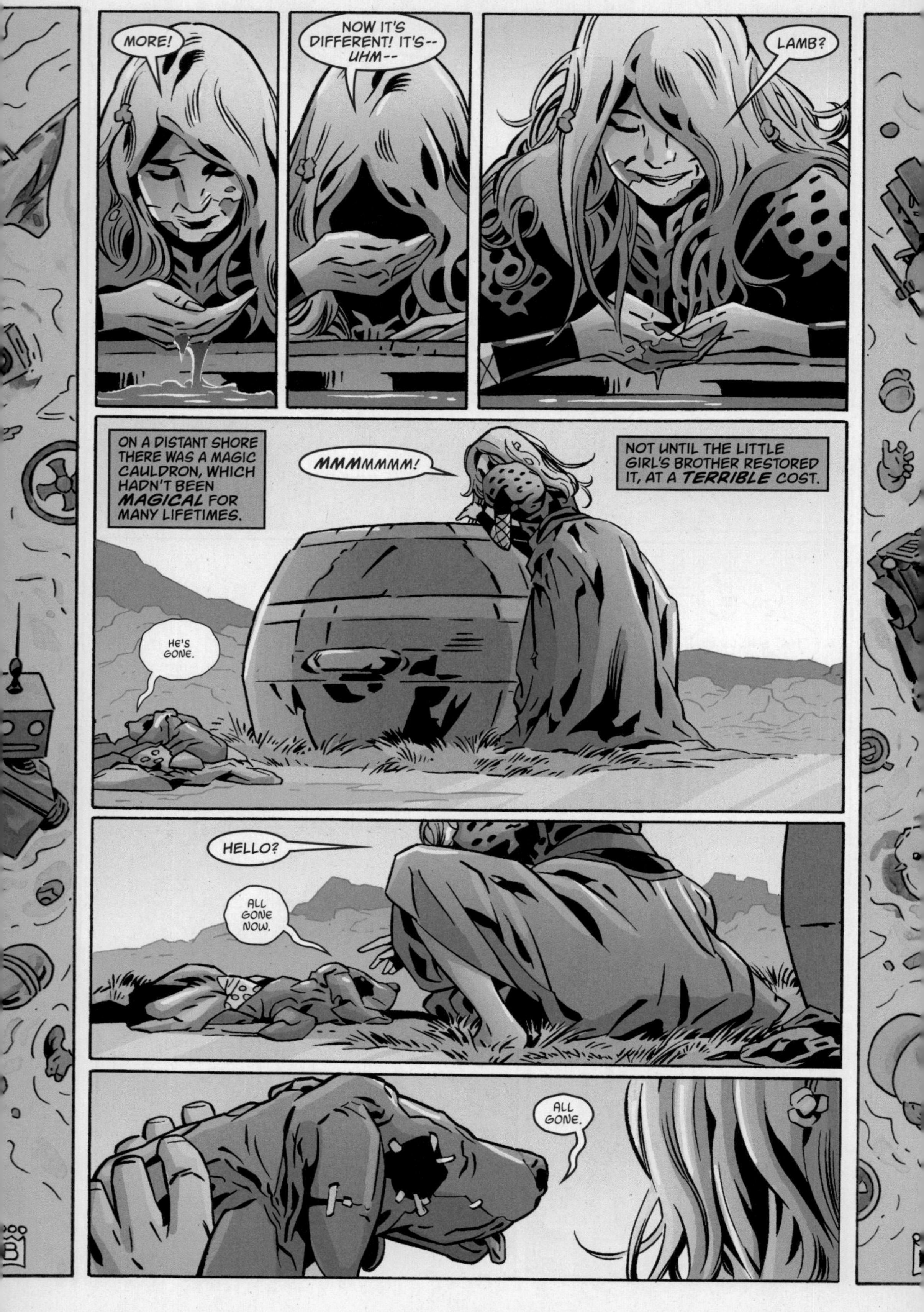
MORE!
NOW IT'S DIFFERENT! IT'S-- UHM--
LAMB?
ON A DISTANT SHORE THERE WAS A MAGIC CAULDRON, WHICH HADN'T BEEN MAGICAL FOR MANY LIFETIMES.
MMMMMMM!
NOT UNTIL THE LITTLE GIRL'S BROTHER RESTORED IT, AT A TERRIBLE COST.
HE'S GONE.
HELLO?
ALL GONE NOW.
ALL GONE.

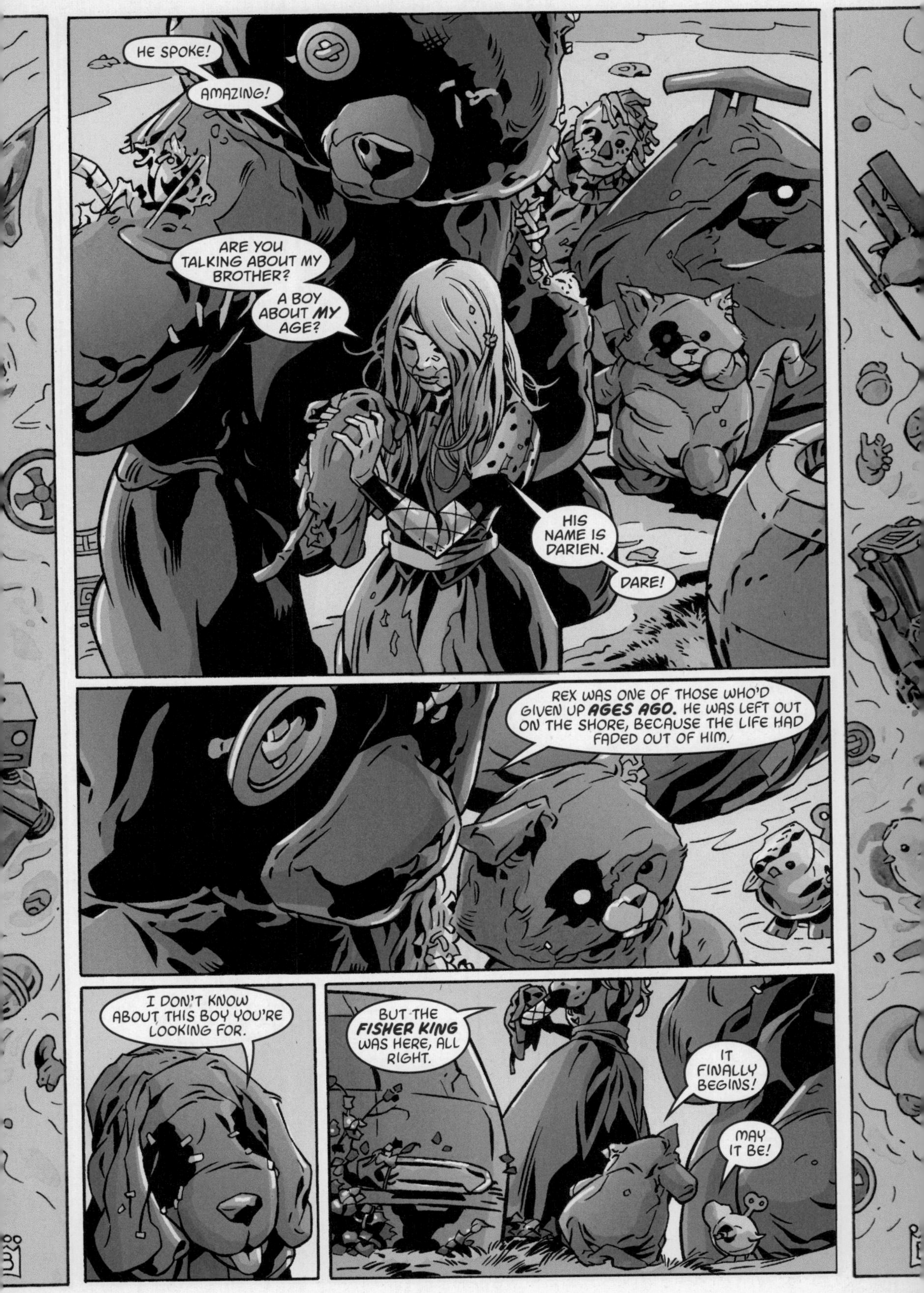

HE SPOKE!
AMAZING!
ARE YOU TALKING ABOUT MY BROTHER?
A BOY ABOUT *MY* AGE?
HIS NAME IS DARIEN.
DARE!
REX WAS ONE OF THOSE WHO'D GIVEN UP **AGES AGO.** HE WAS LEFT OUT ON THE SHORE, BECAUSE THE LIFE HAD FADED OUT OF HIM.
I DON'T KNOW ABOUT THIS BOY YOU'RE LOOKING FOR.
BUT THE ***FISHER KING*** WAS HERE, ALL RIGHT.
IT FINALLY BEGINS!
MAY IT BE!

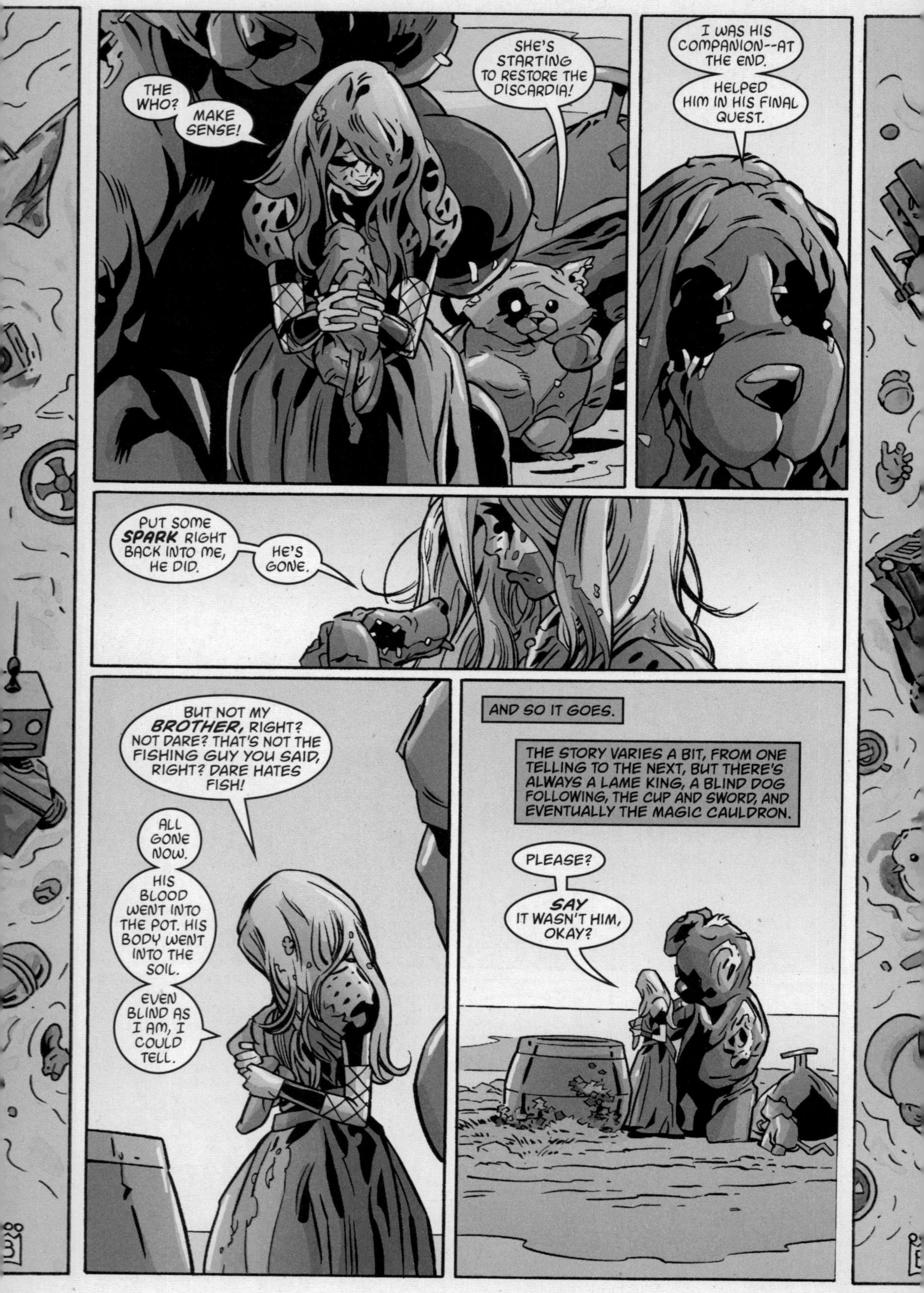
THE WHO? MAKE SENSE!
SHE'S STARTING TO RESTORE THE DISCARDIA!
I WAS HIS COMPANION--AT THE END.
HELPED HIM IN HIS FINAL QUEST.
PUT SOME SPARK RIGHT BACK INTO ME, HE DID.
HE'S GONE.
BUT NOT MY BROTHER, RIGHT? NOT DARE? THAT'S NOT THE FISHING GUY YOU SAID, RIGHT? DARE HATES FISH!
ALL GONE NOW.
HIS BLOOD WENT INTO THE POT. HIS BODY WENT INTO THE SOIL.
EVEN BLIND AS I AM, I COULD TELL.
AND SO IT GOES.
THE STORY VARIES A BIT, FROM ONE TELLING TO THE NEXT, BUT THERE'S ALWAYS A LAME KING, A BLIND DOG FOLLOWING, THE CUP AND SWORD, AND EVENTUALLY THE MAGIC CAULDRON.
PLEASE?
SAY IT WASN'T HIM, OKAY?

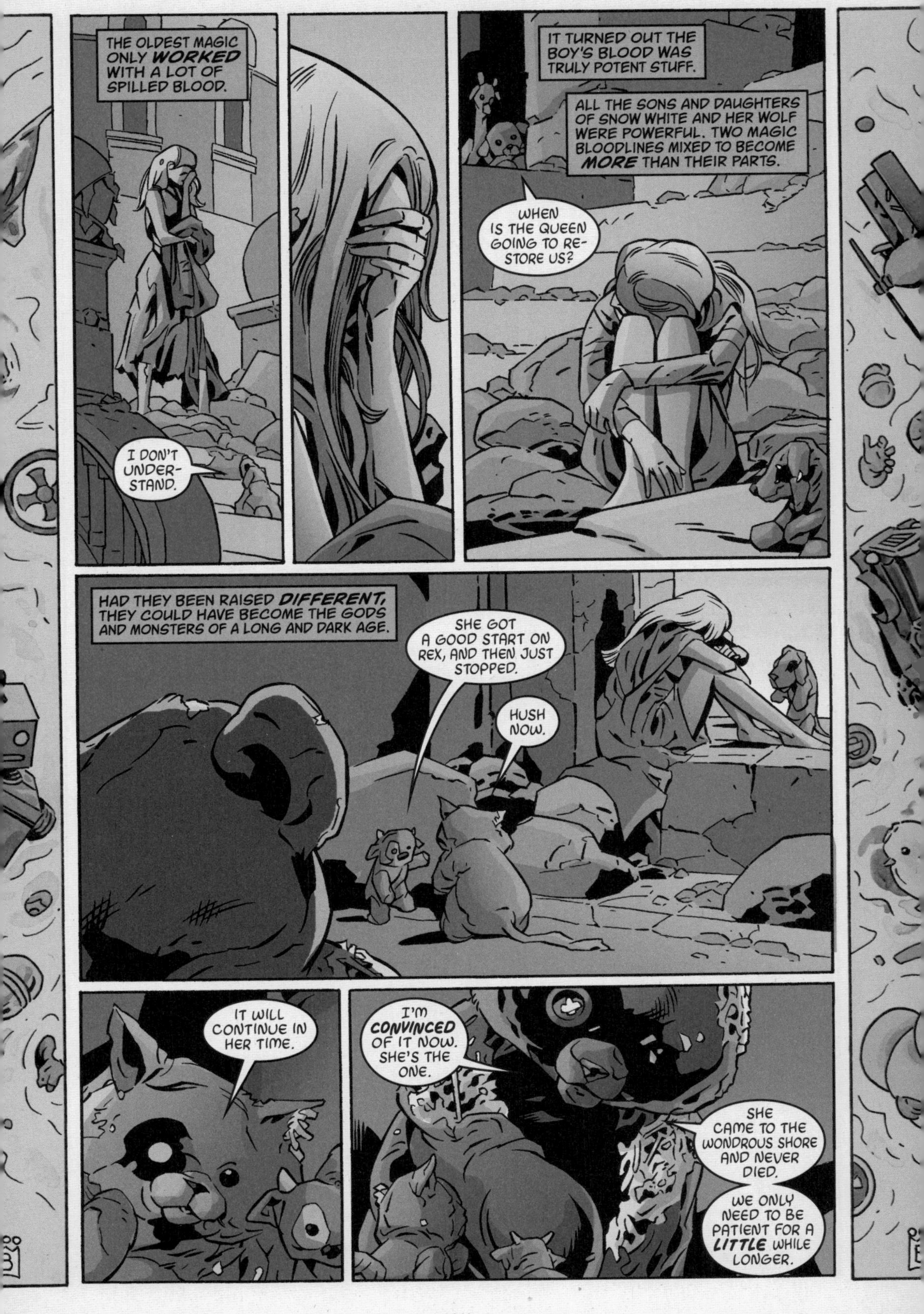

THE OLDEST MAGIC ONLY WORKED WITH A LOT OF SPILLED BLOOD.
I DON'T UNDER-STAND.
IT TURNED OUT THE BOY'S BLOOD WAS TRULY POTENT STUFF.
ALL THE SONS AND DAUGHTERS OF SNOW WHITE AND HER WOLF WERE POWERFUL. TWO MAGIC BLOODLINES MIXED TO BECOME MORE THAN THEIR PARTS.
WHEN IS THE QUEEN GOING TO RE-STORE US?
HAD THEY BEEN RAISED DIFFERENT, THEY COULD HAVE BECOME THE GODS AND MONSTERS OF A LONG AND DARK AGE.
SHE GOT A GOOD START ON REX, AND THEN JUST STOPPED.
HUSH NOW.
IT WILL CONTINUE IN HER TIME.
I'M CONVINCED OF IT NOW. SHE'S THE ONE.
SHE CAME TO THE WONDROUS SHORE AND NEVER DIED.
WE ONLY NEED TO BE PATIENT FOR A LITTLE WHILE LONGER.

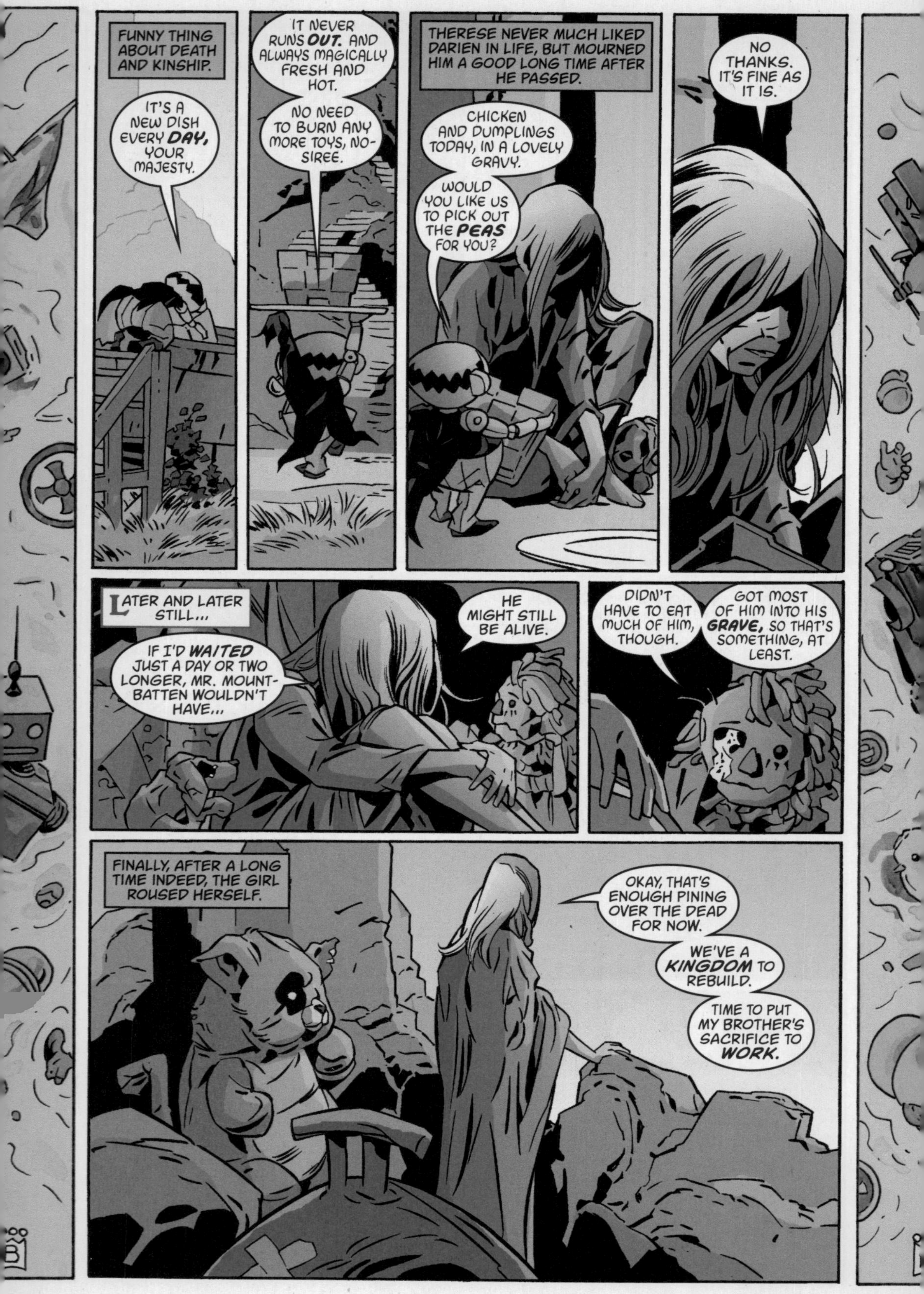
FUNNY THING ABOUT DEATH AND KINSHIP.
IT'S A NEW DISH EVERY DAY, YOUR MAJESTY.
IT NEVER RUNS OUT. AND ALWAYS MAGICALLY FRESH AND HOT.
NO NEED TO BURN ANY MORE TOYS, NO-SIREE.
THERESE NEVER MUCH LIKED DARIEN IN LIFE, BUT MOURNED HIM A GOOD LONG TIME AFTER HE PASSED.
CHICKEN AND DUMPLINGS TODAY, IN A LOVELY GRAVY.
WOULD YOU LIKE US TO PICK OUT THE PEAS FOR YOU?
NO THANKS. IT'S FINE AS IT IS.
LATER AND LATER STILL...
IF I'D WAITED JUST A DAY OR TWO LONGER, MR. MOUNT-BATTEN WOULDN'T HAVE...
HE MIGHT STILL BE ALIVE.
DIDN'T HAVE TO EAT MUCH OF HIM, THOUGH.
GOT MOST OF HIM INTO HIS GRAVE, SO THAT'S SOMETHING, AT LEAST.
FINALLY, AFTER A LONG TIME INDEED, THE GIRL ROUSED HERSELF.
OKAY, THAT'S ENOUGH PINING OVER THE DEAD FOR NOW.
WE'VE A KINGDOM TO REBUILD.
TIME TO PUT MY BROTHER'S SACRIFICE TO WORK.

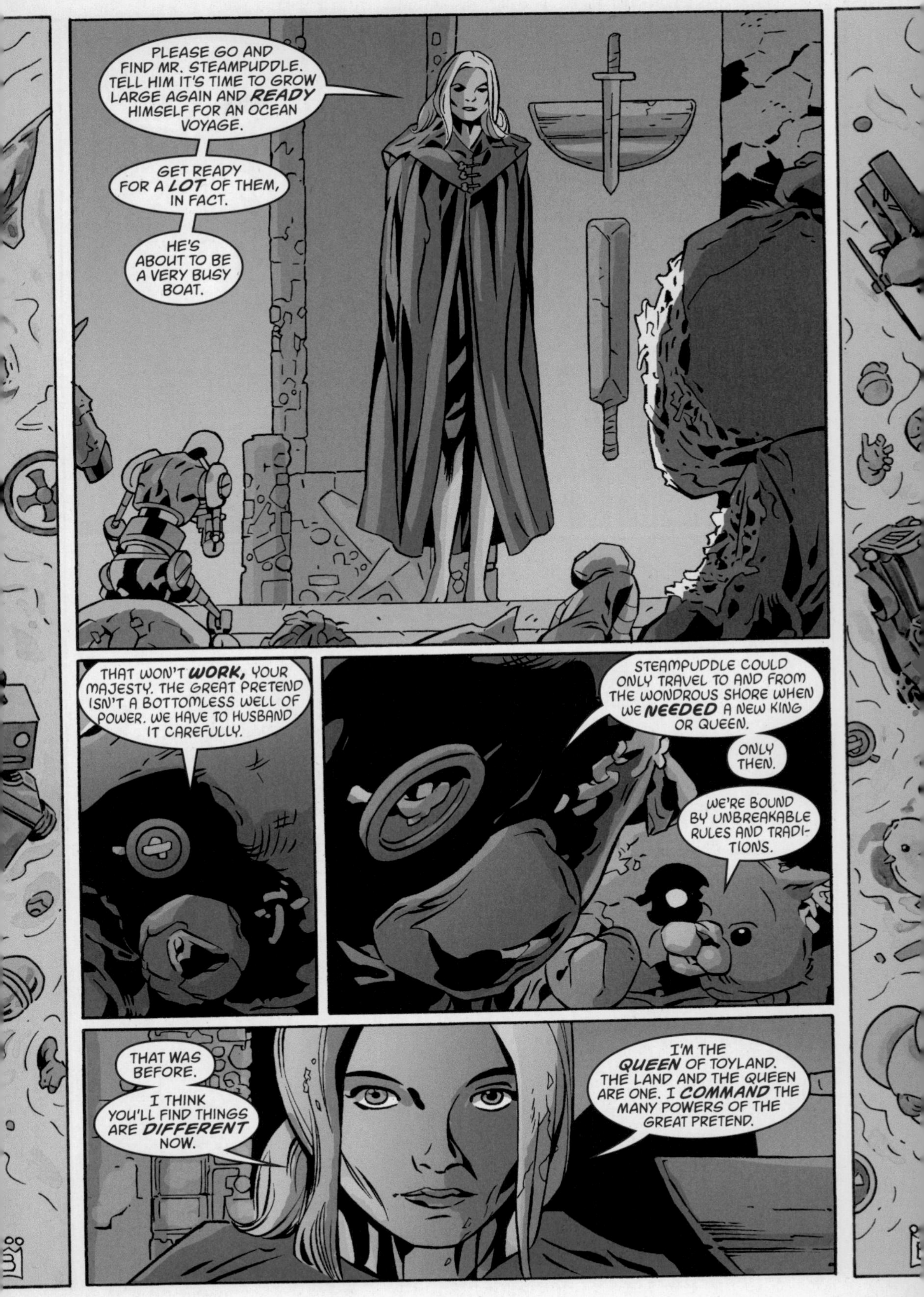
PLEASE GO AND FIND MR. STEAMPUDDLE. TELL HIM IT'S TIME TO GROW LARGE AGAIN AND READY HIMSELF FOR AN OCEAN VOYAGE.
GET READY FOR A LOT OF THEM, IN FACT.
HE'S ABOUT TO BE A VERY BUSY BOAT.
THAT WON'T WORK, YOUR MAJESTY. THE GREAT PRETEND ISN'T A BOTTOMLESS WELL OF POWER. WE HAVE TO HUSBAND IT CAREFULLY.
STEAMPUDDLE COULD ONLY TRAVEL TO AND FROM THE WONDROUS SHORE WHEN WE NEEDED A NEW KING OR QUEEN.
ONLY THEN.
WE'RE BOUND BY UNBREAKABLE RULES AND TRADITIONS.
THAT WAS BEFORE.
I THINK YOU'LL FIND THINGS ARE DIFFERENT NOW.
I'M THE QUEEN OF TOYLAND. THE LAND AND THE QUEEN ARE ONE. I COMMAND THE MANY POWERS OF THE GREAT PRETEND.

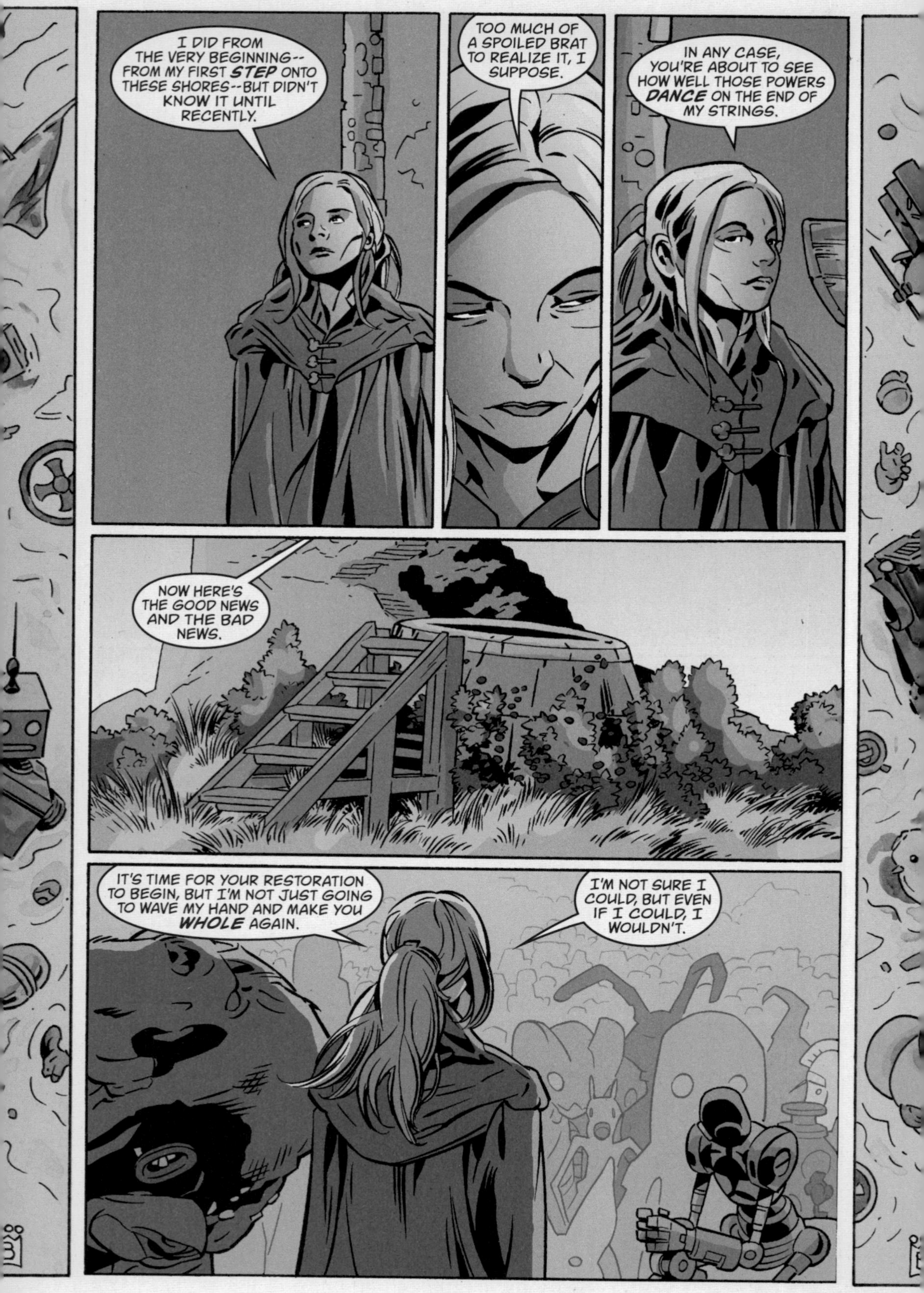
I DID FROM THE VERY BEGINNING-- FROM MY FIRST STEP ONTO THESE SHORES--BUT DIDN'T KNOW IT UNTIL RECENTLY.
TOO MUCH OF A SPOILED BRAT TO REALIZE IT, I SUPPOSE.
IN ANY CASE, YOU'RE ABOUT TO SEE HOW WELL THOSE POWERS DANCE ON THE END OF MY STRINGS.
NOW HERE'S THE GOOD NEWS AND THE BAD NEWS.
IT'S TIME FOR YOUR RESTORATION TO BEGIN, BUT I'M NOT JUST GOING TO WAVE MY HAND AND MAKE YOU WHOLE AGAIN.
I'M NOT SURE I COULD, BUT EVEN IF I COULD, I WOULDN'T.

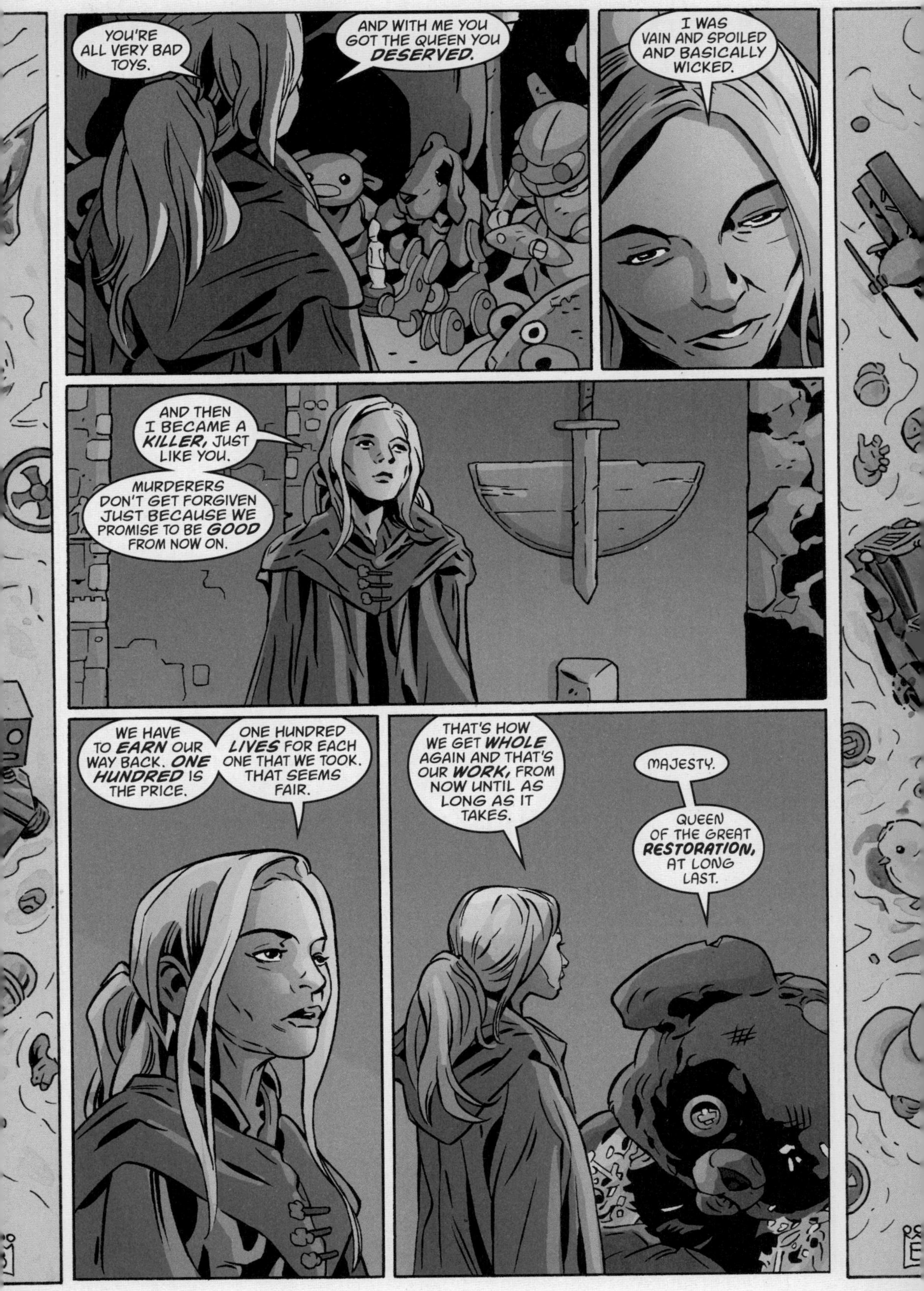
YOU'RE ALL VERY BAD TOYS.
AND WITH ME YOU GOT THE QUEEN YOU DESERVED.
I WAS VAIN AND SPOILED AND BASICALLY WICKED.
AND THEN I BECAME A KILLER, JUST LIKE YOU.
MURDERERS DON'T GET FORGIVEN JUST BECAUSE WE PROMISE TO BE GOOD FROM NOW ON.
WE HAVE TO EARN OUR WAY BACK. ONE HUNDRED IS THE PRICE.
ONE HUNDRED LIVES FOR EACH ONE THAT WE TOOK. THAT SEEMS FAIR.
THAT'S HOW WE GET WHOLE AGAIN AND THAT'S OUR WORK, FROM NOW UNTIL AS LONG AS IT TAKES.
MAJESTY.
QUEEN OF THE GREAT RESTORATION, AT LONG LAST.

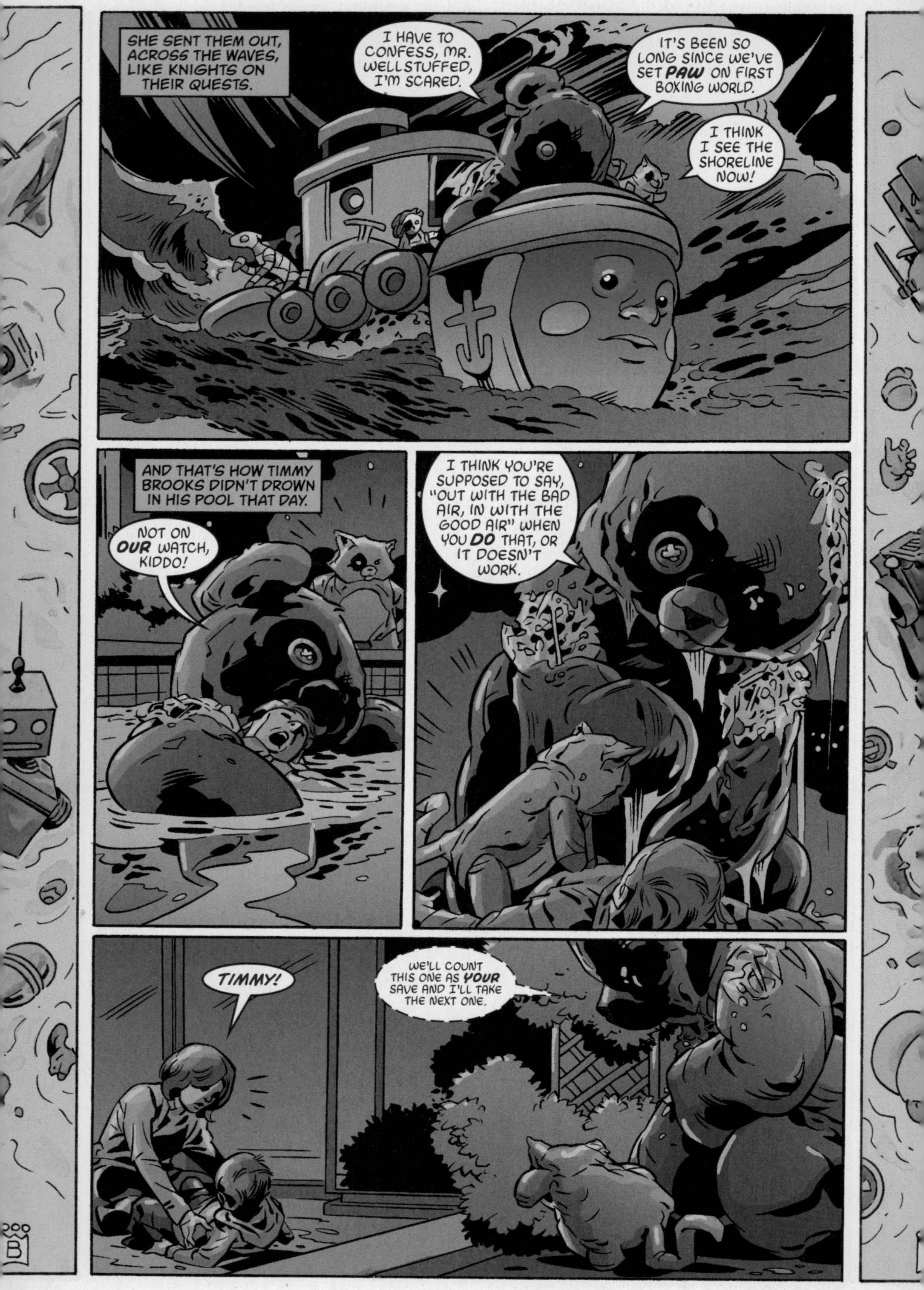
SHE SENT THEM OUT, ACROSS THE WAVES, LIKE KNIGHTS ON THEIR QUESTS.
I HAVE TO CONFESS, MR. WELLSTUFFED, I'M SCARED.
IT'S BEEN SO LONG SINCE WE'VE SET PAW ON FIRST BOXING WORLD.
I THINK I SEE THE SHORELINE NOW!
AND THAT'S HOW TIMMY BROOKS DIDN'T DROWN IN HIS POOL THAT DAY.
NOT ON OUR WATCH, KIDDO!
I THINK YOU'RE SUPPOSED TO SAY, "OUT WITH THE BAD AIR, IN WITH THE GOOD AIR" WHEN YOU DO THAT, OR IT DOESN'T WORK.
TIMMY!
WE'LL COUNT THIS ONE AS YOUR SAVE AND I'LL TAKE THE NEXT ONE.

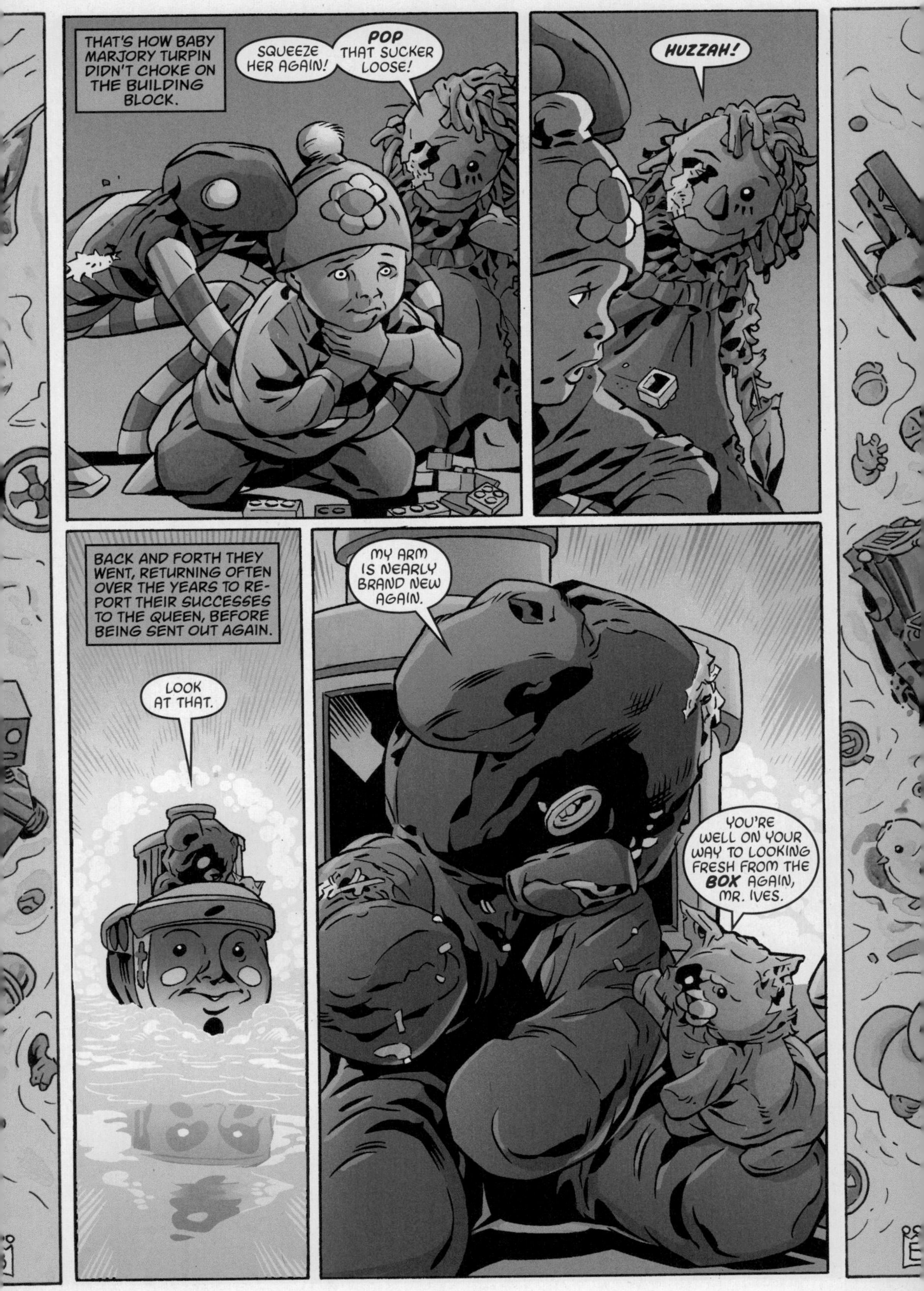
THAT'S HOW BABY MARJORY TURPIN DIDN'T CHOKE ON THE BUILDING BLOCK.
SQUEEZE HER AGAIN!
POP THAT SUCKER LOOSE!
HUZZAH!
BACK AND FORTH THEY WENT, RETURNING OFTEN OVER THE YEARS TO REPORT THEIR SUCCESSES TO THE QUEEN, BEFORE BEING SENT OUT AGAIN.
LOOK AT THAT.
MY ARM IS NEARLY BRAND NEW AGAIN.
YOU'RE WELL ON YOUR WAY TO LOOKING FRESH FROM THE BOX AGAIN, MR. IVES.

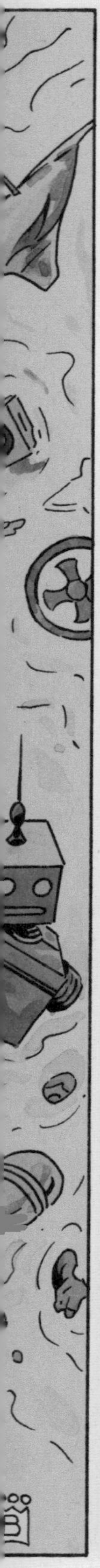

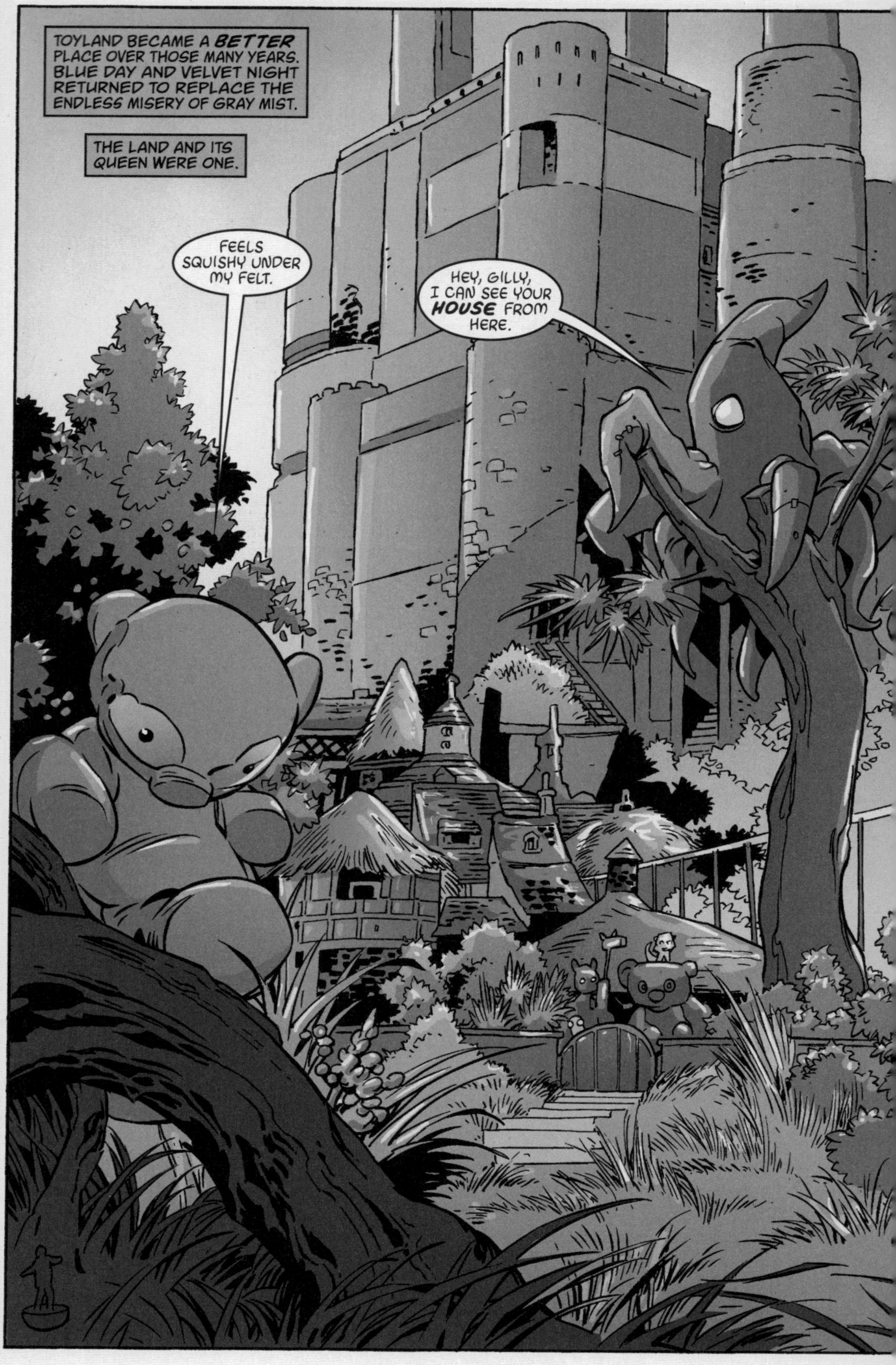

TOYLAND BECAME A BETTER PLACE OVER THOSE MANY YEARS. BLUE DAY AND VELVET NIGHT RETURNED TO REPLACE THE ENDLESS MISERY OF GRAY MIST.
THE LAND AND ITS QUEEN WERE ONE.
FEELS SQUISHY UNDER MY FELT.
HEY, GILLY, I CAN SEE YOUR HOUSE FROM HERE.

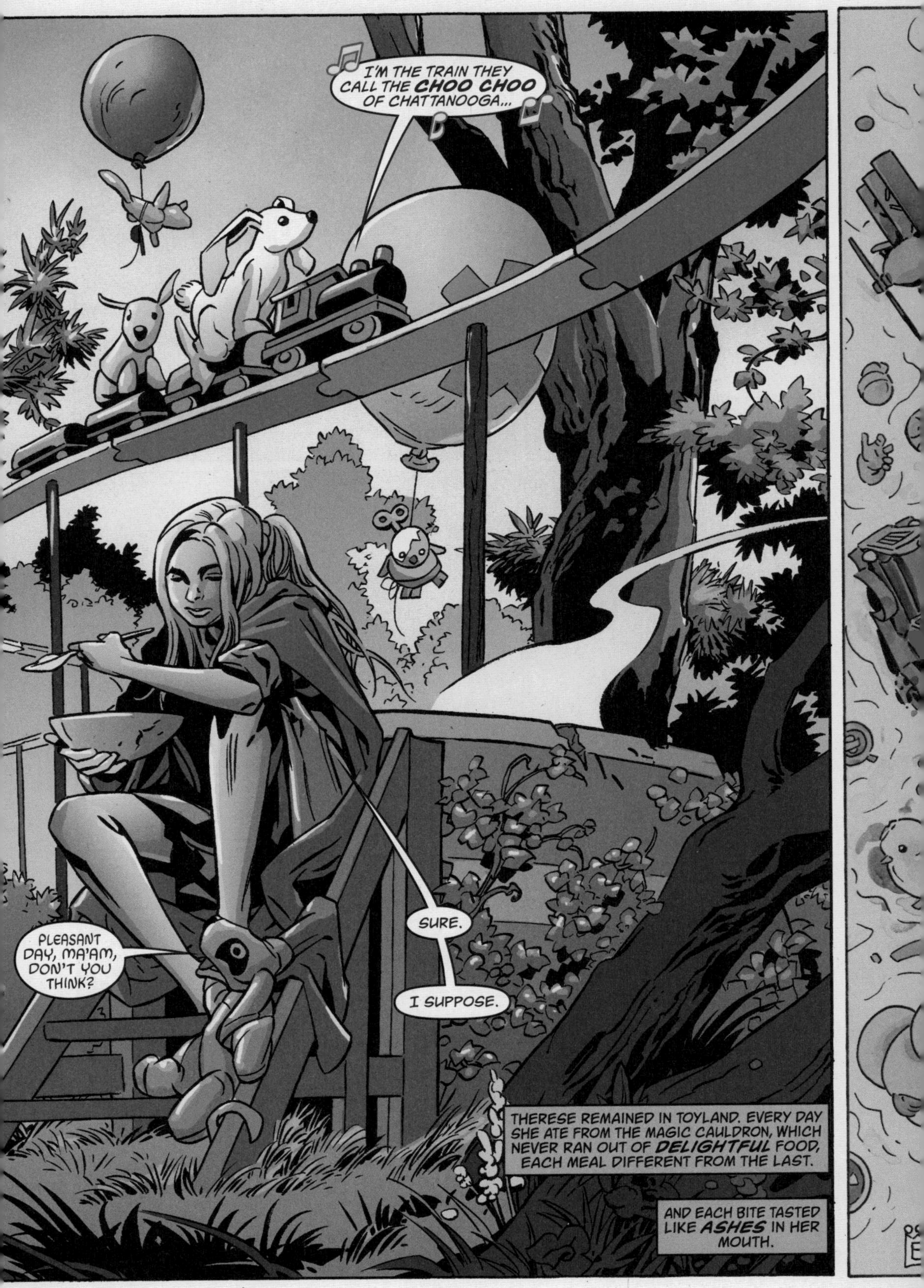
I'M THE TRAIN THEY CALL THE CHOO CHOO OF CHATTANOOGA...
PLEASANT DAY, MA'AM, DON'T YOU THINK?
SURE.
I SUPPOSE.
THERESE REMAINED IN TOYLAND. EVERY DAY SHE ATE FROM THE MAGIC CAULDRON, WHICH NEVER RAN OUT OF DELIGHTFUL FOOD, EACH MEAL DIFFERENT FROM THE LAST.
AND EACH BITE TASTED LIKE ASHES IN HER MOUTH.

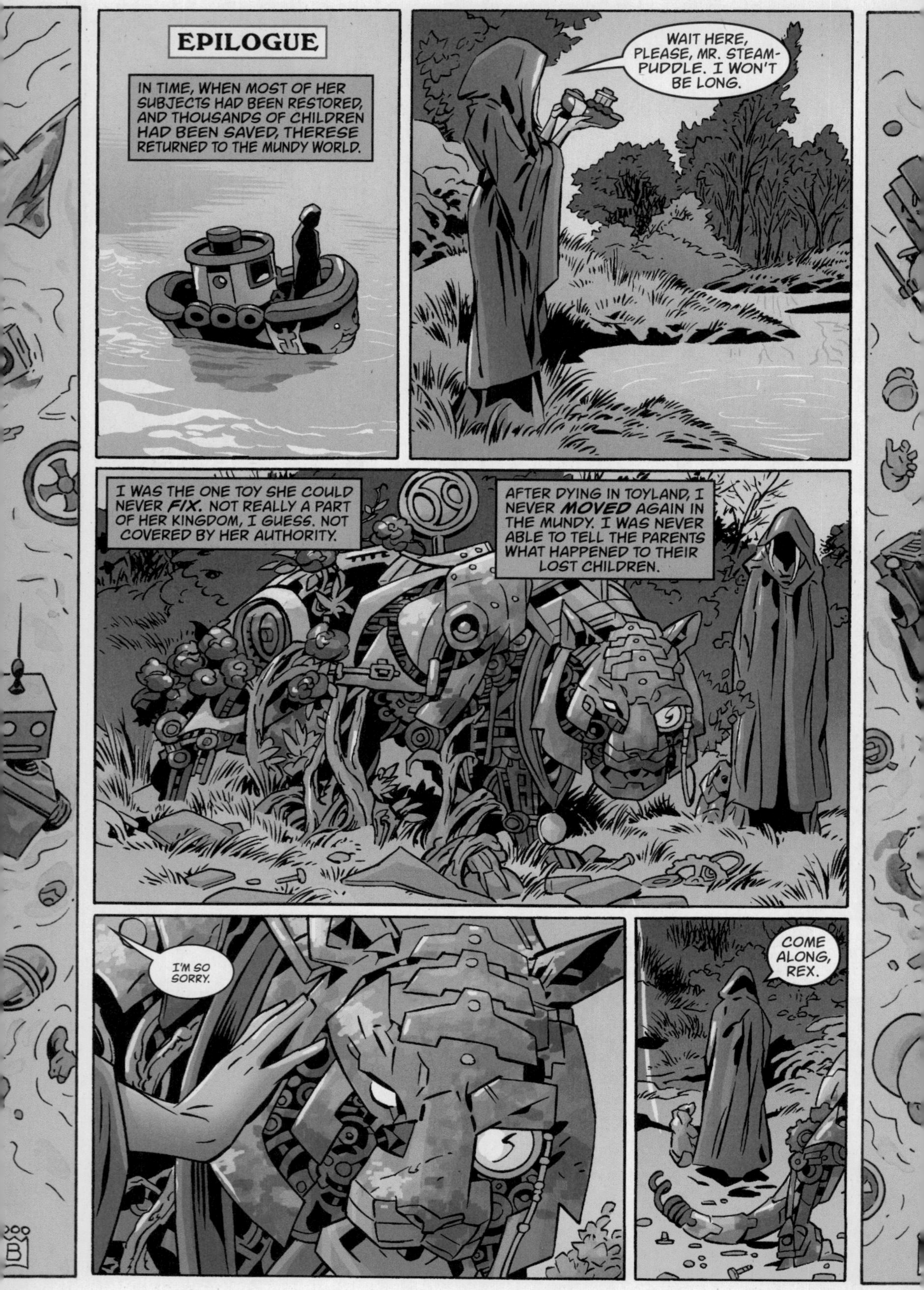

EPILOGUE
IN TIME, WHEN MOST OF HER SUBJECTS HAD BEEN RESTORED, AND THOUSANDS OF CHILDREN HAD BEEN SAVED, THERESE RETURNED TO THE MUNDY WORLD.
WAIT HERE, PLEASE, MR. STEAM-PUDDLE. I WON'T BE LONG.
I WAS THE ONE TOY SHE COULD NEVER FIX. NOT REALLY A PART OF HER KINGDOM, I GUESS. NOT COVERED BY HER AUTHORITY.
AFTER DYING IN TOYLAND, I NEVER MOVED AGAIN IN THE MUNDY. I WAS NEVER ABLE TO TELL THE PARENTS WHAT HAPPENED TO THEIR LOST CHILDREN.
I'M SO SORRY.
COME ALONG, REX.

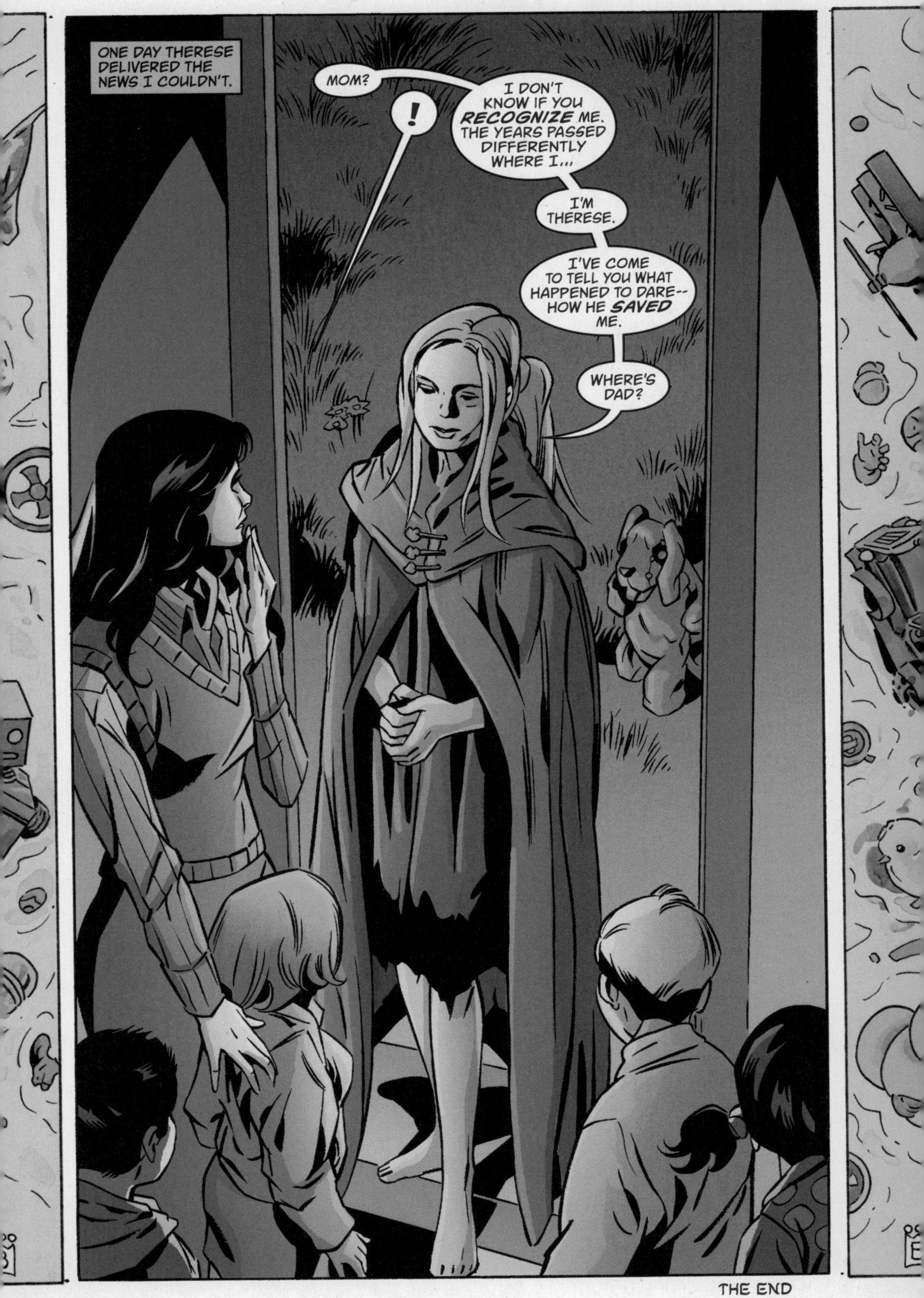
ONE DAY THERESE DELIVERED THE NEWS I COULDN'T.
MOM?
!
I DON'T KNOW IF YOU RECOGNIZE ME. THE YEARS PASSED DIFFERENTLY WHERE I...
I'M THERESE.
I'VE COME TO TELL YOU WHAT HAPPENED TO DARE-- HOW HE SAVED ME.
WHERE'S DAD?

THE END

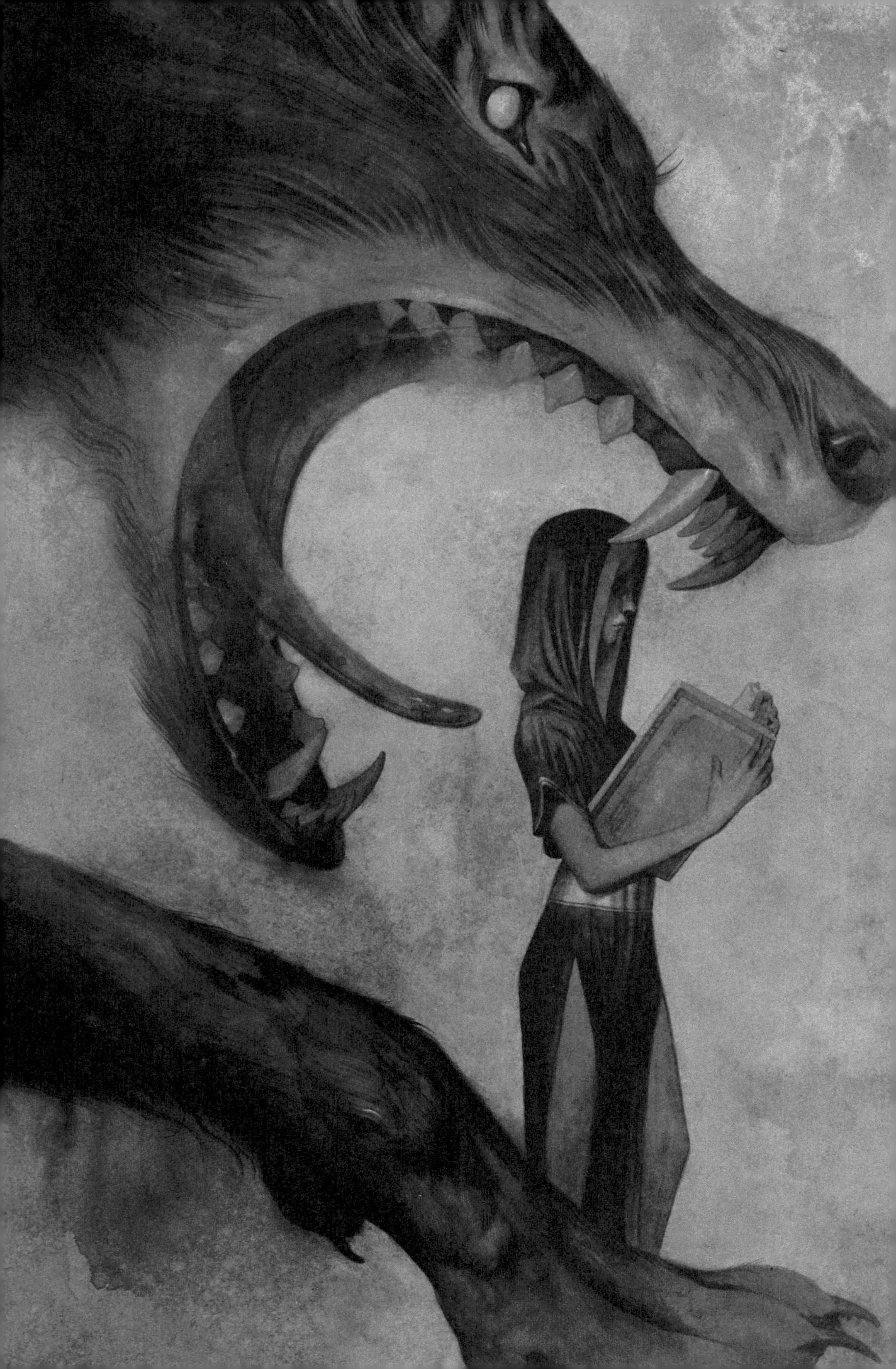

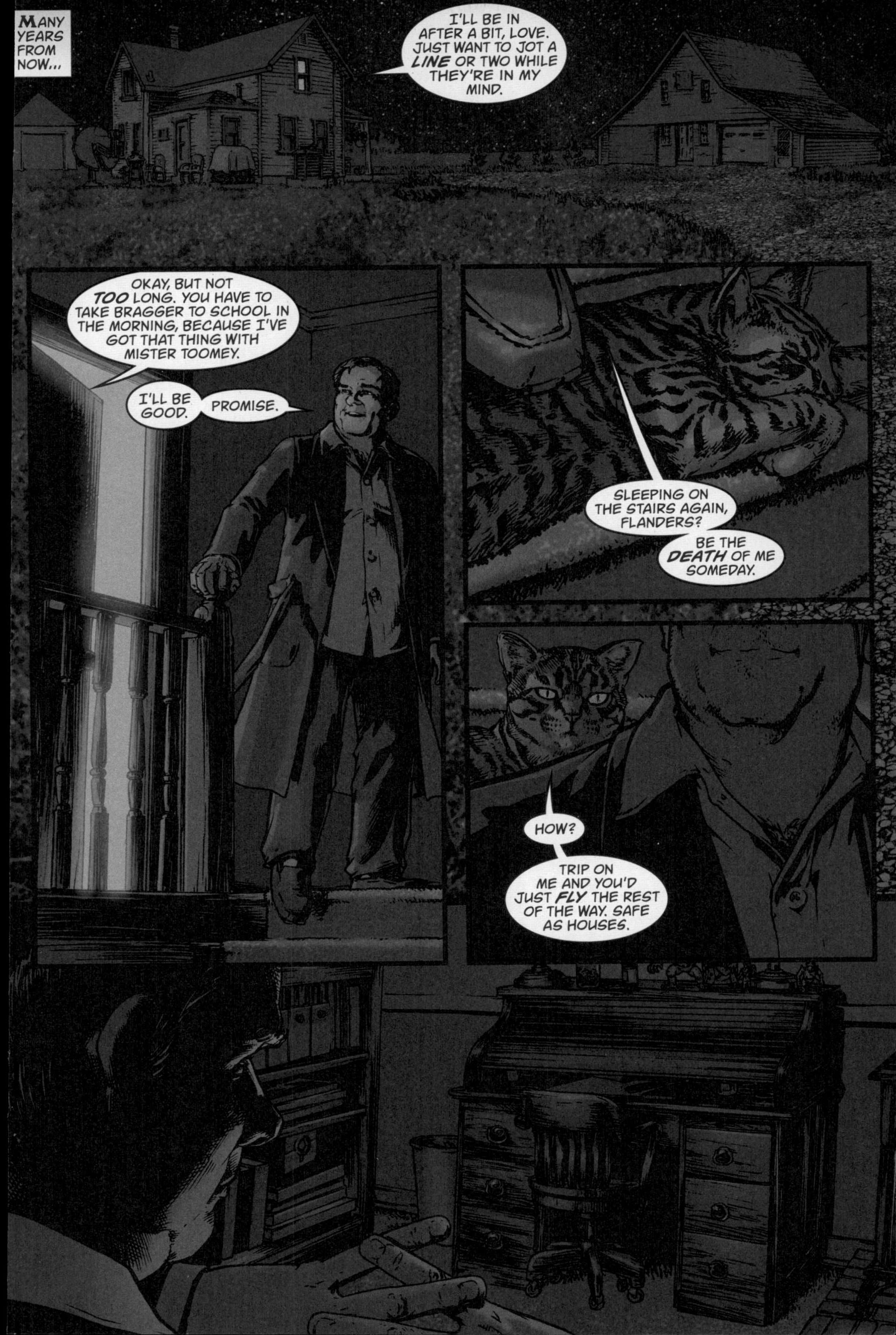
MANY YEARS FROM NOW...
I'LL BE IN AFTER A BIT, LOVE. JUST WANT TO JOT A LINE OR TWO WHILE THEY'RE IN MY MIND.
OKAY, BUT NOT TOO LONG. YOU HAVE TO TAKE BRAGGER TO SCHOOL IN THE MORNING, BECAUSE I'VE GOT THAT THING WITH MISTER TOOMEY.
I'LL BE GOOD.
PROMISE.
SLEEPING ON THE STAIRS AGAIN, FLANDERS?
BE THE DEATH OF ME SOMEDAY.
HOW?
TRIP ON ME AND YOU'D JUST FLY THE REST OF THE WAY. SAFE AS HOUSES.

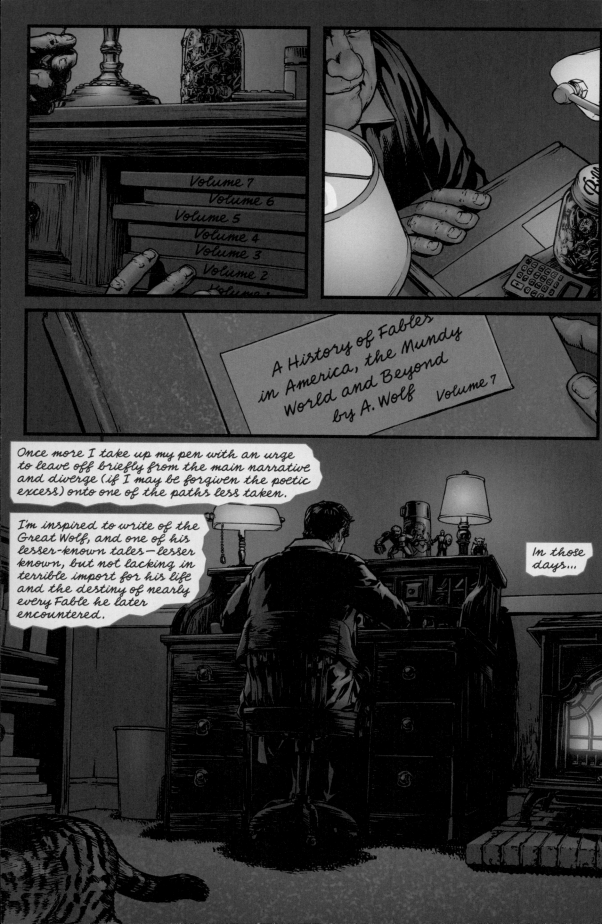

Volume 7
Volume 6
Volume 5
Volume 4
Volume 3
Volume 2
Volume

A History of Fables
in America, the Mundy
World and Beyond
by A. Wolf   Volume 7

Once more I take up my pen with an urge
to leave off briefly from the main narrative
and diverge (if I may be forgiven the poetic
excess) onto one of the paths less taken.

I'm inspired to write of the
Great Wolf, and one of his
lesser-known tales—lesser
known, but not lacking in
terrible import for his life
and the destiny of nearly
every Fable he later
encountered.

In those
days...

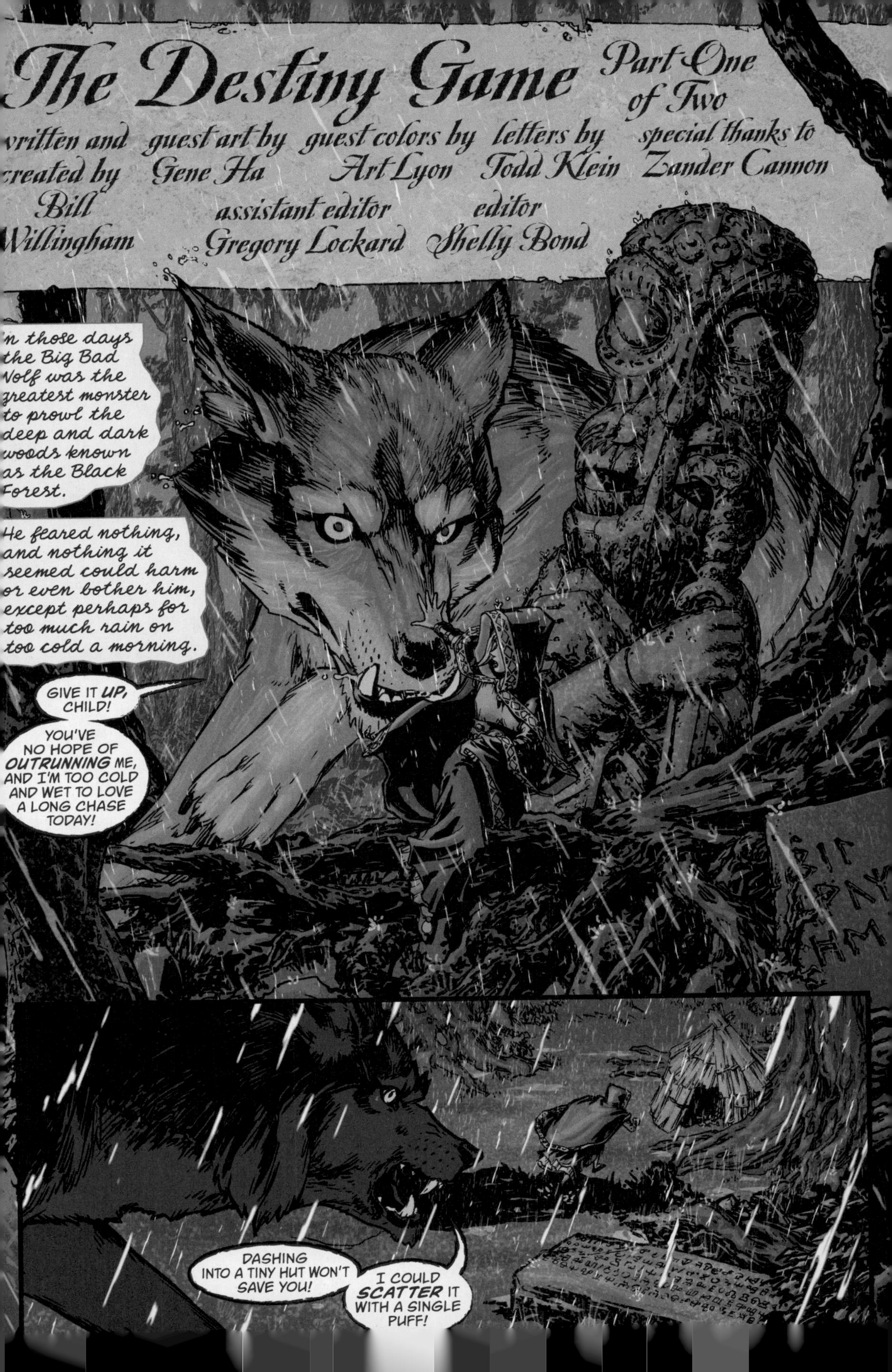
The Destiny Game Part One of Two
written and created by Bill Willingham
guest art by Gene Ha
guest colors by Art Lyon
letters by Todd Klein
special thanks to Zander Cannon
assistant editor Gregory Lockard
editor Shelly Bond
In those days the Big Bad Wolf was the greatest monster to prowl the deep and dark woods known as the Black Forest.
He feared nothing, and nothing it seemed could harm or even bother him, except perhaps for too much rain on too cold a morning.
GIVE IT UP, CHILD!
YOU'VE NO HOPE OF OUTRUNNING ME, AND I'M TOO COLD AND WET TO LOVE A LONG CHASE TODAY!
DASHING INTO A TINY HUT WON'T SAVE YOU!
I COULD SCATTER IT WITH A SINGLE PUFF!

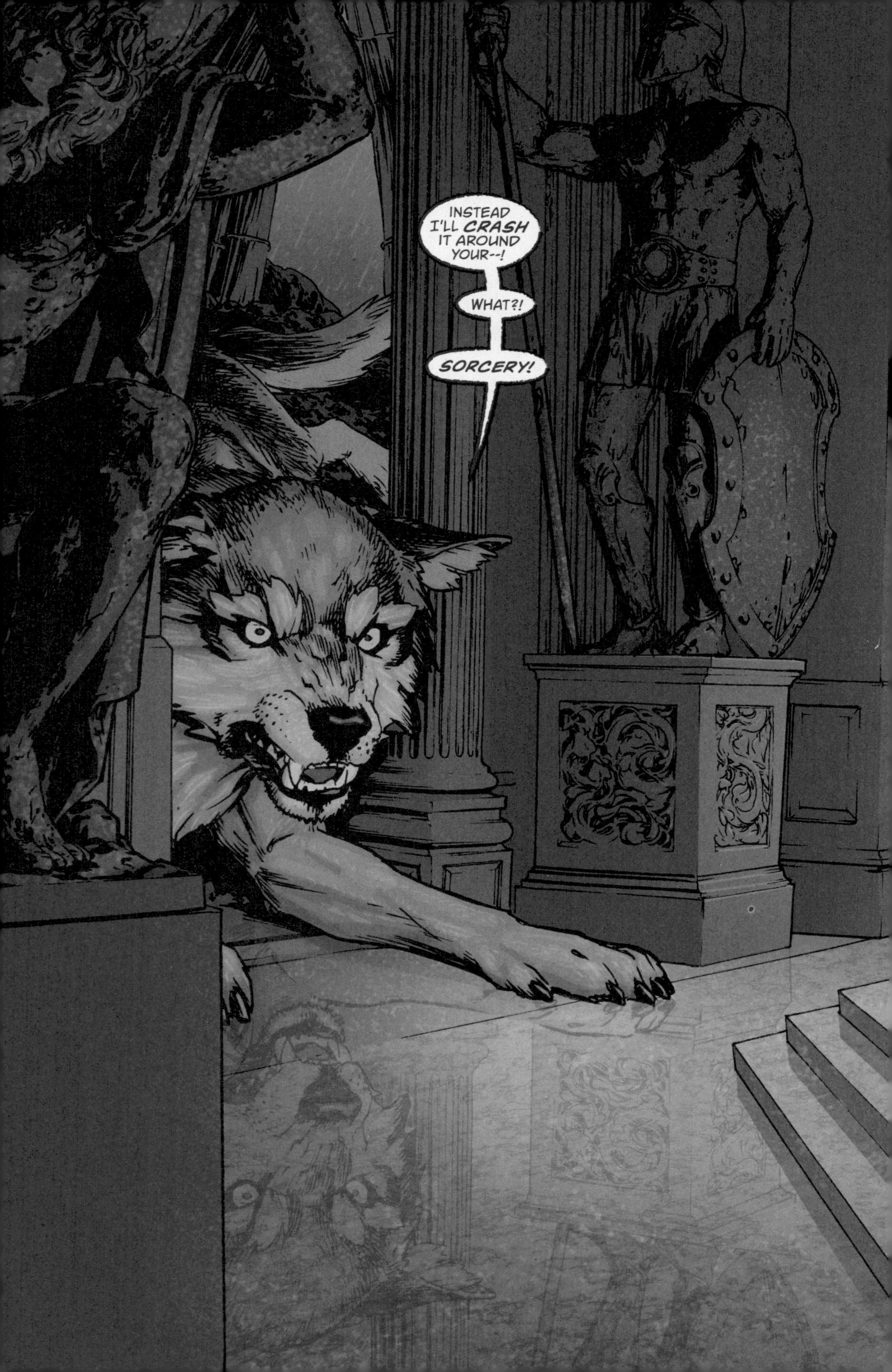
INSTEAD I'LL CRASH IT AROUND YOUR--!
WHAT?!
SORCERY!

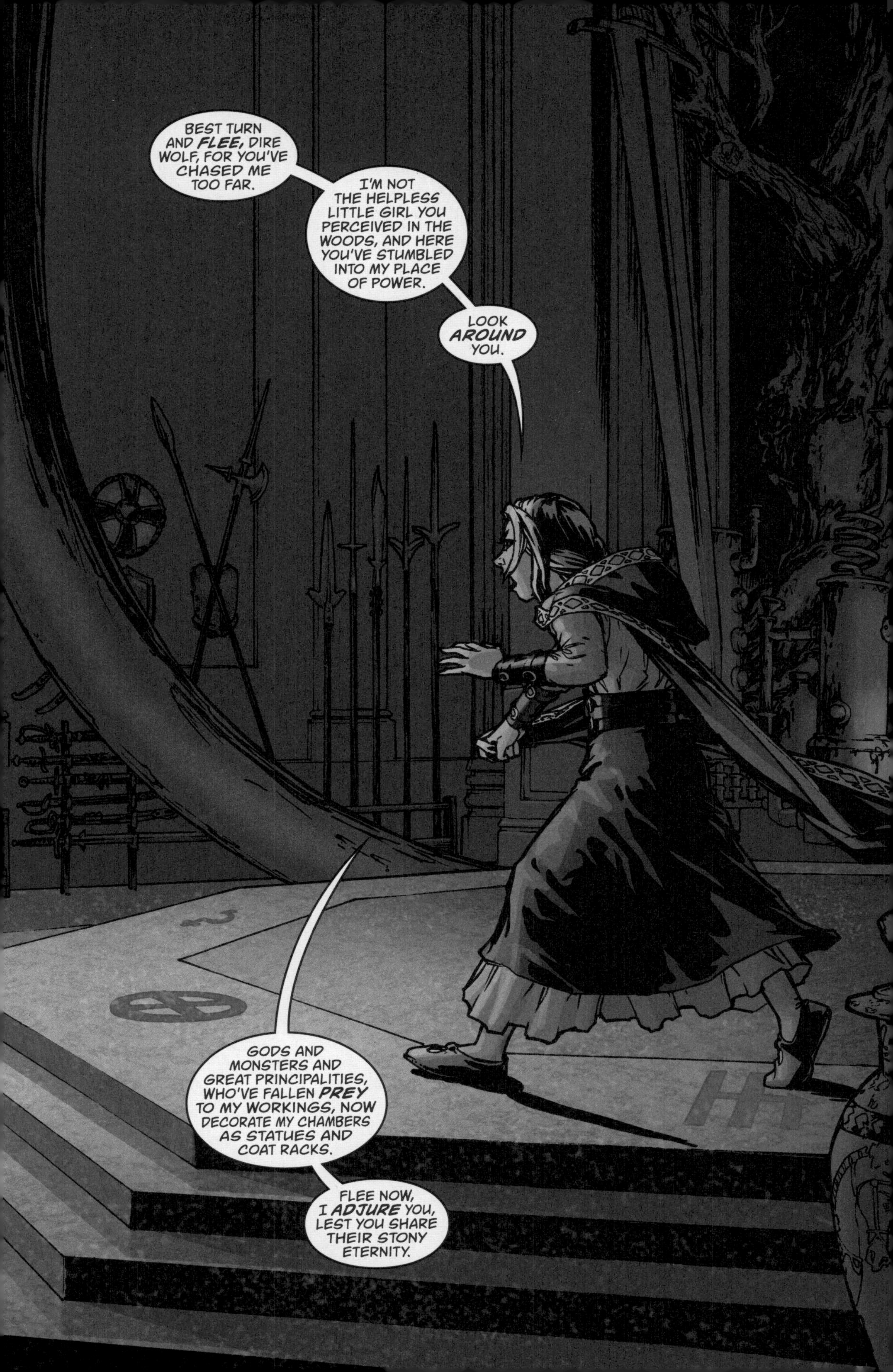

BEST TURN AND FLEE, DIRE WOLF, FOR YOU'VE CHASED ME TOO FAR.
I'M NOT THE HELPLESS LITTLE GIRL YOU PERCEIVED IN THE WOODS, AND HERE YOU'VE STUMBLED INTO MY PLACE OF POWER.
LOOK AROUND YOU.
GODS AND MONSTERS AND GREAT PRINCIPALITIES, WHO'VE FALLEN PREY TO MY WORKINGS, NOW DECORATE MY CHAMBERS AS STATUES AND COAT RACKS.
FLEE NOW, I ADJURE YOU, LEST YOU SHARE THEIR STONY ETERNITY.

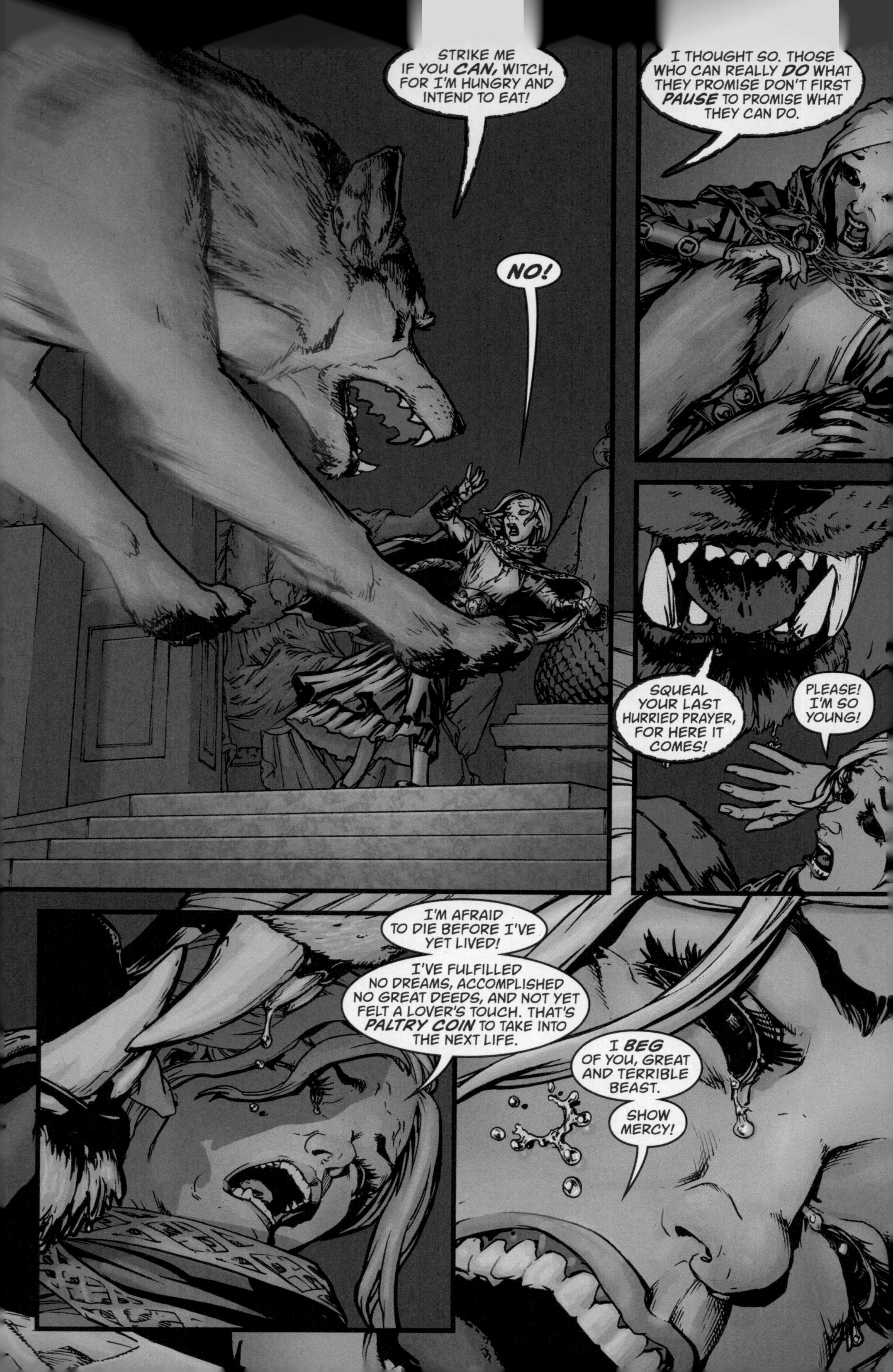
STRIKE ME IF YOU CAN, WITCH, FOR I'M HUNGRY AND INTEND TO EAT!
NO!
I THOUGHT SO. THOSE WHO CAN REALLY DO WHAT THEY PROMISE DON'T FIRST PAUSE TO PROMISE WHAT THEY CAN DO.
SQUEAL YOUR LAST HURRIED PRAYER, FOR HERE IT COMES!
PLEASE! I'M SO YOUNG!
I'M AFRAID TO DIE BEFORE I'VE YET LIVED!
I'VE FULFILLED NO DREAMS, ACCOMPLISHED NO GREAT DEEDS, AND NOT YET FELT A LOVER'S TOUCH. THAT'S PALTRY COIN TO TAKE INTO THE NEXT LIFE.
I BEG OF YOU, GREAT AND TERRIBLE BEAST.
SHOW MERCY!

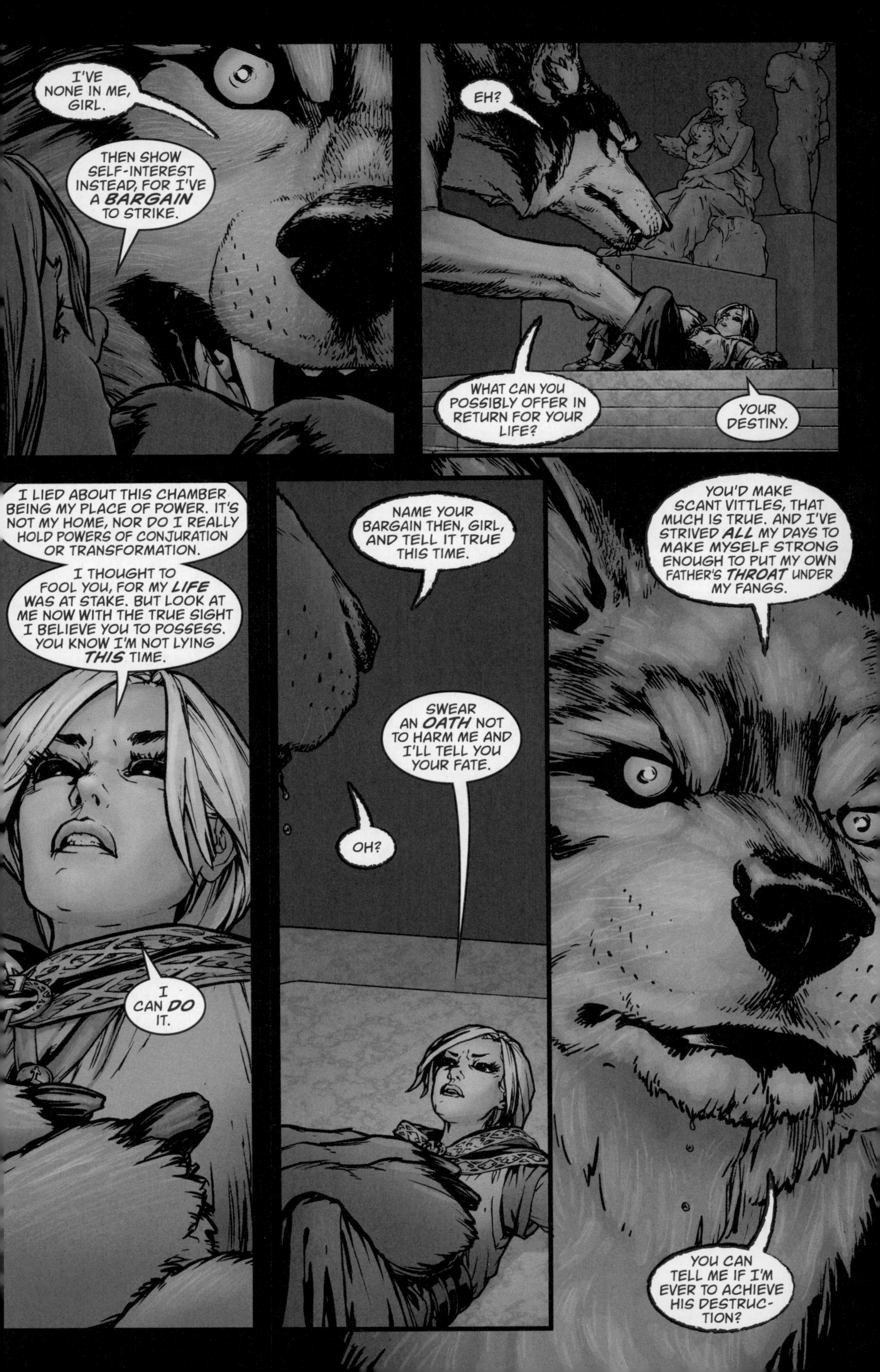
I'VE NONE IN ME, GIRL.
THEN SHOW SELF-INTEREST INSTEAD, FOR I'VE A **BARGAIN** TO STRIKE.
EH?
WHAT CAN YOU POSSIBLY OFFER IN RETURN FOR YOUR LIFE?
YOUR DESTINY.
I LIED ABOUT THIS CHAMBER BEING MY PLACE OF POWER. IT'S NOT MY HOME, NOR DO I REALLY HOLD POWERS OF CONJURATION OR TRANSFORMATION.
I THOUGHT TO FOOL YOU, FOR MY **LIFE** WAS AT STAKE. BUT LOOK AT ME NOW WITH THE TRUE SIGHT I BELIEVE YOU TO POSSESS. YOU KNOW I'M NOT LYING **THIS** TIME.
I CAN **DO** IT.
NAME YOUR BARGAIN THEN, GIRL, AND TELL IT TRUE THIS TIME.
OH?
SWEAR AN **OATH** NOT TO HARM ME AND I'LL TELL YOU YOUR FATE.
YOU'D MAKE SCANT VITTLES, THAT MUCH IS TRUE. AND I'VE STRIVED **ALL** MY DAYS TO MAKE MYSELF STRONG ENOUGH TO PUT MY OWN FATHER'S **THROAT** UNDER MY FANGS.
YOU CAN TELL ME IF I'M EVER TO ACHIEVE HIS DESTRUC-TION?

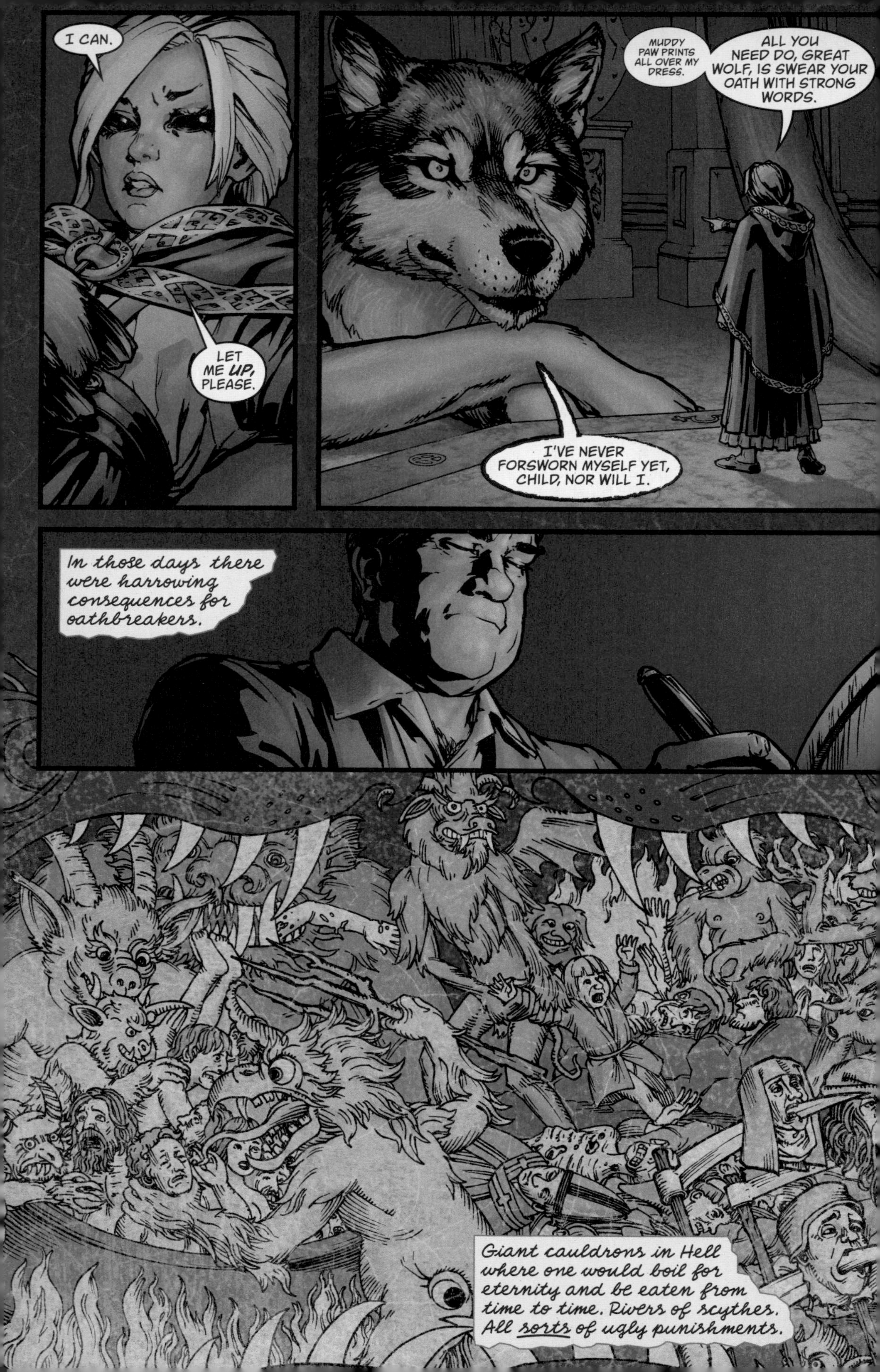
I CAN.
LET ME UP, PLEASE.
MUDDY PAW PRINTS ALL OVER MY DRESS.
ALL YOU NEED DO, GREAT WOLF, IS SWEAR YOUR OATH WITH STRONG WORDS.
I'VE NEVER FORSWORN MYSELF YET, CHILD, NOR WILL I.
In those days there were harrowing consequences for oathbreakers.
Giant cauldrons in Hell where one would boil for eternity and be eaten from time to time. Rivers of scythes. All sorts of ugly punishments.

NOW, MY FATE, GIRL. TELL IT *DIRECT*, WITHOUT THE PRACTITIONER'S USUAL OBSCURE NONSENSE AND CRYPTIC MUMBO JUMBO.

BLUNT AND UNDECORATED?

FINE.

HERE IT IS, THEN.

THREE DAYS FROM NOW YOU *DIE*, TORN TO PIECES BY A TERRIBLE BEAST, AS BIG AND BAD AS YOURSELF.

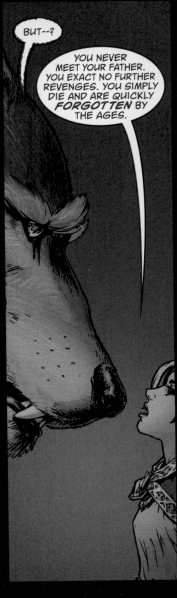

BUT--?

YOU NEVER MEET YOUR FATHER. YOU EXACT NO FURTHER REVENGES. YOU SIMPLY DIE AND ARE QUICKLY *FORGOTTEN* BY THE AGES.

THAT'S IT?

THAT'S IT. NO MERCY. NO REPRIEVE.

NOW PLEASE BE ON YOUR WAY.

The Wolf was stricken to his core. True to his word though, he went on his way, leaving the girl unmolested.

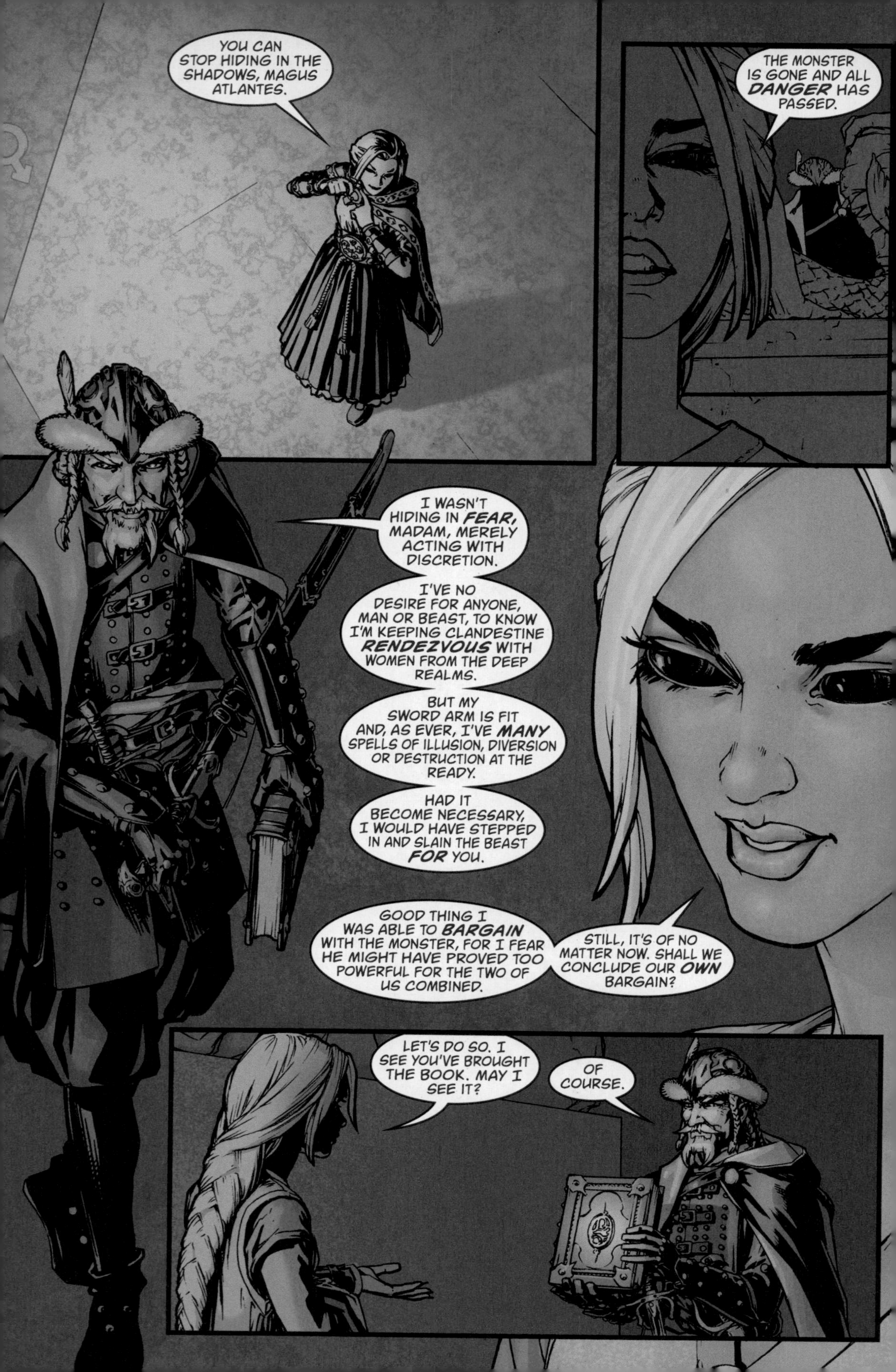

YOU CAN STOP HIDING IN THE SHADOWS, MAGUS ATLANTES.
THE MONSTER IS GONE AND ALL DANGER HAS PASSED.
I WASN'T HIDING IN FEAR, MADAM, MERELY ACTING WITH DISCRETION.
I'VE NO DESIRE FOR ANYONE, MAN OR BEAST, TO KNOW I'M KEEPING CLANDESTINE RENDEZVOUS WITH WOMEN FROM THE DEEP REALMS.
BUT MY SWORD ARM IS FIT AND, AS EVER, I'VE MANY SPELLS OF ILLUSION, DIVERSION OR DESTRUCTION AT THE READY.
HAD IT BECOME NECESSARY, I WOULD HAVE STEPPED IN AND SLAIN THE BEAST FOR YOU.
GOOD THING I WAS ABLE TO BARGAIN WITH THE MONSTER, FOR I FEAR HE MIGHT HAVE PROVED TOO POWERFUL FOR THE TWO OF US COMBINED.
STILL, IT'S OF NO MATTER NOW. SHALL WE CONCLUDE OUR OWN BARGAIN?
LET'S DO SO. I SEE YOU'VE BROUGHT THE BOOK. MAY I SEE IT?
OF COURSE.

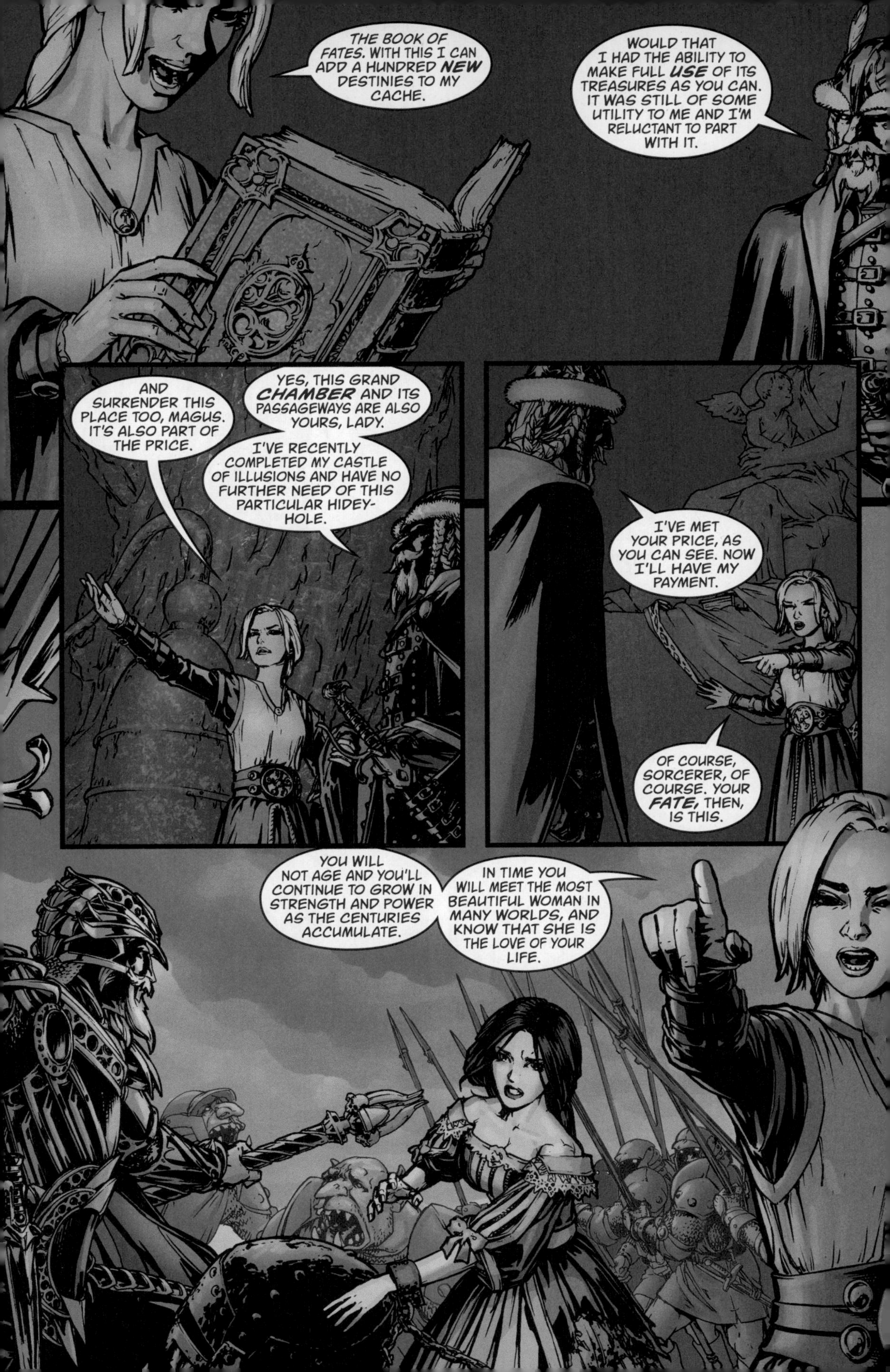
THE BOOK OF FATES. WITH THIS I CAN ADD A HUNDRED NEW DESTINIES TO MY CACHE.
WOULD THAT I HAD THE ABILITY TO MAKE FULL USE OF ITS TREASURES AS YOU CAN. IT WAS STILL OF SOME UTILITY TO ME AND I'M RELUCTANT TO PART WITH IT.
AND SURRENDER THIS PLACE TOO, MAGUS. IT'S ALSO PART OF THE PRICE.
YES, THIS GRAND CHAMBER AND ITS PASSAGEWAYS ARE ALSO YOURS, LADY.
I'VE RECENTLY COMPLETED MY CASTLE OF ILLUSIONS AND HAVE NO FURTHER NEED OF THIS PARTICULAR HIDEY-HOLE.
I'VE MET YOUR PRICE, AS YOU CAN SEE. NOW I'LL HAVE MY PAYMENT.
OF COURSE, SORCERER, OF COURSE. YOUR FATE, THEN, IS THIS.
YOU WILL NOT AGE AND YOU'LL CONTINUE TO GROW IN STRENGTH AND POWER AS THE CENTURIES ACCUMULATE.
IN TIME YOU WILL MEET THE MOST BEAUTIFUL WOMAN IN MANY WORLDS, AND KNOW THAT SHE IS THE LOVE OF YOUR LIFE.

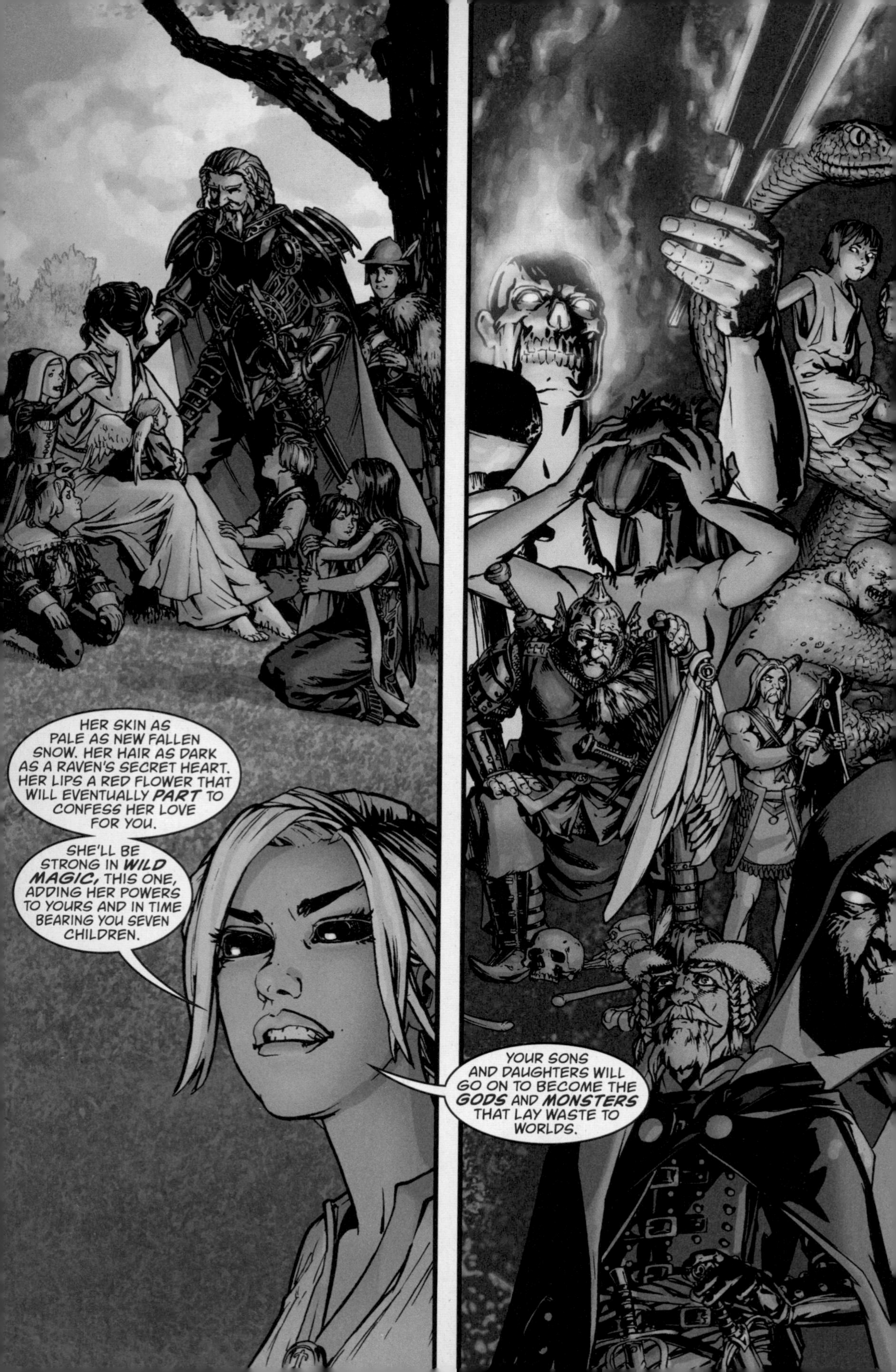
HER SKIN AS PALE AS NEW FALLEN SNOW. HER HAIR AS DARK AS A RAVEN'S SECRET HEART. HER LIPS A RED FLOWER THAT WILL EVENTUALLY PART TO CONFESS HER LOVE FOR YOU.
SHE'LL BE STRONG IN WILD MAGIC, THIS ONE, ADDING HER POWERS TO YOURS AND IN TIME BEARING YOU SEVEN CHILDREN.
YOUR SONS AND DAUGHTERS WILL GO ON TO BECOME THE GODS AND MONSTERS THAT LAY WASTE TO WORLDS.

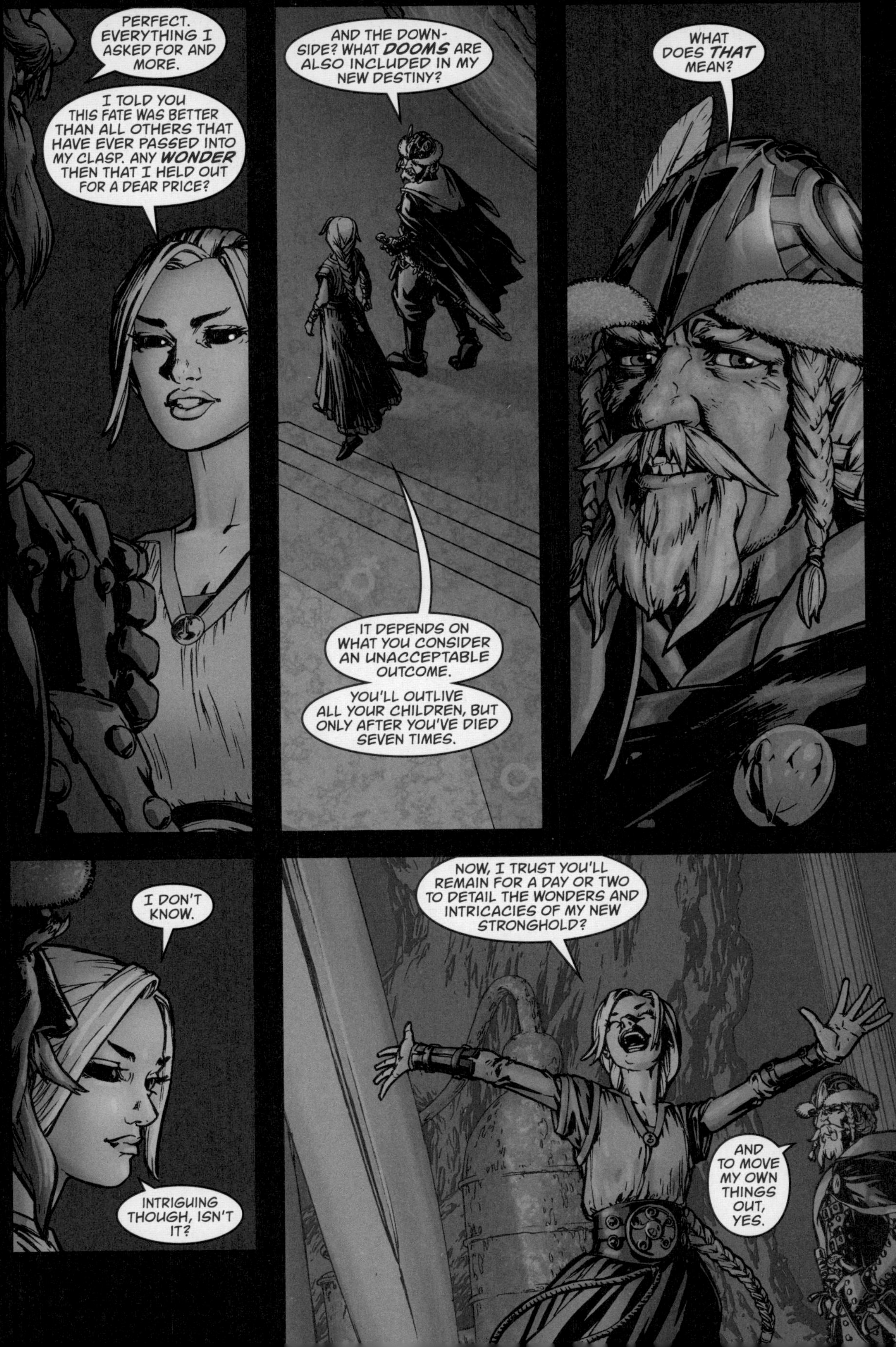
PERFECT. EVERYTHING I ASKED FOR AND MORE.
I TOLD YOU THIS FATE WAS BETTER THAN ALL OTHERS THAT HAVE EVER PASSED INTO MY CLASP. ANY WONDER THEN THAT I HELD OUT FOR A DEAR PRICE?
AND THE DOWN-SIDE? WHAT DOOMS ARE ALSO INCLUDED IN MY NEW DESTINY?
IT DEPENDS ON WHAT YOU CONSIDER AN UNACCEPTABLE OUTCOME.
YOU'LL OUTLIVE ALL YOUR CHILDREN, BUT ONLY AFTER YOU'VE DIED SEVEN TIMES.
WHAT DOES THAT MEAN?
I DON'T KNOW.
INTRIGUING THOUGH, ISN'T IT?
NOW, I TRUST YOU'LL REMAIN FOR A DAY OR TWO TO DETAIL THE WONDERS AND INTRICACIES OF MY NEW STRONGHOLD?
AND TO MOVE MY OWN THINGS OUT, YES.

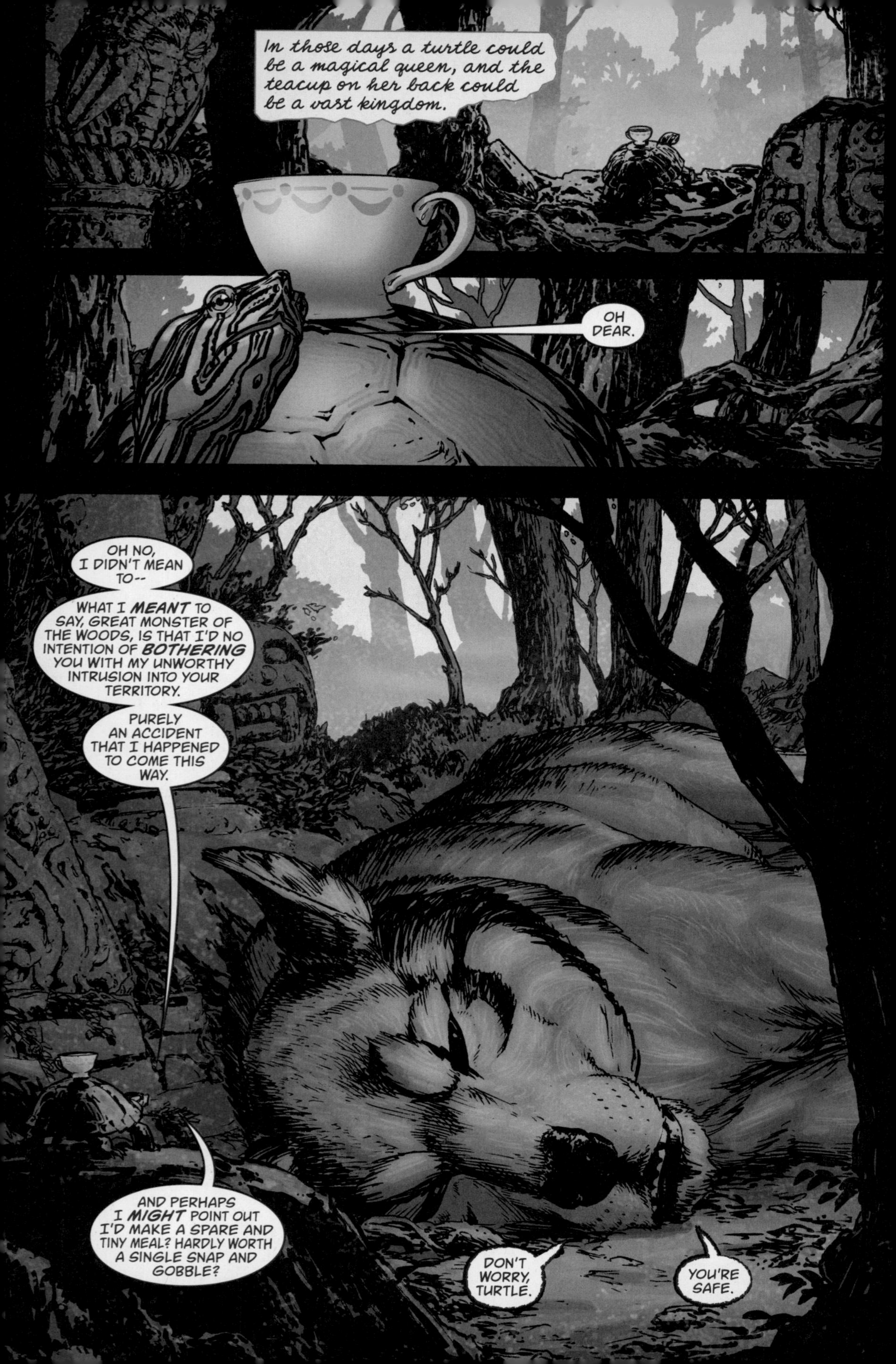
In those days a turtle could be a magical queen, and the teacup on her back could be a vast kingdom.
OH DEAR.
OH NO, I DIDN'T MEAN TO--
WHAT I MEANT TO SAY, GREAT MONSTER OF THE WOODS, IS THAT I'D NO INTENTION OF BOTHERING YOU WITH MY UNWORTHY INTRUSION INTO YOUR TERRITORY.
PURELY AN ACCIDENT THAT I HAPPENED TO COME THIS WAY.
AND PERHAPS I MIGHT POINT OUT I'D MAKE A SPARE AND TINY MEAL? HARDLY WORTH A SINGLE SNAP AND GOBBLE?
DON'T WORRY, TURTLE.
YOU'RE SAFE.

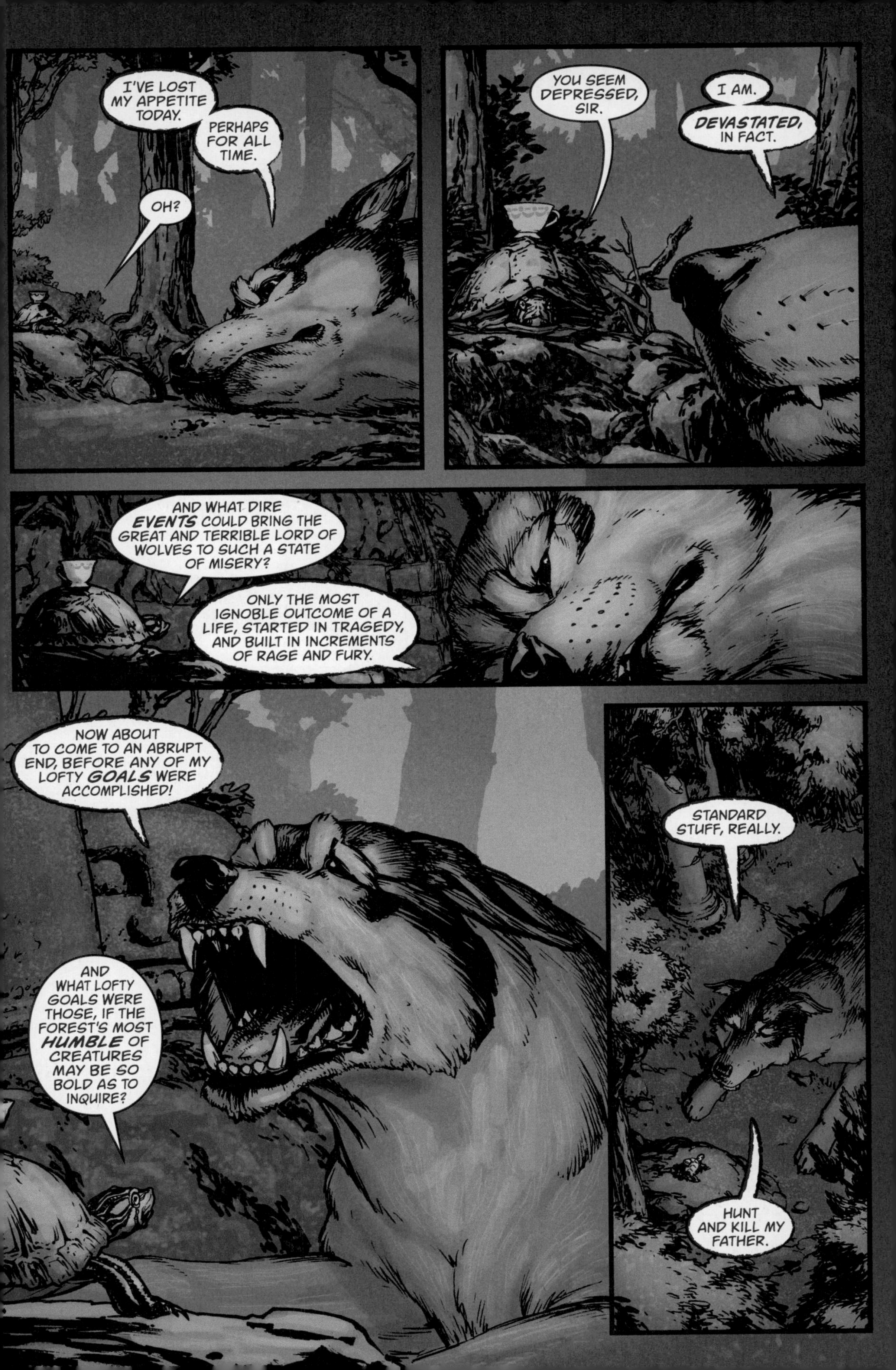
I'VE LOST MY APPETITE TODAY.
PERHAPS FOR ALL TIME.
OH?
YOU SEEM DEPRESSED, SIR.
I AM.
DEVASTATED, IN FACT.
AND WHAT DIRE EVENTS COULD BRING THE GREAT AND TERRIBLE LORD OF WOLVES TO SUCH A STATE OF MISERY?
ONLY THE MOST IGNOBLE OUTCOME OF A LIFE, STARTED IN TRAGEDY, AND BUILT IN INCREMENTS OF RAGE AND FURY.
NOW ABOUT TO COME TO AN ABRUPT END, BEFORE ANY OF MY LOFTY GOALS WERE ACCOMPLISHED!
AND WHAT LOFTY GOALS WERE THOSE, IF THE FOREST'S MOST HUMBLE OF CREATURES MAY BE SO BOLD AS TO INQUIRE?
STANDARD STUFF, REALLY.
HUNT AND KILL MY FATHER.

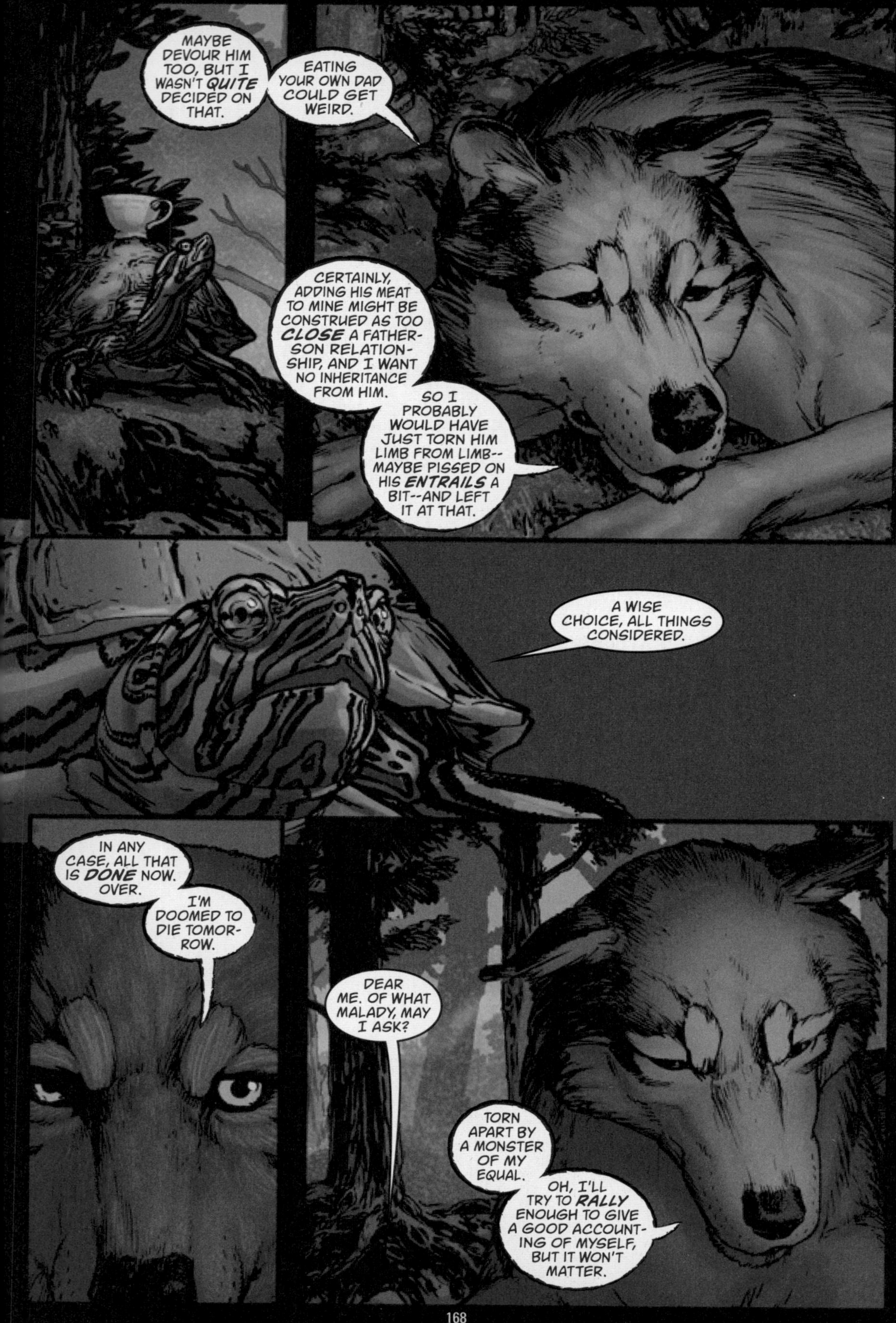
MAYBE DEVOUR HIM TOO, BUT I WASN'T QUITE DECIDED ON THAT.
EATING YOUR OWN DAD COULD GET WEIRD.
CERTAINLY, ADDING HIS MEAT TO MINE MIGHT BE CONSTRUED AS TOO CLOSE A FATHER-SON RELATIONSHIP, AND I WANT NO INHERITANCE FROM HIM.
SO I PROBABLY WOULD HAVE JUST TORN HIM LIMB FROM LIMB--MAYBE PISSED ON HIS ENTRAILS A BIT--AND LEFT IT AT THAT.
A WISE CHOICE, ALL THINGS CONSIDERED.
IN ANY CASE, ALL THAT IS DONE NOW. OVER.
I'M DOOMED TO DIE TOMORROW.
DEAR ME. OF WHAT MALADY, MAY I ASK?
TORN APART BY A MONSTER OF MY EQUAL.
OH, I'LL TRY TO RALLY ENOUGH TO GIVE A GOOD ACCOUNTING OF MYSELF, BUT IT WON'T MATTER.

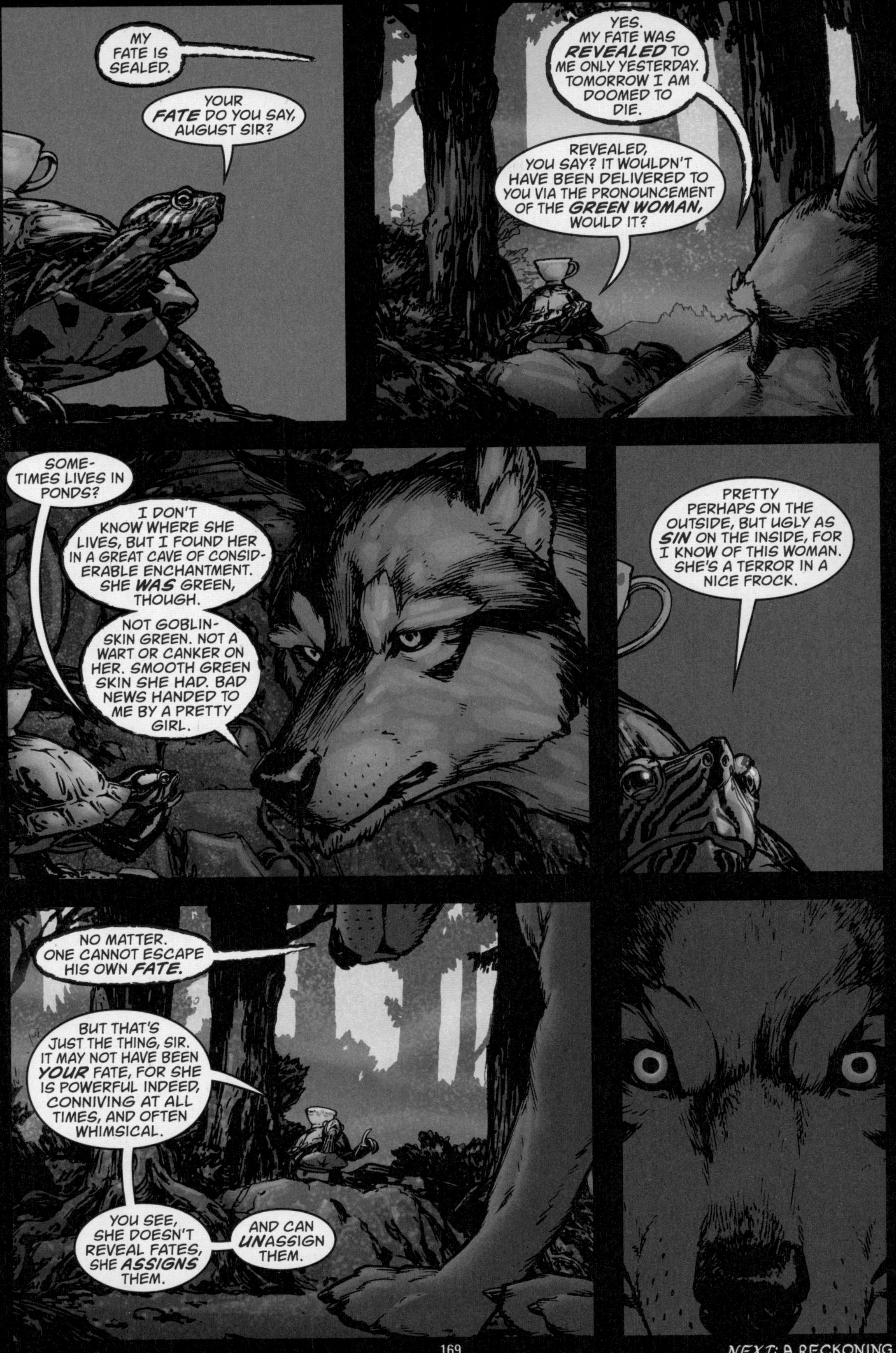
MY FATE IS SEALED.
YOUR *FATE* DO YOU SAY, AUGUST SIR?
YES. MY FATE WAS *REVEALED* TO ME ONLY YESTERDAY. TOMORROW I AM DOOMED TO DIE.
REVEALED, YOU SAY? IT WOULDN'T HAVE BEEN DELIVERED TO YOU VIA THE PRONOUNCEMENT OF THE *GREEN WOMAN,* WOULD IT?
SOME-TIMES LIVES IN PONDS?
I DON'T KNOW WHERE SHE LIVES, BUT I FOUND HER IN A GREAT CAVE OF CONSID-ERABLE ENCHANTMENT. SHE *WAS* GREEN, THOUGH.
NOT GOBLIN-SKIN GREEN. NOT A WART OR CANKER ON HER. SMOOTH GREEN SKIN SHE HAD. BAD NEWS HANDED TO ME BY A PRETTY GIRL.
PRETTY PERHAPS ON THE OUTSIDE, BUT UGLY AS *SIN* ON THE INSIDE, FOR I KNOW OF THIS WOMAN. SHE'S A TERROR IN A NICE FROCK.
NO MATTER. ONE CANNOT ESCAPE HIS OWN *FATE.*
BUT THAT'S JUST THE THING, SIR. IT MAY NOT HAVE BEEN *YOUR* FATE, FOR SHE IS POWERFUL INDEED, CONNIVING AT ALL TIMES, AND OFTEN WHIMSICAL.
YOU SEE, SHE DOESN'T REVEAL FATES, SHE *ASSIGNS* THEM.
AND CAN *UN*ASSIGN THEM.

NEXT: A RECKONING

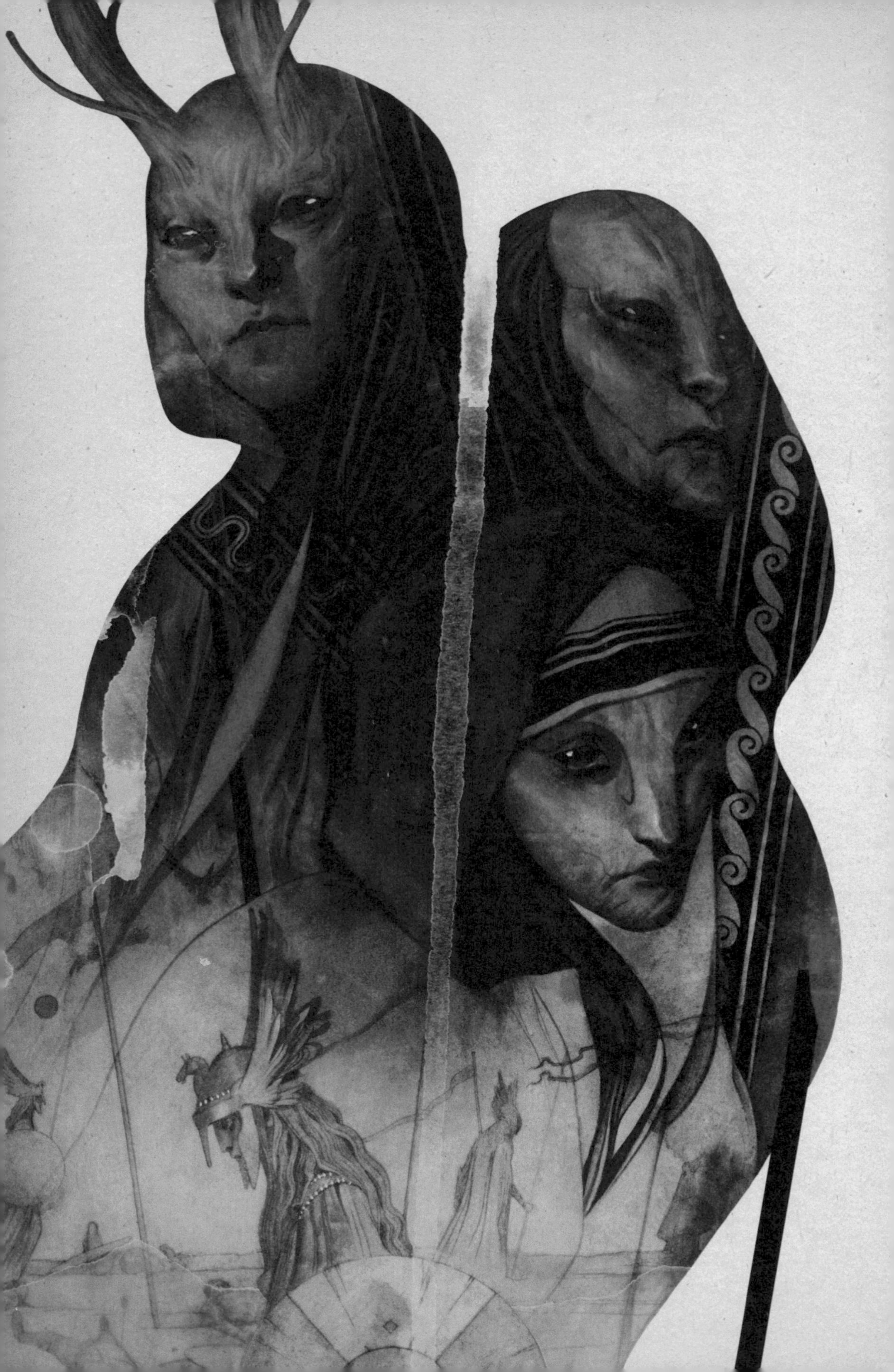

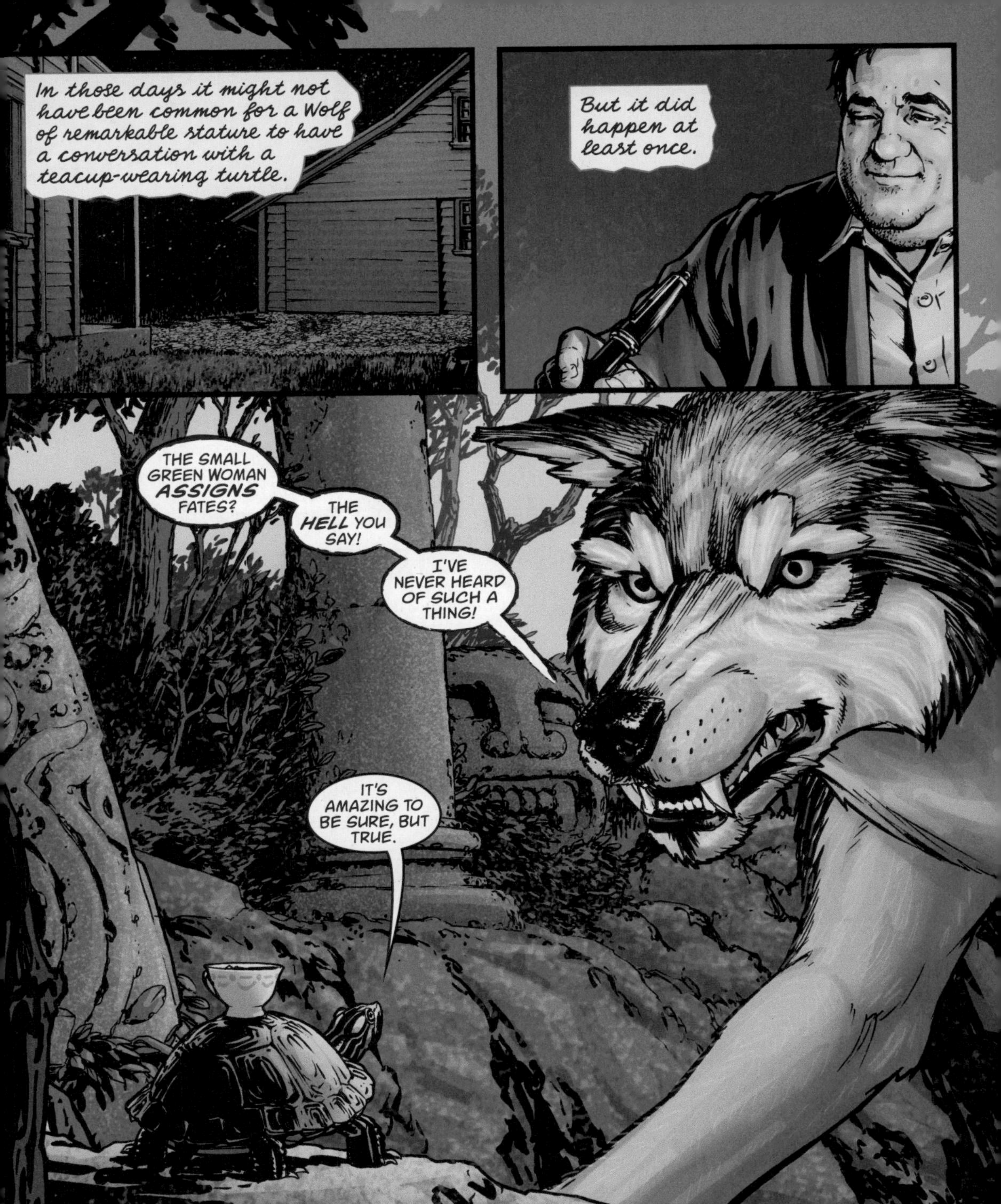
In those days it might not have been common for a Wolf of remarkable stature to have a conversation with a teacup-wearing turtle.
But it did happen at least once.
THE SMALL GREEN WOMAN ASSIGNS FATES?
THE HELL YOU SAY!
I'VE NEVER HEARD OF SUCH A THING!
IT'S AMAZING TO BE SURE, BUT TRUE.

The Destiny Game

Part Two of Two

written and created by Bill Willingham

guest art by Gene Ha

guest colors by Art Lyon

letters by Todd Klein

asst. editor Gregory Lockard

editor Shelly Bond

special thanks to Zander Cannon and Andrew Pepoy

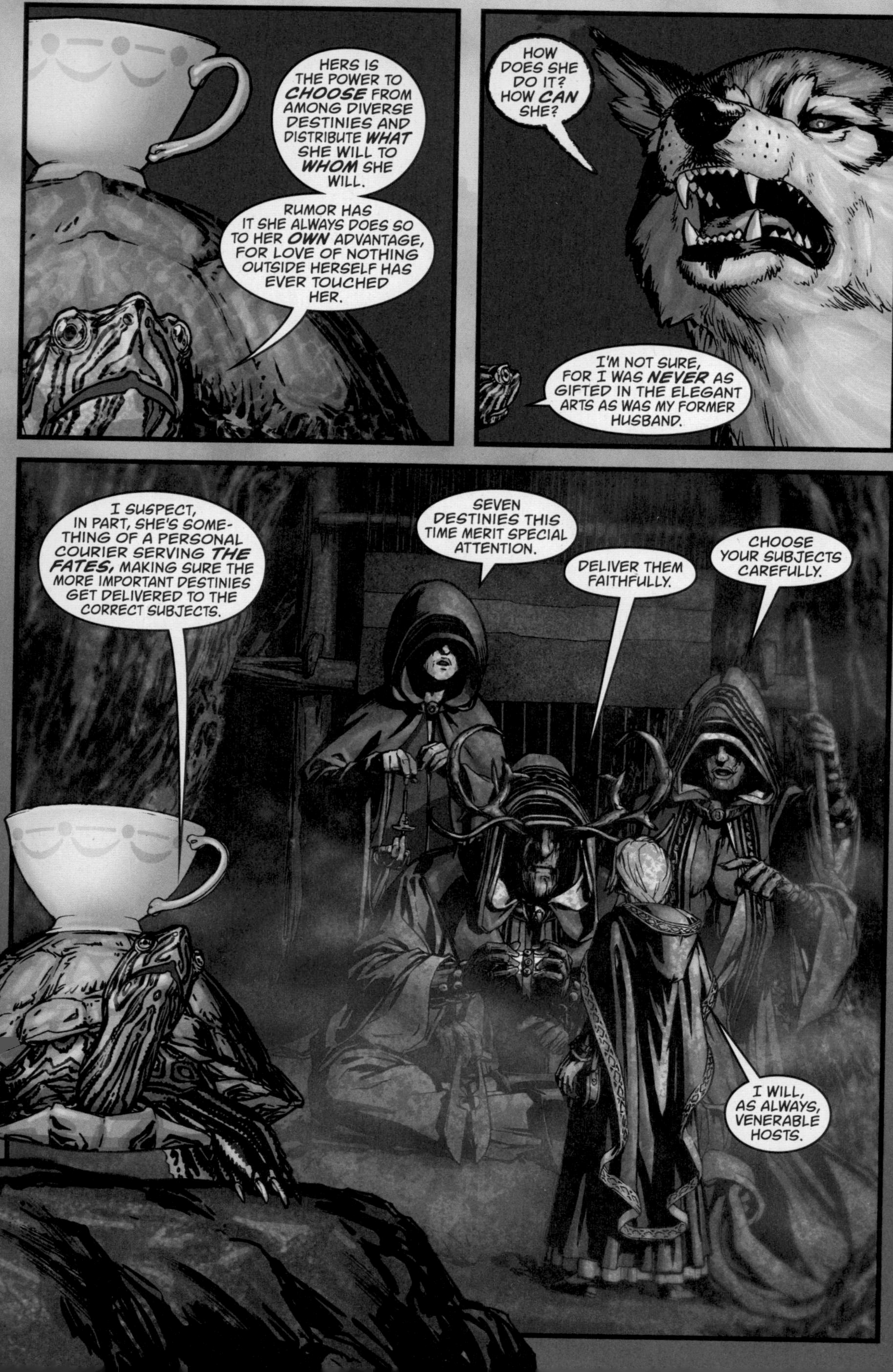
HERS IS THE POWER TO CHOOSE FROM AMONG DIVERSE DESTINIES AND DISTRIBUTE WHAT SHE WILL TO WHOM SHE WILL.
RUMOR HAS IT SHE ALWAYS DOES SO TO HER OWN ADVANTAGE, FOR LOVE OF NOTHING OUTSIDE HERSELF HAS EVER TOUCHED HER.
HOW DOES SHE DO IT? HOW CAN SHE?
I'M NOT SURE, FOR I WAS NEVER AS GIFTED IN THE ELEGANT ARTS AS WAS MY FORMER HUSBAND.
I SUSPECT, IN PART, SHE'S SOMETHING OF A PERSONAL COURIER SERVING THE FATES, MAKING SURE THE MORE IMPORTANT DESTINIES GET DELIVERED TO THE CORRECT SUBJECTS.
SEVEN DESTINIES THIS TIME MERIT SPECIAL ATTENTION.
DELIVER THEM FAITHFULLY.
CHOOSE YOUR SUBJECTS CAREFULLY.
I WILL, AS ALWAYS, VENERABLE HOSTS.

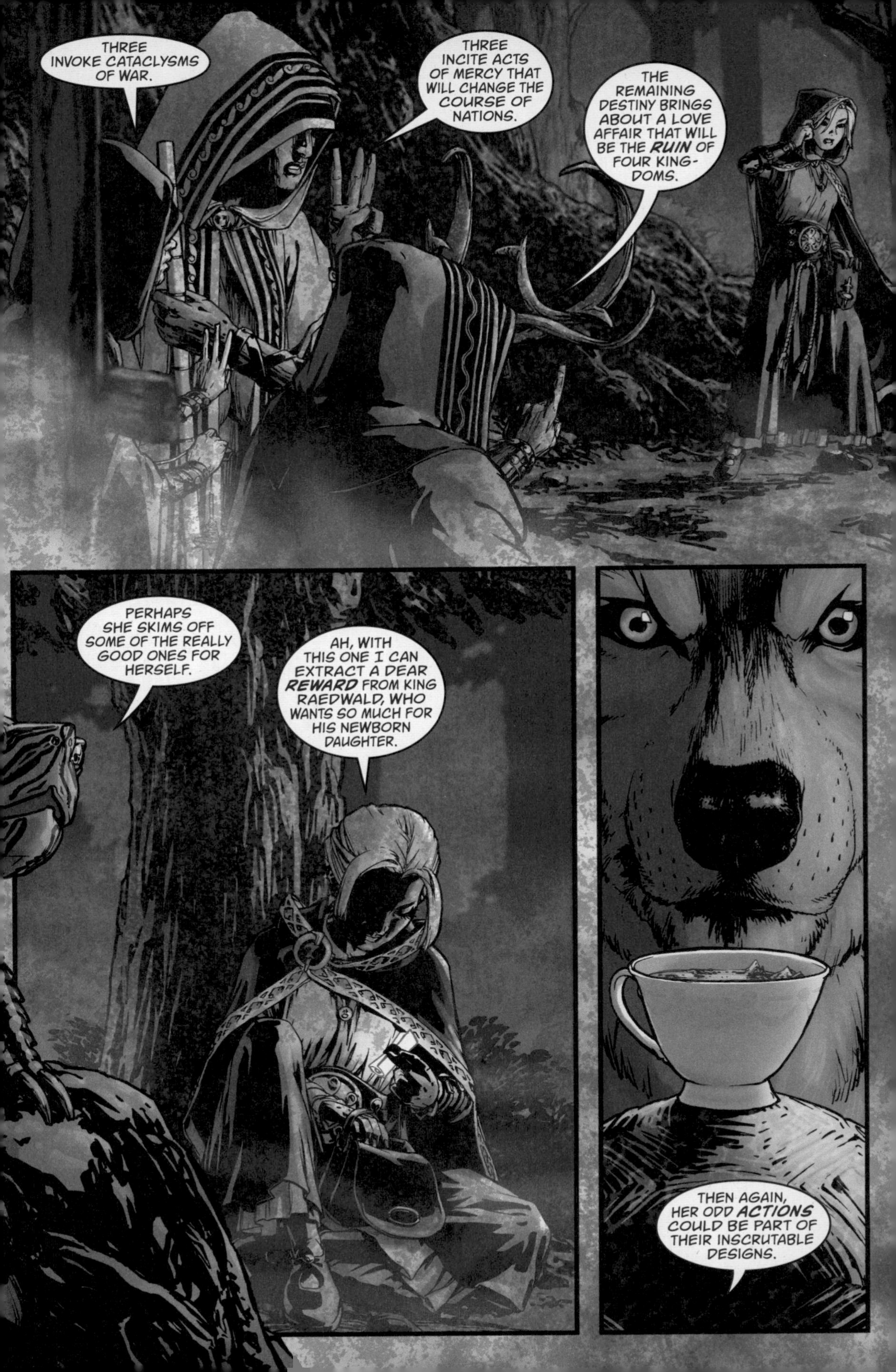
THREE INVOKE CATACLYSMS OF WAR.
THREE INCITE ACTS OF MERCY THAT WILL CHANGE THE COURSE OF NATIONS.
THE REMAINING DESTINY BRINGS ABOUT A LOVE AFFAIR THAT WILL BE THE *RUIN* OF FOUR KING-DOMS.
PERHAPS SHE SKIMS OFF SOME OF THE REALLY GOOD ONES FOR HERSELF.
AH, WITH THIS ONE I CAN EXTRACT A DEAR *REWARD* FROM KING RAEDWALD, WHO WANTS SO MUCH FOR HIS NEWBORN DAUGHTER.
THEN AGAIN, HER ODD *ACTIONS* COULD BE PART OF THEIR INSCRUTABLE DESIGNS.

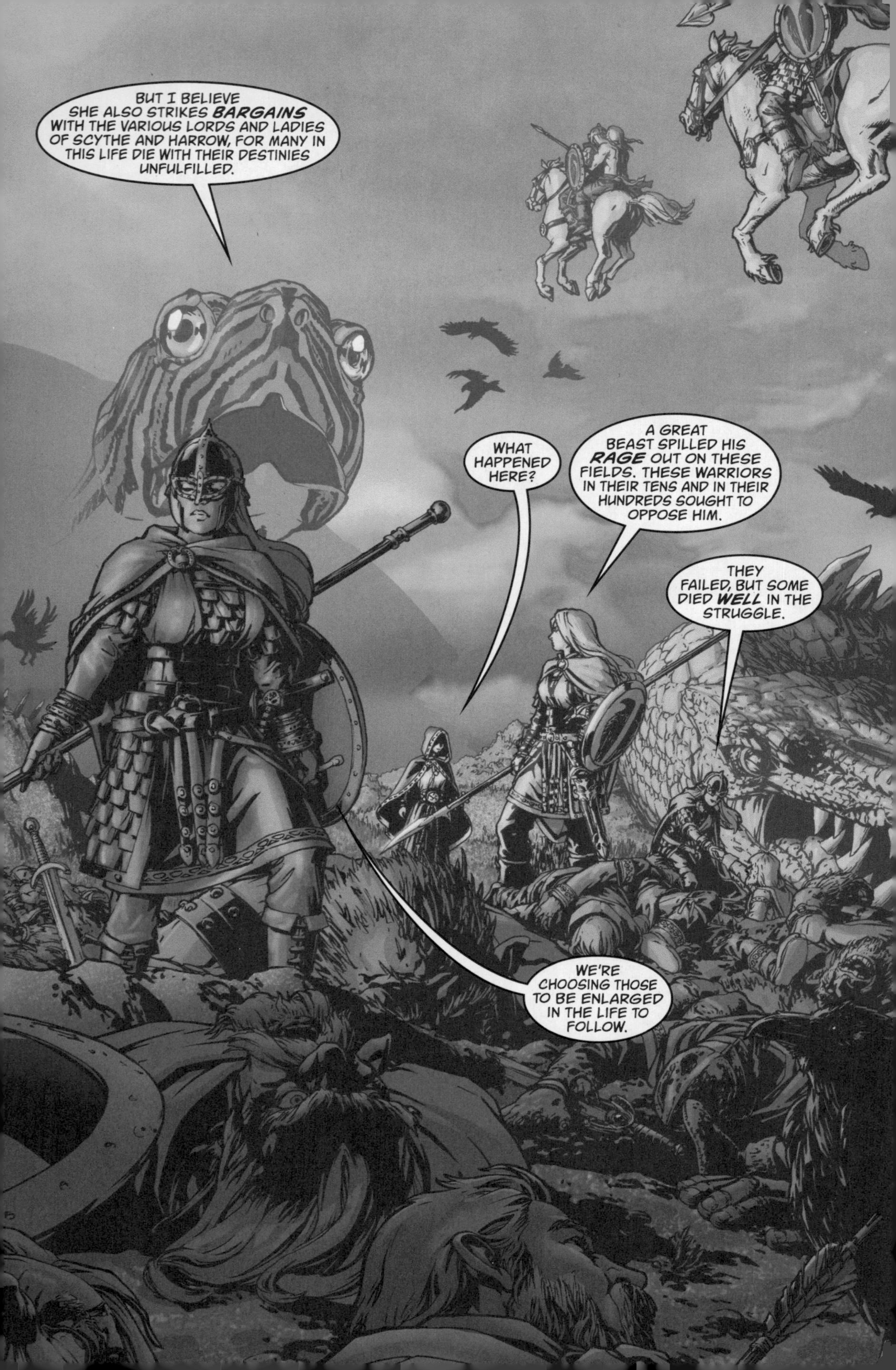
BUT I BELIEVE SHE ALSO STRIKES BARGAINS WITH THE VARIOUS LORDS AND LADIES OF SCYTHE AND HARROW, FOR MANY IN THIS LIFE DIE WITH THEIR DESTINIES UNFULFILLED.
WHAT HAPPENED HERE?
A GREAT BEAST SPILLED HIS RAGE OUT ON THESE FIELDS. THESE WARRIORS IN THEIR TENS AND IN THEIR HUNDREDS SOUGHT TO OPPOSE HIM.
THEY FAILED, BUT SOME DIED WELL IN THE STRUGGLE.
WE'RE CHOOSING THOSE TO BE ENLARGED IN THE LIFE TO FOLLOW.

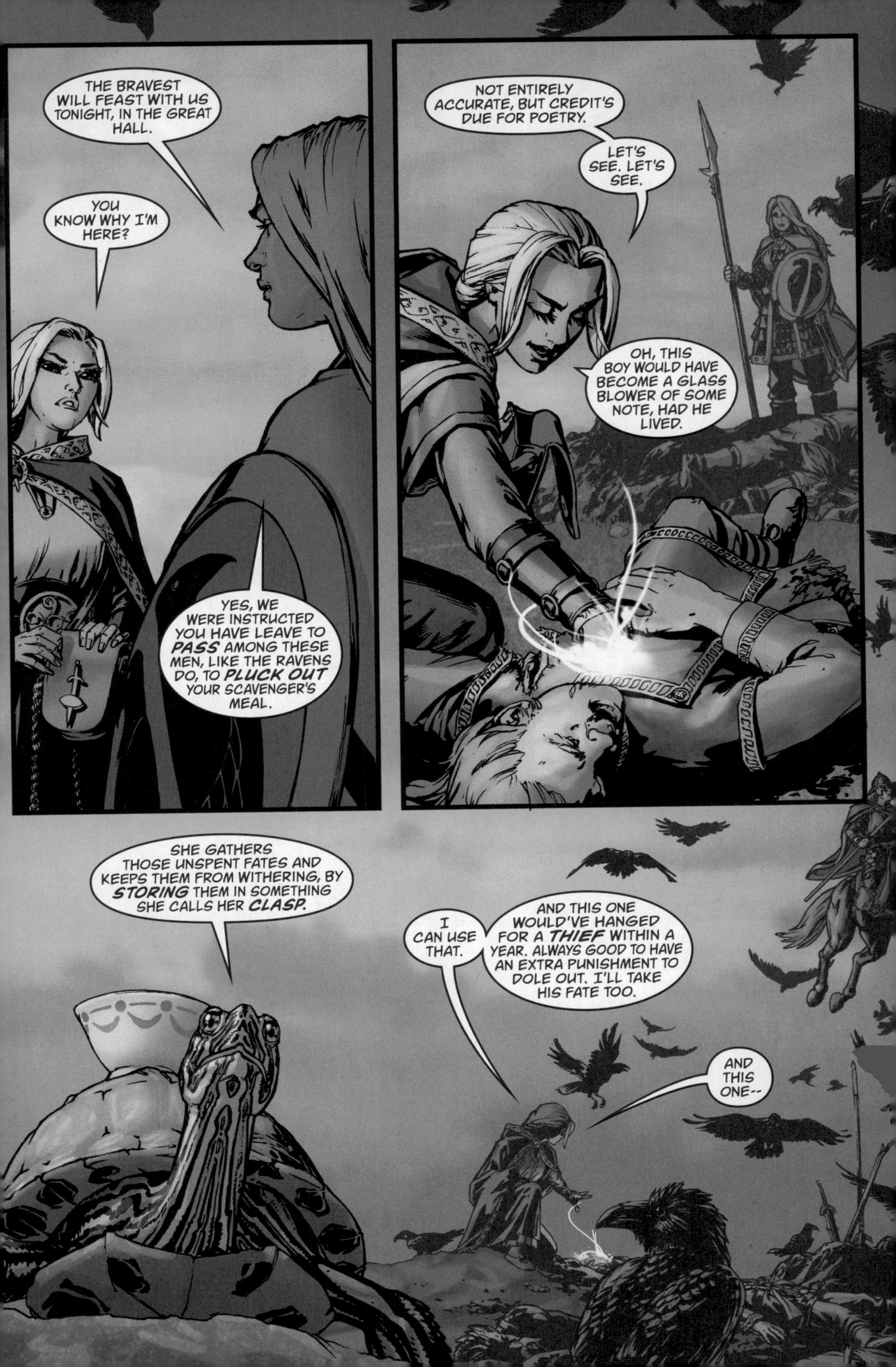
THE BRAVEST WILL FEAST WITH US TONIGHT, IN THE GREAT HALL.
YOU KNOW WHY I'M HERE?
YES, WE WERE INSTRUCTED YOU HAVE LEAVE TO PASS AMONG THESE MEN, LIKE THE RAVENS DO, TO PLUCK OUT YOUR SCAVENGER'S MEAL.
NOT ENTIRELY ACCURATE, BUT CREDIT'S DUE FOR POETRY.
LET'S SEE. LET'S SEE.
OH, THIS BOY WOULD HAVE BECOME A GLASS BLOWER OF SOME NOTE, HAD HE LIVED.
SHE GATHERS THOSE UNSPENT FATES AND KEEPS THEM FROM WITHERING, BY STORING THEM IN SOMETHING SHE CALLS HER CLASP.
AND THIS ONE WOULD'VE HANGED FOR A THIEF WITHIN A YEAR. ALWAYS GOOD TO HAVE AN EXTRA PUNISHMENT TO DOLE OUT. I'LL TAKE HIS FATE TOO.
I CAN USE THAT.
AND THIS ONE--

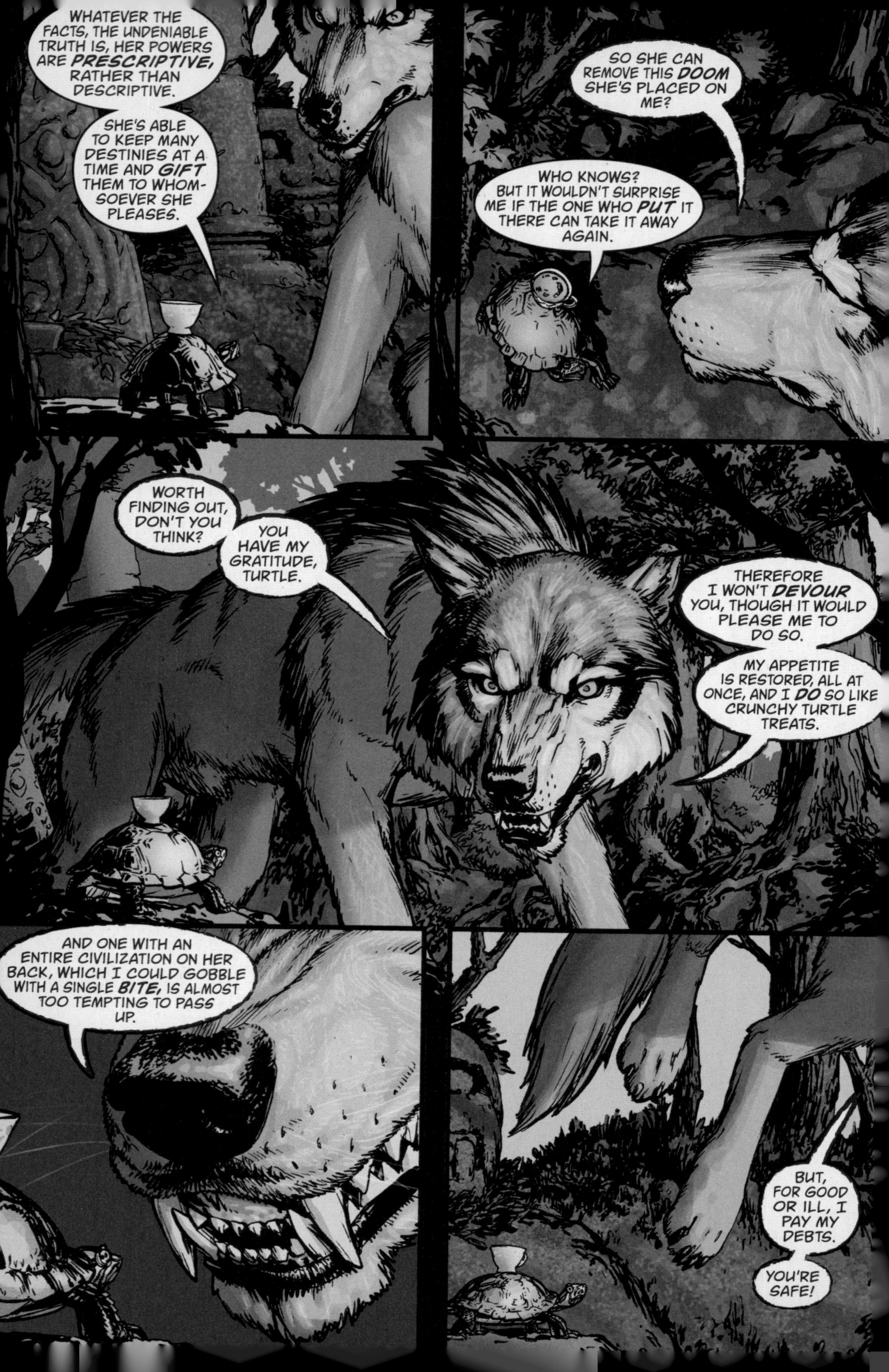
WHATEVER THE FACTS, THE UNDENIABLE TRUTH IS, HER POWERS ARE PRESCRIPTIVE, RATHER THAN DESCRIPTIVE.
SHE'S ABLE TO KEEP MANY DESTINIES AT A TIME AND GIFT THEM TO WHOM-SOEVER SHE PLEASES.
SO SHE CAN REMOVE THIS DOOM SHE'S PLACED ON ME?
WHO KNOWS? BUT IT WOULDN'T SURPRISE ME IF THE ONE WHO PUT IT THERE CAN TAKE IT AWAY AGAIN.
WORTH FINDING OUT, DON'T YOU THINK?
YOU HAVE MY GRATITUDE, TURTLE.
THEREFORE I WON'T DEVOUR YOU, THOUGH IT WOULD PLEASE ME TO DO SO.
MY APPETITE IS RESTORED, ALL AT ONCE, AND I DO SO LIKE CRUNCHY TURTLE TREATS.
AND ONE WITH AN ENTIRE CIVILIZATION ON HER BACK, WHICH I COULD GOBBLE WITH A SINGLE BITE, IS ALMOST TOO TEMPTING TO PASS UP.
BUT, FOR GOOD OR ILL, I PAY MY DEBTS.
YOU'RE SAFE!

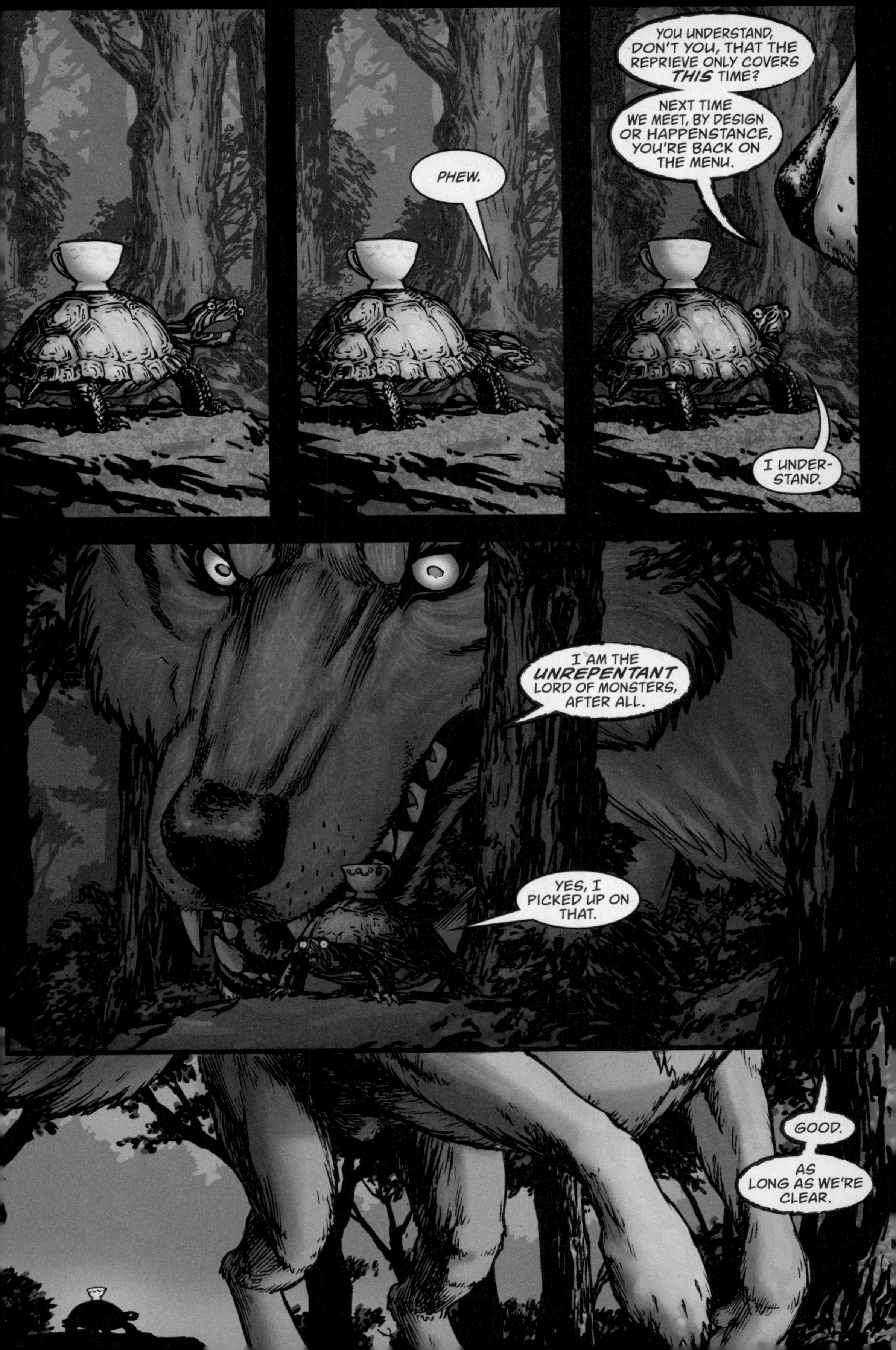
PHEW.
YOU UNDERSTAND, DON'T YOU, THAT THE REPRIEVE ONLY COVERS *THIS* TIME?
NEXT TIME WE MEET, BY DESIGN OR HAPPENSTANCE, YOU'RE BACK ON THE MENU.
I UNDER-STAND.
I AM THE *UNREPENTANT* LORD OF MONSTERS, AFTER ALL.
YES, I PICKED UP ON THAT.
GOOD.
AS LONG AS WE'RE CLEAR.

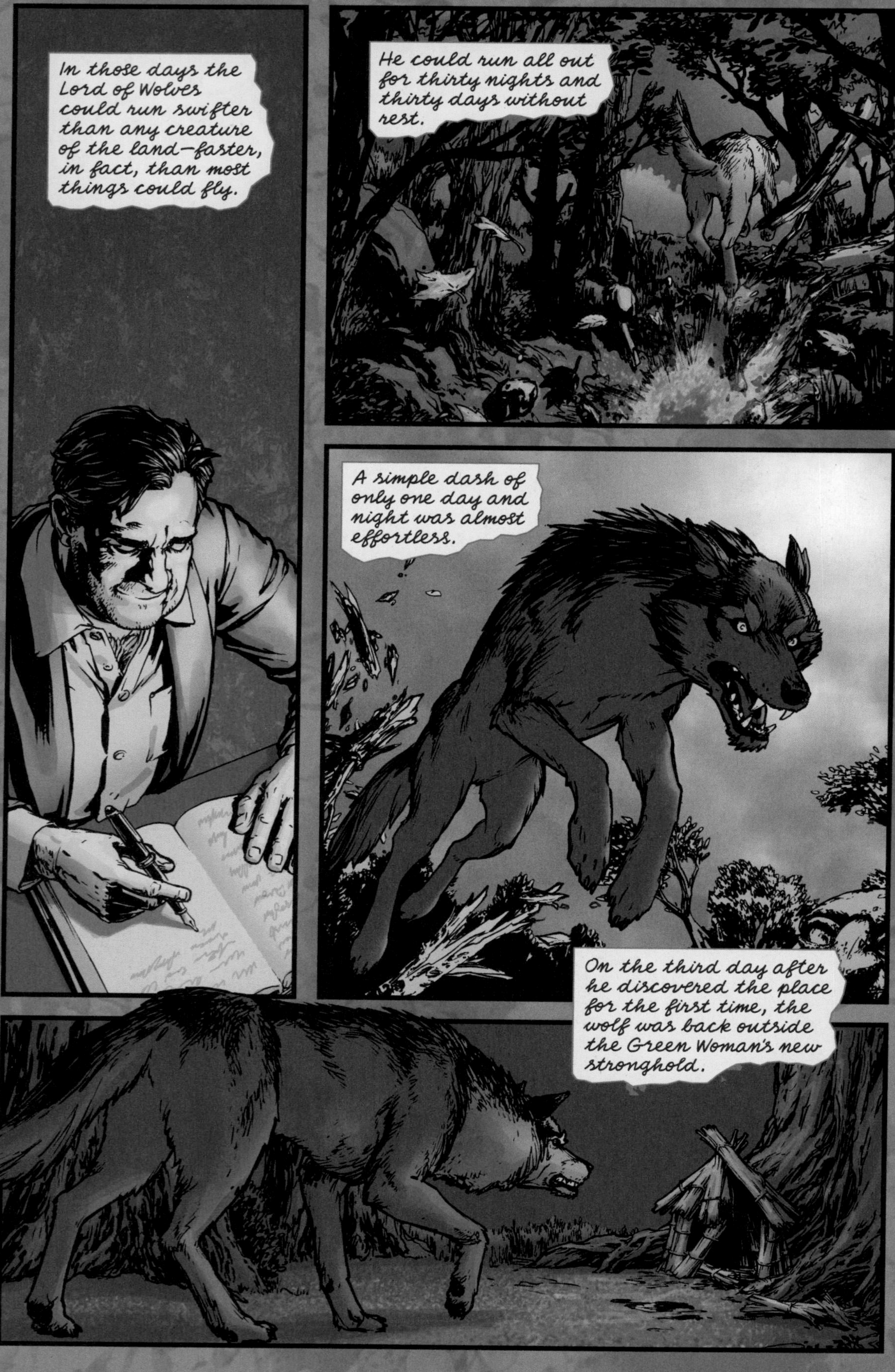
In those days the Lord of Wolves could run swifter than any creature of the land—faster, in fact, than most things could fly.
He could run all out for thirty nights and thirty days without rest.
A simple dash of only one day and night was almost effortless.
On the third day after he discovered the place for the first time, the wolf was back outside the Green Woman's new stronghold.

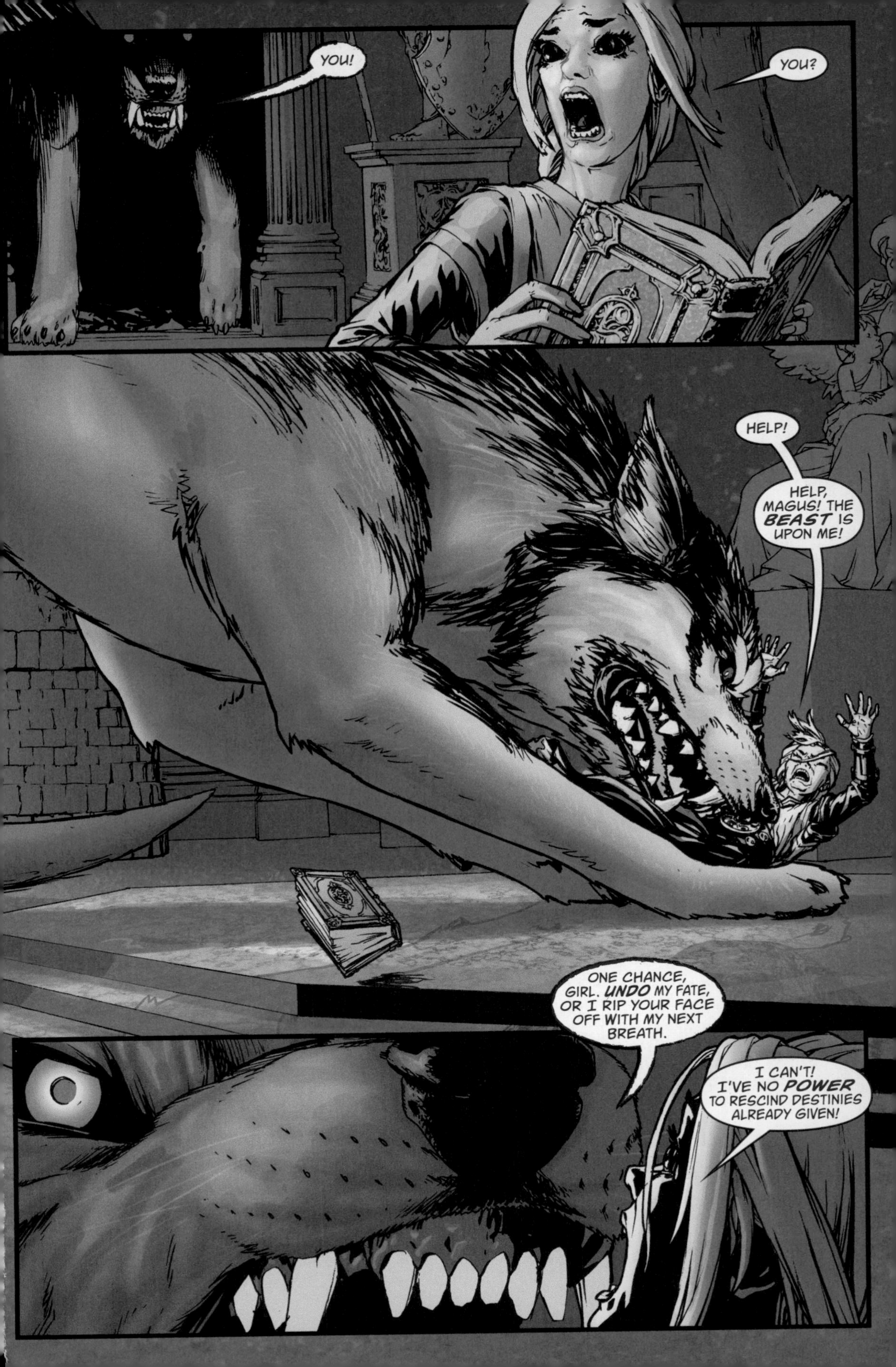
YOU!
YOU?
HELP!
HELP, MAGUS! THE BEAST IS UPON ME!
ONE CHANCE, GIRL. UNDO MY FATE, OR I RIP YOUR FACE OFF WITH MY NEXT BREATH.
I CAN'T! I'VE NO POWER TO RESCIND DESTINIES ALREADY GIVEN!

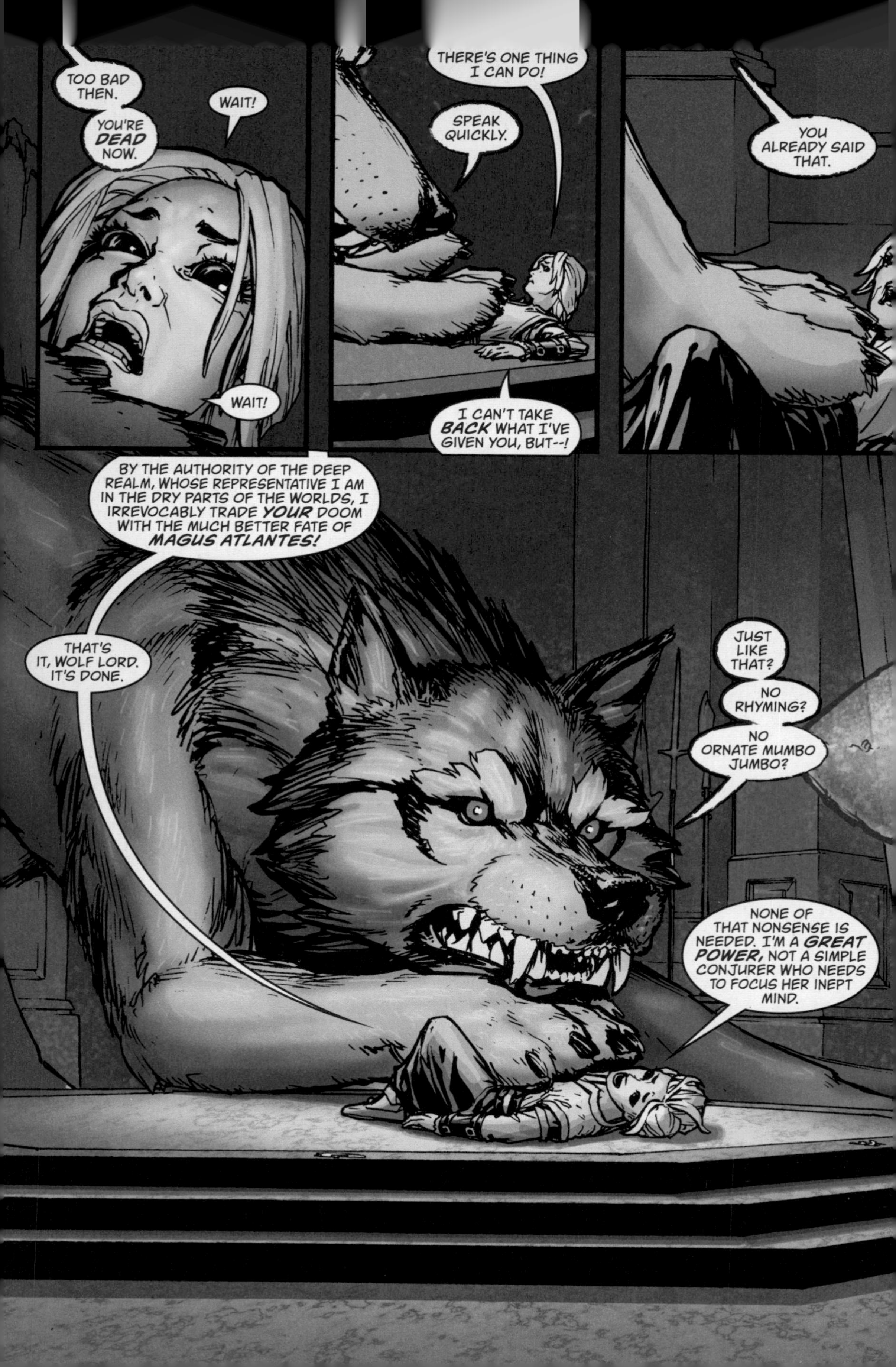
TOO BAD THEN.
YOU'RE DEAD NOW.
WAIT!
WAIT!
SPEAK QUICKLY.
THERE'S ONE THING I CAN DO!
I CAN'T TAKE BACK WHAT I'VE GIVEN YOU, BUT--!
YOU ALREADY SAID THAT.
BY THE AUTHORITY OF THE DEEP REALM, WHOSE REPRESENTATIVE I AM IN THE DRY PARTS OF THE WORLDS, I IRREVOCABLY TRADE YOUR DOOM WITH THE MUCH BETTER FATE OF MAGUS ATLANTES!
THAT'S IT, WOLF LORD. IT'S DONE.
JUST LIKE THAT?
NO RHYMING?
NO ORNATE MUMBO JUMBO?
NONE OF THAT NONSENSE IS NEEDED. I'M A GREAT POWER, NOT A SIMPLE CONJURER WHO NEEDS TO FOCUS HER INEPT MIND.

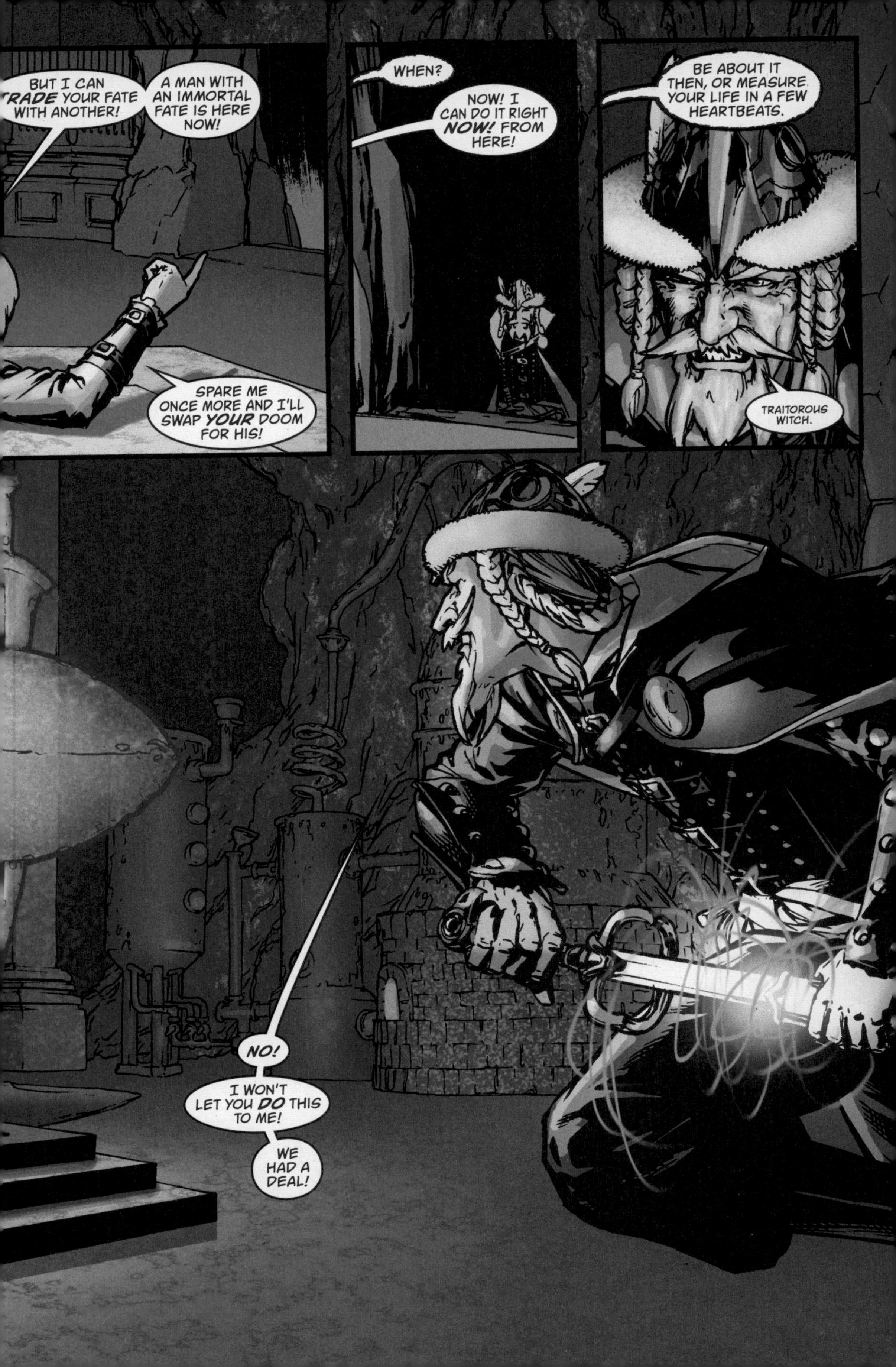
BUT I CAN TRADE YOUR FATE WITH ANOTHER!
A MAN WITH AN IMMORTAL FATE IS HERE NOW!
SPARE ME ONCE MORE AND I'LL SWAP YOUR DOOM FOR HIS!
WHEN?
NOW! I CAN DO IT RIGHT NOW! FROM HERE!
BE ABOUT IT THEN, OR MEASURE YOUR LIFE IN A FEW HEARTBEATS.
TRAITOROUS WITCH.
NO!
I WON'T LET YOU DO THIS TO ME!
WE HAD A DEAL!

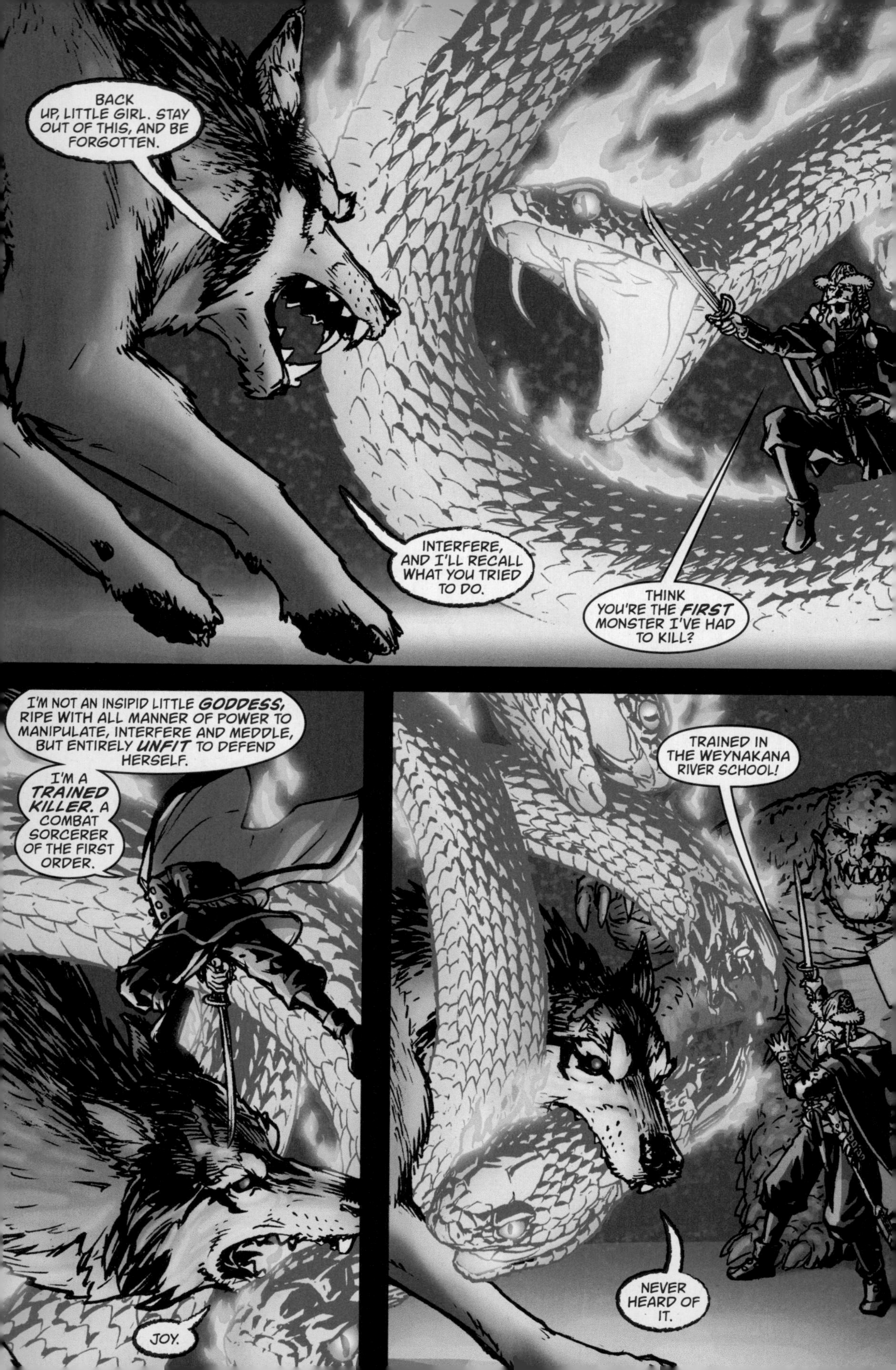
BACK UP, LITTLE GIRL. STAY OUT OF THIS, AND BE FORGOTTEN.
INTERFERE, AND I'LL RECALL WHAT YOU TRIED TO DO.
THINK YOU'RE THE FIRST MONSTER I'VE HAD TO KILL?
I'M NOT AN INSIPID LITTLE GODDESS, RIPE WITH ALL MANNER OF POWER TO MANIPULATE, INTERFERE AND MEDDLE, BUT ENTIRELY UNFIT TO DEFEND HERSELF.
I'M A TRAINED KILLER. A COMBAT SORCERER OF THE FIRST ORDER.
JOY.
TRAINED IN THE WEYNAKANA RIVER SCHOOL!
NEVER HEARD OF IT.

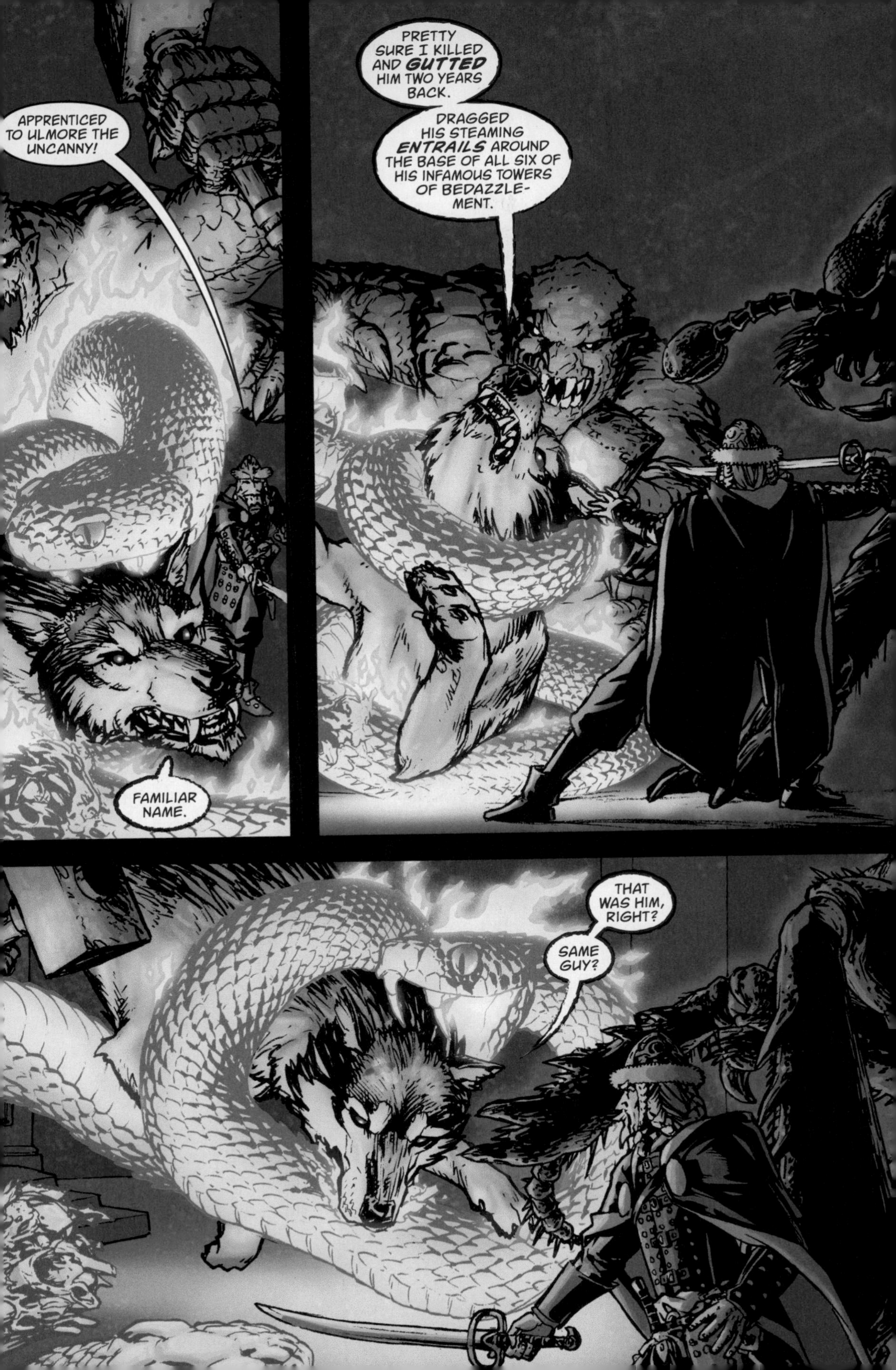
APPRENTICED TO ULMORE THE UNCANNY!
FAMILIAR NAME.
PRETTY SURE I KILLED AND GUTTED HIM TWO YEARS BACK.
DRAGGED HIS STEAMING ENTRAILS AROUND THE BASE OF ALL SIX OF HIS INFAMOUS TOWERS OF BEDAZZLE-MENT.
THAT WAS HIM, RIGHT?
SAME GUY?

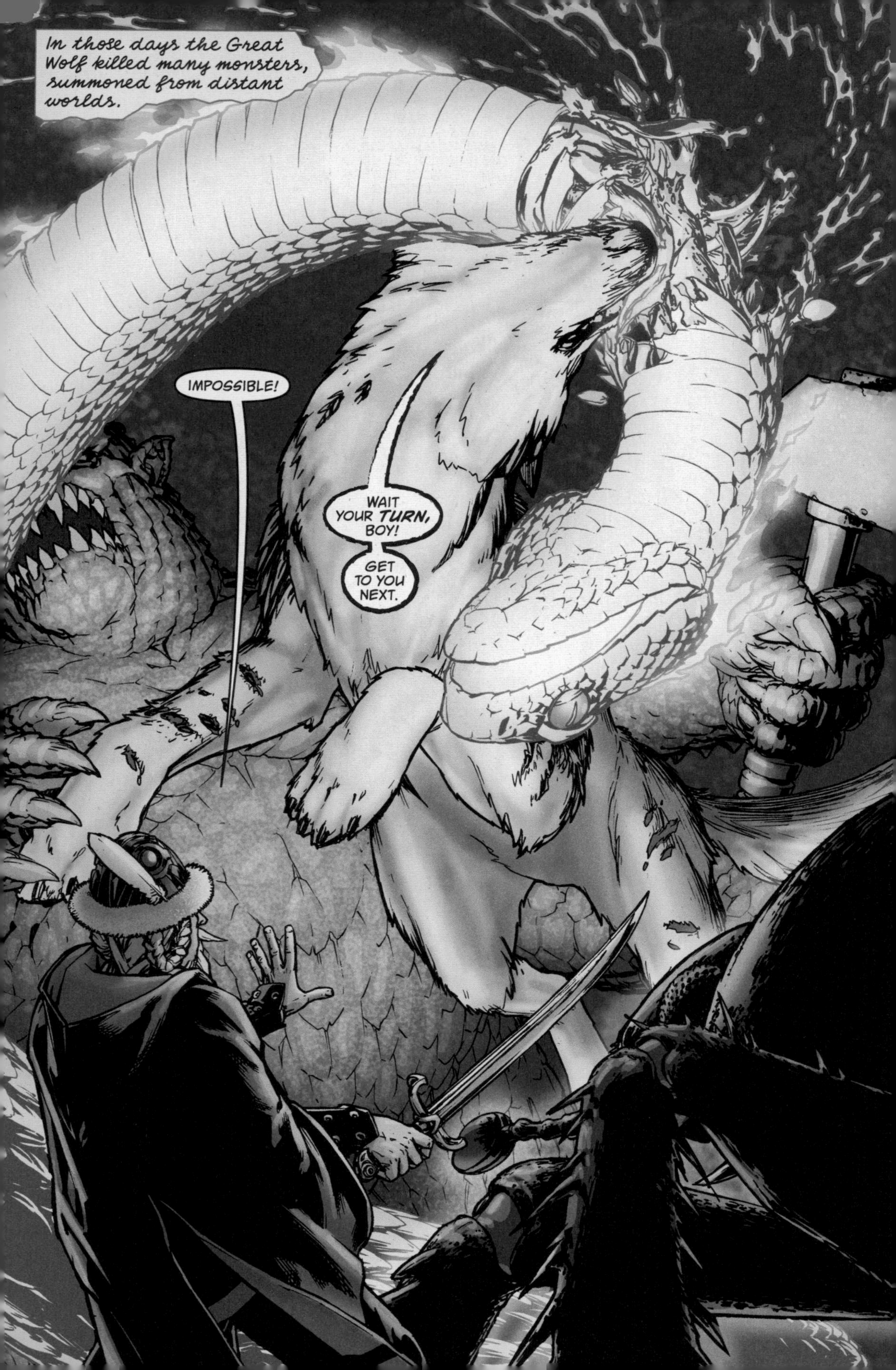
In those days the Great Wolf killed many monsters, summoned from distant worlds.
IMPOSSIBLE!
WAIT YOUR TURN, BOY!
GET TO YOU NEXT.

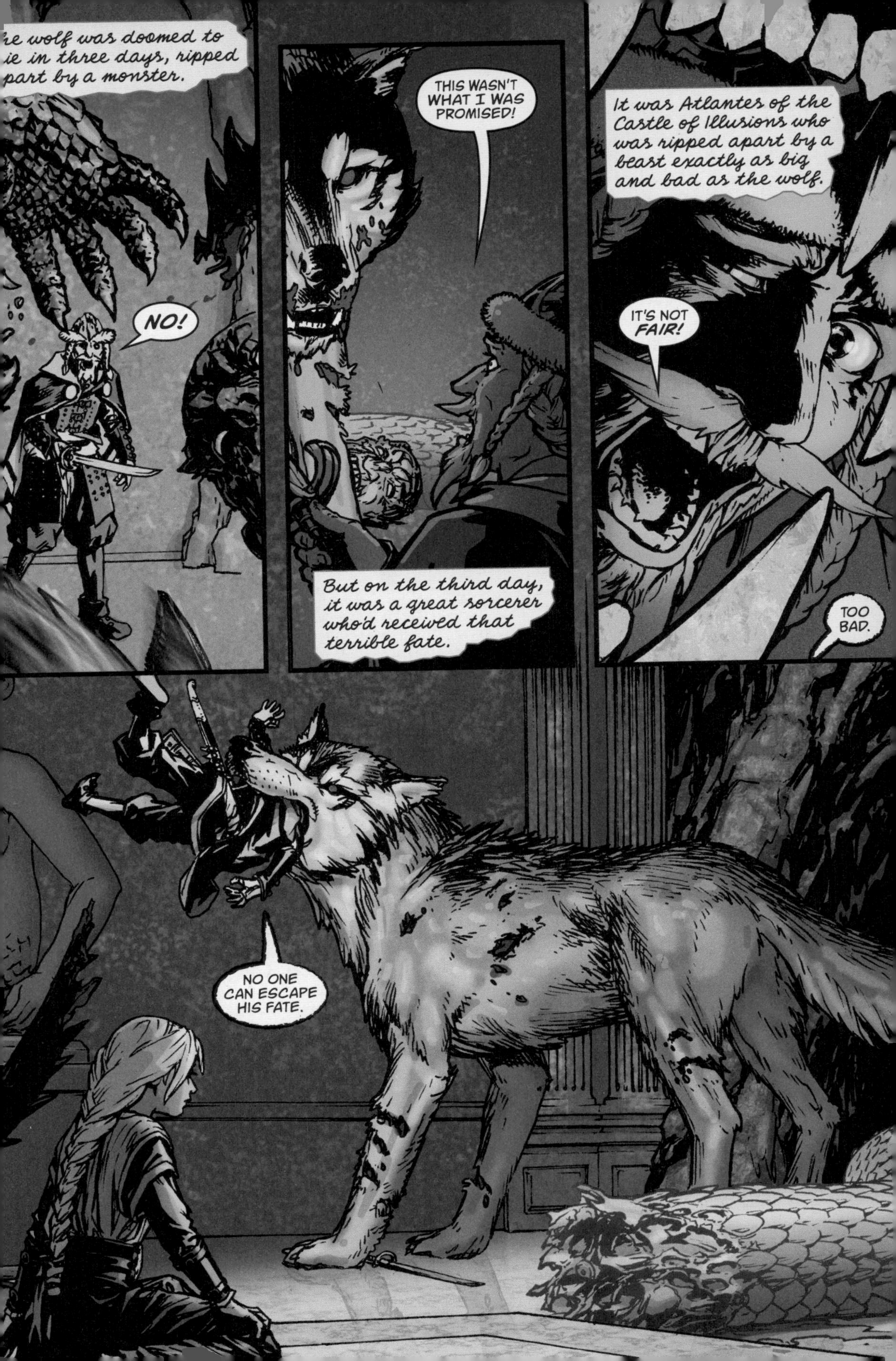
he wolf was doomed to
ie in three days, ripped
part by a monster.
NO!
THIS WASN'T WHAT I WAS PROMISED!
But on the third day, it was a great sorcerer who'd received that terrible fate.
It was Atlantes of the Castle of Illusions who was ripped apart by a beast exactly as big and bad as the wolf.
IT'S NOT FAIR!
TOO BAD.
NO ONE CAN ESCAPE HIS FATE.

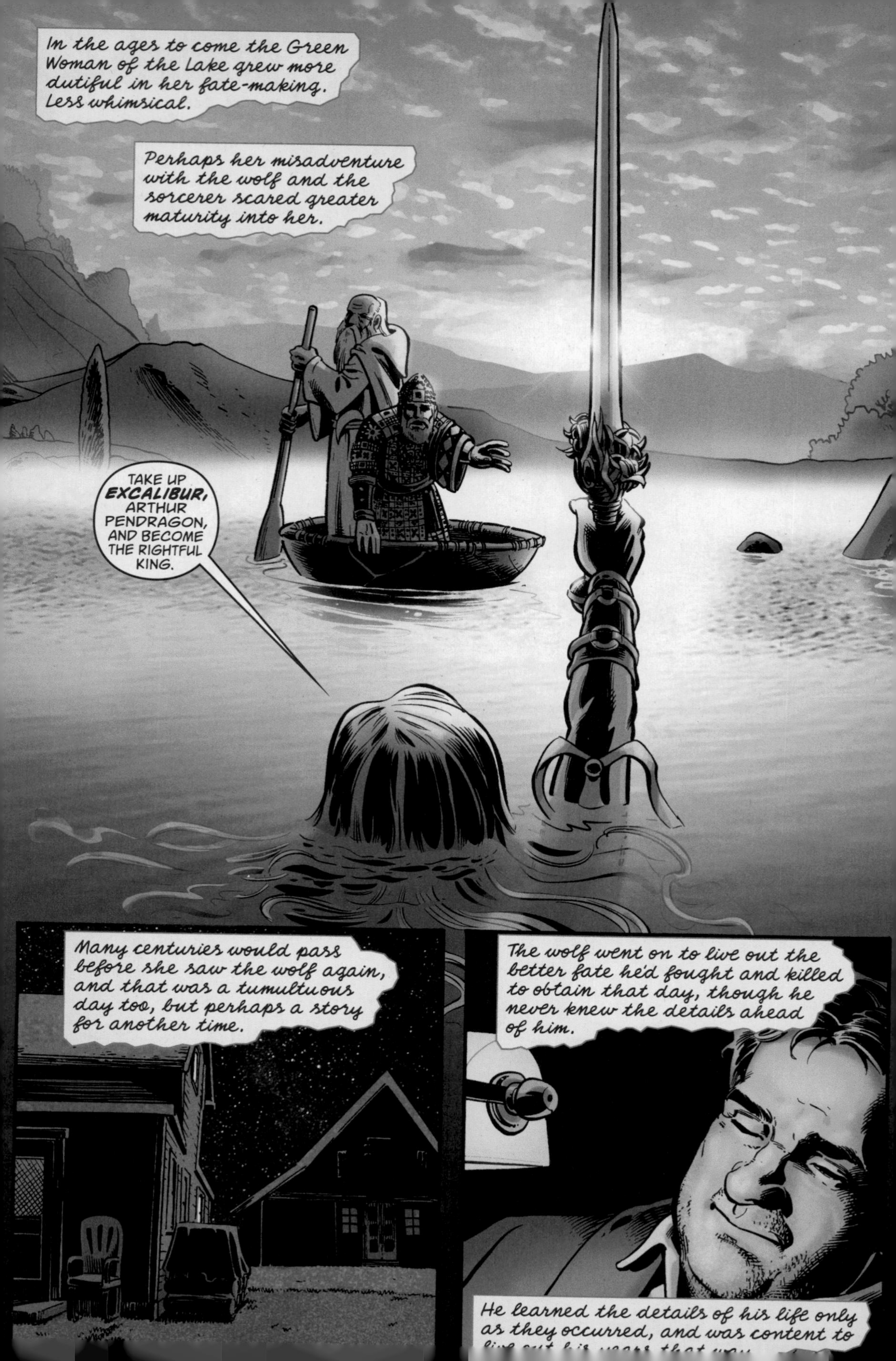

In the ages to come the Green Woman of the Lake grew more dutiful in her fate-making. Less whimsical.
Perhaps her misadventure with the wolf and the sorcerer scared greater maturity into her.
TAKE UP **EXCALIBUR,** ARTHUR PENDRAGON, AND BECOME THE RIGHTFUL KING.
Many centuries would pass before she saw the wolf again, and that was a tumultuous day too, but perhaps a story for another time.
The wolf went on to live out the better fate he'd fought and killed to obtain that day, though he never knew the details ahead of him.
He learned the details of his life only as they occurred, and was content to

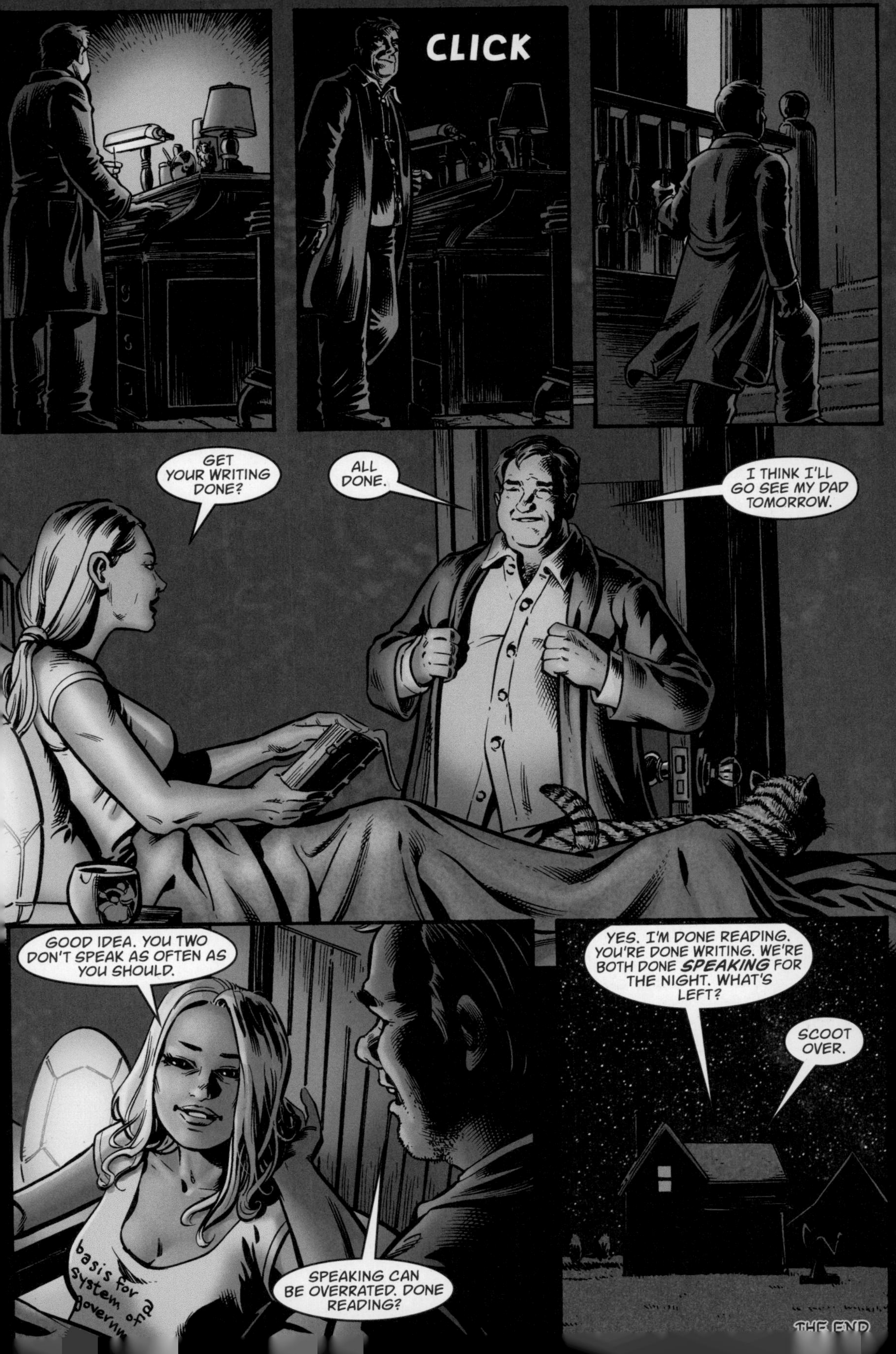
CLICK
GET YOUR WRITING DONE?
ALL DONE.
I THINK I'LL GO SEE MY DAD TOMORROW.
GOOD IDEA. YOU TWO DON'T SPEAK AS OFTEN AS YOU SHOULD.
SPEAKING CAN BE OVERRATED. DONE READING?
YES. I'M DONE READING. YOU'RE DONE WRITING. WE'RE BOTH DONE *SPEAKING* FOR THE NIGHT. WHAT'S LEFT?
SCOOT OVER.
THE END

PATCHWORK

CHARACTER DESIGNS AND PRELIMINARY ART BY MARK BUCKINGHAM

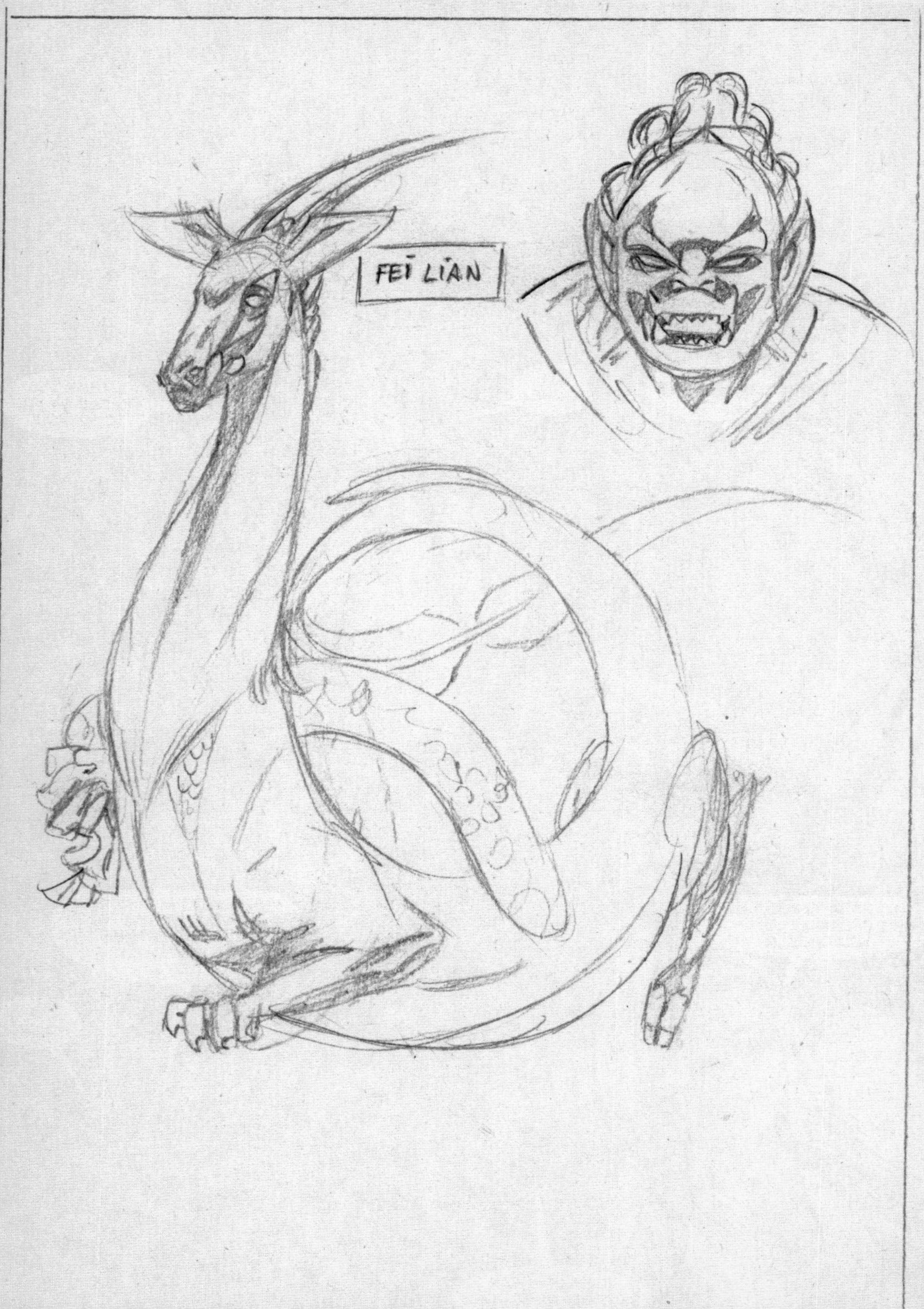
FEI LIAN

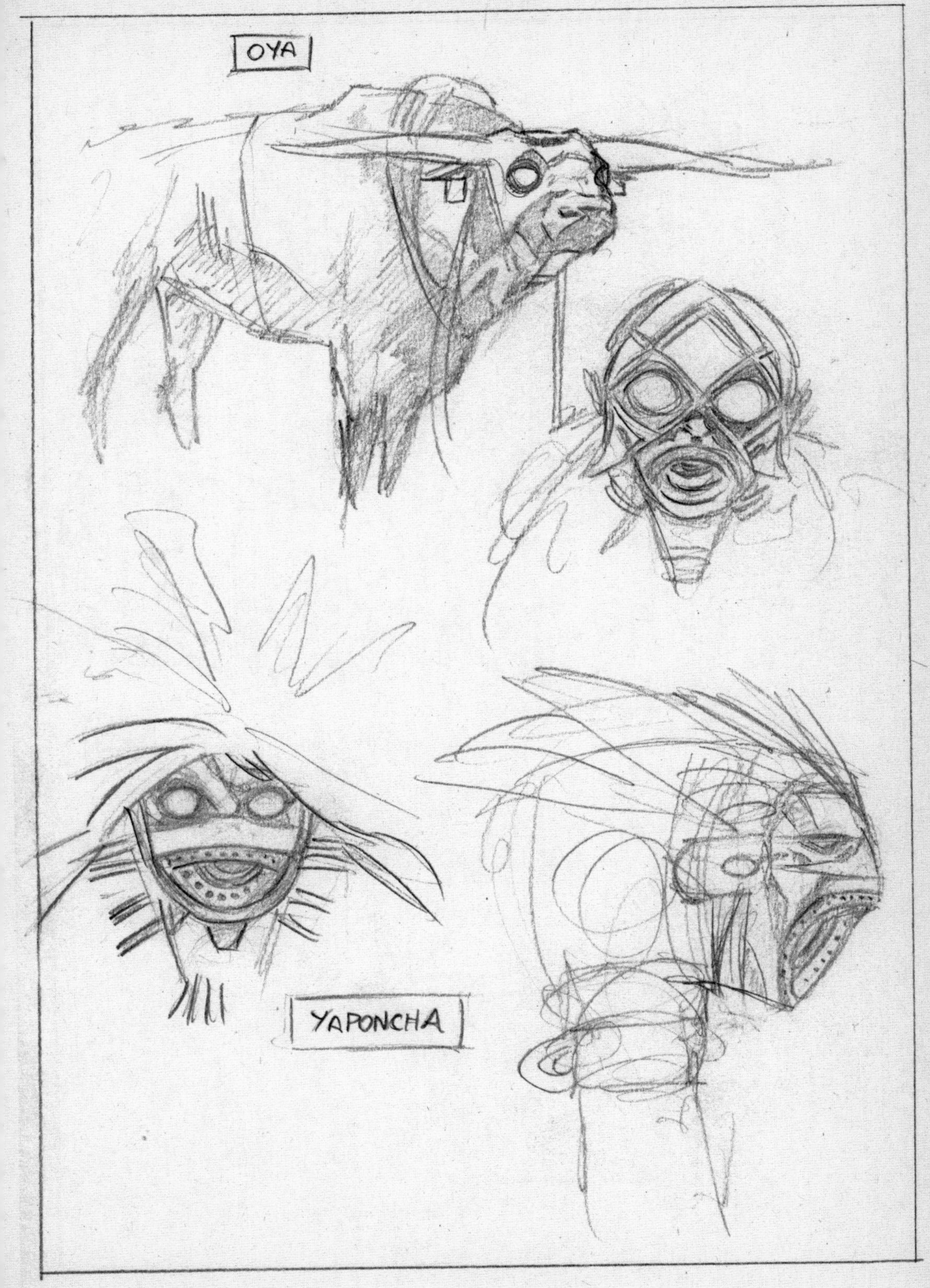

OYA
YAPONCHA

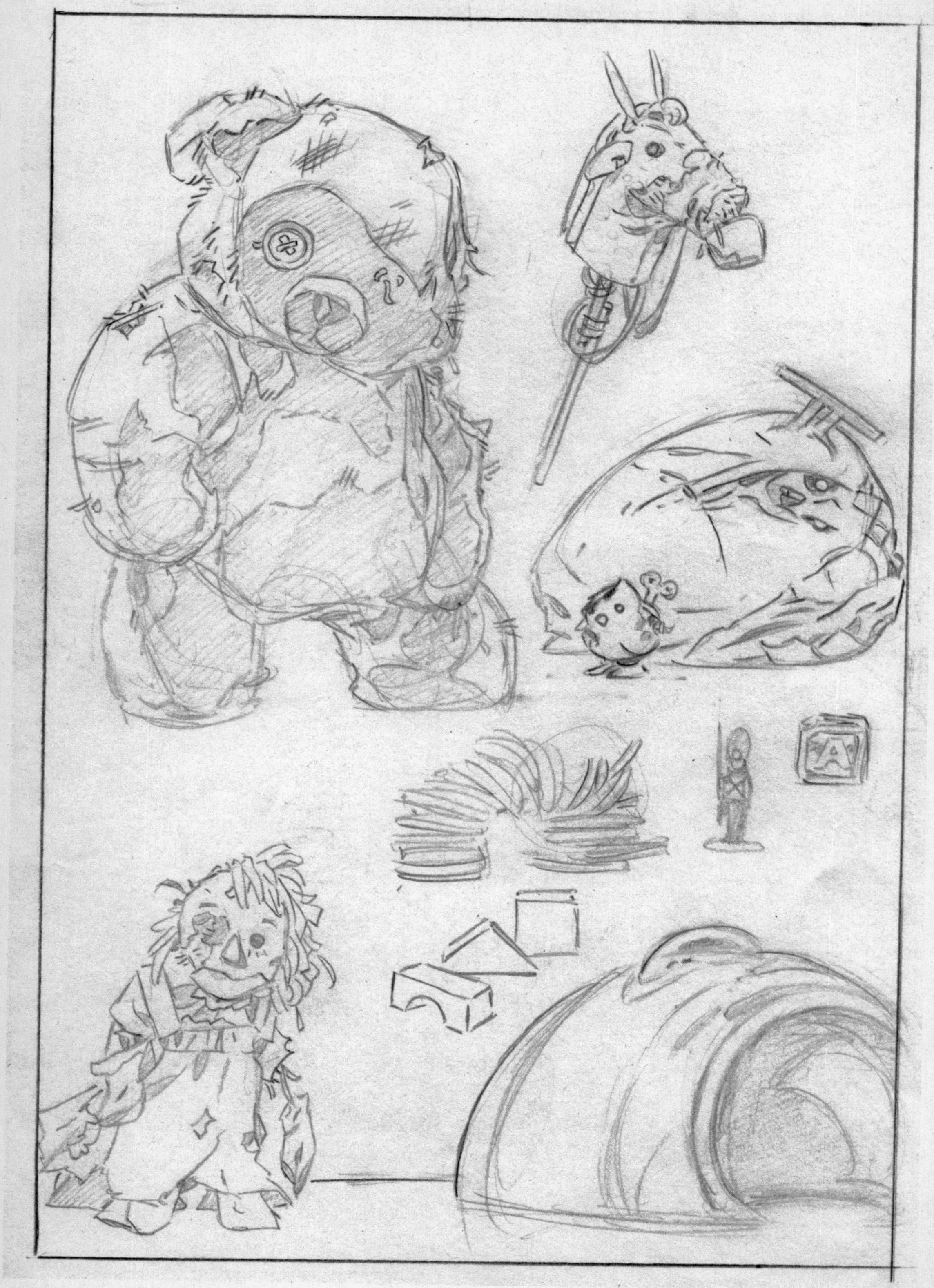
A

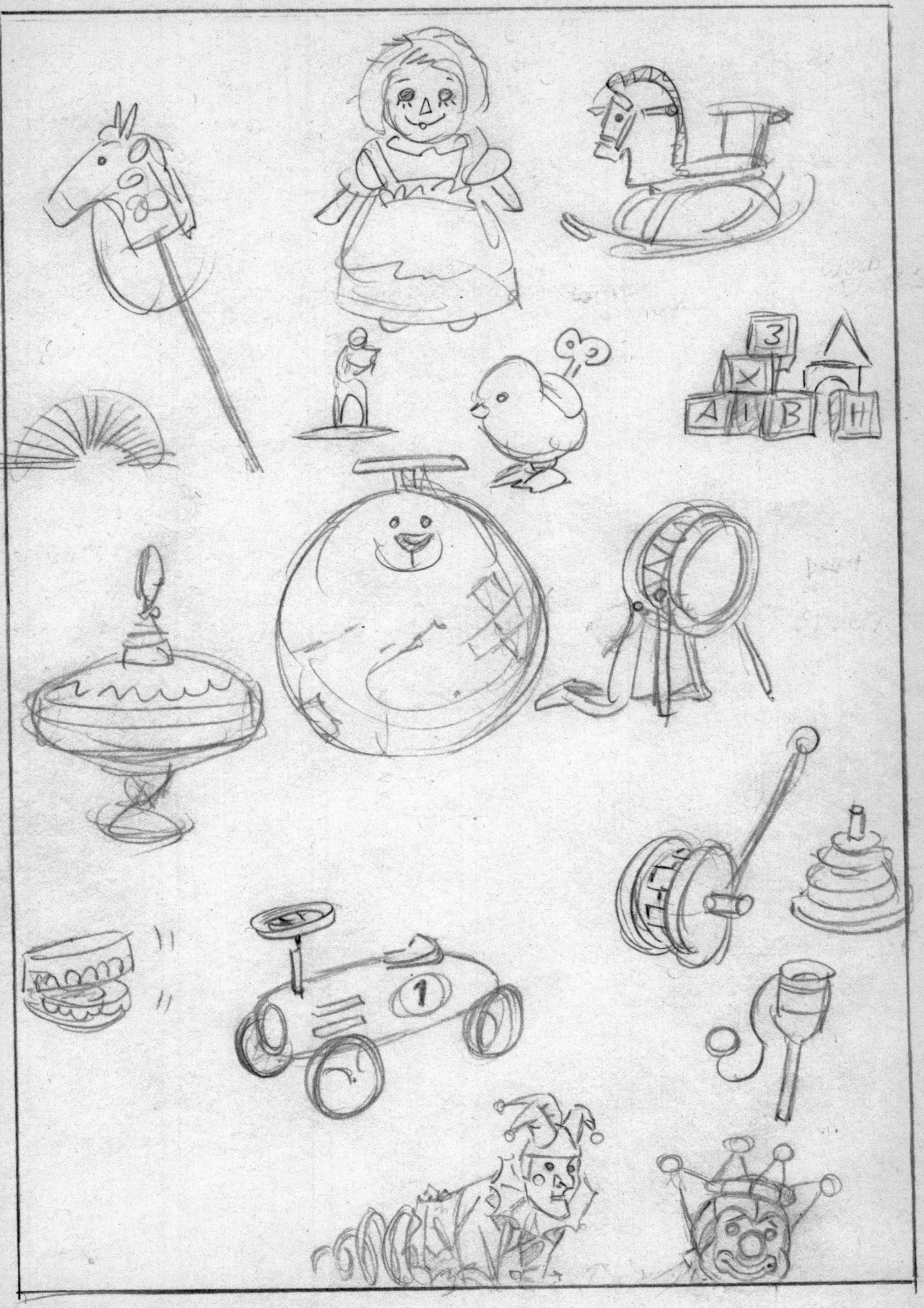

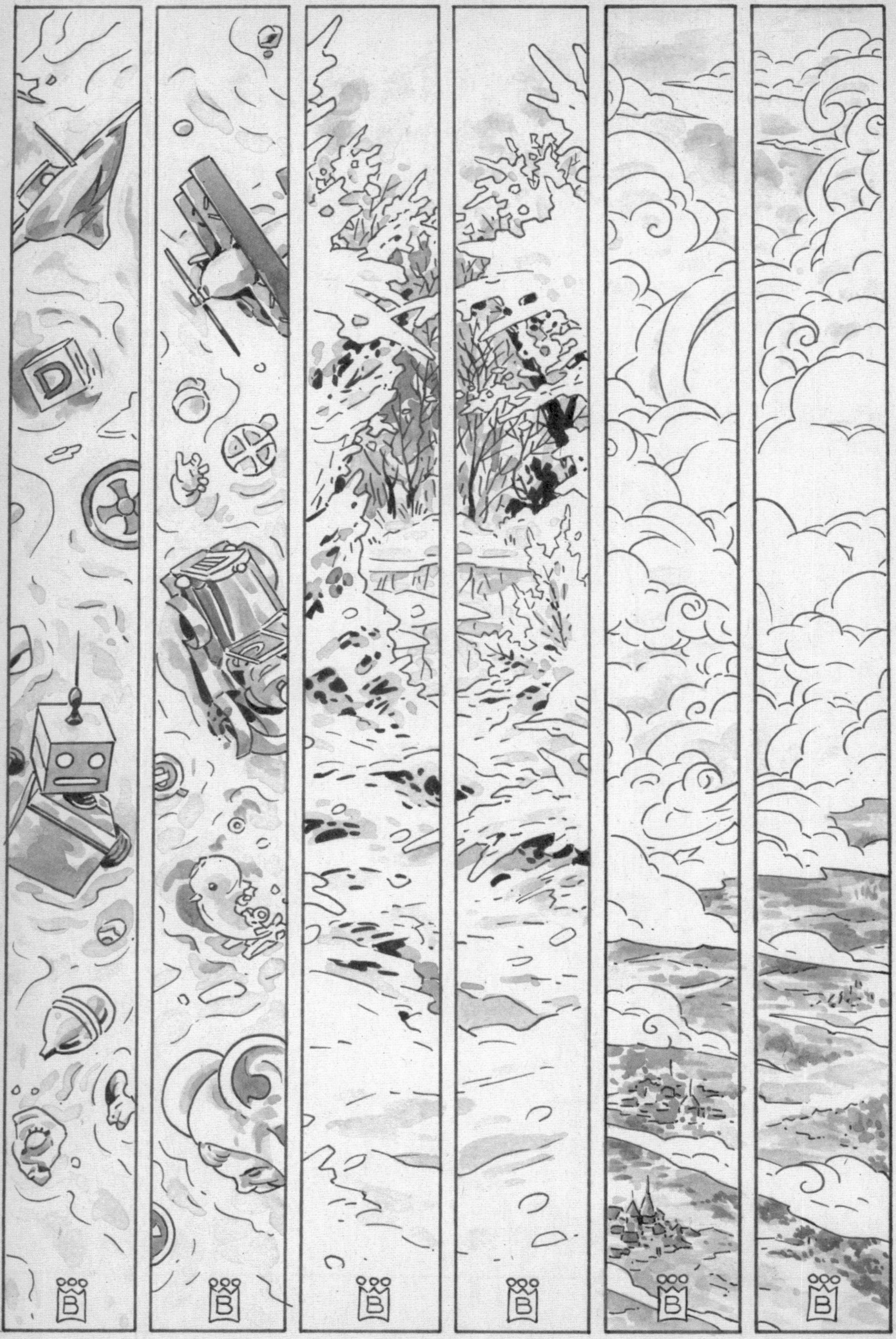